AF607794

THE ALL-ENCOMPASSING EYE OF UKRAINE

MAXIM TARNAWSKY

The All-Encompassing Eye of Ukraine

Ivan Nechui-Levyts'kyi's Realist Prose

UNIVERSITY OF TORONTO PRESS
Toronto Buffalo London

Toronto Buffalo London
www.utppublishing.com

ISBN 978-1-4426-5008-4 (cloth)

Library and Archives Canada Cataloguing in Publication

Tarnawsky, Maxim, author
The all-encompassing eye of Ukraine : Ivan Nechui-Levyts'kyi's realist prose / Maxim Tarnawsky.

Includes bibliographical references and index.
ISBN 978-1-4426-5008-4 (bound)

1. Nechui-Levyts'kyi, I. S. (Ivan Semenovych), 1837–1918 – Criticism and interpretation. 2. Realism in literature. I. Title.

PG3948.L47Z55 2015 891.7'932 C2015-901296-1

This book has been published with the help of a grant from the Federation for the Humanities and Social Sciences, through the Awards to Scholarly Publications Program, using funds provided by the Social Sciences and Humanities Research Council of Canada.

University of Toronto Press acknowledges the financial assistance to its publishing program of the Canada Council for the Arts and the Ontario Arts Council, an agency of the Government of Ontario.

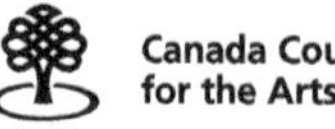

University of Toronto Press acknowledges the financial support of the Government of Canada through the Canada Book Fund for its publishing activities.

To Uliana

Contents

THE ALL-ENCOMPASSING EYE OF UKRAINE

Introduction

As I was completing work on the last chapter of this book, I received as a gift from Leonid Ushkalov his most recent work, *Realizm – tse eskhatolohiia: Panas Myrnyi* (Realism is eschatology: Panas Myrnyi).[1] This act of generosity and friendship by one of Ukraine's foremost literary scholars was a great joy to me. Of course, getting an unexpected gift is always a pleasure and a good book is especially welcome, but I was very pleased by this book for reasons beyond the pleasure of receiving a gift. Here was a book by a very prominent scholar about a writer from the era of Ukrainian literary realism! That is a very uncommon event! My colleague's gift was not only enjoyable and enlightening reading, but also a good omen concerning the scholarly fate of Ukrainian realism.

Ivan Nechui-Levyts'kyi, whom I shall call Nechui, is the major figure in the period of Ukrainian literary realism. Leonid Ushkalov would likely say that Nechui shares this position with Panas Myrnyi. Perhaps so. The point is not worth arguing. Both writers played a vitally important role in the development of Ukrainian literature in the second half of the nineteenth century, a period when literary realism was the vehicle of a cultural movement that shaped the course of the Ukrainian nation in its social, historical, and political development. With the future of Ukrainian national identity in the balance as a result of repressive, indeed genocidal, policies in the Russian Empire, the question of the relative importance of these two writers is irrelevant, perhaps even morally and intellectually unjustified. Each played a vital role. But that's not to say they played the same role, or even a similar one.

It is not particularly enlightening to say that Nechui was a unique figure in his day. The number of activists working for the advancement of Ukrainian culture on both sides of the border dividing Ukrainian territory in the second half of the nineteenth century was not small, but it was certainly not large enough to treat its various figures as mere representatives of a particular trend, as one of the "y" subset of the "x" group of Ukrainian cultural activists. They were all unique, and their contribution to the cause they were trying to promote was always personal, singular, individual, peculiar, and unusual. But this is not how the realist era is viewed in Ukrainian cultural, and particularly literary, history.

There are two dominant views. The first, a positive view, lionizes the Ukrainian cultural activists of the late nineteenth century for their perseverance and struggle against the insurmountable obstacles that were thrown up against them. They kept the faith with the culture of the Ukrainian masses when the situation was most bleak, and their efforts allowed the next generation of leaders – better educated, better trained, and using better, more forceful, modern, and politically astute methods – to continue the struggle and make the significant gains that characterized the Ukrainian movement in the first decades of the twentieth century. The second, a critical view, holds that the cultural activists of the older generation of the late nineteenth century were patriotic individuals who did their best under difficult circumstances for the cause of maintaining a national identity, but, limited by their antiquated world view and a failure to understand the new cultural and political realities, they created a limited and false model of Ukrainian culture that was incapable of providing national identity to the newly emerging, Europe-oriented, and politically, culturally, and socially more sophisticated intellectuals that dominated the Ukrainian national movement in the second decade of the twentieth century and beyond.

These two views of Ukrainian realism share an obvious defect: they measure the past through the prism of succeeding developments. Naturally, they find it wanting. Measured by modernist principles, realism, whether in Ukrainian literature or any other literature, will always seem a complete failure. Ukrainian realism needs and deserves a thorough re-evaluation based on principles that derive from its own aesthetic, historical, social, and philosophical circumstances, not those of the next generation. But there is another serious defect in these general views of Ukrainian realism: they assume the phenomenon has a unified character that is clearly delineated and reasonably well understood. This is not the case. Realism in Ukrainian literature is a weak and problematical cultural development. While there certainly are some general features that characterize the era, the writers who formed its cultural profile were, by and large, solitary, individuals who were working alone, without much cooperation, without universal cultural institutions, and without the public debate that is necessary to harmonize the activity of diverse creative individuals. Ukrainian realism needs and deserves a series of discreet re-examinations of the individual writers who worked in this era with a focus on their unique characteristics, on the peculiarities of their creative techniques and intellectual concerns. The canvas of the general landscape will remain confusing so long as the figures in the scene are all drawn from the same prototype, rather than from specific, individualized portraits.

The goal of this monograph is to create such an individualized portrait of Nechui. My particular goal is to uncover a writer who is largely unknown, to reveal a voice that has been largely unheard, to unmask a creative artist who has been obscured by an accumulated build-up of ideological dirt, historical rust, and aesthetic mould, to clean, grind, and polish the ossified remains of Ivan Semenovych Nechui-Levyts'kyi until a more lifelike and colourful Nechui emerges. In order to accomplish this goal, the chapters of this monograph will answer a handful of very elementary questions: Who was Nechui? What did he write about, both as subject and as theme? How did he write? What peculiarities of method and subject do his works reveal? These questions are not meant to be exhaustive nor is this work meant to offer a complete and definitive reading of Nechui and his works. Quite the contrary, my goal is to disturb the apparent complacency surrounding this author, to focus on those qualities of his person, his thinking, and his writing that are least known, poorly explored, and most surprising. I hope as a result to make meaningful and enlightening the characteristic uniqueness of one of Ukrainian literature's foremost realist writers, and thereby to stimulate a renewed interest in his works and in the era to which he contributed.

Of course, for the English reader, Nechui cannot be made new because he has never had a chance to get old. Hardly anything has been written about him in English, and only one work, the novel *Mykola Dzheria*, exists in an English translation. So while keeping the focus on what is unusual, unknown, and misunderstood in Nechui, I have kept an eye out for the reader who is not familiar with his works at all and have maintained, I hope, a balance between writing for readers who know his works well and writing for readers who had never heard of him before. But no matter how much or how little familiarity my reader may have with Nechui, the newness of Nechui that is emphasized in this book is entirely a matter of ideas, interpretations, and perspective. There are no new discoveries of literary or biographical materials in this monograph. All of the evidence used in constructing both the biography and the literary interpretation of Nechui in this volume is well established. I have found no biographical facts that were previously unknown (or at least unknowable), nor any new texts, whether belletristic, essayistic, or personal. I cannot even claim to have gained access to all the known works, although I have managed, with the help of colleagues, to pull a few rarely seen texts into the light of day, or, at least, the glowing pixels of Internet republication.[2] Nechui's obscurity is not a matter of the absence of facts and data, although I am certain that further research will produce new discoveries, and I am hopeful that scholars in Ukraine will undertake this work. The unknown Nechui I reveal in this volume does not need to be discovered; he's hiding in plain sight. Years ago, when I first began work on this project, my intention was to pursue archival research that would excavate new evidence about Nechui that I still believe is hidden in archives and repositories in Ukraine. But my grant applications on this topic received a sceptical reception: Nechui and basic archival research are not fashionable in today's scholarship. However, I gradually realized that such research, while potentially fruitful, was not necessary to correct the misunderstanding of Nechui. The situation was clear enough without new facts or discoveries, so I abandoned the game of granstmanship and concentrated on undoing the existing misrepresentations of Nechui, on clearing up the portrait of this creative artist that was hidden beneath a century of accumulated distortions and misreadings.

The archetype and fountainhead of Nechui studies is the biography of the writer by Serhii Iefremov. In the 1920s, Iefremov produced a remarkable series of literary biographies, among them portraits of the modernist Mykhailo Kotsiubyns'kyi, the actor and playwright Ivan Karpenko-Karyi, and the realist Panas Myrnyi.[3] Working directly from the papers Nechui had bequeathed to the Chernihiv Historical Museum (which Nechui called the Tarnovs'kyi Museum, in honour of its major benefactor), and in parallel with the first major posthumous edition of Nechui's works, Iefremov was in an unusually good position to produce a definitive work despite the ideological and material difficulties of the early Soviet regime. Iefremov's reputation as a champion of populist principles in culture merely enhanced the authority of his work, assuring, as it were, a sympathetic reading of the old populists: Myrnyi, Nechui, and Karpenko-Karyi. Eventually, Stalinist terror destroyed Iefremov and made his name and work unmentionable in Soviet scholarship. Nevertheless, those Soviet scholars who wrote on Nechui followed in his footsteps, repeating his ideas and reacting to his interpretations, even if they could not acknowledge this in their works. Nowhere, neither inside nor outside the Soviet Union, was there any indication that Iefremov's work was seriously flawed. There was not even any reaction to the somewhat peculiar selection of letters that Iefremov added as an addendum (along with other previously unknown items) to the monograph. In particular, no one pointed out that the letters he reproduced seemed to be particularly selected to answer complaints by Nechui directed at Iefremov's earlier efforts, while the author was still alive, to publish his works. In what was taken to be a friendly biography, one would expect Iefremov to be somewhat more reticent, or perhaps even forgiving, in discussing Nechui's angry reaction to the manipulation of his texts by Vik (The age), the publishing house Iefremov had founded. But that was not the case. Not at all! Iefremov simply added editorial footnotes to Nechui's letters declaring that the charges were "a complete fantasy" on the part of the author.[4] The suspicions raised by this unfriendly, subjective, and bold dismissiveness are a major part of the impetus that brought me to the writing of this book.

Chapter 1 of this book is devoted to exploring Nechui's biography against the background of the controversial relationship between Nechui and Iefremov, his biographer. In the absence of any major new biographical studies of Nechui (in any language), I have attempted to give as complete a presentation of the facts of his life as possible. Yet, surely, much more should be known about a man who lived for eighty years at the end of the nineteenth century and the beginning of the twentieth! So many questions go begging for answers! What was the nature of the relations in the family home? What was the character of Nechui's relationship with Panteleimon Kulish? What did he do as a student in Kyiv? Whom did he know? Why did he leave Siedlce? What really happened in Kishinev as far as Ukrainian activities were concerned? Who were his friends and enemies at the Kyiv *Hromada*? How much did he know about the activities of the organization? Was there more than mere linguistic sparring in his sudden turn against Hrushevs'kyi? Were there any intimate or very close personal friends in his daily life? The available evidence does not provide satisfactory answers to these questions. I hope the biography presented here spurs interest in finding the evidence that might provide more answers and greater insight into Nechui's actions, feelings, and ideas.

Chapters 2 and 3 look at Nechui's depiction of Ukraine – the first, the foremost, and, indeed, the only subject of his literary works. In a tribute on the occasion of the thirty-fifth jubilee of Nechui's writing career, Ivan Franko characterized him as the "all-encompassing eye of Ukraine," an author who captured the details of an entire nation.[5] Chapter 2 explores Nechui's personal geography and the social stratification he depicts in his works. These are topics where Nechui's established reputation is largely on the mark, where he is less unknown than elsewhere: Nechui really is the Balzacian chronicler of Ukrainian territory and Ukrainian society. But for readers who assume he writes only about villages and peasants, and writes about them in a familiar populist spirit, chapter 2 is required reading – his villages and their inhabitants offer many surprises. Another surprise: Nechui's depictions of Kyiv and of the urban middle class are far more important and conspicuous than many readers imagine. In chapter 3, where the nationality question is the central concern, Nechui's fervent patriotism should not be a surprise to anyone. His list of enemies here includes all the usual suspects: on the one hand, the social and economic policies of the Russian Empire – serfdom, conscription, industrial capitalism; and, on the other, the groups that many Ukrainians thought of as oppressors – Poles, Russians, and Jews. The unknown Nechui, however, or at least the less well-known one, devotes very considerable attention to Ukrainians who abandon, disrespect, or ignore their own nationality. And, in at least one of his works, he takes on the issue of cosmopolitanism in a direct challenge to those Ukrainian intellectuals of his time (read: Drahomanov and Franko) who chastised him for what they perceived as his parochial world view. This is a Nechui that very few critics have seriously examined.

The last three chapters of this volume focus directly on the unknown qualities of Nechui's writing. Studies that focus on the writing technique of any Ukrainian realist authors are extremely rare, and Nechui is no exception. The existing work on Nechui often focuses on language use or folkloric borrowings. These studies yield predictable results that only confirm what readers can clearly see without a detailed analysis. The very few comments on the mechanics of Nechui's prose style that do exist are largely critical, focusing on what are assumed to be errors or infelicities in writing. Chapter 4 opens with an examination of these presumed errors and proceeds to focus on three central qualities of Nechui's writing: repetition, pacing, and the absence of purposeful construction. The intention here is not to make judgments about the strengths and weaknesses of his writing but rather to point out its essential features. For better or worse, Nechui writes in a manner entirely his own, which must be described before it can be evaluated. The chapter then concludes with a discussion of Nechui's response to modernism as embodied in his parody of a modernist story.

The most unusual characteristic of Nechui's belletristic prose is its focus on women and on a woman's sensual and amorous pleasure or joy. That is the topic of chapter 5, which shines a spotlight on a group of lesser-known works by Nechui, particularly his short novel *Ne toi stav*, where women's issues appear in a variety of manifestations, from religious holidays to conjugal pleasures. Nechui's understanding of these issues derives from a fundamentally joyful outlook, a sensibility that grows from an essentially positive moral judgment of human desires and the pursuit of happiness. Chapter 6, the last in the volume (aside from the conclusion), looks at Nechui's historical writing, both novels and essays. These are among the least-known works in his oeuvre: most of them are not reprinted in the ten-volume edition of his works that is still (for good reason) the primary source of his texts. These historical works add a significant dimension to our understanding of Nechui as a writer and intellectual, even though they are not a radical departure in style or philosophy from his better-known literary works.

This book has been a very long time in coming. If scholarly projects aged along with their authors, this one would likely show signs of arthritis. Over the long course of its slow development, the project and its author have reaped great benefits from various individuals and institutions that offered support, encouragement, critical assessments, and assistance, particularly with obscure texts and sources. Almost thirty years ago, when I was still a graduate student, the late Omelian Pritsak reacted to my expression of interest in Nechui by pointing me in the direction of an important memoiristic essay by Maria Hrinchenkova, which figures prominently in chapter 1. It led to my first published essay on Nechui, which appeared in Pritsak's sixty-fifth birthday Festschrift. Between then and now, many individuals have given me assistance, for which I am very grateful. I particularly wish to thank those who helped locate rare texts: Johannes Remy, Andrii Danylenko, Ksenya Kiebuzinski, and the many dedicated librarians of the Harvard College Library. I also express my gratitude to the Ukrainian Research Institute of Harvard University, which offered me a Shklar Research Fellowship in 2007 that led to an acceleration of this project and allowed for its eventual completion. I am grateful to all of my colleagues who generously offered assistance and encouragement. And I am especially grateful to my wife, Uliana Pasicznyk, and our two sons, Ivan and Stefan, who have always offered the strongest support and encouragement, along with a large measure of understanding, patience, and tolerance.

1 The Unknown Nechui

In the introduction to his monograph on Nechui-Levyts'kyi, Serhii Iefremov describes what he calls the dual life of a typical Ukrainian writer of the nineteenth century.[1] By day, says Iefremov, these individuals toiled at the mundane tasks of supporting their existence, while in the remaining hours they struggled for the glorious Ukrainian cause they so passionately advocated. By day they served the oppressive regime in a variety of civil service jobs as teachers, government bureaucrats, or public functionaries. In their leisure hours, they sacrificed their time, health, and energies to literature. Here, says the biographer, "is the permanent, endless collision, the source of the tragic shattering of the human being, the squandering of noble intentions and broad plans, the dissolution of the self in trivialities."[2] For Iefremov, the Ukrainian writer of the nineteenth century combines the features of an anti-establishmentarian revolutionary and a Chaplinesque human toiling automaton, a mere cog in a great machine. The struggle of this individual is particularly difficult, since his or her goal is the attainment of an aesthetic ideal. The physically and emotionally oppressive circumstances in which this task is undertaken are singularly ill-suited to the refined and delicate work of the writer and intellectual. Thus, the nineteenth century Ukrainian writer becomes, in Iefremov's view, a paragon of the suffering intellectual freedom fighter, a pathetic David struggling against an invincible Goliath, without hope and without the dignity of public and personal identification with the struggle.

As illustration, Iefremov offers a quote from Mykhailo Kotsiubyns'kyi. Citing his own biography of the modernist writer, Iefremov quotes from a letter Kotsiubyns'kyi wrote to one of his friends, Volodymyr Hnatiuk: "Damned office work has caught me in its firm grip [leaving me] incapable of doing anything."[3] Iefremov's biography of Kotsiubyns'kyi had appeared two years before the monograph on Nechui and was reissued alongside the Nechui biography in 1924, so the reference to Kotsiubyns'kyi was understandable. No doubt, Iefremov also considered it quite a natural juxtaposition. But this comparison of Nechui to Kotsiubyns'kyi is misleading. Kotsiubyns'kyi is better known for his vacations in Capri than for his office drudgery and Iefremov's comparison of the two writers has the unintended consequence of highlighting how entirely wrong Iefremov's assessment really is.

Kotsiubyns'kyi and Nechui are comparable only in the most superficial generalities. In their writing, in their thinking, in their personalities, in their private lives, and even in the world they inhabited and represented, these two writers were very different. Kotsiubyns'kyi, twenty-six years younger than Levyts'kyi, belongs to a different generation of writers, to a different social and aesthetic milieu. He was something of a pampered intellectual dandy. Introspective and delicate in personality, he was indeed a man for whom the difficulties of daily existence could impinge on his writing. He was not at all averse to complaining about his health, his material circumstances, and the ineluctable drudgery of quotidian existence – all of which conspired to prevent him from achieving the intellectual and emotional serenity that are required for true art and creativity. These complaints, however, were not the symptoms of pathetic suffering but simply the intuitive response of a delicate disposition enthralled by the majesty of modernist high aesthetics. Kotsiubyns'kyi's material circumstances were never very easy, especially in his early life, but he was not enslaved to a cruel fate that prevented him from reaching his potential as a writer.

While in Kotsiubyns'kyi's case Iefremov's characterization merely misrepresents the nature of that writer's complaints about drudgery, in the case of Nechui, the very notion of a serious divide between his daily life and his literary career is mistaken. Ivan Semenovych Levyts'kyi, a schoolteacher in the Russian Empire's western provinces, did indeed keep his writing and his teaching separate. As a writer he used a pseudonym, and no doubt he did not advertise to his superiors in the government bureaucracy that he was writing works of Ukrainian literature and having them published in a foreign country. This would likely have endangered his career and pension as a teacher. But this was a practical, politic choice, not a reflection of some inherent principles of his world view. At his postings as a teacher in Siedlce and later in Kishinev there were colleagues with whom Nechui shared his literary and cultural interests and his works. Later, after his retirement to Kyiv, even the semblance of a division between the man and the writer disappeared. In Kyiv, Nechui lived a quiet, retired life unconstrained by any conflict between his roles as a citizen and as a Ukrainian intellectual. Of course, he did not go out of his way to inform the authorities that he was a Ukrainophile (and thus subject to government surveillance or even arrest), but his life was essentially of a piece. For better or worse, in his own eyes and in the eyes of those who knew him he was the Ukrainian novelist Ivan Nechui-Levyts'kyi, the creator of Omel'ko and Marusia Kaidash, of Baba Paraska and Baba Palazhka, and of countless other characters and scenes of life in Ukraine.

All of this would hardly be worth saying if it were not for the extraordinary weight Iefremov's biography carries and the lasting pernicious effect of his views. Iefremov's notion of the Ukrainian intellectual and writer of the nineteenth century may be appropriate for Taras Shevchenko or other early romantics, whose identities as Ukrainian writers were not always in harmony with their identities as public individuals, but this is not the case with Nechui. He was not a man suffering and struggling against himself in a crusade on behalf of Ukrainian culture or Ukrainian peasants. Quite the contrary, he was a man at home with both his cultural activism and the simple, hard facts of the lives of Ukrainian peasants. He was an educated man, at home among the intellectual elites of Ukraine, Russia, and Europe, but he was deeply attached – emotionally, ideologically, aesthetically, philosophically, and convivially – to the *narod*, the simple folk, the common man. He spent the bulk of his life in urban centres, but he loved the countryside and took every opportunity to vacation there and visit family and old friends. On questions of national identity, Nechui was a patriot, unabashedly pro-Ukrainian, who never failed to point out wrongs done to Ukrainians by Russians and Poles. But his patriotism was generally confined by two limits: he was not politically active, and his attention was focused on Ukrainians in the Russian Empire. These limits would often put him at odds with other Ukrainophiles, but in his own outlook these were largely consistent principles. In his general understanding of culture, nationality, society, and art, Nechui's views were unified, consistent, and coherent. He was neither a spiritually troubled romantic nor an intellectually challenged modernist. Nechui was not a philosopher. He did and said things that were inconsistent and contradictory, as most people do. But these were merely instances of human foibles, not the product of inherent dualities or tensions. And foibles and peculiarities were qualities with which Nechui was especially blessed.

The most significant of these peculiarities concerns his advocacy of his own personal variant of proper Ukrainian. In the first decade of the twentieth century, Nechui suddenly developed the view that inferior and improper western Ukrainian linguistic forms were being deliberately introduced into the language in a conspiracy by an influential cabal of intellectuals that included the respected historian and future president of Ukraine, Mykhailo Hrushevs'kyi, and Serhii Iefremov. While some of Nechui's comments made sense, many of his pronouncements were not only wrong but actually contradicted his own earlier practices. Nevertheless, the aging Nechui advanced his views with great passion and energy along with enormous obstinance and ill will, provoking very serious disagreements with a number of important individuals. The inconsistency and passionate hostility Nechui displayed on this issue were certainly unusual for the otherwise mild-mannered schoolteacher. Since the bulk of the people with whom he argued were younger than he, and since his views were obviously capricious in so many details, the incident provoked more pity than genuine anger. Iefremov, in particular, understood it in such a manner, and this understanding further coloured his presentation of Nechui as a pitiable, suffering, and self-contradictory figure. In the last half decade of his life, the aging and solitary Nechui may indeed have been a pitiable figure, but this last snapshot of the writer should not be allowed to obscure and depreciate the person or his accomplishments. During his long productive life Nechui had earned his place as a major figure in the development of Ukrainian culture, and his literary and historical measure should not be taken in his final years when the frailties of old age had reduced his productivity and his spirit.

Nechui's eighty-year lifespan included a variety of personal and professional twists and turns, but he was not a man whose biography is marked by dramatic experiences or very unusual events. The appearance of an uneventful life is reinforced by the relative paucity, for a man of such importance and longevity, of biographical materials.[4] Despite its apparent simplicity and tranquillity, Nechui's biography needs careful attention and continued research, not only to counteract the distorted image of his person but also to help crack open the fossilized scheme of interpretation that has reduced his work to a sequence of platitudes in the curriculum of primary schools in Ukraine. With a more balanced image of the writer and a fuller appreciation of the themes that dominate his works, those schoolchildren and their teachers just might be surprised by what they discover.

Ukrainian culture of the late nineteenth century is rich in intellectuals whose origins are found in the lower or middle strata of society. But their ascent of the social pyramid is not indicative of a social climate that favoured or encouraged such upward mobility. Quite the contrary, the restrictions on access to education in the Russian Empire were an effective deterrent to such advancement. Thus, it is no surprise that many of those who did advance in social standing were the sons of clergymen, who enjoyed special privileges in the form of guaranteed access to education in religious schools. If being the son of a clergyman was an advantage in Ukraine, Ivan Semenovych Levyts'kyi had a very large inheritance of this asset. As far back as memory reaches, for a minimum of four generations, his male ancestors were all priests.[5]

The first in this series of clergymen, Nechui's great-great-grandfather Ioann Leontovych, may have been from a noble family. In 1748 he was ordained a Ukrainian Greek Catholic priest and assigned pastor of the church of St Nicholas in Stebliv. In 1768 he converted to the Orthodox faith. St Nicholas officially became an Orthodox parish in 1794. This was a time of growing Russian-Polish and thus also Ukrainian-Polish animosity and conflict. The year 1768 witnessed the outbreak of the bloody Ukrainian, anti-Polish, and anti-Catholic uprising, the Koliivshchyna as well as the Polish Bar Confederation, which tried to reverse growing Russian influence in Poland. In 1793 Stebliv and the entire Right Bank of Ukraine were incorporated into the Russian Empire as part of the second partition of Poland. By that time, the pastor of St Nicholas was Ioann's son, Petro, who secured this position thanks to the support of the parishioners. No doubt, this popular support was only enhanced by the fact that he changed his surname from Leontovych (which sounds foreign, aristocratic, and Polish) to Levyts'kyi (which sounds less so), as reported in the documents of his ordination in 1777. In his autobiographical "Zhyttiepys'," Nechui, quoting his father, explains this change in surname as something Father Petro did because it was in fashion (10:7). This terse understatement is repeated and further muddled in the autobiographical letter to Oleksander Konys'kyi, where Nechui relates that Uniates (Greek Catholics) and Poles had tried to force his grandfather to join the Union (the Greek Catholic Church) by smoking him out of his house, but he had remained faithful to Orthodoxy (10:263).

This version of events is somewhat misleading. Father Petro clung faithfully to Orthodoxy, but his father, Ioann, had been a Uniate priest for many years. To present the change of surname as a matter of "fashion" is to hide the fact that it was a deliberate step to Ukrainize a foreign-sounding surname. If Nechui was embarrassed by this fact, he could easily have just left it out. He certainly knew enough history to put his grandfather's decision in its proper context. Nechui was never shy about his own anti-Polish, anti-aristocratic, and anti-Uniate sentiments, and was likely embarassed that his family's clerical traditions started in the Greek Catholic Church under Polish rule. Perhaps he even knew of some aristocratic family roots. In any event, the family history he presents is a sanitized version of what must have actually taken place. His understanding and appreciation of this family history is an important factor in examining those of his fictional works that portray the family life of clergymen in contemporary and preceding generations.

Ioann begat Petro, Petro begat Stefan, Stefan begat Symeon (Semen), and Symeon begat Ivan Semenovych Levyts'kyi, that is, Nechui. All but the last were priests. Nechui's younger brother, Amvrosii, also became a clergyman, as did Amvrosii's youngest son, Apolinarii. This was a clergy family in the grand tradition. In most generations it was not the first-born son who became a priest, so there was nothing particularly extraordinary in the fact that Ivan didn't. Generally, only one son took orders and inherited what must have been thought of as the "family" parish, which after 1803 was no longer St Nicholas (it was closed) but the church of the Transfiguration of the Lord (Preobrazhenniia Hospodn'oho) in Stebliv. In the early years of the nineteenth century, the Levyts'kyi clergymen married village girls and their children were christened in the arms of village peasants. Stefan, who succeeded his father Petro after 1813, married a peasant girl but had his children christened in the arms of local aristocrats. Later generations were more likely to socialize with other clergymen from surrounding villages.[6] Nechui's father, Semen, took over the parish in the 1830s and married Anna Lukianivna Trezvins'ka, the daughter of a priest who served at the Lebedyn Women's Monastery. As Nechui recalls, his maternal grandfather was a simple *kozak* (cossack, that is, a free man, not an enserfed peasant) from the Poltava region who travelled to this area with his brother. and they both became priests and adopted (different) aristocratic surnames. Nechui's uncle Ievtrop, Anna's brother, was also a priest, although he did not succeed his father at the Lebedyn Monastery but received a parish of his own in Semyhory, not far from Stebliv. Surrounded thus on all sides by clergymen, Nechui was more than just the son of an Orthodox priest – he was the product of an ecclesiastical dynasty. This was a social category with specific markings. It was not, however, an indicator of extraordinary religiosity or devotion. Nechui was a secular man for whom religious life was first and foremost a familiar personal experience and a congenial milieu.

Expansive in their conquest of time, the Levyts'kyi clan was very localized in its geography. Stebliv is a village on the Ros' River, located at the bend where the tributaries Borovytsia and Khorobra flow into it. The high banks of the river and the plentiful vegetation of the rich soil make for a colourful and pleasant natural landscape. Today it is an urbanized village (*selyshche mis'koho typu*) with a population of 3,791 located in Cherkasy oblast, sixteen kilometres west of the regional centre, Korsun'-Shevchenkivs'kyi.[7] It lies roughly 180 kilometres south of Kyiv, fifty kilometres southwest of Kaniv, and seventy kilometres west of Cherkasy. In the nineteenth century, under different administrative divisions (after 1837), Stebliv belonged to the Kaniv district of Kyiv *gubernia*. A cloth mill was established in the village in 1845, a sugar mill in 1844.

Stebliv can trace its history at least as far back as 1036, when Iaroslav the Wise built a fortress on this spot, but the history that Nechui absorbed from his native surroundings was tied to later events. The territory of modern Cherkasy oblast was the scene of many important historical events in the long period of conflicts between Ukrainians and Poles. In his autobiographical letter to Konys'kyi mentioned above, Nechui recalls that on trips outside the village his father would relate stories about incidents that happened in the places they were passing (10:262). There was a ravine named "Slaughter" and a road named for Nalyvaiko, the Cossack rebel leader of the 1590s. There were the ramparts where hetman Bohdan Khmel'nyts'kyi camped while planning his crossing of the Ros' River. And all around were the living memories of the Koliivshchyna uprising of 1778, which, as we have seen, played a role in the Levyts'kyi family fortunes as well. Nechui, born sixty years after those events, would have heard about them from his father, from his grandfather Stefan (who lived until 1872, when Nechui was thirty-four), from his extended family, and from his neighbours. But the bloody uprising of the previous century was not only an oral memory circulated among family members and local inhabitants. It was a formative event in Ukrainian history and culture.

Stebliv is only twenty-five kilometres from Kyrylivka (today called Shevchenkove), the village where Taras Shevchenko lived as a child. Moryntsi, where Shevchenko was born. is even closer. In 1838, when Nechui was born, Shevchenko's freedom had just been bought from his owner and his career as a writer and painter was beginning. His reputation spread very rapidly after the publication of the *Kobzar* in 1840, so even as a child Nechui would have known about the famous poet from a nearby village. Of course, Shevchenko himself absorbed the same geographical history that Nechui did, particularly regarding the Koliivshchyna uprising, to which he devoted one of his best-known works, the long poem *Haidamaky*. Lebedyn, where Shevchenko's hero rescues his sweetheart Oksana, is the town where Nechui's uncle served as a priest at the monastery. The geography of Nechui's origins left a prominent historical imprint in his consciousness, just as it did with Shevchenko before him. But the younger man had an additional benefit. The geography of his era carried a powerful additional stamp – that of Shevchenko himself. Nechui's development as a writer owes much to both of these elements.

The greatest influence on Nechui, of course, came from his immediate family. Ivan (no doubt in memory of his great-great-grandfather Ioan but also remembering other Ivans in the family) was born on 13 November 1838 (i.e., on 25 November according to the Gregorian calendar used elsewhere but not in the Russian Empire until 1918). He was the first child of Semen (Father Symeon) and Anna, who had eight other children. Of these eight, only four, two pairs of twins, survived past early childhood. Amvrosii, who was later ordained a priest, and Anna (named just like her mother), who later married an orthodox priest, Hryhorii Radziievs'kyi, were born in 1842. Dmytro and Fedir were born in 1849, but Dmytro died when he was seven. Maksym was born in 1840 but died of smallpox after seven months. Three daughters, Oleksandra, Mariia, and Olena, were born in 1844, 1845, and 1847, but they did not survive their first year.

When Semen Levyts'kyi took over the parish of the Transfiguration, his father, Rev. Stefan was still relatively young, so the freshly ordained priest and his new bride bought themselves a separate house. The building was near the church, on the cliff overlooking the Ros' River. Today it is the Nechui-Levyts'kyi Museum honouring the writer who grew up within its walls. Nechui describes it as a small and cosy home where he and his siblings, the twins, slept on the kitchen floor alongside their nanny, Baba Motria, a distant relative of their mother. Later, his father added two more rooms to the house and the children moved into the living quarters (10:9). Nechui's childhood was not marked by particular hardship or want. In comparison to the neighbouring peasants, the priest's family enjoyed comfort and bounty. Most important, they were free, which distinguished them from the bulk of the enserfed peasant population. Viewed from the perspective of the successful rural gentry, however, the life of the clergy was not very genteel and only slightly better than that of the peasants. In Right-Bank Ukraine in the mid-nineteenth century, clergy families like the Levyts'kyis occupied a middle rung on the social scale between the Polish Catholic *szlachta* (gentry) and the Ukrainian Orthodox peasants, but culturally they were much closer to their peasant parishioners.

Like many memoirists, Nechui wrote about his youth in a nostalgic spirit and coloured his experiences with the tint of his adult views on social and cultural issues: his own village was a corner of paradise, the schools were unbelievably bad, and the simple folk were generally kind and fun-loving people. But the accent Nechui puts on his recollections also gives us important clues about his personality and his relations with his family and others as a child. The most important portraits, of course, are those of his parents. Through the eyes of his first-born son Rev. Semen Levyts'kyi appears as a somewhat severe and unfriendly figure but also as a learned man, a patriot, and a well-intentioned social reformer. In the earliest of his biographical sketches, written at a time when his father was still alive, Nechui describes his father thus: "My father did not have an influence on me. Phlegmatic, stuttering when he spoke but not when reading or preaching, he sat, or more often lay, in his room with a book and seldom came out to us nor did he allow us to come in to his room. He did not like domestic chores. He always sat with his books and was better suited to a bookish life. The household was run entirely by my mother, who managed everything herself and thus shortened her life" (10:263). This passage begs for a Freudian reading, which Valerian Pidmohyl'nyi later provided, and we shall return to that interpretation in a later chapter dealing with Nechui's depiction of female characters. Clearly, Nechui felt his father lacked paternal warmth and affection for his children. But Nechui's dissatisfaction with his father's emotional austerity and physical indolence was balanced by an abiding respect for his interest in Ukrainian culture. As Nechui was growing up, Semen Levyts'kyi organized a school for the local children in his own home. When the local landowner learned of it, he had it closed and put the pupils to work in his cloth mill. Nechui quotes the landlord telling his father "if you teach the peasants to read, you and I will end up working in the fields and the peasants won't want to" (10:265). The clergyman's unique middle social rank made him a potential partner for both the upper and the lower classes. The establishment of the school was not necessarily the result of profoundly reformist social views – it may have grown out of the priest's need to educate his own children and it no doubt had a strong Ukrainian and perhaps even an anti-Polish character. But in mid-nineteenth-century Russia any attempt to educate peasants, whether inspired by idealism or mere charity, marked this rural clergyman as an unusual figure. The landlord's objection was obviously founded on far more familiar motives – unenlightened greed and self-interest – but it may also have reflected a national prejudice. Any schooling for peasants would be objectionable. Schooling that was likely Ukrainian in spirit and content was all that much worse.

Semen Levyts'kyi's interest in Ukrainian culture is further documented in his work as a collector of folklore. The romantic sensibility that came from the West to Eastern Europe, particularly to Kharkiv University in the early years of the century, eventually spread as far as the parish of Stebliv. Here, Semen Levyts'kyi was actively collecting folklore and sharing it with other collectors, most notably Panteleimon Kulish. Specifically, in 1845, when Nechui was only seven, his father sent Kulish a description of a Ukrainian wedding.[8] Twenty-five years later in an anonymous editorial note to a story in *Pravda*, which he was then editing, Kulish recounted (writing about himself in the third person):

> A long time ago, Mr Kulish, exploring Kyiv gubernia on foot and on horseback, made the acquaintance of an intelligent village priest. Later this priest collected for Mr Kulish songs, tales, and sayings from among the common folk, and he gave them to his young son to transcribe so that they could be mailed. This little boy, having acquired from the common people a taste for language, has now turned out to be the famous Nechui.[9]

That description of a wedding, which Kulish forwarded to another folklorist, Osyp Bodians'kyi, from whose archive Oleksii Dei published it,[10] contains the texts of many folk songs, some of which later became material in Nechui's stories. If the seven-year-old Nechui could actually transcribe this text, his father must have spent more time teaching him than he did lying around on the couch in his study. In any event, this weddding description helps illustrate the scope and origins of the Ukrainian sentiments in the Nechui household. Although the text is written in Russian, as would then be considered fitting for a serious, formal description of peasant customs, Father Semen Levyts'kyi, at least in his younger years, delivered sermons in Ukrainian. He even collected them and sent them off to the Kyiv Metropolitan, but the sermons were deemed unbefitting the dignity of an Orthodox pulpit, because they were in Ukrainian (10:8). Nechui proudly underscored his father's Ukrainian patriotism, explaining that his library included *Istoriia malorosiii* and *Litopys samovydtsia* but nothing by Pushkin or Gogol (10:263). The fact that Nechui does not mention his father's contacts with Kulish in his memoirs may be tied to Kulish's shrinking reputation among Ukrainian intellectuals at the turn of the century. Nechui himself had extensive contacts with Kulish later in his life, and these are not mentioned either.

Every male Ukrainian writer of the nineteenth century, it seems, owes an enormous debt to his mother and/or nannies. Nechui is no exception. The logic is quite simple. Writers must be educated, a step that cannot take place without a father's desire for career advancement for his son. Education (except for possible village schools, like the one attempted by Nechui's father) was invariably in the Russian language and thus pulled the young man away from his Ukrainian roots and was likely to drive him away from the backward peasant customs, including the language, of his Ukrainian origins. Gogol illustrates the situation admirably. An inclination to the finer elements of culture, another prerequisite for a writer, further aggravates this estrangement. But despite these challenges – for reasons that may include a romantic fascination with the folk, a political desire to promote things Ukrainian, a prosaic interest in depicting the life of the lower classes – the budding writer chooses to write in Ukrainian. Where else can this writer find the linguistic, descriptive, thematic, and ideological material for his writing, as well as the emotional support for his unusual choice, except in the warm and fuzzy memories of his childhood upbringing, which, no doubt, included a mechanism for direct contact with the oral literary production of the *narod*. This latter role was surely the prerogative of mother, nanny, childhood playmates, or other native carriers of Ukrainian traditions.

As we have seen, Nechui's father provided some of this cultural grounding through his interest in folklore. But in Nechui's memoirs, it is his mother and nanny that receive special praise in this regard. Where his father was cold and forbidding, Nechui depicts his mother, Anna, as an exceptionally friendly person. She was a tall, happy, and convivial woman. She grew up by the Lebedyn monastery, where she learned to read Church Slavonic and developed her strong religious inclination. She enjoyed reading The Lives of the Saints and performed the full ritual of religious observances – prayers, worship, fasting – in which she later involved her children. Nechui emphasizes his emotional link to his mother. Reading the life of the biblical Joseph who was sold into slavery by his brothers, his mother cried and so did Ivan (10:264). Nechui recalls that he was his mother's favourite and so was particularly saddened by her early death when he was only thirteen. He makes a point of blaming her death on hard work and the deleterious effect of bearing two sets of twins. He emphasizes that she was the one who took care of all the practical details and work around the house. He also points out that she did not speak Russian (10:263; but she could read Church Slavonic). This was also true of his paternal grandfather, Rev. Stepan, and his maternal grandmother, both of whom lived with Nechui's family until their deaths at an advanced age. Naturally, everyone in the home spoke Ukrainian.

Another source of pleasant childhood memories and Ukrainian cultural underpinnings was Baba Motria, the nanny. Like Nechui's mother, she too sang Ukrainian songs, told stories, associated with other villagers, and generally kept the children exposed to and involved in the simple life of Ukrainian peasants (10:264–5). But the significance of women in Nechui's childhood is not confined to reinforcing Ukrainian identity. We have already noted that Nechui's memoirs depict a contrasting image of a cold and withdrawn father and a warm and loving mother and nanny. This is probably not unusual for male childhood recollections, but in Nechui's case the pattern extends to other men and women that appear in his autobiographical writings. In particular, Nechui describes the widow Hapka Shulzhykha and her niece, Palazhka Shulzhivna, the housekeepers in the dormitory of the Bohuslav school. These surrogate mother figures are friendly and caring towards their charges, the boarding pupils, providing tasty and nutritious meals, laundry services, and even personal hygiene – Nechui describes a weekly head washing in the traditional village manner (10:34). His feelings towards these women clearly mirror those for his mother. Analogously, many of the men who appear in his recollections, particularly those in authority at the school, are depicted as cold and heartless, if not outright cruel. For a man who was a schoolteacher for twenty years, Nechui has very little good to say about his own education – the primary subject of his memoirs.

In accordance with a change in regulations regarding the children of Orthodox clergy that lowered the starting age from twelve to eight, at age seven Ivan was sent off to his maternal uncle, Ievtropii Trezvins'kyi, a teacher in the Bohuslav school, to prepare him privately for entrance into grade school. Thanks to his father's earlier efforts and the year of further instruction with his uncle, Ivan was well prepared and in 1847 entered directly into the first grade of the school in Bohuslav, rather than into the preparatory grade. The six-year program included the study of arithmetic, geography, Latin, Greek, Russian, Church Slavonic, sacred texts, catechism, church history, music, and other subjects.

Although he mentions his school years in all his autobiographical writings, it is in the "Uryvky z moikh memuariv i zhadok" that he gives the most details about this period. This text, written when Nechui was seventy-six, was one of the last things he ever wrote. The text exhibits more sentimentality and nostalgia than Nechui's earlier memoirs – perhaps because its author is older – but it also introduces some new recollections and new themes that had not previously appeared in any of Nechui's memoirs. As in earlier recollections, the depiction of the educational experience in Bohuslav is very negative. Nechui even repeats a story he had told in his "Zhyttiepys'" about the intoxicated school principal who visits the pupils in their dormitory during lunch and spoils their food by sprinkling tobacco into their soup. True, the memoirist's credibility is somewhat undermined by the fact that in an earlier text (10:12) he had named the principal Troits'kyi whereas now he asserts that the drunken boor was a Russian named Strakhov (10:29). Regardless of the confusion, this incident, as well as the memories of cruel and frequent corporal punishment and the crushing boredom of a pedagogical system based on the memorization of texts, gives ample evidence for the negative view Nechui often expressed of educational methods in the Russian Empire. But this text also offers a glimpse of another side of Nechui's personality that is less often visible in his memoirs: his joyful and friendly disposition. Details about other pupils in Bohuslav and their activities outside the classroom give the text its nostalgic quality and show the young Ivan as a bright, cheerful, and impressionable child. He is happy to help his friends, trading his superior intellectual skills for items of food sent to the pupils by their parents. He is troubled by the brutality of the teachers and the poverty of many of the pupils (although this is likely a sentiment of the memoirist rather than the child). But most of all, and here we are at the intersection of the child and the remembering adult, Nechui is thrilled by the small wonders of childhood. He describes a midnight outing through the snow, when the bored children run barefoot and in their bedclothes through the monastery grounds to the school and back to their dormitory: his focus is on the bright moonlight illuminating the fresh white snow and the enchantment it brings when he looks into the school windows and sees witches or when he peers down into the ravine of the Ros' River, where he sees the white rabbits of moonbeams flitting about above the churning waters (10:32–4). The episode has such an impact on the boy that after their return to the dormitory, he has a powerful dream about witches and rabbit-like moonbeams. The dream has such an impact on the sleeping child that he literally falls out of his bed (10:37).

Nechui's reputation as a stodgy old grumbler – earned in his orthographic quarrelling – obscures what is perhaps the single most important feature of his personality and his writing: joy. Iefremov's image of Nechui as a suffering patriot in the romantic tradition has many pernicious consequences, but none worse than the distortion of his cheerful, fun-loving disposition. Except for his later years, when advancing age diminished his strength and his optimism, Nechui was characteristically a man who practised and advocated good cheer. This is not to say that he was a raucous "party animal." He most certainly was not. He was a conservative and restrained man with no inclination to exuberance, let alone excess. He was punctilious and methodical to a fault, and he did not indulge in any particular vices, or at least there is no record of such behaviour. He did not seek out pleasures, and he could easily deny himself comforts. But he was happy and cheerful. He understood, whether consciously and philosophically or, more likely, silently and instinctively, that happiness was the basic and most important state of the human condition. He created his literary characters on that fundamental principle. In the Jeffersonian triad of values – life, liberty, and the pursuit of happiness – Nechui would, no doubt, start with the last and derive the two others from it. In his own life, the pleasures he sought were invariably modest, and more often than not, aesthetic in nature. Where other memoirists retell moments of dramatic emotional experiences – their loves, their conflicts, their successes and failures – Nechui relates the powerful impression left on his consciousness by dancing moonbeams on the icy riverbank by a gurgling waterfall or the light-hearted games and distractions at a springtime school holiday in a meadow outside of town. Among other happy recollections were singing in the school choir, where he was a member, decorating the school with fresh greenery for Pentecost, and marvelling at the personal handicrafts of his fellow schoolchildren, which included decorated pen cases, key chains, and bird cages.

Whatever the balance of sentiments here between the experiencing child and the recollecting adult, it is clear that Nechui preferred to take delight in the beauty and felicity of what is, was, and could be than to bemoan what is not or was not as it should be. For a nineteenth-century realist writer, social inequalities were a staple element of the thematic menu, and Nechui's appetite for this fare is clearly evident in his works. This theme also appears in his memoirs, but it is not the major focus. The class differences between the pupils in Bohuslav were likely insignificant because they were all products of clergy or religious families.[11] The major injustice challenging the good cheer of Nechui's recollections is the brutality and stupidity of some of the teachers and administrators, noted earlier. But these concerns do not dominate the text. In "Uryvky," the most memorable students are not victims of cruelty, like Demianovs'kyi (10:20–1), who died after a beating from a teacher, but those, like Iakym Netups'kyi or Maksym Kolomats'kyi, who stood out from among the others, who were outsiders, distinguished by a mark of alterity. Netups'kyi was a giant, a seventeen-year-old among the ten-year-old first-graders. Kolomats'kyi, on the other hand, was physically deformed, with a small and weak body and an oversized, conical head on wide shoulders. Both were good students. Nechui's friendship with these two unusual boys underscores his compassionate and friendly disposition, his own abilities as a student, and likely tells us something about his own sense of identity. Perhaps he, too, considered himself something of an outsider and identified with others like himself. In any case, we are a long way from the images of social discrimination that often characterize the experiences of children as narrated by realists with a social agenda. The protagonist of Franko's "Olivets'" (The pencil), for example, is a victim of poverty and social conditions as well as of a brutal schoolteacher. Like Franko, Nechui also condemns the cruelty practised in schools, but his focus is more on the human, the personal side of problems, rather than on their social dimensions. Even his description of the tobacco-sprinkling inspector is not devoid of sympathy for a man who is clearly lost in a world of personal emptiness and hopelessness. Nechui was certainly not indifferent to the corrosion of class discrimination, but this was not the context in which he usually framed his views.

The six years Nechui spent in elementary school in Bohuslav are better represented in his memoirs than any other period in his life. Indeed, there is very little evidence of any kind regarding his years as a student in Kyiv. In the spring of 1853, he finally got to see the city about which he had heard so many fantastic tales, but it did not make a very positive impression. The dark churches with their grotesque imagery did not appeal to him (10:12). At the Kyiv Theological Seminary, where Nechui was enrolled, students were not beaten or whipped, but it was only somewhat less cruel and certainly not much more advanced intellectually than his previous school: the pedagogy was stale and bookish despite some younger teachers who encouraged the students to work on their own. But Kyiv had its own attractions. Students were required to sign a pledge that they would avoid the company of girls and would not marry before they completed their studies. Of course, despite this promise, the students did not forego the pleasures of the big city, and Nechui readily took part in parties and outings with his fellow students.[12] But for Nechui the real pleasures of Kyiv meant books. One day during his first year at the seminary, at the Kontrakty market right in front of the Kyiv Theological Academy (where he would enrol eight years later), Nechui was attracted by the cover illustration of a devil on a volume displayed in a French bookstore. It was a small book and inexpensive, and since the students were learning French, Nechui found the courage to buy it. It turned out to be Alain-René Lesage's *Le Diable boiteux* (1707; variously translated as *The Devil on Two Sticks*, *The Devil on Crutches*, or *The Lame Devil*). Afterwards, according to his memoirs, he went on to buy illustrated French editions of Jacques-Henri Bernardin de Saint-Pierre's *Paul et Virginie* (1788), Cervantes's *Don Quixote* (1605–14), Chateaubriand's *Atala* (1801), *Les Natchez* (1826), and *Génie du christianisme* (1802), Dante's *Divine Comedy* (1308–21), Eugène Sue's *Envie* (1848) from his *Les Sept Péchés Capitaux* (The Seven Deadly Sins) (10:14), and Sir Walter Scott's *The Fair Maid of Perth* (1828) (10:267). He liked Dante most of all. He also discovered Shevchenko at this time, but the text, he specifically says, came from his father, not from his own contacts in Kyiv. Contemporary Russian literature, specifically Pushkin and Gogol, Nechui claimed, did not form a part of his reading until the upper grades of the seminary.

Thus, it was in the period of Nechui's studies in Kyiv at the seminary that his interest in literature awoke. Of course, the specific details of this experience may be subject to some doubt. His emphasis on French and generally Western European texts rather than Russian ones fits very neatly with his adult views on the foreignness of Russian culture among rural Ukrainians. And it seems likely that his reading knowledge of French and German took longer to develop than the first few months of education at the seminary. Nevertheless, the general outline of Nechui's literary initiation is clear. The major texts were classics of the Western European canon. Contemporary writing meant romanticism, even if this was not the last word among trendy readers in Paris or London. Russian writers, whether earlier or later in their arrival on his reading list, were evidently not making a large impression. Most importantly, Ukrainian literature is almost invisible.

The issue of *Lastivka*, Ievhen Hrebinka's almanac of Ukrainian literature that Nechui mentions as his first encounter with Shevchenko, came out in St Petersburg in 1841, that is, twelve years before Nechui arrived in Kyiv. Of course, Shevchenko had also published two editions of his *Kobzar* by this time. Most importantly, Shevchenko's works, and the works of other writers, circulated privately among the Ukrainian intelligentsia. Nechui does not reveal any contact with such publications or any private sources of Ukrainian literature. Shevchenko came to Nechui not through the Ukrainian circles of Kyiv, although he says Shevchenko's works circulated among the students at the seminary, but through personal and geographical connections in Stebliv (10:268). Shevchenko was in Ukraine and in Kyiv during the summer of 1859 and his presence, no doubt, helped promote Ukrainophile sentiments and activities. In his years at the seminary and later at the Theological Academy, Nechui might have been in contact with a developing Ukrainophile community and movement in Kyiv. Tsar Nicholas I had ruled with an authoritarian disposition, evident in the severe punishment he handed out to Shevchenko and the other members of the Cyrillo-Methodian Brotherhood, but after his death in 1855 the situation improved somewhat. Kyiv in the late 1850s and early 1860s saw a growing, albeit small and self-contained, movement of Ukrainian cultural activists who took up the challenge of defending Ukrainian culture from imperial repression and neglect.[13] The Kyiv Theological Academy played an important, if unwilling and unwitting, role as a source of these activists. The children of the clergy were precisely the right social group for this mission – they were inherently closer to the culture of the Ukrainian peasants, and, by virtue of their education, they were most likely to see the need for cultural development and education. Nechui was squarely in this category, but nowhere in the available record – neither in his memoirs nor in those of any other activists – does he figure as one of these activists. This may, of course, be a question of pragmatic discretion. The Ukrainophile movement was persecuted by the authorities, and in his memoirs from 1876 through 1890 Nechui might have avoided mentioning such contacts to forestall any accusations of wrongdoing. But this is unlikely. It is far more probable that Nechui was simply not part of this movement. He was not a man with a revolutionary inclination. The Ukrainophiles were not, of course, revolutionaries in any real sense, but the choice to work on behalf of the Ukrainian cause and of the Ukrainian lower classes required a passionate inclination to political activism that doubtless was alien to Nechui's deliberate and restrained personality. There may have been other factors as well.

Nechui finished his studies at the seminary in 1859, but he was in such poor health that he returned to Stebliv to recuperate. He had lived in rented urban quarters near the canal in the Podil – Kyiv's geographically and socially lower town along the river – and the unhealthy environment left its mark on his health, not particularly robust to begin with. He was a long time recovering. Perhaps the twenty-year-old needed not only physical recovery but also some time to think about what he would do next. Whatever the reasons, after a period of recuperation, Nechui found himself back in his familiar Bohuslav monastery school, only now not as a pupil but as a teacher. He was hired as a teacher of grammar, geography, and arithmetic, and he served in this capacity from 22 April 1860 until 20 September 1861, perhaps with an earlier period as a volunteer. This brief stint as a teacher in Bohuslav would serve Nechui well twenty-five years later, in 1885, when at the tender age of forty-six he became eligible for a teacher's pension after a quarter century of service to Russian imperial pedagogy. Apparently he was a well-liked teacher in Bohuslav: at least he was held to be one of the better young teachers by Pavlo Klebanovs'kyi, who published a very descriptive memoir about his studies at the school. Klebanovs'kyi, in his last year when Nechui was a teacher, describes a wave of young new dedicated teachers, among them Nechui, who brought a more purposeful educational spirit to the school. Nechui, in particular, says Klebanovs'kyi, argued strongly against corporal punishment and the exploitation of younger students by older ones. He also gave the pupils French books to read, thereby encouraging them to move beyond the narrow confines of the antiquated program of study despite the derisive reaction of the school principal.[14]

While Nechui was handing out literature in French to his pupils in Bohuslav, he was also preparing for his own entrance into the Theological

Academy in Kyiv, where he began his higher education in the autumn of 1861. Returning to school meant reneging on the terms of an agreement with the seminary, which had given him a thirty-ruble grant to help him start his career as a teacher. The administration of the seminary had his last two months' salary from Bohuslav garnisheed as partial repayment of the grant.[15] Although the academy had a glorious past stretching back to its founding in 1632 by Petro Mohyla, the school that Nechui enrolled in was no longer a leading scholarly institution. It was fundamentally a religious school run by the Orthodox Church for its own purposes. The serious institution of higher education and scholarship in the city was Kyiv University, but Nechui apparently did not consider this option.

While Nechui, as noted above, was not an active participant in the various student groups at the academy that were working for social change, he was aware of their existence. The most important consequence of Nechui's studies at the Theological Academy was his novel *Khmary* (The clouds), which depicts the lives of students and professors at the school. As in the novel, so in reality the antiquated scholastic education provided there was not of the highest calibre, except, perhaps, in religious studies. Furthermore, this was a time of heightened social activism. Slavery (serfdom) was abolished in the same year Nechui entered the academy. The old-fashioned religious school was at odds with the sentiments of those among its students who were inclined to use their education for the benefit of society, particularly the newly liberated but still impoverished and oppressed peasants. In his novel Nechui depicts such a character in his hero, Radiuk, who was in fact modelled on two such activists whom Nechui knew as a student at the academy (10:441). Of course, Nechui's depiction of his hero may not coincide with the understanding these activists themselves had of their activities. Nechui was criticized for the feeble energy and political confusion of Radiuk's activism, but this anaemic hero is just further evidence that the writer was not personally involved in such activities. Had he been politically active, he likely would not have received so many commendations from the academy's principal and faculty not only for his good grades but also for his exemplary behaviour and modesty.[16]

Besides the reform of serfdom, 1861 was also memorable in Ukraine for the publication of the first Ukrainian periodical, *Osnova*. Although it lasted for only a year, the journal's influence was great, signalling to many the idea that Ukrainian culture and specifically Ukrainian literature were legitimate social and intellectual ideas. Nechui was clearly among those who interpreted the periodical in such a spirit, mentioning it specifically in his memoirs as a stimulus to his own writing. But it ceased publication after fourteen issues, before he could realize his intentions and make a submission (10:15). Nechui's experience at the Theological Academy brought two issues into sharper focus for him, literature and nationality. The first two years of the academy's program included philosophy, world and Russian history, Russian and German literature, aesthetics, and church history. Nechui pursued a historical program of study, so mathematics was not required, to his own delight. Theology was taught only in the last two years (10:325). The academy's library was poor, but students kept up with contemporary writers by subscribing to popular journals. In this atmosphere, Nechui no doubt felt a growing attraction to literary creativity. Nationality, on the other hand, was reinforced with a negative accent. The academy attracted students from across the spectrum of Orthodox nations. In addition to Ukrainians, there were many Russians studying with Nechui, but also Serbs, Bulgarians, Moldavians, Greeks, and Georgians. Conflicts over issues of Ukrainian national identity arose among the students and professors, particularly after the appearance of Mykola Kostomarov's essay "Dve russkija narodnosti" ["Two Rus'ian Nations"] in the third issue of *Osnova* for 1861. The Russian students and professors were generally hostile to the idea of education or literature in Ukrainian, according to Nechui (10:268), Nechui quotes one professor as telling the students that in the interest of the state, it would be best to burn all Ukrainian literature (10:16). The ethnic tensions in the Kyiv Academy were only a small part of a general awakening of national identities in the Russian Empire that took place in the third quarter of the nineteenth century. Ukrainians, Russians, and Poles were all becoming more conscious of their own nationality and of the differences and antagonisms between them. The Polish uprising of 1863, another instance of these growing national antagonisms, did not directly affect Nechui at the time and had no place in an Orthodox religious institution, but it had important and direct consequences for his career and for the Ukrainian movement as a whole.

Nechui graduated from the Kyiv Theological Academy with a master's degree in theology in the spring of 1865. Whether or not he had ever entertained a notion of entering religious orders, he was clearly not so inclined now. His education had prepared him for a career as a teacher in the Orthodox seminaries, and he hoped for an appointment in Kyiv. Instead, he was given an assignment at the seminary in Poltava as a teacher of Russian language and literature. Here, as in Bohuslav, he was well liked by his students, and one memoirist even recalls his emotional readings of Shevchenko in class.[17] But the salary earned by teachers in Orthodox seminaries was very small, and Nechui realized that staying there would condemn him to terrible poverty. No wonder the turnover among teachers in Bohuslav had been so great! There was another factor, as well. In Poltava, Nechui began to write. In fact, he created his first work, a story (*povist'*) entitled "Dvi moskovky" (Two soldiers' wives). But he was writing in Ukrainian! That was not an activity that could be comfortably pursued within the bounds of an Orthodox religious institution in Russia. Nechui needed a position that paid better and offered more personal freedom. Ironically, the opportunity arose as a result of the Polish uprising.

Russian imperial authorities took a number of repressive steps following the uprising to prevent any recurrence of such disturbances in the future. One step was to inculcate loyalty to the empire by better controlling the education Polish children received in their schools. Of course, teachers in these outlying and potentially hostile provinces (from a Russian perspective) would be paid better than those who enjoyed the comforts of home territory. Moreover, each year of service in these areas would count as one and one-third years in pension calculations.[18]

But not all the children living in what was considered Polish territory were Poles. Many were Ukrainians. So an opportunity arose for Ukrainian teachers to exploit this Russificatory policy to their own advantage. Nechui asked two of his former professors at the Kyiv Theological Academy, Teofil Lebedyntsev, the historian and future editor of the journal *Kievskaia starina* who was then serving as the supervisor of the Kholm school district, and Ievhen Kryzhanovs'kyi, who was taking up a position as a supervisor of the school administration in Podlasie (Podlachia), to find him a position in the town of Bila (Biala Podlaska), 147 kilometres east of Warsaw, in an area with a sizeable Ukrainian population. Lebedyntsev did manage to place Serhii Hrushevs'kyi, the father of the future historian Mykhailo Hrushevs'kyi, in the Kholm schools, but Nechui did not get the position he wanted. He was appointed to a girl's high school in Kalisz, 207 kilometres west of Warsaw,[19] which was not even remotely a Ukrainian area. Nechui found himself in the heart of Poland, teaching Polish girls Russian language, literature, history, and geography. Not surprisingly, he asked to be transferred. In June 1867, after just one year in Kalisz, he took up a similar position in Siedlce, eighty-nine kilometres east of Warsaw, also at a girl's high school, but this time one for Uniates – that is, for Ukrainian girls. Nechui felt more comfortable here and participated in activities with his students that went beyond his formal duties as a Russian teacher. He even accepted the position of school librarian, which entailed a small salary bonus. Where the salary for a seminary teacher in Poltava had been, according to Nechui himself, 250 rubles (10:269), in Siedlce he was reportedly earning 1,200.[20]

For Nechui, better pay and more freedom were not the only advantages of teaching in the schools of Congress Poland. Now, he was practically on the doorstep of the Ukrainian lands of the Austro-Hungarian Empire! For a Ukrainian writer, this was no small matter. In 1863 the Russian tsar had signed a secret instruction to imperial censors that prohibited the publication of certain books in Ukrainian. This instruction, known as the Valuev circular, was not a blanket prohibition of publishing in Ukrainian, and its specific terms were somewhat ambiguous.[21] The circular specifically prohibited the publication of any non-belletristic books in Ukrainian, but it also prohibited any books in Ukrainian that were intended for mass reading. This could be interpreted to exclude belletristic works as well. However it was interpreted in practice, the circular had a strong dampening effect on the development of Ukrainian literature through the clear implication that writing in Ukrainian, even if not legally prohibited, was suspicious, undesirable, perhaps even reprehensible.

There is no historical record of Nechui's reaction to the Valuev circular or any indication that he submitted works for publication in the Russian Empire before 1873. Thus, he did not test the provisions of the Valuev circular. In this he was not unique. The number of belletristic titles published in Ukrainian in Russia fell markedly after the new rules were implemented.[22] No one has compiled the evidence of what was submitted only to be rejected, but Mykhailo Drahomanov famously reproached Ukrainians in the Russian Empire for their failure to publish belletristic literature in Ukrainian under the provisions of these rules.[23] Evidently, neither Nechui nor other Ukrainian writers in Russia felt comfortable attempting publication at that time. Despite Drahomanov's admonitions about inertia and timidity among Ukrainian writers, Nechui was, in fact, writing. But he published elsewhere, outside of Russia. Establishing connections with those who could get his works published in Austria was possible in Kyiv, but, as we have noted, Nechui was apparently not seriously involved with Ukrainian activists when he was a student there. It was his proximity to Warsaw that gave him this opportunity.

Among the officials involved in ratifying the plans that Lebedyntsev and Kryzhanovs'kyi were formulating for schools in Uniate eparchies were former members of the Cyrillo-Methodian Brotherhood, Vasyl' Bilozers'kyi and Panteleimon Kulish, who had been rehabilitated and were now officials on imperial service in Warsaw.[24] Nechui thus learned that Panteleimon Kulish was living in Warsaw, where he held a Russian imperial bureaucratic post from 1864 to 1867. Kulish would have been an attractive contact for Nechui not only on account of his large reputation in Ukrainian literary circles as publisher, editor, and author, but also in light of the earlier cooperation with Nechui's father. Nechui might even have remembered meeting him as a child. In any event, towards the end of 1867 Nechui set out for Warsaw, where he visited Kulish. The meeting is described in a letter Nechui wrote about Kulish to the Russian literary historian and Gogol specialist Vladimir Shenrok on 7 January 1898,[25] which Shenrok used as a source in a biographical sketch of Kulish.[26] Since Warsaw was only three stops by train from Siedlce, Nechui visited Kulish several times. As Nechui says in his memoirs, the meetings with Kulish, his wife Hanna Barvinok, and her brother, Vasyl' Bilozers'kyi – like Kulish, a former member of the Cyrillo-Methodian Brotherhood – gave him a moral boost that helped him find his way in a foreign land. They did that and much more. Kulish put Nechui in touch with the contacts he had in western Ukraine, in the Austro-Hungarian Empire. There, the situation for Ukrainian publishing was very different from that in Russia. There were no restrictions on the Ukrainian language in Austria. There were obstacles, but they were financial and practical: a lack of money and of the skilled human resources necessary to maintain a publishing program. Eastern and western Ukrainians met in a marriage of mutual convenience. The west supplied the freedom to publish; the east provided financial support, writers, and cultural and political sophistication.

By the time Nechui met with Kulish, he had two manuscripts that he could show him: "Dvi moskovky" (which Nechui had written back in Poltava) and a short story entitled "Horyslavs'ka nich, abo rybalka Panas Krut'" (A memorable night, or the fisherman Panas Krut' – in later redactions the title was shortened to "Rybalka Panas Krut'") – written in Kalisz (10:270). Two more non-fiction works were written during the first half of 1868,[27] during the time Nechui and Kulish were meeting in Warsaw: a review of two published historical dramas and the first part of a lengthy study of Ukrainian mythology entitled *Svitohliad ukrains'koho narodu v prykladi do sehochasnosti*, which Nechui would continue in later years. Kulish judged Nechui's works positively, particularly their reliance on an authentic Ukrainian language. No doubt he advised Nechui to publish these works in Lviv in the newly established journal *Pravda*, which Kulish himself was instrumental in supporting and which in its nearly thirty-year existence became one of the great institutional pillars on which a modern Ukrainian literature was established. With the help of an intermediary, Levko Lopatyns'kyi, these four works made their way to Lviv, where they all appeared in *Pravda* in the course of 1868, the first full year of the journal's appearance. "Dvi moskovky" appeared first, in issues 8 through 13, then "Panas Krut'" in 23–6, the review in 29–32, and the study in folk mythology in 35–47. Nechui barely left the journal's pages during the whole year. It was an auspicious beginning for a new author, a new journal, and a new era in the history of Ukrainian culture. Despite repression and prohibitions in Russia, Ukrainians were to have a literature in their own language. Despite internal strife and social underdevelopment, western Ukrainians in the Austro-Hungarian Empire were joining their counterparts across the border in the promotion of a single, modern cultural identity. Ivan Nechui-Levyts'kyi was not among the activists on whose political and organizational skills this effort was founded, but he was from the very start a key participant. He and a handful of other writers were the creators of the cultural product that would set the tone and establish the model for a literature that would become the cultural, aesthetic, and intellectual expression of an entire nation. A generation later Ukrainian literature would grow to be more diverse in its aesthetics and its intentions, but in the late 1860s, if Ukrainian literature were to survive, it needed three things: institutionalization, aesthetic quality, and widespread popularity or appeal. *Pravda* provided the first, Nechui the latter two.

These publications on the pages of *Pravda* were the first works published by this author, but the person of the author was not disclosed in the journal. The pieces were signed with the pseudonym "Nechui." Later in his life, Ivan Levyts'kyi signed his works with a combination of his pseudonym and surname, Nechui-Levyts'kyi, and it is under this combined form that he became generally known. Nechui's use of a pseudonym does not signify any particular psychological or publicistic feint. It was a common practice among Ukrainian writers who were citizens of the Russian Empire. In publishing their works, particularly abroad, they used pseudonyms to avoid the possible negative consequences of writing and publishing in what the Valuev circular had clearly marked as a dangerous language. The government had made writing in Ukrainian a quasi-legal undertaking, and it was natural for authors to protect themselves with a pseudonym. While a great number of people would have known who the author of the stories in *Pravda* actually was, Nechui did not advertise this fact among the people he lived and worked with. Indeed, he tells us in his memoirs, even his father did not know (10:17).

The choice of pseudonyms is not addressed anywhere in Nechui's own writing nor have subsequent critics explained it. It remains something of a mystery. The word itself does not appear in dictionaries, but it is obviously a combination of the negative particle with the stem of the verb for hearing, feeling, or otherwise sensing (*ne chuty*). As a name, it has the character of old Ukrainian Cossack appellations, which often focused on an individual's physical or behavioural characteristics. In this spirit, it might have been used for a deaf cossack. Valerian Pidmohyl'nyi famously understood it as "do not hear" and, combining this speculation with Nechui's comments about his father, assumed that it stemmed from an Oedipal complex in which the son was, among other things, hiding his literary activities from his father.[28] While this interpretation makes for exciting reading and raises important issues, it stretches credulity beyond the breaking point. The word can also be construed as a nominalization of the quality of insensitivity (not to feel), understood as untroubled, undisturbed, undemonstrative, or unexcitable rather than callous, hard-hearted, or unsympathetic. In Ukrainian folk medicine a flowering plant, *Hieracium pilosella* (mouse-ear hawkweed), is commonly called *nechui-viter* (or *nechuiviter*), likely underscoring the plant's hardiness and insensitivity to wind (*viter*), since its leaves are at the base and its stolons creep along the ground. Perhaps Nechui adopted his pseudonym with this understanding of the term, but such an interpretation is mere speculation and still leaves much to be explained.

In connection with Nechui's meetings with Kulish, we also learn of Nechui's other travels at this time. As a teacher Nechui had the summer months free. He generally took advantage of this time to go home and visit his family, relatives, and friends in the Bohuslav and Stebliv area. But in the summer of 1868, he made a trip to Russia proper, visiting Vilnius and Riga, and then St Petersburg and Moscow. In St Petersburg he met with Mykola Kostomarov, from whom he picked up one of Kulish's manuscripts that the author had asked be returned. Apparently Nechui did not go home to Stebliv that summer, since in February 1869 his aunt wrote to him and complained that his younger brother had not shared with her Nechui's letter recounting his journey.[29] Had he gone home after the trip, he likely would not have needed to write letters about it later. In any event, in the summer of 1869 Nechui was travelling again, this time in the opposite direction. He set off for Europe with Hryhorii Sol's'kyi, a former classmate from the Kyiv Academy and now a fellow teacher in the girls' high school in Siedlce. Apparently the initial goal was Italy, but, says Nechui (10:326–7), in Vienna he met with Kulish, who advised him that Italy was too hot in the summer and recommended Switzerland, so he went there instead. Unfortunately, Nechui did not leave any recollections about his travels in Western Europe, although Mykola Taranenko cites a fragment from an unpublished work where Nechui recalls a conversation with some Slovaks on a train: they spoke Slovak while he spoke Ukrainian and everyone understood each other perfectly.[30]

If Nechui did not leave reflections on his holidays, it was not for a want of energy. Quite the contrary, the thirty-year-old Nechui was at the peak of his creativity and productivity in Siedlce. Having established contact with leading cultural figures in Lviv, he was busy producing material for them to publish. Nechui was writing up a storm, even though he had a full-time job as a teacher. As his first works were being published in 1868 he was already working on his next major work, the novel *Prychepa* (The cocklebur), a work depicting the moral decay, financial ruin, and denationalization that result from the social climbing and materialistic ambitions of the spoiled children of Ukrainian families. Like his previous works, this one appeared in *Pravda*, in issues 12–46 for 1869, that is, from late March to mid-December. This time, however, Kulish not only gave it his blessing, he gave it a very substantial edit. As Mykhailo Vozniak has shown, Kulish made major changes to the language and orthography of the first six (of twelve) chapters of the novel.[31] Indeed, Meliton Buchyns'kyi, who was closely involved with the publication of *Pravda*, later said in a letter to Mykhailo Drahomanov that the manuscript was "so massacred by editorial corrections in red that it was pitiful and frightening to see."[32] Kulish was so thoroughly taken with this work that he even marked stress on many of the words in the manuscript.

Another of Nechui's works from this time had a far less productive connection to Kulish. In a letter to Mykhailo Hrushevs'kyi of 29 November 1900, Nechui explains the delay in submitting a manuscript by the need to make a copy. Without photocopies, of course, Nechui literally had to write out the text again by hand or hire someone to do it. The need for copies, he goes on in the letter, was confirmed by his experience with an earlier manuscript entitled "Naimyt Iarosh Dzheria" (Iarosh Dzheria, hired hand), which had been stolen from Kulish at the train station in Kraków (10:369). The story of Kulish's loss, whether by theft or otherwise, of a briefcase containing unique copies of his own and Nechui's manuscripts is documented (if not fully clarified) in the correspondence between Kulish and the editors of *Pravda*. Oles' Fedoruk gives the best-researched reconstruction of events, which puts the manuscript of *Iarosh Dzheria* in Kulish's hands in Vienna no later than August of 1870, after which it is lost in Kraków in December of that year. The title of the lost work suggests, of course, that this was an early version of the novel *Mykola Dzheria*, perhaps Nechui's best-known work. In a letter from 1871 Kulish reported that Nechui has almost completed recreating the novel and would soon be submitting it for publication. In fact, the manuscript is dated 1 January 1876 and was not published until 1878. Nechui probably wrote a variant of this short novel twice in the years 1868–71, but the final version, which depicts the hero working as a fisherman in the Kishinev area, was no doubt modified after August 1873, when he began teaching in that city.

Yet another major work that Nechui wrote in this period was the novel *Khmary*, which depicts the environment of the Kyiv Theological Academy. One of the early versions of the novel is dated 24 May 1871 (2:379). Excerpts from this novel appeared in *Pravda* in 1873 and 1874 and the first complete publication was in Kyiv in 1874. It seems unusual that Nechui would initiate such a project in Siedlce, so far from Kyiv and five or six years after graduating from the academy, with no particular events at that time to stimulate these memories. Perhaps it was something he had been planning earlier and brought to fruition in the creative burst of energy that characterized his time in Siedlce. It was a work that he would continue to tweak and edit for many years to come.

Nechui also wrote other works in his years as a teacher in Russian-ruled Poland. In 1870 he sent to the editors of *Pravda* four items for publication: (1) a translation of an essay by the Russian historian and ethnographer Ivan Gavrilovich Pryzhov (1827–85) on Ukrainian literary history that had appeared in the Voronezh *Filologicheskie zapiski* in 1869;[33] (2) translations of two stories by Mikhail Saltykov-Shchedrin, "Povest' o tom, kak odin muzhik dvukh generalov prokormil" (A tale about a peasant who fed two generals) and "Dikii pomeshchik" (Wild landowner), both of which had appeared in *Otechestvennie zapiski* (co-edited by Saltykov) during 1869; (3) a translation of parts of Mykola Kostomarov's Russian-language historical treatise on the *Last Years of Poland*; and (4) a chronicle of events in Ukraine.[34] Of these, only two were published in *Pravda*. Saltykov's two hungry generals and Kostomarov's work on Polish history appeared in the journal early in 1870, before the journal closed down that summer for lack of funding. The chronicle of news from Ukraine was not published and apparently has not survived. Nechui's translation of Pryzhov's work could not be included because Natal Vakhnianyn's translation of it had already appeared. Saltykov's second story probably would have appeared but for the suspension of the journal's publication. By 1872, when publication resumed, *Pravda* had new editors and other materials to publish, and Saltykov's story may not have seemed as fresh as it would have been two years earlier.[35]

As this list of materials shows, Nechui was pursuing a specific purpose. As Mykhailo Drahomanov said in so many of his publications, Ukrainians in Austria were not well acquainted with Russian cultural developments. Translations of a liberal Russian writer, translations of Russian-language historical writing about Poland or Ukraine, and a news summary can all be seen as part of a deliberate effort to acquaint Galician Ukrainians with the best of Russian scholarship and culture. It was also, as Nechui makes clear in the introduction to his translation of Saltykov (2:386), an attempt to show that the Russophile orientation among Ukrainians in Galicia was focused on precisely the most backward and ossified elements of Russian culture. Perhaps with some prompting from Kulish, Nechui could not have failed to observe the gulf between Ukrainians on either side of the imperial border. Promoting familiarity with Russian culture, particularly in matters concerning Ukraine, was not an effort to foster harmony or neighbourly fraternity between Ukrainians and Russians – it was an effort both to educate benighted Galician Ukrainians about cultural developments everywhere in Europe, including Russia, and also to clarify the very sensitive issue of Ukrainian identity. In this latter context, advancing familiarity with Russia meant undermining the Russophile orientation. With this goal in mind, and with the pages of *Pravda* silent, Nechui submitted his next essay, entitled "Orhany rosiis'kykh partii" (The press of the Russian parties), to another Lviv publication, *Osnova*, a populist semi-weekly that existed briefly during the period of *Pravda*'s inactivity. The essay examines the popular press in Russia at the time and shows Nechui's interest in the politics of the era. In a somewhat simplistic and didactic tone it praises a liberal European orientation and criticizes the conservative view from a perspective that was very common among liberal intellectuals in Russia. The essay is an indictment of tsarist authoritarianism and Russian chauvinism that goes a long way towards dispelling a popular stereotype of Nechui as a provincial bumpkin and secular anchorite. Perhaps in his later years Nechui did not keep up with the times and was not aware of what appeared in the newspapers and journals, as some memoirists assert, but this essay testifies that in his Siedlce years he was a reasonably well-informed observer of contemporary Russian (and not just Russian!) politics and intellectual trends.

In addition to fiction and cultural politics, Nechui's pen was also aimed, as we have noted, at folklore and ethnography. Exploring the unfamiliar territory of Podlasie where he found himself, Nechui naturally turned this experience into raw material for his writing. In 1872 a renewed *Pravda* published an ethnographic description of his wanderings in this region.[36] His primary interest was in its Ukrainian population, their customs and habits, their language, and their understanding of their own identity. He evidently made a number of such excursions, including some to local historical landmarks. In later works – for instance, in his novel *Kniaz' Ieremiia Vyshnevets'kyi* (Prince Ieremiia Vyshnevets'kyi), written in 1896–7 – he used his memories of these visits to construct vivid descriptions.[37]

Beyond these activities, Nechui was also busy as a teacher. Newspaper reviews and other sources speak of an amateur theatrical production in Siedlce of Ivan Kotliarevs'kyi's *Natalka Poltavka* in late 1868 in which Nechui played the role of the romantic hero, Petro. Teachers from the high school filled a number of roles, and one teacher's wife played Natalka. The roles called for talent as both actor and as singer, and Nechui apparently carried off his stage debut with success.[38] In later years visitors observed on Nechui's piano a portrait in costume of the actress who played Natalka. There were some who understood this picture as a memento of an actual old flame of Nechui's, not just a keepsake from a theatrical performance.[39] Furthermore, Maria Zahirnia (Hrinchenkova) reported that when she and her mother, who was of similar age to Nechui, asked the elderly writer whether he had ever loved any women, he replied that there had been two, both in Siedlce. In both cases, Nechui said, he was talked out of marriage. In the first instance, the school principal told him that it was inappropriate for a teacher to marry a woman who rode around on horseback with officers. In the second, his sister told him that his earnings as a teacher would be too meagre to support a family. Also, the woman would want to have dresses appropriate for attending balls, she told him, and he could not afford that on one hundred rubles.[40]

Nechui may well have related such a tale to Hrinchenkova and her mother, but it hardly seems credible that a man intending to propose marriage could be talked out of his intentions with such foolish arguments. And, as noted earlier, in Siedlce Nechui was making twelve hundred rubles, not one hundred, and was living quite comfortably. If he did in fact buy a piano in advance of making a marriage proposal, as Hrinchenkova says he told her, he obviously would have had the funds to buy his wife a dress or two. The whole episode sounds much more like something from one of his novels (specifically *Prychepa*) than from Nechui's own experience.

Another surprising story concerning Nechui in his Siedlce period arises from contemporary correspondence rather than memoirs. Ukrainian civic and political figures in Lviv were so taken with Nechui that they actually considered the feasibility of securing him a professorship of Russian literature at Lviv University. The suggestion appears in a number of letters[41] between correspondents in Lviv in 1869–70. Whether or not this was a realistic possibility, it is clear that Nechui, who had only appeared on the scene a year or two earlier, had dazzled his readers and acquaintances. No doubt this good impression was strengthened in personal meetings. In the course of his years in Podlasie, Nechui visited Lviv, perhaps more than once but certainly in the spring of 1871, when he met with various notable figures and even arranged for the publication of his first book, consisting of the materials already published in *Pravda*. It is worth noting, parenthetically, that Nechui and other Ukrainians from Russia paid the costs of publishing out of their own pocket in advance and then recovered some of this investment from the proceeds of books as they were sold. If he could afford to publish his own books, likely he could afford to get married as well. In any event, between his publications in Lviv journals and his personal acquaintances there, Nechui was making a good impression. The teaching assignment in Siedlce had been a most fortuitous development for him.

Of course, Nechui's growing reputation was not confined to western Ukraine. In October of 1871, Mykhailo Drahomanov, who was generally very well informed and frequently travelled to Western Europe (the letter in question is from Heidelberg), was already seeking more information about Nechui, whom he praises, for an article on current Ukrainian literature. But he claims not to know the identity of the person behind the pseudonym.[42] After Buchyns'kyi tells him, Drahomanov answers that he actually knew the name from Kulish and Nomys but was seeking Nechui's address in order to write to him personally.[43] Just over a year later, in January 1873, however, Drahomanov is less enthusiastic and compares Nechui unfavourably with Panas Myrnyi.[44] The change in sentiments no doubt had any number of causes, including souring relations with Kulish, whose protégé Nechui was understood to be; nevertheless, it confirms Drahomanov's growing familiarity with Nechui's work. And, of course, if Drahomanov is following Nechui's writing, it is an obvious corollary that his friends in Kyiv must also be familiar with these works.

Specific details of Nechui's popularity in Ukraine at this time are not readily available. The fact that Drahomanov mentions the folklorist Nomys (Matvii Symonov) as a source in 1871 indicates that Nechui's reputation was spreading, since Symonov lived in Lubny. It seems likely that this popularity was not just a matter of reading his works at a distance. Although Nechui's summer travels have not been thoroughly catalogued, it is well established that he liked to go home to his native Stebliv and Bohuslav during holidays and vacations, particularly in the summer months. Mykola Taranenko says he visited Odessa during the summers of 1871, 1872, and 1873.[45] Whatever the destination – home, vacation, or both – many of these travels might readily have included or accommodated a stopover in Kyiv. The itinerary he describes in the first paragraph of his later work "Zhyvtsem pokhovani" (Buried alive) is precisely such a trip from Siedlce through Kyiv, to his native region. A former student of the Kyiv Academy who was one of the few Ukrainian writers actively publishing works of literature must have been a very welcome acquaintance for the expanding circle of Ukrainian activists in Kyiv in the early 1870s. They could hardly have let such an interesting fellow slip past them to his home village without trying to make his acquaintance. Indeed, Nechui himself was just as likely to have wanted to make their acquaintance. The first letter, from 23 April 1872, in Nechui's ten-volume *Works*, is to Pavlo Zhytets'kyi, a leading figure among the Kyiv Ukrainophiles (10:255). In it he speaks of a virtual acquaintance, indicating that he had not yet met with Zhytets'kyi, but he also expresses his regret that he did not meet with Lev Lopatyns'kyi when he was in Kyiv during the vacation. It is likely, then, that he visited

Kyiv and its Ukrainian activists either in the summer of 1871 or during the Christmas and New Year's holidays in January 1872. Whether or not he visited, he had certainly written to Zhytets'kyi earlier. In a letter to Mykhailo Drahomanov (then still in Western Europe) on 7 February 1872 Zhytets'kyi reports that he received a letter from Nechui two days before in which Nechui proposed that the Hromada publish his manuscript of over a hundred pages.[46] It is not clear which work this might have been, but Zhytets'kyi praises Nechui as a writer and suggests putting off other works for later in order to publish Nechui. In fact, however, nothing of Nechui's appeared in Kyiv until 1874.

In the years following the Valuev circular, the work of activists in the cause of spreading Ukrainian culture – Ukrainophiles, as they would eventually be called in police investigations – was in decline. The enthusiasm that had produced the Sunday school initiatives in 1859–62 was sorely tested by the government's repressive measures.[47] Only gradually, in the late 1860s, was the courage and energy found for renewed group initiatives. These took the form of modest secret meetings in private homes of a group of individuals focused on literary and educational goals. Among their projects was the compiling of a grammar and dictionary of Ukrainian. Among the key activists were the historians Volodymyr Antonovych and Mykhailo Drahomanov, the composer Mykola Lysenko, and the linguist, ethnographer, and former student of the Kyiv Theological Academy, Pavlo Zhytets'kyi. Zhytets'kyi had been expelled from the Theological Academy for his Ukrainian activities before Nechui started attending, and it seems unlikely the two were acquainted in the early 1860s. In any event, Zhytets'kyi was reassigned as a teacher from Kamianets'-Podils'kyi to Kyiv in July 1868, and his presence in Kyiv helped create the critical mass necessary to reinitiate the activity of what would become known as the Kyiv Old Hromada. Chronologically, the renewal of Ukrainophile activities in Kyiv corresponds precisely with Nechui's steeply climbing career as a writer and teacher in Siedlce. The fact that Nechui was writing to Zhytets'kyi was no accident or coincidence.

Beyond mentioning an earlier visit to Kyiv, Nechui's published letter from April 1872 offers additional clues of an existing relationship that extended further than just publishing. Nechui is explicitly thanking Zhytets'kyi for his "participation in my case" (in Russian, "dobroe uchastie v moem dele"). Since the letter is about finding a teaching position in Kyiv, perhaps Zhytets'kyi made some efforts to help in this matter. That means, of course, that there must have been previous communication on this issue as well, which is also signalled by Nechui's specific comments on particular types of teaching positions, as if in answer to suggestions in an unknown earlier letter from Zhytets'kyi. Furthermore, Nechui speaks frankly about money. Considering the possibility of accepting a position that pays less than he currently earns, he says it would have to lead to something better in short order, because "precisely at this time," he says, it would be inconvenient. The willingness to discuss finances and the reference to special conditions at precisely this time clearly imply that Zhytets'kyi knew more about Nechui than what is said in this letter. They had corresponded before this about more than just publications.

Another possible conduit for Nechui's connection to the Hromada was the composer Mykola Lysenko, who was an active participant in Hromada affairs when he was in Kyiv. In 1874 Nechui and Lysenko exchanged letters regarding their collaboration on the operetta *Marusia Bohuslavka*. The letters contain a very dynamic discussion of the plot structure, with Lysenko even suggesting an entire detailed outline for an opera that differs substantially from the eventually completed work.[48] The tone of the letters suggests an ongoing friendship. The earliest dated letter, from Nechui, begins with the words "Having taken your advice" (10:256), clearly indicating a previous communication. In Lysenko's letter of 23 August 1874 he informs Nechui that he and his wife have gone to St Petersburg "as I boasted in last year's winter" (torishn'oi zymy).[49] This presumably dates their communication to 1873 or perhaps even 1872, if we understand the phrase "last year's winter" written in August to mean a winter before the current calendar year. The possibility of an earlier acquaintance is further advanced by their mutual contacts with Panteleimon Kulish, who also wrote a work about Marusia Bohuslavka and may have been the original source of the idea of a musical work about her. Nechui first met Kulish, as we have seen, in 1867–8 in Warsaw. Lysenko and his wife made a similar pilgrimage to meet Kulish in 1869 in Dresden. Perhaps this mutual connection with Kulish later helped establish the friendship between Nechui and Lysenko.

Whatever paths Nechui traversed in his approaches to the Kyiv Ukrainophiles, those links were getting stronger. He was in Kyiv again in the summer of 1873. In July of 1874 the letter to Lysenko is from the village of Trushky, not very far south of Kyiv. And when the members of the Kyiv Hromada assemble for a group photograph during the Archaeographic Conference that they organized in Kyiv in August 1874, a very young-looking Nechui (he's thirty-five) is among them, seated quite prominently near the centre of the picture.[50] On 11 September 1874 Nechui is formally admitted as a member of the Kyiv Hromada.[51] Since he was not a resident of Kyiv he cannot have been a very active participant in their ongoing activities, but his membership put him in touch with a highly influential group of Ukrainian cultural figures.

Nechui's writing had now enrolled him in the two most important circles of Ukrainian activists of the 1860s–1890s, the Galician intellectuals and the Kyiv Hromada. It is the combined efforts of these two groups, as mentioned above, that represents the high point in the development of Ukrainian cultural activities in the last third of the nineteenth century. Although Nechui was one of the few people with a foot in each of these two camps, he was not one of the major players, at least not from an organizational perspective. Yes, he was an important writer, and certainly one of the most prolific and capable in these circles, but he was not a leader. As a citizen of the Russian Empire, his place was clearly on the eastern, Kyiv side of this Ukrainian-Galician connection, but he did not set the direction for organizational activity, nor was he a strategist or conspirator in the clandestine projects of the Kyiv Hromada. He was a loyal, dedicated, and skilled foot soldier in the battle to establish a Ukrainian cultural identity. Just as his work in the Siedlce period of his creativity in some measure showed the influence of Panteleimon Kulish, so his subsequent work would show the influence of his new Kyiv associates.

In the early and mid-1870s, the Kyiv Hromada sought various means of promoting Ukrainian history and culture. It was a covert organization consisting of intellectuals who shared a common interest in Ukrainian culture and scholarship but not a single political strategy. Thus, it was understandable that the primary goal was the publication of all sorts of materials, from belles-lettres to scholarship and including everything in between. The methods and strategies to achieve their goals varied widely, from completely legal and public gestures, such as the establishment of the Southwestern Branch of the Imperial Geographical Society – effectively a front for the activities of the Hromada – to underhanded and secret endeavours, such as bribing the censors to allow publications banned under the Valuev rules. Although the Hromada was very eager to promote Ukrainian publications in Galicia, this was a Kyiv organization and its first priority was to promote Ukrainian culture in the Russian Empire. At least before the Ems Ukaz of 1876, which effectively prohibited nearly all publishing in Ukrainian and even closed down publications about Ukraine in Russian, the Hromada was looking for ways to bring Ukrainian literature and materials about Ukrainian culture and history out into the open in Russia. This domestic orientation influenced Nechui as well.

Ironically, the last major accomplishment of Nechui's Seidlce period, the establishment of contacts with the Kyiv Hromada, symbolically undermined his earlier success, or at least reversed its orientation. Having established his reputation by publishing in Galician journals and even adjusting his writing to some degree (by translating from Russian) in order to meet the specific conditions of a Galician audience, Nechui now turned his attention away from the Ruthenian lands of Austria-Hungary and back to Ukraine (in the terminology of that day), back to the historical lands of the cossacks and Orthodoxy, and back to an imperial political and cultural climate that saw all things Ukrainian as heresy, treason, and secessionism. While Nechui was always a loyal patriot of his own half of Ukraine, especially of his own little corner in the southern reaches of Kyiv gubernia, there can be little doubt that the change in orientation came from his contacts with the Kyiv Hromada. It was from them that he acquired a taste for Cossack history and an inclination to brave the intimidating bulwarks of Russian imperial censorship. In 1872 he published his first book in Lviv. Perhaps the Hromada contributed financially to this publication. (The eight thoussand rubles from Ielysaveta Myloradovych to establish a press came a year later.) It was, after all, the Hromada's financial support that had allowed *Pravda* to resume publication in that year. Nechui's first volume, titled *Povisti* (Tales), had an unsigned introduction likely written by Kulish and contained the works he had previously published in *Pravda*. It was the culmination of his Siedlce era. Although he would continue to publish in Galicia, particularly after the Ems Ukaz made it impossible in Russia, his attention was now on Ukraine. His writing would not change in any fundamental way, but he would be taking up suggestions that came from his new friends in Kyiv, particularly a focus on history and on the common people.

According to Nechui himself, the Siedlce period of his life came to an abrupt and unexpected end in 1873, when he returned from the summer holidays and discovered that as a result of curriculum changes and staff intrigues, he had been reassigned to a different school – in Suwalki, 220 kilometres north of Siedlce. In the unfriendly and tense atmosphere that ensued, Nechui asked for and received an assignment for a school in the Odessa school district, specifically, the boys' high school in Kishinev, today's Chişinău, the capital of Moldova (10:16–17). The story has all the requisite ingredients of a good Ukrainian soap opera: a scheming, lovelorn daughter of a general, an old Russian hag of a school principal, a confused and irascible school administrator, a supporting cast of good-hearted friends, etc. But while the characters and storyline may well be based on fact, the truth of the matter seems less simple than Nechui suggests. Elsewhere in his memoirs Nechui merely says he left the Warsaw school district after an insult regarding his work and service ("distavshy obydu za sluzhbu i robotu," 10:270). No doubt Nechui had some particular cause to leave Siedlce when he did, but, as we have seen from the April 1872 letter to Zhytets'kyi, Nechui was already looking for a new teaching assignment more than a year earlier. Documents indicate that the transfer to Suwalki was from 1 July 1873 and the assignment to Kishinev on 11 August, barely more than a month later. If these official dates are accurate, and if Nechui only learned of this matter upon his return from vacation (early August?), there is simply not enough time for all the necessary bureaucratic actions and postal communications to have taken place. Surely Nechui must have been planning a transfer and when his situation in Siedlce blew up in his face, he could fall back on preparations already underway. The high school in Kishinev had a tradition of Ukrainian staffing, and he may have been able to call on the assistance of friends in securing a position there.[52]

Whatever the mechanics of Nechui's transfer to Kishinev, the move raises questions about his intentions. Siedlce, as we have seen, was very good for Nechui as a writer, and he was working in a Ukrainian environment. Kishinev was not a Ukrainian city (despite Nechui's claims – no urban area was Ukrainian), and if Nechui felt uncomfortable as an agent of imperial Russification on Polish territory, where he was in fact teaching Ukrainian children, he would presumably feel even less comfortable among the children of the leading families of Bessarabia. In the autobiographical letter to Ohonovs'kyi from 1890 Nechui puts yet a different interpretation on this transfer:

> I did not like the Podlasian plain, so wet and muddy, the frequent rains, the humid air, the gloomy pine forests almost like a cemetery. I was drawn to the poetic south, where there is more light, where nature is finer. I wanted back to Ukraine ... Kishinev felt more like home, because there were many Ukrainians there. The area around Kishinev is mountainous and scenic, there are orchards and vineyards everywhere. My life was pleasant. (10:327)

The way Nechui describes its attractions, Kishinev might be in southern Italy. Regardless of the facts – whether Kishinev might indeed have felt more Ukrainian than Siedlce or whether the Podlasian plains were funereal and humid – this explanation of Nechui's move to Kishinev reverses the logic of the previous account. Apparently, he wanted to leave Podlasie. The rude shove he got from the school administrator was merely the last straw that finally prompted him to act on his desire to move south. Without additional information, it's impossible to guess what really made Nechui uncomfortable in Siedlce. Perhaps there were personal matters that drove him away. It is unlikely, however, that Nechui left Siedlce because his career as a Ukrainian writer was in conflict with his other obligations there. In the six years he spent there, he had achieved very considerable success and fame with his writing. He was now one of Ukraine's foremost writers.

In 1873 Kishinev was a rapidly growing city with a population close to one hundred thousand. Much of this growth came through immigrants from other lands of the Russian Empire, so there were certainly many Ukrainians and Jews from Ukraine in the city. But it was not a centre of Ukrainian cultural activity. There was no branch of the Hromada there. It was closer to Kyiv than Siedlce had been, and much closer to Odessa, but it was much further from Lviv. It could not be matters of Ukrainian culture that attracted Nechui to this location. Perhaps it was simply the urban atmosphere. Nechui, at thirty-five, was still young. Perhaps he felt stifled in the provincial atmosphere of a small Polish town. The teaching in Kishinev was not much different than in Siedlce. He taught Russian language and literature, Old Church Slavonic, and Latin. His salary was thirteen hundred rubles. He was apparently a good teacher, attentive and compassionate towards his pupils and well liked by them.[53]

Altogether Nechui spent twelve years in Kishinev, twice as long as he did in Siedlce, yet the biographical data available from this period is not as extensive. The contacts he had established in Kyiv were bearing fruit and his writing took off in new directions: the libretto *Marusia Bohuslavka*, noted above, is one example. He wrote another dramatic (but not musical) work, *Na kozhum'iakakh* (In the Kozhumiaky section of Kyiv), at the same time and both were published in the Fritz printshop (Typographia Fritsa) in Kyiv in 1875, most likely with the financial support of the Hromada. This latter play, a comedy about the family of a social-climbing merchant in Kyiv who wants to marry his daughter to an upstart fraud, was later reworked by the dramatist Mykhailo

Staryts'kyi and retitled *Za dvoma zaitsiamy* (Chasing two hares). It became a very successful theatrical production and then later, in Soviet times, a popular movie. Drama, however, was not a rewarding genre for Nechui. Later, after his retirement, he would write a two-act vaudeville entitled *Holodnomu i open'ky miaso* (For the hungry, even mushrooms are meat) in 1886 and two minor theatrical sketches, but none of his theatrical works (except in Staryts'kyi's revised version) were successful. Although his general ideas were good, Nechui's practical understanding of the requirements of theatrical writing left something to be desired. His version of both the libretto and the comedy needed further work before they could be used effectively.[54] Lysenko wrote music for parts of *Marusia Bohuslavka*, but later used this music in a different work and the operetta never materialized.[55]

Nechui had somewhat greater success with another new genre he took up in Kishinev as a result of his membership in the Hromada. As part of its activities the Hromada had always put an emphasis on education for the general masses, starting with the Sunday schools a decade earlier. Now, the Hromada decided to implement a plan of producing and disseminating pamphlets on various topics in Ukrainian history. These popular booklets, which they called *metelyky* (butterflies), were to be aimed at an audience of common folk – they were to be simple, short, and in Ukrainian. It isn't precisely clear how this project got started or how Nechui got involved in it, but in 1875–6 the first set of these butterflies appeared in Kyiv and the authors were Nechui and Drahomanov. Nechui's contributions were titled *Uniia i Petro Mohyla, kyivs'kyi mytropolyt* (The [church] union and Petro Mohyla, Kyiv metropolitan), *Pershi kyivs'ki kniazi: Oleh, Ihor, Sviatoslav i sviatyi Volodymyr i ioho potomky* (The first princes of Kyiv: Oleh, Ihor, Sviatioslav, and Saint Volodymyr and his successors), and *Tatary i Lytva na Ukraini* (The Tatars and the Lithuanian period in Ukraine). The first two were again printed at the Fritz printshop, the third at Eremeiev. Of course, it is important to note that these works – short pamphlets in Ukrainian about Ukrainian history and clearly aimed at a less-educated reader – were still prohibited under the terms of the Valuev censorship rules. The fact that they were passed by the Kyiv censor was not a result of Nechui's diplomatic skills or good luck, but rather of the Hromada's financial muscle and the corruptibility of the censor, who was later dismissed for taking bribes.[56] In joining the Hromada, Nechui had moved into a circle of activists who were willing to do what was necessary to advance the cause of Ukrainian culture. In the Russian Empire, that meant stepping beyond the law. For a man of Nechui's honest and forthright character this was probably a rather large step. The simple deviousness of the Old Hromada would eventually get swamped by a tidal wave of forceful and even violent revolutionary actions of a younger generation, but for the gentlemen activists of Nechui's generation, even simple bribery and subterfuge required considerable courage. When it came to Ukrainophile activies, the authorities were inefficient and corruptible – some were even sympathetic – but on the whole, the government was not lenient towards what was officially considered a dangerous and treasonous orientation.

Nechui's foray into history writing under the umbrella of the Kyiv Hromada was a new direction for him as a writer, but one in which he soon found himself quite comfortable. In the course of the next thirty years he would write and publish about a dozen historical essays, ranging in size from journal articles of ten pages to small monographs of 150 pages. But perhaps the most important consequence of Nechui's Hromada-prompted interest in history was his historical fiction. The libretto for *Marusia Bohuslavka* was based more on legend than real history, but in his later years Nechui would write a novel and a play about Hetman Ivan Vyhovs'kyi and another novel about Ieremiia Vyshnevets'kyi (or Jeremi Wiśniowiecki, as he is better known) in which historical facts would become key ingredients. While Nechui's interest in Ukrainian history was not suddenly acquired in his contacts with the Hromada, there can be little doubt that the experience of writing popular historical essays prepared and encouraged him to try his hand at historical fiction.

Another new direction in Nechui's writing that coincided with his departure from Siedlce was comic satire. His earlier works had already revealed the lighter side of his personality, his penchant for breezy, lighthearted narrative and humorous anecdotes within works of a generally sombre and serious spirit. But the first work he published in Ukrainian in Kyiv was a masterful comic sketch that introduced his most famous and enduring characters, the malicious village crackpot Baba Paraska Hryshykha and her equally foolish and mean-spirited nemesis, Baba Palazhka Solov'ikha.[57] The success of the first story led to another about the two hags, and then a cameo appearance in a larger work and then two more stories written much later, after Nechui's retirement. This new comic mode did not mark a radical change of direction for Nechui, but it did signal a subtle reassessment of his audience and of his own skills. Nechui was gradually moving away from models borrowed from

Shevchenko and Marko Vovchok towards an idiom of his own, one that put language at the aesthetic centre of a work, favoured national over social issues, and focused on individual personalities rather than social types or psychological categories. These different priorities were not entirely new, but their relative weight in his writing was increasing.

Membership in the Kyiv Hromada opened new creative avenues for Nechui but it also afforded him an opportunity to continue on the paths he had already established and even to reissue in Kyiv works he had previously published in Austria. With the Hromada's backing the Fritz printshop in Kyiv issued his second book, titled *Povisti*, as had been done for his first book in Lviv the previous year. This one contained a new work, entitled *Khmary*, one of Nechui's best-known novels in which he depicts the Kyiv Theological Academy where he had studied. Nechui had written this novel in 1870–1. A selection from it had appeared in *Pravda* before Nechui had moved to Kishinev and that excerpt was included in his Lviv volume. Another part appeared later in *Pravda*. This Kyiv edition, however, was the first full publication of the work. That should read "almost full," since even with the Hromada's backing the censors cut significant passages from the text where the clergy or their school was presented in a negative light. Perhaps that is why Nechui and the Hromada sent his next book to the censors in St Petersburg. It would include the works he had published earlier in Lviv. But if they were hoping for a more lenient censor, they were disappointed. The manuscript came back to Nechui in Kishinev in May of 1876 with numerous cuts. "They even cut the word 'ridni' [native] in the expression 'ridni ukrains'ki pisni' [native Ukrainian songs]," he complains in a letter (10:271). In that same month Nechui is cheerfully answering a request from Oleksander Konys'kyi to provide materials and a biography for an anthology that Konys'kyi was planning. Nechui sent him an extensive autobiography and boasted that he had already written one in Russian for another planned publication (10:261). The school year was ending and Nechui would take the approved manuscript of his book to Kyiv himself, where he could meet his Hromada friends and bask in his growing reputation.

But before Nechui left for Kyiv, disaster struck – a complete catastrophe! The fates were merciless to this Ukrainian writer. No sooner had Nechui gained a reputation, established himself with the Kyiv Hromada, published a few works in Kyiv, and settled down in the poetic southern comforts of Kishinev, than the Russian tsar and the entire machinery of the imperial police state decided to attack the very heart and soul of his existence. Ukrainian literature was to be no more, at least not in the Russian Empire. On 18 May 1876 Tsar Alexander II, vacationing in Bad Ems in Germany, signed a decree that expanded the prohibitions of the Valuev censorship rules.[58] Henceforth, all publications in Ukrainian were prohibited, as was the importing of Ukrainian-language publications from abroad. And since this regulation was the deliberate work of the enemies of the Kyiv Hromada, the edict included a few other points as well. The newspaper of the Kyiv Hromada, *Kievskii telegraf*, was ordered closed. The scholarly organization that served as a legitimate public front for the Kyiv Hromada, the Southwestern Branch of the Imperial Russian Geographical Society, was ordered disbanded. Mykhailo Drahomanov, a professor at Kyiv University and one of the leading figures – certainly the most spirited and activist member – of the Kyiv Hromada, was ordered dismissed from his position and exiled from the empire. No sooner had Nechui got his foot in the door than the empire had struck back. The enemies of the Hromada – Ukrainians themselves in some cases, most notably in the person of Mykhailo Iuzefovych, the prime mover behind the Ems edict – had settled their personal scores with the Hromada by convincing the authorities to issue a genocidal prohibition whose purpose was to prevent the development of Ukrainian culture. The edict even provided financial support for the publications of the Russophile camp of Ukrainians in Austria, further underscoring the edict's essential ideological postulate: the only good Ukrainian was a Russian one. The brief resurgence of Ukrainian cultural activities in Kyiv was over.

It is difficult to imagine how this edict affected Nechui. For the more experienced members of the Hromada, the *Lex Juzefoviana*, as they almost invariably called it in their correspondence, was a heavy blow, yet also a return to the familiar difficulties of the late 1860s when their activities had been stifled by the authorities. But Nechui, whose sedate and contemplative character had earned him the nickname Vladyka (His Holiness, i.e., the customary title of a bishop) among Hromada members,[59] had not experienced the repressions in Kyiv in the late 1860s. This situation was new to him and the edict must have seemed a measure aimed squarely at his own person. The second volume of his works planned for publication in Kyiv was now doomed. So, too, was Konys'kyi's anthology. Gone were the hopes he had cherished of building a career as a Ukrainian writer in Ukraine. His turn away from Lviv towards Kyiv now looked much less promising. Now his career as a Ukrainian writer no doubt seemed questionable and even risky.

His new friends in Kyiv were no longer a firm foundation on which to base his hopes. Correspondence among the Hromada members in the summer of 1876 shows remarkable courage and resilience. Everyone, including His Holiness, was pledging to continue their efforts as best they could. But it must have been an extraordinarily bitter and dispirited man who returned to the classroom in Kishinev in the fall of 1876 to resume his duties as a propagator of Russian culture in Bessarabia. Not yet at the midpoint of what would be an eighty-year lifespan, he must have felt his brief meteoric career as a Ukrainian writer to be at an ebb. His country had condemned his culture and his hopes as a writer to extinction.

Not surprisingly, 1877 was a lean year for Nechui. Not a thing of his was published anywhere. No letters of his from that year have survived. He was teaching his pupils, licking his wounds, and, no doubt, seething in anger. In his biography of Nechui, Serhii Iefremov cites information provided to him by a Kishinev resident, D. Shchehlov, regarding Nechui's activities there in the immediate aftermath of the Ems edict.[60] Apparently Nechui was at the centre of a small group of high school teachers who gathered occasionally, much like the Kyiv Hromada, to exchange ideas and discuss issues. There is no mention and no record of public activity by this group. There is, however, a police report from 1881 indicating that Nechui was under suspicion for being a "a rabid Ukrainophile" (*zavziatyi khokhloman*, using a pejorative term for Ukrainians). The author of the report knows Nechui's pseudonym and knows about his connections with Drahomanov. He also mentions that this teacher panders to students and speaks Ukrainian to them.[61] What the police report doesn't mention, but Iefremov does, is that the meetings of the teachers' group in 1877 involved discussions of an essay Nechui had written entitled "Nepotribnist' velykorus'koi literatury dlia Ukrainy i dlia Slavianshchyny" (The undesirability [lit. unnecessariness] of Great Russian literature for Ukraine and for all Slavic lands), a long-winded and complex treatise about the nature of literature and its relation to a national culture. In a nutshell, Nechui argued that Russian culture and Ukrainian culture are different and the only literature that is appropriate for Ukrainians is Ukrainian literature. He said much more than that, but that argument alone was, and still is, enough to cause quite a commotion.

A Ukrainian culture completely independent of Russian culture? For many, the idea is simply unthinkable. In Soviet times, it was unspeakable. This essay was the thousand-pound gorilla that made working on Nechui so politically dangerous for Soviet Ukrainian literary scholars. They could praise Nechui's socially conscious writing, they could point to all his achievements as a writer, but they had to castigate him for this essay. It was bourgeois nationalism. It was a denial of the hallmark of Soviet Ukrainian cultural orthodoxy – the leading role that Russian culture has had and must have in relation to Ukrainian culture. One after another, Soviet Ukrainian literary scholars stumbled when they got to this essay, which, of course, could never be reprinted in Soviet times. For better critics, it was reason enough to stay away from Nechui. Of those who did mention it, very few ever managed it without completely losing all measure of scholarly integrity and good sense. Only Oleksander Bilets'kyi, a critic with an enormous scholarly reputation and impeccable ideological credentials, ever found a formula that wasn't completely foolish. He didn't excuse or accept the ideas in Nechui's essay, but he understood their emotional origins. "It's not a product of critical thinking," says Bilets'kyi, "but a product of emotion, deeply scarred by the harsh measures of tsarism ... boiling over from the insult ... It was a shriek from the 'prison of nations'."[62] On this point, Bilets'kyi hit the mark. The ideas in the essay are not quite as irrational as he might have thought, but the essay was indeed the shriek of a badly injured soul, an angry, vengeful tirade from His Holiness Nechui, the self-appointed keeper of the flame of Ukrainian cultural identity.

From the start, the essay was fated to be troublesome. Nechui sent it to *Pravda*, where the editors were evidently at a loss for what to do with it. The first part was published as an editorial in a supplement to the regular issues, under the title "S'ohochasne literaturne priamuvannia," (The direction of contemporary literature) in 1878. *Pravda* experienced financial and editorial difficulties at that time and appeared very irregularly in the next decade. Part two of Nechui's essay did not appear until 1884, when it was included in a single-volume annual issue of the journal edited by Ivan Franko. Franko's involvement is somewhat ironic, because when the first part of the essay appeared six years earlier, he published a sharply critical review of it. While the essay was unsigned, Franko knew who the author was, although he did not reveal this in his review. This exchange between Nechui and Franko marks the beginning of a long-running polemical debate between the conservative Nechui and his more radical critics, particularly Franko and Drahomanov.[63] The debate was largely informal, and on Nechui's part, it was conducted mostly in his fictional works.

Even the greatest calamities eventually dissipate, and Nechui, like all other Ukrainian cultural activists, needed to find ways to continue his work after the Ems Ukaz. He re-established his links to *Pravda* and eventually to other Galician journals. The work whose manuscript Kulish had lost in 1870 was rewritten and published as *Mykola Dzheria* in *Pravda* in 1878. The historical essays Nechui had been preparing for publication in Kyiv were published in Lviv. Most importantly, there were new works: a manuscript entitled *Burlachka* (The vagabond girl) that had been completed in February 1876, before the Ems edict, and a comic novel completed in 1878 entitled *Kaidasheva sim'ia* (Kaidash's family), featuring Baba Paraska in a cameo role. Nechui and the Hromada were not ready to give up completely. According to the censorship rules decreed in Ems, a work in Ukrainian literature could only appear if it were written using Russian spelling. Nechui submitted all three new works to the imperial censors in such variants, and *Burlachka* was allowed and appeared in Kyiv in 1880, *Mykola Dzheria* in 1883. The comic antics of Kaidash's family, however, were apparently too much for the censors and that work appeared only in Lviv. The work that saw the greatest effort in adapting to the new rules was a novel Nechui envisioned in 1876 about the life of the country clergy.[64] The manuscript of *Starosvits'ki batiushky ta matushky* (Old-world pastors and their wives) was completed in 1880 (10:282). In 1882, the Kyiv Hromada founded a Russian-language journal, *Kievskaia starina*, where members continued their publishing activities in support of Ukrainian culture. The editor, Feofan Lebedyntsev, translated Nechui's novel into Russian and included it in the journal in 1884. The Ukrainian text did not appear until 1888 in Lviv.

The Kyiv Hromada was gradually coming back to life under the new rules, and Ukrainian literary works were occasionally slipping through the imperial censorship. Despite financial difficulties, the circumstances for publishing Ukrainian works in Lviv were improving. There were more journals now, and more opportunities. Drahomanov, exiled from Russia, was using Hromada financial resources to publish Ukrainian works and works about Ukraine in Western Europe. But Nechui's remarkable energy and productivity diminished. The causes of this decline may have been various. Perhaps he never recovered from the profound sense of personal outrage that the Ems edict must have elicited. But his letters from the early 1880s do not support such a view. He is animated, involved, ready to help, and eager to work. In a letter to Kostomarov in December 1880 he even suggests that the prohibitions of the Ems edict are not as terrible as they actually were. After detailing his own experience with the Petersburg censors, he strikes an optimistic note: "There is no prohibition on belles-lettres," he tells Kostomarov, "Grigor'iev's rejections of my novels were a result of his own evil intentions as an inveterate russifier opposed to all human rights" (10:284). Since he is actually asking Kostomarov to intervene with the new director of the censorship administration to allow his submitted manuscripts to be published, perhaps Nechui is deliberately playing a naive, loyalist charade before the eminent historian. Although the Ems edict was a secret order that was not formally made public, Nechui and the Hromada members were aware of its actual contents. In July 1876 *Pravda* had even published passages from the instructions sent out by the imperial censorship office after the edict.[65]

The decline in Nechui's productivity in Kishinev is likely tied to other factors. As he mentions in letters (10:290), his workload as a high school teacher was not trivial.[66] His growing reputation came with its own obligations. A young Borys Hrinchenko, for example, sends his works to Nechui for comment and evaluation. No doubt there were other, less-skilled writers who also pleaded for attention and sought his opinion. Nechui was characteristically gracious and encouraging in these circumstances.[67] But the real cause of Nechui's decline was his health. The archival records of the Kishinev high school indicate that his "lengthy and frequently recurring illness" is affecting the fulfilment of the school's teaching program.[68] In addition to his usual Christmas and summer trips to Kyiv (which meant a trip home as well), in the summer of 1884 Nechui asked for permission to travel to Szczawnica, a resort town in southern Poland with a mineral springs spa. Of course, once in Austria, he took advantage of the trip to stop in Lviv and meet with various people there (10:394) and also to explore the locale for use in future literary works. But this was not an excuse for a scenic holiday. Nechui's letter of 4 September 1884 to Oleksander Konys'kyi, while still full of his usual high spirits about writing and visiting new places, makes clear that the mineral springs have not cured his stomach ailment. Although only forty-five at the time, Nechui tells his colleague that after the next school year he will retire from teaching and settle in Kyiv. In his valiant effort to cleanse Nechui's image of un-Marxist and un-Soviet blemishes, Oleksander Bilets'kyi suggested that Nechui's early retirement from teaching may have been tied to his Ukrainian activities in Kishinev.[69] Bilets'kyi, who likely did not know about the Kishinev police reports regarding Nechui, speculated, with perceptible echoes of Iefremov, that this teacher by day but clandestine writer by night may have experienced recriminations or confrontations with the school principal over his Ukrainophile sentiments and activities and that these unpleasantries may have been a contributing factor in his decision to take an early retirement. But as the published police report makes clear,[70] the former principal of the school "vouched absolutely" for Nechui's reliability. There is an episode in Nechui's later novel, *Nad Chornym Morem* (At the Black Sea), of a political confrontation between a teacher and a principal where the principal suggests retirement to resolve a conflict. If this scene had an actual antecedent in Nechui's life, it could just as likely have occurred in Siedlce as in Kishinev.

A few months later, shortly after the new year,[71] Nechui did indeed take early retirement. His doctor advised him to leave Kishinev. He made a return visit to Szczawnica and to Lviv, where he was again meeting with Ivan Franko, Ivan Belei, Oleksander Konys'kyi, and others. He took advantage of this, his last trip abroad, for another round of small excursions. But his health was still poor and he had difficulty writing. He tells his correspondents: "I don't have the strength to work" (10:195), "This is not a time to think about writing" (10:299), and "I haven't been able to write at all for two years" (10:300). In the fall of 1885 he settled in Kyiv, taking quarters at 31 Velyka Pidval'na Street. His pension was set at a paltry two hundred rubles but was later increased (10:304, 10:534). He was actively trying to get his works published both in Lviv and in Kyiv, particularly *Starosvits'ki batiushky ta matushky*, which had not yet appeared in Ukrainian, but these were works he had written earlier. In 1885 he wrote only a couple of short stories. He had written very little since 1881. This creative drought would continue for the first few years in Kyiv.

From his retirement to his death in 1918, thirty-three years later, Nechui lived in Kyiv – much, much longer than he lived anywhere else. If we add the years he spent in Kyiv as a student, he spent more than half his life in that city. And yet, in the popular imagination Nechui is seldom associated with any urban space. More than a few of his works are set in Kyiv, his descriptions of the city are vivid and colourful, and they are among the earliest that exist in Ukrainian literature, yet he is seldom credited with having a special affiliation to Kyiv, although he lived there far longer than other writers – Valerian Pidmohyl'nyi, for example – whose names are routinely tied to the city. This is, of course, partly a result of the contrived reputation he endures that pigeonholes him as an ethnographic realist. But it is also a consequence of the invisible life he chose to live there.

Despite his previous experience there and his membership in the Kyiv Hromada, Nechui moved to Kyiv as something of an outsider. In poor health and with a severely reduced income, he lived quietly and modestly. Even when both these conditions improved, Nechui was not a man who would become an energetic group leader or activist. He certainly participated in various cultural activities, particularly those connected with the Kyiv Hromada, but this organization was changing. Younger activists with new ideas were gradually taking leadership positions in the Ukrainian community. The cultural mission of the Old Hromada had proven inadequate in the face of government authoritarianism and repressions. The Ukrainian question was evolving from a cultural mission into a political struggle. This was true of many issues in the Russian Empire, where the last decades of the nineteenth century witnessed a radicalization of efforts to achieve social change, a politicization of issues that had previously been regarded in a broader context. In a climate where change was imminent and revolution was the watchword, the cautious cultural activism of the original members of the Kyiv Hromada from the 1860s and 1870s now seemed outdated to many younger Ukrainians. The Old Hromada was slowly transforming into a new Hromada, with younger members inclined towards direct political action. The old guard had worked to establish scholarly organizations and journals. It had worked within the limited sphere that government restrictions allowed. Its projects focused on education for the masses, on compiling dictionaries, on publishing ethnographic studies. A new generation of activists wanted something more and was willing to use various means, legal or not, to achieve these goals. The Ukrainian question was no longer about identity, but about freedom. The goal was no longer to inform the world of the existence of a Ukrainian nation, but to replace the existing social and legal structures with new ones that would allow this nation to enjoy the rights to which all nations are entitled.

These new developments led to occasional friction between the young radicals and the Old Hromada. Even within the Old Hromada itself, there had been radical elements. The break between Mykhailo Drahomanov and the other members of the Hromada highlighted such divisions within this older, more conservative group. In 1888 Nechui's health and circumstances improved somewhat, allowing him to complete work on another significant novel, *Nad Chornym Morem*, in which he addressed some of the new social realities. Nechui was only fifty years old, but he was not only very clearly aligned with the Old

Hromada, he was on the conservative end of that group. In his view, the questions that agitated Ukrainian intellectuals were essentially cultural in nature. He did not entertain the possibility of political activism, his priorities clearly focused on the maintenance and development of Ukrainian identity, not on the sophistication of this identity, not on its harmonization among social classes, not on its role in the universal family of nations. Ukrainian cultural identity was a very well defined concept for Nechui, and his loyalties were tied to its defence. At the core of this identity was language, which occupied, beyond any doubt, the central pedestal in Nechui's pantheon of values. For him, anything that threatened or challenged this language was deleterious, if not outright evil. He built his life and identity on service to this great ideal. As a writer, language was not only an abstract ideal to be cherished, it was the tool he relied on to achieve his goals and the vehicle that took him in that direction. It was a first principle, an unalterable postulate, the foundation on which all other values are built.

Nechui's defence of this simple and perhaps simplistic position put him at odds with the general scheme of social, cultural, and political developments in Ukraine in the later years of the nineteenth century. In a world where revolutionaries could justifiably claim that even the assassination of the tsar had not led to social change, Nechui's insistence on his cultural and linguistic priorities necessarily set him apart from those who saw change in a political context. His younger colleagues no doubt had sincere respect for him and for his accomplishments, but they thought of him as a relic from a previous age. Even when younger colleagues were engaged in activities of a cultural nature, essentially continuing the work of older predecessors, their attitude was respectful indulgence. For example, Liudmyla Staryts'ka-Cherniakhivs'ka, the daughter of Nechui's friend, playwright, and fellow member of the Kyiv Hromada, Mykhailo Staryts'kyi, describes in her memoirs the meetings of the young Kyiv literary activists in the early autumn of 1891 or 1892. Among those present are Nechui, Antonovych, Pchilka, Konys'kyi, and Staryts'kyi, but they are clearly the "elder statesmen" of the meeting, not really members of the same group as the youngsters. They are from a previous era.[72]

But Nechui was not yet fading into oblivion. In 1888 he moved to a different apartment, in the courtyard of a building at 19 Novo-Ielyzavetyns'ka Street. Even before Nechui moved out this street was renamed Pushkins'ka as it is still called today. It is just north and parallel to Khreshchatyk, which is Kyiv's main thoroughfare today but was then still developing as a major axis in the city. He lived there for more than twenty years, until 1909. The owner was a Mr Sehet, the director of the Kyiv Mutual Credit Society, who died in 1904 (10:413), but his widow kept the property for a few more years before selling it to new owners, who tore it down and constructed a new building there. Most of the friends and visitors who later wrote reminiscences about Nechui mention this apartment, its convenient, central location, and its sparse but very orderly furnishings, including a piano, and note its diminutive, overly formal and polite, but generally cheerful inhabitant. Nechui lived alone in a very measured, routine existence, developing habits and patterns that were notoriously predictable. As his health and resources allowed, he continued his creative work and publishing. The censorship of Ukrainian publications in Russia had always been somewhat haphazard. Although the provisions of the Ems edict remained in force – indeed, they were never rescinded – various Ukrainian books were permitted on an individual, ad hoc basis even before the major relaxation that took place in 1905. The situation must have been maddening for Nechui as well as other writers, who devoted countless hours to correspondence and submissions only to discover that the decisions of the censors were arbitrary and unpredictable. But Nechui, patient and meticulous, kept submitting his works, both new and old, for publication. Mostly this was to Lviv, to his friend Ivan Belei, who was editing the newspaper *Dilo* (The deed), or to Vasyl' Lukych, who was responsible for the journal of the Shevchenko Scientific Society, titled *Zoria*. But some of his works also appeared in *Kievskaia starina* in Kyiv, or in almanacs and anthologies appearing in St Petersburg, Kharkiv, Odessa, and elsewhere in the Russian Empire.

Although not as productive in retirement as he had been in Siedlce, Nechui was not only writing more than he had in Kishinev, he was writing in a variety of genres. In 1890 he completed *Afons'kyi proidysvit* (The vagabond from Athos), a tale about a swindler preying on the monks of a Kyiv monastery, and he also completed *Ukrains'ki humorysty ta shtukari* (Ukrainian humorists and tricksters), a long ethnographic study in fictionalized form of comic traditions in Ukraine. The next year saw the completion of a short novel set in Kishinev, *Navizhena* (The demented woman), something of a sequel to *Nad Chornym Morem*, as well as the publication of Nechui's second major essay on the national character of Ukrainian literature and its relationship to Russian culture. The essay was entitled "Ukrainstvo na literaturnykh pozvakh z Moskovshchynoiu" (Ukrainianness in a literary duel with Muscovy). It was published, of course, in Lviv and signed with a new evocative pseudonym, Bashtovyi, the sentinel on the watchtower in cossack times who was to light a signal fire at the approach of Tatar raiders. Like the earlier essay, "Nepotribnist ...," this essay showed more passion than well-reasoned argument, but it did reveal Nechui's abiding interest in questions of cultural modelling and Ukrainian-Russian differentiation.

In the spring of 1893, Nechui received an invitation from Natalia Kobryns'ka to contribute to an almanac focused on women's themes. His reply expressed a genuine interest but politely put off an actual committment; he was busy, he said, and would perhaps come up with something later. But the idea of writing on women's themes apparently stayed with Nechui. In November of the same year, at the end of a letter requesting the correction of mistakes in the text of his new work, *Pomizh vorohamy* (Among enemies), which was being serialized in *Zoria* and would then be reprinted as a book, he tells Lukych that a story he's now writing, *Ne toi stav* (He's not the same), would be short but that he would likely not finish it very soon (10:342). He was right about one thing. He didn't finish it until 23 January 1894 (6:464). It turned out to be a significant work for Nechui, staking out his interest in popular new themes. Nechui himself apparently thought well of this novel. He delayed sending this novel to *Zoria* while waiting for permission to publish in Kyiv. As he explained in another letter to Lukych, no Ukrainian work could appear in Russia if it had first appeared in Austria. After a long journey through the bureacracy, the St Petersburg censorhip office approved the novel (in Russian spelling) and it appeared in 1896 in both Kyiv and in Lviv. It was an unusual triumph for Nechui, for Ukrainian literature, and for women's themes.[73]

Meanwhile, Nechui had other celebratory moments as well. In the spring of 1894, Mykola Lysenko initiated a combined jubilee celebration of twenty-five years of literary work by Ivan Nechui-Levyts'kyi and by the playwright Mykhailo Staryts'kyi.[74] In both cases, it isn't entirely clear how the calculation was made. Nechui's first work was published in 1868 and Staryts'kyi's in 1865, neither of which was twenty-five years from 1894, but Lysenko's idea succeeded and the writers were honoured in a number of cities. The available sources do not give further details, but apparently some form of public celebration was held at least in Kyiv and Kharkiv. In any event, Nechui received so many congratulatory letters and telegrams – apparently a whole bundle from Kharkiv – that he felt he could not answer them all; instead he chose to acknowledge them in a public notice in the journal *Zoria* for 1 (13) December 1894.[75]

He thanked all his well-wishers, singling out in particular those who had sent greetings from Galicia and Bukovyna, that is, from abroad.

In the 1890s and 1900s Nechui was active in a number of initiatives beyond his own writing. In a letter to Mykhailo Komarov in 1893, Mykola Lysenko says Nechui will be funding a prize of five hundred rubles for the best work of dramatic literature about the cossack or early Rus' period.[76] On 10 January 1896 Nechui writes to Borys Hrinchenko, greeting him with the new year and enclosing the 250-ruble prize for his *Iasni zori* (Bright stars), a play about the legendary Marusia Bohuslavka, whom Nechui had also written about. Nechui also informs him that the first prize went to Mykhailo Staryts'kyi for his play *Bohdan Khmel'nyts'kyi*. Nechui also took his own advice about historical writing, although his own works were narrative, not dramatic. In 1895 he completed a novel about Ivan Vyhovs'kyi, the Ukrainian hetman who in 1657–9 who tried to realign the cossack state away from Muscovy. Two years later Nechui completed his novel about Jeremi Korybut Wiśniowiecki, the scourge of Ukrainians during the Khmelnyts'kyi uprising and the grandson of Baida Vyshnevets'kyi, founder of the cossack Sich.

Another important project, though this one did not come to fruition, was a plan to publish a Ukrainian-language journal titled *Promin'* under the nominal editorship of Nechui. It is not clear who the project's backers and principal movers were – Nechui could not have undertaken this on his own – but it was Nechui who applied for permission to publish such a journal to the censorship authorities in St Petersburg. The application was turned down.[77] Mykola Taranenko also claims that in 1891 Nechui edited a complete edition of the works of Ivan Kotliarevs'kyi,[78] but this has proven impossible to verify. We do know that Nechui was not present in 1903 at the opening of the Kotliarevs'kyi monument in Poltava, where so many Ukrainian writers from both sides of the border were in attendance. Perhaps his health did not permit him to travel – he was sixty-four at the time. Staryts'kyi, only two years younger, did make the trip. Nechui did step forward, however, for another major project for which he was particularly well suited. Panteleimon Kulish had died on 14 February 1897, leaving unfinished the Ukrainian translation of the Bible that he had undertaken for the British and Foreign Bible Society in London. Nechui took over the project in 1900 and completed it in 1901, translating, by his own count, roughly one-quarter of the text (10:373). Nechui was very good at languages and consulted various existing translations into European languages, particularly the German Lutheran translation (10:443). However, he did not know

Hebrew or Aramaic. Ivan Puliui, who served as the intermediary between Nechui and the Bible Society, had an extensive correspondence with Nechui regarding the details – linguistic, canonical, practical, and financial – of this project. After many complications, in January 1903 Nechui reported receiving payment from the Bible Society's for the translation: 2999 rubles for Kulish's widow, and 444.50 for Nechui (10:403). Nechui deposited the money in a Kyiv bank and earmarked it in his will for the support of poor Ukrainian students at Lviv University (10:408–9). Since a Ukrainian translation of scripture was very expressly prohibited in Russia, he gave instructions that most of the gratis copies given him by the Bible Society be distributed among colleagues in Lviv. Nechui's efforts, and those of Kulish, had a limited impact. The translation could be distributed only in Galicia, Bukovyna, and among the Ukrainian emigrants to North America. Because of the difference in views on the canonicity of various texts of scripture between Western Christians and Orthodox Christians, some portions of Old Testament text translated by Nechui were not included in the version published by the Bible Society in Vienna in 1903.

Among his other projects, Nechui also found time for some topics that were not part of his familiar repertoire. Ukrainians in Austria published a German-language journal in Vienna entitled *Ruthenische Revue*. In October of 1905 this journal published an essay of Nechui's entitled "Die Anzahl der Ruthenen in Europa, Asien und America" (The number of Ukrainians [Ruthenians] in Europe, Asia, and America) which was, as the title makes plain, a demographic study focused on counting the number of Ukrainians in the world. Apparently Nechui intended this essay for the Lviv *Literaturno-naukovyi visnyk*, but once he had agreed to its publication (in translation) in the *Revue*, it no longer made sense to the editors in Lviv to duplicate it in *Visnyk* (10:447). In the same letter to Mykhailo Hrushevs'kyi where he mentions his demographic essay, he also mentions two others, "The Celts and their literature" and "From Kyiv to Mykolaiv" (10:448). Neither of these is known to exist. The second essay had been written at the request of Drahomanov (10:449) before 1880, when Nechui mentioned it in a letter to Volodymyr Barvins'kyi, the editor of *Pravda* (10:279). In the letter to Hrushevs'kyi he says a shortened version of the essay was included in the work of the eminent French geographer Élisée Reclus in his volume on Russia, in a chapter on the Ros' River valley. Volume 5 of Reclus's *Europe*, part of his monumental *Nouvelle géographie universelle: la terre et les hommes*, does have a lengthy and very Ukrainophile-friendly chapter on the southern

Dnipro River basin, but there is no chapter on the Ros' River valley and there is no attribution of any borrowing. Perhaps Nechui's essay was merely background reading for Reclus or someone assisting him.

While attending to these and other public projects, Nechui was also busy, as always, with the publication and republication of his own works. Matters took a turn for the better in 1898, when Nechui received permission from the censorship office to publish the first two volumes in what was conceived as a multivolume edition of his works. In the published correspondence, Nechui first mentions this plan and outlines the contents of the initial four volumes in a letter to Hrushevs'ky of 2 January 1899 (10:355). According to Serhii Iefremov, the impetus for a large multivolume collection of Nechui's complete works came from a group of young activists at the Vik publishing enterprise.[79] This group included Iefremov himself, as well as Volodymyr Durdukivs'kyi, Oleksander Lotots'kyi, and others. The claim is something of an anachronistic exaggeration, since a complete edition of Nechui's works – one that would include his essays on Russian-Ukrainian literary relations – was simply inconceivable in Russia at that time. Even his early novel *Prychepa* was initially banned in 1898 (10:355), leading to the amalgamation of volumes 1 and 2 into a single volume. The details of how this multivolume edition was planned and executed are not clear – information about who initiated the project and who published the first volume is incomplete. The substance of Nechui's letters to Petro Stebnyts'kyi, a Ukrainian writer living in St Petersburg, where volume 1 appeared, suggests that Stebnyts'kyi was the intermediary between publisher and author. Stebnyts'kyi's unpublished letters to Nechui in the Kyiv archives (10:542) may explain who the publisher was and how this edition was planned, arranged, and financed. Apparently Nechui personally handled the permissions from the censorship office and released the rights for the first two volumes for a mere one hundred rubles (10:356). Volume 1, a very substantial book of 757 pages, appeared in St Petersburg in 1899. Volumes 2 and 3, each over 450 pages, came out in Kyiv in 1900 and 1901, respectively. Volume 2 contained the novel *Starosvits'ki batiushky ta matushky*, originally intended for volume 3, while volume 3 contained *Prychepa* (planned for volume 2 but banned by the censors) under a different title, *Nakhaba*, as required by the censors when they finally gave approval for its publication. These two volumes were definitely published by Iefremov's Vik, as Nechui makes clear in his letters (10:427). That was, unfortunately, the beginning of a disastrous relationship.

In his account of these events, Iefremov does not disguise the tough, hard-headed approach that Vik took in dealing with Nechui. Working under the difficult conditions of Russian censorship and repression, and with weak finances, these patriots were engaged in a battle for the future of Ukrainian culture. The old-fashioned, silly foibles of a doddering old man were not going to stand in their way. To demonstrate these foibles, Iefremov quotes a passage from one of Nechui's letters to Stebnyts'kyi in which Nechui argues that the books should be the same size as the 1866 edition of Shevchenko's *Kobzar*, because "a large and long book is awkward to hold in your hands, particularly lying down. It's always twisting and bending and vexatious for the reader."[80] Iefremov's citing of this quote is puzzling. Vik specialized in publishing small brochures of a few dozen pages that were meant for mass consumption. Why should an author's concern for a reader-friendly packaging of his books be seen as silly, especially since Nechui's volumes were indeed quite large? Before ridiculing Nechui, Iefremov might have considered some letters that another client author had writtten to him. Panas Myrnyi, whose works Vik was also publishing, wrote to Iefremov on 4 March 1901 about his own forthcoming volume and specifically compares it to Nechui's: "I'd like the book to be convenient for reading – it shouldn't break your hands with its weight, like the first volume of Levyts'kyi."[81] Apparently, other authors also had the same silly concern about the size of their books that Nechui had expressed. But there is yet a further problem with Iefremov's quote. The letter he cites does not exist in the published collection of Nechui's letters and no such passage is found there.[82] Of course, Iefremov could have had access to letters that later Soviet editors either did not find or chose to ignore or to censor. This matter, it seems, must be added to the list of unanswered questions regarding Nechui.

Whether or not Nechui wrote such a letter, the real difficulty between Vik and Nechui was not the author's insistence on the details of the books' shape and size but on the text of the works to be published. Iefremov recalls that Nechui was editing and rewriting the texts of his novels, often to the detriment (at least in Iefremov's view) of the works themselves. But the real problem was orthography. Nechui had developed his own rules for Ukrainian spelling, and he was insisting on them. When given proofs of the volumes to check, he discovered his wishes had not been followed, and he sent back the proofs with corrections. "And then," continues Iefremov, "the youths [i.e., Iefremov and others at Vik] would often restore the original text (as to style) or would completely ignore the idiosyncracies of the old writer (as to orthography). At first he did not notice this silent war on the proof pages. But eventually he did and got upset."[83] Indeed he did. He not only got angry, but he eventually launched a small-scale war of his own, in which Iefremov was one of the primary enemies. Nechui, who had battled imperial censors all his life, now had another censor preventing him from publishing what he had written. When Nechui received copies of the finished books and complained that his changes had been ignored, Iefremov told him, "But they're already printed!" (10:427). After Vik did the same thing with a new edition of his *Rybalka Panas Krut'* in 1903, Nechui lost patience and Vik and Iefremov lost his trust. "I don't believe them, they can't be believed. For them, any means are good, as long as it turns out their way. They'll subvert you with trickery, so long as it comes out their way" (10:428). Nechui would not cooperate with what he called despotism. Despite his passionate commitment to the Ukrainian cause and his great desire to have his works published, Nechui felt that his author's rights gave him control over his own texts, including their orthography.

Another identical conflict offers an instructive comparison. In response to an invitation from Mykhailo Kotsiubyns'kyi, Nechui submitted his story "Gastroli" (On tour) for the almanac entitled *Z potoku zhyttia* (From the stream of life). He had already raised the issue of orthography with Kotsiubyns'kyi regarding an earlier almanac entitled *Dubove lystie* ([*sic*]; Oak leaves) and had instructed the younger writer: "If you are thinking of making any changes in authors' works, first ask the authors for their permission, otherwise you'll insult them." Referring to projects implementing what he calls "Galician orthography," he continued, "excuse me if I don't agree to take part in such publications" (10:406). Kotsiubyns'kyi's replies are a model of tolerance and good sense. While maintaining that it seems foolish to publish an almanac where every work follows a different orthography, he assures Nechui that an author's rights are absolute.[84] Indeed, despite his obvious misgivings about Nechui's orthographic principles and his poor opinion of Nechui's story,[85] Kotsiubyns'kyi instructed his collaborator, Mykola Cherniavs'kyi, to pay particular attention to Nechui's orthography and to publish the story as Nechui requested.[86] Cherniavs'kyi deliberately ignored this request[87] and standardized the orthography in the published volume. Nechui was, of course, upset (10:463), but Kotsiubyns'kyi's subsequent apology was heartfelt, honest, and flattering. He tells Nechui that if there were indeed (as Nechui constantly asserted) readers that would not touch books published in the "Galician orthography," then "they would deny themselves the pleasure of Nechui's 'Gastroli.'"[88] Kotsiubyns'kyi's disarming flattery and civility insured a continuing friendship between the two writers. He treated Nechui with the respect and tact accorded a living writer, whose authorial rights and personal feelings required attention. For Iefremov and the "youth" at Vik, the old man and his texts were, no doubt, a piece of history – ossified monuments on the road to Ukrainian cultural autonomy.

Nechui's role as just this kind of living monument became even clearer during the celebration of his thirty-fifth jubilee in 1904. For a number of years the Ukrainian community had turned available opportunities for public celebration into rallying points for the promotion of Ukrainian culture. The largest and most important of these was the opening of the monument to Ivan Kotliarevskyi in Poltava in 1903, but smaller events were no less important, particularly when they took place in Kyiv. In December 1903 the thirty-fifth jubilee of the creative work of Mykola Lysenko took place in Kyiv. A public collection for a gift was announced to which Nechui contributed.[89] There was a public commemoration and a performance of Lysenko's opera *Rizdviana nich.* Nechui was quite impressed by these events, including the income generated at the opera (10:408). Lysenko himself then helped organize a jubilee celebration for Nechui. The events took place on 18 through 20 December 1904. The first evening saw a performance of *Za dvoma zaitsiamy,* the play that Staryts'kyi and Nechui had reworked from Nechui's original *Na kozhum'iakakh.* The jubilee celebration itself was held on the second day. On December 20th the festivities concluded with an evening performance at Lysenko's newly constituted school of music, which was established with the funds given to Lysenko at his jubilee.[90]

Nechui's jubilee celebration is one of the best-known events in Nechui's life, thanks to Iefremov's biography and the memoirs of Maria Hrinchenkova, both of which appeared in 1924. In both accounts, the most memorable and regrettable moment was the premature departure of the honoree. As Iefremov describes it, "Nechui spoiled his jubilee in 1904 by getting up from the table during one of the congratulatory speeches because 'It's ten o'clock – I can't any more, I'm sleepy.'" Hrinchenkova tells a similar tale, with a few more details.[91] The sixty-six-year-old Nechui was undoubtedly a quirky man with some of the bad habits and rough edges of lifelong solitude, but his premature departure may have been less dramatic and less disruptive than his biographers suggest. Nechui's jubilee had at least one guest who wasn't invited:

a police spy. On reports that Galician Ukrainophiles were expected to attend, including Ivan Franko (who did not come[92]), the authorities ordered surveillance of Nechui's jubilee celebrations. The resulting police report gives a good idea of what actually happened.[93] The events on the second day began at 1:00 p.m. at the Literary-Artistic Society. There were about 250 people present, including delegates from Poltava, Chrenihiv, Odessa, Kharkiv, Moscow, Warsaw, St Petersburg, and from Galicia. Speeches were made by various individuals. The event lasted until 5:00 p.m. At 7:00 p.m. a group of seventy-six persons assembled at a private dining room in the Hotel Continentale. There they again made speeches, initiated petitions, and raised toasts, including some that demanded "political freedom." The evening ended at midnight, except, says the police report, that the master of ceremonies, Nechui, and three other writers left a half hour earlier. Thus, Iefremov and the police spy agree on the fact that Nechui left early, but the police report makes his departure sound far less disruptive.

It was in the nature of these events that they consisted of two parts, a public ceremony in the afternoon and a private one in the evening.[94] This division allowed the Ukrainian activists to speak more freely at the second, private event. Thus it was at the unveiling of the Kotliarevs'kyi monument, where the authorities had prohibited the use of Ukrainian by citizens of the Russian Empire during the afternoon, public ceremony, but could do nothing about the use of Ukrainian in the private ceremony that followed in the evening. At Nechui's jubilee, the afternoon ceremony, hosted by Olena Pchilka (Ol'ha Drahomanov-Kosach – mother of Lesia Ukrainka and sister of Mykhailo Drahomanov), consisted of speeches and tributes by various colleagues and communities of Ukrainians. This was the place for formal tributes, and the program included a response from the honoree expressing his gratitude.[95] The private event in the evening – with the police spy stationed outside the door, perhaps questioning the waiters and hotel staff to identify voices he could only overhear – would naturally have had a less formal character and would have included food and drink. Speeches here would have been more personal and more emotional, perhaps with increasing passion as the evening wore on (and more spirits were consumed). If, as the police report maintains, the company had reached the point of calling for political independence, a sentiment growing more common in the politically charged atmosphere leading to the revolutionary events of 1905 but still not something that could safely be said in public, then the event had clearly taken its predictable course, from honouring Nechui himself to using his jubilee as a pretext for political agitation and discussion. Perhaps Nechui's early departure from the evening festivities is more appropriately understood as the normal response of an elderly teetotaller[96] after a long day to a party growing more boisterous by the minute.

There is yet another source of information about Nechui's jubilee that raises questions about Iefremov's and Hrinchenkova's accounts of the evening. That source is, ironically enough, Iefremov himself. In the February 1905 issue of *Kievskaia starina*, a journal that generally reflected the milieu of the Ukrainophile movement, Serhii Iefremov reported on the events of Nechui's thirty-fifth jubilee. Writing in Russian in the "Notes on Current Events" section of the journal, Iefremov discusses recent efforts by the Ukrainian intelligentsia to rescind the crippling restrictions of the Ems Ukaz of 1876. "First of all," he explains, "the Ukrainian intelligentstia, having gathered in Kyiv in December of the previous year [i.e., 1904] to honour the jubilee of I.S. Levyts'kyi, could not help but note, once they were speaking of the accomplishments of a Ukrainian writer, that such accomplishments were circumscribed by unbearable restrictions."[97] He then goes on to reproduce a petition to the minister of the interior detailing the harm inflicted on Ukrainian culture by the Emz Ukaz and calling for its annulment. Iefremov's account of this event and the petition is by no means unique. Similar descriptions appeared in the *Ruthenische Revue*, the *Literaturno-naukovyi visnyk*, and elsewhere.[98] Iefremov, of all people, would have been acutely aware that the event from which Nechui departed somewhat early was not – or at least was no longer – a celebration of his accomplishments as a writer but rather a political caucus of young activists formulating a petition and delegation to the government. No wonder there was a police spy at the door. Perhaps Nechui's departure reflected recognition that the part of the event devoted to him was over and that he was no longer needed there. The versions of Nechui's jubilee told by Iefremov and Hrinchenkova make excellent anecdotal material, but they are deliberately coloured by the particular image of Nechui as a quirky crackpot that these two writers are trying to project.

This impression is further supported by another anecdote Hrinchenkova tells in her recollections of Nechui. The revolutionary events in Russia in 1905 included various attempts by Ukrainian activists to advance their cause. Among these was an attempt to establish in Kyiv a daily Ukrainian newspaper. Eventually, the first Ukrainian daily newspaper, *Hromads'ka dumka*, began to appear in Kyiv. Financial backing for the paper came from Ievhen Chykalenko, but the principals in its creation and publication were a group of activists that included Serhii Iefremov and Borys and Maria Hrinchenko in very prominent roles. Naturally, in establishing the paper they turned to a large circle of individuals for support and cooperation. They asked Nechui as well, and his answer was negative. Hrinchenkova's anecdote begins with Iefremov's Ukrainian-language editorial against the pogroms in Kyiv. The editorial had just been published when Hrinchenkova went to invite Nechui to cooperate with the planned newspaper. Nechui focused on the linguistic faults of Iefremov's editorial, as he saw them. Hrinchenkova quotes her own response: "At this great historic moment, instead of helping the Ukrainian cause with your authoritative name and your work, you not only refuse to do so, but you make fun of those people who want to insure we do not miss this opportunity."[99] Thus appeared the legend that Nechui, the old codger, did not appreciate the importance of publishing a Ukrainian newspaper, that he would not cooperate with this noble patriotic venture because of his peculiar spelling rules. But as we have seen, only a few years ealier, in 1901, Nechui had actually put in an unsuccessful proposal for a periodical of his own named *Promin'*, and he published his works in other newspapers. Perhaps it was only the newspaper in which Iefremov was a key player that he refused to cooperate with. He had broken with Vik because of the abuse of his authorial rights in their publications: perhaps it was the people behind it that Nechui found objectionable, not the paper itself. A few years later, when this paper had been reconfigured as *Rada*, Nechui took the trouble to send Chykalenko a marked-up copy of an issue of the newspaper with all of the purported orthographic and vocabulary faults noted (10:481–3). The orthography is now much better than it had been in *Hromads'ka dumka*, he wries, but still not perfect (10:481). Apparently he thought highly enough of this paper, and newspapers in general, to attempt to persuade them to follow his own orthography. Needless to say, they did nothing of the sort. It's a good thing they didn't.

Nechui's orthographic and linguistic crusade is surely the low point in the writer's biography. What makes it so is neither the fact that he took an interest in formulating linguistic standards nor the actual principles that he advocated. What made Nechui an embarassment to his friends, a ridiculous blockhead to his enemies, and a pitiable old kook to the majority of readers was the passion, the vehemence, and the uncontrolled and irrational ferocity with which he pursued this cause.

May the gods of temperance and moderation one day forgive this linguistic bigot. Unfortunately, he set an example that far too many have since followed.

At the end of the nineteenth and beginning of the twentieth century, the Ukrainian language was not in a well-ordered condition.[100] Although spoken by millions, it was a language without the usual mechanisms of linguistic harmonization and control that were typical of modern European languages. In the Russian Empire, Ukrainian was not taught in schools. For the most part, it was not used in cities. It did not penetrate polite or intellectual society except as a curiosity. There were few dictionaries, grammars, or other elements of scholarly analysis or linguistic control, and those that did exist did not have universal authority. The government's edicts made sure it stayed that way. The situation in western Ukraine was better but still far from adequate. The fact that one of the large ongoing projects of the Old Hromada was the compilation of a dictionary speaks clearly of the preception of Ukrainian activists in Kyiv regarding the state of the language. Further complicating the situation was the very substantial linguistic difference between eastern and western Ukraine, between that part of Ukraine that was within the Russian Empire and the other part that was in the Austro-Hungarian Empire. Once eastern Ukrainians, under pressure from a repressive government, turned to western Ukraine to provide a forum for their publications, linguistic contact between these two disparate regions inevitably led to conflicts and, gradually, to a process of reconciliation. When the repressive measures in Russia began to dissolve in the 1900s, the primary locus of cultural activities moved back from Lviv to Kyiv and the influence of western Ukrainian linguistic features was now felt directly in eastern Ukraine. Conflict and controversy were unavoidable. Eventually they would lead to harmonization and the adoption of standard norms for the language. The key issue for many Ukrainian activists was to find compromises and temporary solutions that would allow cultural activity to continue while the slow and unregulated process of linguistic standardization ran its course. The times called for patience, toleration, mutual respect, and a sense of fair play. But on this issue Nechui did not know how to play ball in a friendly competitive game. Like a Ukrainian Dr Jekyll and Mr Hyde, when this unassuming, fun-loving, gentle old man set foot on the pitch of linguistic debate, he morphed into a fanatical gladiator convinced that winning the game depended more on bloodying the opponents than on advancing the ball. Perhaps it was his lifelong solitude that numbed the natural instinct to avoid insulting colleagues. Perhaps it was the humiliation he felt at the hands of Iefremov and Vik, who ignored his authorial rights. Perhaps it was just the emotional calcification of an old man feeling increasingly helpless in a changing world. Likely it was all of these and other factors as well that drove Nechui into a pattern of vicious personal attacks against his opponents. It was certainly not good sense or justified righteousness.

The linguistic debates that erupted in the first decades of the twentieth century in Ukraine had one central issue, standardization, but at least three essential but interrelated lines of argument: regionalism, national authenticity, and social class. In determining which linguistic forms were to be deemed normative and which should be judged substandard, the first issue was, of course, a matter of regional variants. This factor was apparent in its simplest form in the natural distinctions between geographic locations. Ukrainians in Poltava used forms that were not current in Vinnytsia. But the important distinction was between east and west, between the Ukrainian that had developed in western Ukraine (with obvious Polish influences) and the Ukrainian spoken in eastern Ukraine (with obvious Russian influences). Since the locus of major activity had shifted eastward, to eastern Ukraine, where there were far more Ukrainians than in western Ukraine, the eventual standard would necessarily need to be acceptable to easterners, which left Galician forms at an obvious disadvantage. The ideological focus on central Ukraine as the essential home territory of the Ukrainian nation also gave eastern forms an advantage. National authenticity, even in western Ukraine, was invariably a quality of the central territories. Ukrainians were the nation that had produced the Zaporozhian cossacks, the cossack state, Kyivan scholars and churches, the Haidamaks, and Shevchenko. All the trump cards of national identity were in the east. But in practical terms, the west was considerably further along on the road of developing a modern language than was the east. A generation of publishing and public utilization in the west – while the east had been suffering under imperial linguistic repression – had produced a profound imbalance in the development and use of a modern sophisticated vocabulary. The language of the east, despite various attempts to move upward, was the language of the peasant masses. It was the language of Shevchenko, who did not write about science, or business, or philosophy, or politics, or technology. In western Ukraine, Ukrainian was still a socially restricted language, but it had made significant inroads into public usage beyond the peasant household. A generation of Ukrainian intellectuals had learned to use this language in intellectual debate, in commerce, in politics, and, to some extent, in higher social circles. If Ukrainian was to succeed as a modern language, it needed to serve the needs of all Ukrainians, not just the lower classes and the writers who wrote about them. In this regard, western Ukrainian linguistic forms had a very distinct advantage. When institutions such as the Shevchenko Scientific Society began publishing in Kyiv, naturally, they used many of the linguistic forms they had already been using in Lviv. But would linguistic goods made in Galicia pass muster with customers in the east?

If the customer was Nechui, they certainly wouldn't. Throughout his entire life Nechui consistently emphasized the national primacy of the *narod*. Raised in a social system in which upward mobility meant denationalization, Nechui felt that the only true embodiment of national identity was the Ukrainian peasant. This principle applied to language as well. In his view, standard Ukrainian should necessarily be modelled on the language of Ukrainian villagers, the only authentic carriers of the language. This view was less unreasonable than it may seem today. The assimilatory pressure on upwardly mobile Ukrainians produced in the nineteenth century – just as it would in the twentieth and does today – linguistic forms that are not a natural outgrowth of language development but a product of language mixing based on faulty knowledge. Nechui, a former high school language teacher, wanted everyone to use good Ukrainian, just as he had taught his pupils to use good Russian. The problem, of course, was to determine what "good Ukrainian" was. Nechui thought that the village was the only uncorrupted source of the living language. But which village?

In actual practice, Nechui's prescriptions for "proper" Ukrainian were inconsistent, haphazard, and unscientific.[101] Although a well-read and intelligent man with a reasonably good knowledge of a number of languages, Nechui was not a linguist, and he had no particular skills in solving complex problems of etymology, morphology, or the history of the language. He simply relied on his own knowledge and preferences. But he did justify these prejudices with two relatively consistent arguments. His chief complaint was always against Galician forms. He was passionately opposed to the idea that vocabularly, spelling, or grammar from western Ukrainian might supplant eastern forms. Only rarely did he admit that a Galician neologism was acceptable. His linguistic tirades almost invariably consisted of enormous lists of words and phrases that he found objectionable. Typically, he would cite a

Galician form and then provide an example of how an eastern villager would misunderstand it, as when he suggested that the word "vidsotok," which means per cent, would be misunderstood as referring to a "sotka," the smallest measure for the sale of vodka in eastern Ukraine. Nechui thought the only proper term was "protsent." The word "vidsotok" actually had another stroke against it: it included the prefix (and preposition) "vid" (meaning "from"), which, Nechui argued, should be consistently replaced with "od."

Galician sins were not limited to vocabulary, of course. Galician spelling norms were also unacceptable. For instance, Nechui objected to separating the reflexive particle "sia" from the basic form of the verb, a prejudice later accepted in standard Ukrainian. He also objected to the softening of the consonant "ts" to "s" in many words, such as the demonstrative pronoun "tsei" – this too was later adopted as normative. Some of Nechui's most comical objections, however, were to the double-dotted "ї" for the iotated vowel "ji" and the use of the apostrophe. He ridicules these forms as scholarly gobbledygook (should there be two, three, or four dots above the genetive form of the feminine singular pronoun [її]?), on the same order as the various diacritical markings in Old Slavonic or classical Greek. Modern languages did not need such confusing monstrosities, argued Nechui, unaware that later authorities would side with his oponents.

The objection to peculiar symbols points to the other consistent complaint in Nechui's linguistic system: his objection to what he considered archaic forms. Despite the claims of Shevelov, Bilodid, and other linguists that Nechui was the enemy of linguistic innovation, in fact he generally spoke out in favour of innovation and against what he considered archaic forms.[102] He objected to anything that seemed to be derived from a deliberate adherence to historical forms. Nechui considered Galician usage to be heavily influenced by the need to fend off the Russophile cultural orientation, and he assumed that many western grammatical and morphological forms were deliberate archaisms meant to attract adherents of this Moscow-oriented camp. Another example of his focus on innovative forms was his support for simplified spelling in certain inflected forms. Thus he advocated the use of a simple "i" ending in feminine singular adjectives in the locative case. In standard Ukrainian, this form requires a glide at the end (e.g., *na zelenii̯ travi*), but this glide is often ignored in pronunciation by many speakers, and Nechui thought that standard orthography should not enforce a form erased in common usage. The thousands of pupils in Ukrainian grade schools who are to this day regularly penalized by their teachers for making this mistake would no doubt think better of Nechui if they knew he had advocated this simplification.

Although Nechui had expressed opinions on matters of vocabulary and orthography in his letters before 1903, these were occasional, ad hoc judgments on very specific matters. After his experience with Iefremov and Vik, however, the frequency, purposefulness, and vehemence of his linguistic proclamations suddenly increased. Almost every letter now contained some comment or complaint about linguistic matters. Some letters had no other purpose. He even wrote to the secretary of the British Bible Society requesting that the next edition of his translation of scripture be published not in the Galician dialect but in the Ukrainian language (10:473–4). Eventually, he could not resist writing long essays and even entire books addressing the various linguistic errors he encountered everywhere he turned. The result was three major works. The first was "S'ohochasna chasopysna mova na Ukraini" (The language of periodicals in Ukraine at this time), which appeared in 1907 across 155 pages of the newly launched journal *Ukraina*, intended as a Ukrainian-language continuation of what had been *Kievskaia starina*.[103] A few years later, in 1912, Nechui made another attempt at revealing the dangers of Galician influence on Ukrainian, this time in the form of a small monograph of ninety-six pages entitled *Kryve dzerkalo ukrains'koi movy* (The distorted mirror of Ukrainian language). Finally, on the very eve of the First World War (which led to wartime censorship and a renewed ban on Ukrainian publications in the Russian Empire and occupied territories, i.e., Galicia) Nechui published his final linguistic treatise and last original work, *Hramatyka ukrains'koho iazyka*. Intended as a high school textbook, it consisted of two parts: the first was titled "Etymology" and included a substantial glossary, and the second was titled "Syntax."

It has proved impossible to produce a simple summary of the argument in Nechui's linguistic works. Shevelov's six-point synopsis of the 1912 monograph is a deliberate misrepresentation, focusing only on what is ridiculous.[104] Zhovtobriukh's friendly description of the grammar avoids Shevelov's deliberate hostility, but it only gives an overview, not an analysis.[105] Nechui's linguistic essays defy synopsis because they are disorganized, impressionistic, and repetitious. These are not carefully crafted arguments but very long and tedious recitations of what Nechui considers linguistic faults. Like most of Nechui's writings, they try to be light-hearted, using humour, sarcasm, and colourful expressions to convey the argument, but they often lose their easy manner and descend into interminable lists, dubious historical explanations, and spiteful accusations against the malefactors who pollute the Ukrainian language with Galicianisms.

The chief characteristic of Nechui's linguistic works, the quality that makes them unbearable, even painful, for the reader is his absolute conviction that the spread of Galicianisms in Ukrainian publications in eastern Ukraine is the deliberate and malicious enterprise of specific individuals. Nechui does not see linguistic interaction as a natural result of historical circumstances. Galicianisms are not a consequence of more active communication between the two halves of Ukrainian territory. No, they are the result of a conspiracy launched by particular villains to spread these despicable linguistic features. In the first work Nechui points his accusatory finger at some familiar targets: primarily Iefremov and his colleagues at Vik, but also Mykola Cherniavs'kyi, who ignored Kotsiubyns'kyi's instructions, and other editors of specific periodicals and anthologies. But in the second work, Nechui goes beyond his familiar attacks on Iefremov and, indeed, far beyond all bounds of reasonable debate, in attacking a single individual as the leader and promoter of the conspiracy, the Darth Vader, so to speak, of the evil Galician linguistic empire stretching its destructive tentacles into Ukraine. This time, the principal villain is no longer Iefremov but Mykhailo Hrushevs'kyi, the acclaimed historian and future president of an independent Ukrainian state.

Nechui's relations with Hrushevs'kyi began in 1884 when the hopeful young scholar, then only eighteen, wrote to the well-known author from Tbilisi, where he had just graduated from high school. Hrushevs'kyi had begun to write short stories, and he sent them to Nechui for critical appraisal. Nechui was gracious and encouraging in his response. The twenty-three letters he wrote to the historian between 1884 and 1906 were always cordial and respectful, even when he was making suggestions about vocabulary and grammar. But in *Kryve dzerkalo* that friendly tone disappears. While commending Hrushevs'kyi for his energetic work in founding important institutions and for his historical scholarship, Nechui accuses him of a plot to undermine all the progress that Ukrainian culture had made in the preceding decades. The move from Lviv to Kyiv of the Shevchenko Scientific Society's publication program is interpreted negatively. All the various publications that were founded by Hrushevs'kyi or included him in a leading role are doing Ukrainian culture a disservice, says Nechui. On balance, according to Nechui,

Hrushevs'kyi is doing more harm than good. Given Nechui's earlier friendly relations with Hrushevs'kyi, it is hard to imagine what could have caused such a reversal. The opening pages of this bellicose rant refer to an essay Hrushevs'kyi had published in the *Literaturno-naukovyi visnyk* in 1911 entitled "Na Ukraini." Although no such essay appears there, Hrushevs'kyi, says Nechui, had complained that in Ukraine, too much attention was being devoted to squabbling over trivial linguistic matters. Nechui would have understood this as a personal attack, since he was obviously one of the key figures in the linguistic debates. And for Nechui, language issues could never be trivial.

In the last years before the outbreak of war, the aging Nechui had clearly lost his intellectual balance and good judgment. His writing no longer had any sparkle. It was a tedious diatribe from an irascible old man. Just when Ukrainian cultural and political affairs had made great strides and reached the eve of an important breakthrough, a period all those who lived through it would remember well, Nechui was unable to see the larger picture. Because this period in Ukrainian history led to great and memorable changes and because Nechui's public posture at this time was so far out of step with these changes, the recollections of Nechui that survived among those who knew him often focused on this discrepancy, on the psychological and intellectual distance between this linguistically fixated curmudgeon and the exciting, uplifting events that culminated in the establishment, albeit only briefly, of an independent Ukrainian state. But how would these memoirists reconcile Nechui's considerable achievements as a writer with this foolish orthographic preoccupation of his later years? Among those who respected Nechui's achievements as a writer, the simplest solution was pathos. Nechui's foibles could be excused by depicting him as a victim whose suffering both ennobled him and excused his peculiarities. The aging Nechui could be converted into a hopelessly isolated, pitiful bachelor septuagenarian, helpless and lost in the raging torrent of modern political and cultural change. For those who had personally been the victims of Nechui's wrath, this depiction seemed to be a generous solution that avoided angry recriminations. Iefremov's biography falls into this pattern, as does Hrinchenkova's memoir.

Other memoirists replicated this perspective and even repeated some of the same stories. Ievhen Krotevych, for example, describes Nechui as a generous, friendly, and fun-loving man, but cannot resist retelling the story of the spoiled jubilee, although he admits he was not there.[106] In his version, however, the hour of Nechui's premature departure is moved up to nine o'clock. Perhaps ten o'clock didn't seem sufficiently unreasonable to Krotevych, who was himself approaching eighty when he wrote his memoirs. Another story about Nechui relates directly to the attack on Hrushevs'kyi. In December 1928 an important exhibit honouring Nechui's memory was held at the Muzei Ukrains'kykh Diiachiv Nauky i Mystetstva. Hryhorii Kovalenko-Kolomats'kyi wrote a brief report on the museum exhibit, even copying sample entries from Nechui's personal log of household expenses. But the highlight of the piece is a story about Nechui's panicked flight from a disgruntled admirer of Hrushevs'kyi, who was angered by Nechui's *Kryve dzerkalo*.[107] This admirer, says Kovalenko-Kolomats'kyi, an American named Borodai, eventually caught up with Nechui just outside the doors of the *Literaturno-naukovyi visnyk* (*LNV*) bookstore, where he angrily accosted the writer and berated him for his attack on Hrushevs'kyi. The diminutive and elderly Nechui fled from the broad-shouldered American by retreating into the bookstore, where he sought the protection of the bookstore clerk, to whom he explained his predicament. Inevitably, continues Kovalenko-Kolomats'kyi, this led Nechui into his usual linguistic rant, and he began explaining to the clerk that it was not just Hrushevs'kyi himself who was at fault but also his Galician minions, including one Iurii Siryi, editor of the newspaper *Selo*. "But that's me," said the bookstore clerk, since Siryi was then in charge of the *LNV* bookstore. Thus does Kovalenko-Kolomats'kyi conclude his anecdote triumphantly, cementing the image of Nechui as an isolated anachronism who did not even know the important figures in the younger generation of Ukrainian activists.

Some twenty years later, this same Iurii Siryi, who was in fact Iurii Tyshchenko, the publisher who later left Ukraine and ended up in the United States after the Second World War, gave his own account of this encounter in an émigré publication from the Displaced Persons camps in post-war Germany.[108] In his version, there were two separate events. Siryi/Tyshchenko knew Nechui and had visited him at his home in 1908, where he was surprised to discover that this literary giant was in fact a rather diminutive (and very pedantic) man. Nechui welcomed him graciously but nevertheless read him a lecture on the orthographic faults of the *LNV* publications program, for which Siryi was responsible. The two met occasionally at the *LNV* offices, where Nechui came to purchase journals or newspapers. Thus it was a great surprise for Siryi to encounter Nechui on Duma Square in Kyiv one day and to hear him launch into a tirade against "that Hrushevs'kyi and this satanic Siryi" who were infecting Ukraine with the Galician virus. He had not recognized Siryi, and when appraised of this error Nechui made excuses about his failing eyesight. The incident with Borodai is also described somewhat differently. It begins with Siryi, alerted by a commotion, racing out of the *LNV* offices onto the sidewalk to discover Borodai towering above Nechui, who is bent over and cowering with his hands over his head. Borodai is yelling at him and holding a raised walking stick over his head, while Borodai's wife pleads with her husband to calm down. Borodai, explains Siryi, was notorious for his quick temper and irrational behaviour. That's why Vynnychenko had used him as a model for his story "Umirkovanyi ta shchyryi" (The "Moderate" One and the "Earnest" One). "Having spent over twenty years in America," says Siryi, "and having earned the professional qualifications of an engineer, O.I. Borodai returned to Ukraine without having acquired any restraint in his relations with people who thought differently than he did."[109] Nechui, Siryi continues, lamented that he had met Borodai by chance before the *LNV* offices and wanted to make him a present of his latest book when the latter had begun yelling and chasing him with his stick. Siryi's account thus raises some doubts about how unreasonable Nechui's behaviour was in this incident.

Other evidence from Nechui's later years in Kyiv also points to a more balanced portrait. Bedevilled and bewildered by the imagined conspiracy against his beloved language, Nechui nevertheless did not, despite the claims of some memoirists, lose touch with reality, nor did he lose the other qualities that, for better or worse, characterized his personality. One of these qualities was his good heart, and even the victims of his wrath could not but notice it. Oleksander Lotots'kyi, one of the principal malefactors in the Vik affair – he was the editor who ignored Nechui's instructions on galley proofs – puts this quality in a revealing context. He says of Nechui: "This was a person with an unusually beautiful soul [*nadzvychaino khoroshoi dushi*] – the kind that illuminates the clean works of this author, unbesmirched by life's dirt."[110] When Roman Zaklyns'kyi wrote to Nechui in 1912 that his son, Rostyslav, had been arrested by the tsarist police for "living under a false passport," Nechui not only visited the young man in the Kyiv prison, but brought him books, conveyed messages from his father (10:489), and agreed to store some of his belongings, which he later had shipped abroad to Rostyslav, after his release from prison.[111]

Nechui's final years are characterized by Iefremov, Hrinchenkova, and others as having been lived in misery and destitution. No doubt anyone who relied on a government pension, as Nechui did, would have experienced financial difficulties after the outbreak of the First World War and the eventual dissolution of the government that paid the pension. An elderly man living alone during the war would have experienced serious problems, including where to take his meals and how to get medical attention. But the picture of Nechui that arises from his correspondence in these years does not consist exclusively of such dark colours. Around 1909, Nechui finally had to abandon his apartment on Pushkins'ka when the building was to be torn down. He moved a few times in his last years, living at 5 Volodymyrs'ka Street, then 41 L'vivs'ka, and finally at 8 Dionisiis'kyi proulok. Eventually he was taken to a facility for the care of the infirm. After 1913 linguistic battles fade from his correspondence: he is now more often concerned about his health and gives very considerable attention to the disposition of his property upon his death. Although the sums he mentions are not large, Nechui was not destitute. For many years he had been publishing his own books and had invested the earnings from these and other publications (including the Bible translation) in bank accounts that paid interest. In a sequence of psychologically revealing letters to Illia Shrah in 1915 (10:497–502), Nechui makes clear that he has a few thousand rubles in bank accounts, which he has bequeathed to the Chernihiv Historical Museum with the understanding that they will use these funds to complete the publication of a multivolume edition of his works. He gives clear instructions and suggestions on various matters, including how to arrange the works into volumes, what the minimum press runs should be to avoid financial loss, and how to make use of various minor works still in his notebooks. He even tells Shrah that his two linguistic publications, *S'ohochasna chasopysna mova* and *Kryve dzerkalo*, should not be reprinted, as their importance was only temporary and ad hoc. In matters of practical and financial importance Nechui had never been as sharp as Panas Myrnyi, a professional accountant, but even in his later years Nechui still had a rational sense of practical realities and a clear and reasonable understanding of what he wanted to accomplish. He also knew what he did not want done. In the last of his known letters, written in 1917, he tells an unnamed correspondent (the letter was not sent) that he would rather not hold another proposed jubilee celebration, which would produce only saccharine and insincere sentiments. "And if something must indeed be said about me," he continues, "there will soon be an opportunity – the cemetery is longing for me." Nechui died on 2 April 1918, old style, that is, on 15 April by the Gregorian calendar, and he was interred at the Baikove Cemetery in Kyiv after funeral rites at St Sophia Cathedral. These were the final weeks of the existence of the Ukrainian National Republic, shortly before the coup that put Hetman Skoropads'kyi at the head of a German-supported government in Kyiv. Nechui died quietly in the Dehteriv hospital,[112] with very modest public recognition of his passing. Even those who remembered him and noted his passing betrayed weak familiarity with the old writer. For instance, the anonymous author of the obituary that appeared in the *Literaturno-naukovyi visnyk* speaks explicitly of a personal acquaintanece with Nechui, but also says that he was eighty-five when he died.[113] He was, in fact, seventy-nine.

Nechui's legacy, unlike his passing, was acknowledged soon after his death, but his works have had mixed fortune. Nechui was fortunate in the 1920s during the years of the Soviet Ukrainian literary renaissance. Iefremov composed his biography. Iurii Mezhenko assembled a multivolume collection of his works, a task made considerably easier by Nechui's having put many of his writings in order in his later years. A museum exhibit of photographs, manuscripts, letters, and personal effects was put on in 1928, as noted above. But Nechui's memory suffered on two accounts: the personal recollections of those who knew him only as a pitiful old man and the newly constructed Soviet ideology, which could not overlook two grievous sins in his works. At a time when other writers, including Ivan Franko and Panas Myrnyi, had clearly focused on class struggles, Nechui had never seen it as a simple, overriding issue. And after the renaissance of the 1920s when the Communist Party wanted to re-establish the dominance of Russian culture in Ukraine, Nechui's consistent denunciations of Russian culture as a foreign import into Ukraine made him a dangerous enemy. Any appraisal of Nechui had to walk a fine ideological line, exaggerating his social revolutionary sentiments and minimizing his anti-Russian pronouncements.

Soviet Ukraine experienced an ideological thaw in the 1960s and scholarly work on Nechui made some advances, but these advances were still governed by ideological strictures. The ten-volume edition of his works published in 1965–8 was a major achievement, but it was far from complete and deliberately hobbled to avoid political difficulties. A few studies of Nechui's life and works were published, but these were generally simplifications and naive summaries intended for schoolchildren. There was no serious attempt to interpret his works or compose a biography. The situation has hardly changed today. Although there are no longer any impediments to a serious, comprehensive, scholarly reassessment of Nechui's life and work, there is very little interest in him in contemporary Ukraine. Some attention has been given to the works that were banned outright in Soviet times – the literary essays and the historical works – but these have been very limited in their goals and importance.

Nechui cries out for attention. His biography alone raises very many unanswered questions that might be resolved with further research. Many of his texts have not been republished, let alone assembled in a scholarly edition. What needs attention most of all, however, is our understanding of his role in Ukrainian literature. Much of our understanding of his works is based on notions that arise from a very unscholarly approach to his texts. As we have seen, his biography is not quite as clear and simple as the existing interpretation of him suggests. In the chapters that follow we shall see that much the same holds true for his works.

2 Describing Ukraine

The primary and most basic question about Nechui's writing is also the simplest to answer: "What did he write about?" Ukraine, of course. He wrote about Ukraine always, exclusively, and invariably. Although no such country existed during his lifetime – the territory of what is Ukraine today was then divided between two foreign empires, the Russian and the Austro-Hungarian – Nechui was always very certain and very clear about the existence of Ukraine. Modern scholarly notions of the arbitrary, provisional, or imagined nature of nations notwithstanding, Nechui had no doubts about Ukraine, its existential reality and permanence. Although he never actually explained what Ukraine meant to him, it is clear enough from his writing how he understood the concept: Ukraine was a territory, it was a nation (i.e., a people), it was a culture, and it was an identity. For Nechui, these were indisputable and unalterable facts. As a Ukrainian writer, his role was to write about these facts, to describe Ukraine in all its breadth, complexity, and peculiarity. He acknowledged this commitment explicitly.

In his controversial programmatic essay about the status of Ukrainian literature, "Nepotribnist' velykorus'koi literatury dlia Ukrainy i dlia Slavianshchyny," Nechui employs the traditional Shakespearean metaphor and argues that a writer should hold a mirror to his community:

> The realist artist-writer should be such a lens for his community, and the Ukrainian writer should be such an instance of concave or convex glass for Ukraine. In his soul, the Ukrainian life that boils and vegetates around him should be reflected and transformed. If a writer feels himself at least slightly a Ukrainian citizen, a fragment of the Ukrainian nation and the Ukrainian community, he should feel a sacred obligation to reflect in his

imagination, in his heart, the community that bustles around him, to rejoice in its happiness, to cry its tears, and not to climb fences into foreign gardens and not to position his soul in relation to images of foreign, non-Ukrainian life. The Ukrainian writer should not worry that there will be little work for him in Ukraine. Ukrainian life is an untapped underground ore deposit, although it has already been explored by such great talents as Shevchenko. It has endless material that just waits for its workers, entire schools of workers in this literary field. Before them stretches the wide canvas of Ukrainian peasant life from the Caucasus and Volga to the very mouth of the Danube, from the Carpathians and beyond to the forests of Hrodna and Minsk. Some will say that the simple folk give but modest material for literature, in which individuality is poorly developed, in which the poet will not find a wide variety of types and characters, that the life of the common folk is governed almost entirely by nature, and that peasants are all similar, like one insect is indistinguishable from another. Let it even be so, but the Ukrainian people will nevertheless give the Ukrainian writer a wealth of material. The life of the people cannot be identical across the wide expanse from the Caucasus to beyond the Carpathians. The Kuban cossack, descendant of the Zaporozhians, the Saratov or Astrakhan peasant, is very different from the Hungarian peasant. The Carpathian Hutsul, Lemko, or Boyko is very different from the farmer of Kyiv and Poltava because in the Carpathians they don't sow or reap but instead they gather in their granaries … milk and cheese, like the ancient patriarchs. The residents of the forests of Hrodna, Minsk, Mahileu, Volyn, or Siedlce do not resemble their fellow-countrymen from the Dnipro basin, even in their dress, with their ruddy or white woollen caps, in their grey shirts, narrow pants, and bast shoes. The stories of Osyp Fed'kovych, which describe the life of Ukrainian peasants in Bukovyna, in the Carpathians, show clearly that their lifestyle is not similar to the lifestyle of those Ukrainians that live in the plains. The Ukrainian people, spread out across such a wide expanse, offer an equally wide expanse of subjects for the Ukrainian realist writer.[1]

In this programmatic text Nechui emphasizes the expansiveness and diversity of Ukraine. Indeed, his geography is distinctly inclusive: the toponyms he mentions are mostly outside the borders of present-day Ukraine. But his point is simple and clear, if somewhat Whitmanesque in its comprehensiveness: everything that is Ukrainian in one way or another is appropriate matter for the Ukrainian writer. While this particular passage emphasizes the lower classes, the *narod*, Nechui also emphatically asserts the need for Ukrainian writers to encompass all the social classes, from the lowest to the highest. In a letter to Mykhailo Kotsiubyns'kyi of 20 January 1903 he writes:

> I agree with you that Ukrainian writers must not limit themselves to describing only village life ... In our time the Ukrainian book has many readers among the intelligentsia. For such a reader there must be works about himself, describing his own skin and bones, truthfully and realistically, as he really is ... Naturally, our writers need to care about their own country, to describe all the social levels, all the life, all the people, that can be found on the territory of the Ukrainian tribe.[2]

The consequences of this explicit policy are evident throughout Nechui's works. Like Balzac (with his own connection to Ukraine) who chose to depict all of French society, Nechui had clearly set himself an ambitious goal: to describe as much of Ukraine, particularly its people, as he could. Of course, like any writer, he wrote most about what he knew best. The Ukraine he describes is the one he experienced: Nechui seldom ventured into fictional geography or places he had not seen with his own eyes. In its territory, material and behavioural culture, social classes, and character types, Nechui had in fact seen very much of Ukraine, and his works reflect this breadth.

Stebliv, Nechui's native village, situated along the banks of the Ros' River, a Right-Bank tributary of the Dnipro, is the setting for many of his works, including "Rybalka Panas Krut'," *Burlachka*, *Mykola Dzheria*, *Kaidasheva sim'ia*, *Starosvits'ki batiushky ta matushky*, "Baba Paraska ta baba Palazhka" (Baba Paraska and baba Palazhka), "Zhyvtsem pokhovani," "Gastroli," *Na gastroliakh v Mykytianakh* (On tour in Mykytiany), and several other fiction and non-fiction works. Among these works, the precision and significance of geographical descriptions varies. The most important and revealing are in *Mykola Dzheria*. The novel begins in the village of Verbivka on the Rastavytsia River – better known as the Rostavytsia – which flows from the southern extremity of Zhytomyr oblast in an easterly direction and empties into the Ros' at Bila Tserkva. There is, in fact, a village called Verbivka on the Rostavytsia, but the one in Nechui's novel is actually based on the village of Trushky, seventeen kilometres south-west of Bila Tserkva.[3] The plot of the novel follows a group of runaway serfs from Verbivka as they wander first to Stebliv, where they work in the sugar mill, then on to another mill in the vicinity of Cherkasy, and finally across the steppe in a southwesterly direction to the city of Akerman (Akkerman, today's Bilhorod-Dnistrovs'kyi) at the mouth of the Dnister River in Bessarabia, a territory that had been ceded to Russia by the Ottoman Empire in 1812. Nechui was familiar with Bessarabia, of course, because from 1873 to 1885 he worked as a schoolteacher in Kishinev, then the capital of Bessarabia. The setting of *Mykola Dzheria* thus corresponds entirely to Nechui's personal geography – that is, places he had visited or where he had lived.

This link between Nechui's fictional and personal geography is a prominent feature of his works, and it applies to more than just the area where he grew up. As we have seen, Nechui spent many years in Kyiv, first as a student of the seminary and the academy and later, in his retirement, as a permanent resident. The novel *Khmary* is not only set in Kyiv but focuses precisely on the Kyiv Theological Academy where Nechui studied, a school that is now and had formerly been the prestigious Kyiv Mohyla Academy but in the nineteenth century was, as Nechui describes it in the novel, a far less intellectually sophisticated Orthodox religious school providing higher education mostly to the male children of the clergy and to prospective clergymen. Kyiv is also the setting for his *Afons'kyi proidysvit* (1890) and *Kyivs'ki prokhachi* (Kyiv beggars, 1901), works that focus on the religious institutions of the city. In *Neodnakovymy stezhkamy* (Different paths, 1902), the setting moves between Kyiv and the country estate of the Hukovyches across the Dnipro, not far from the city. As noted, Nechui lived in Kishinev for a number of years and this city, along with nearby Odessa, which Nechui is known to have visited, appear as the settings in his *Nad Chornym Morem* (1888) and *Navizhena* (1891), works that very deliberately assert a Ukrainian presence among the multinational residents of these cities and Ukraine's southern coast overall. The personal nature of Nechui's fictional geography is also evident in some of the minor settings in his works. In *Khmary*, Radiuk visits his family home in a village called Zhurbani, near Poltava. While the village itself may be an invention, Nechui was familiar with Poltava, having taught at the Poltava Seminary during the 1865–6 school year. Another reflection of personal geography occurs in Nechui's historical novel *Kniaz' Ieremiia Vyshnevets'kyi*. In a letter to Ivan Belei in February 1902, Nechui explains that he based his description of the Jesuit monastery in Lviv where Vyshnevets'kyi is educated on the recollections of his own visit in 1872 to the archaeological remains of a similar monastery in Drehochyn (10:395). He adds that the description of Vyshnevets'kyi's palace in Lubny is based on his recollections of the excellently preserved Radziwiłł palace in Biała (Biała Podlaska, Nechui's Bila) that he saw on the same excursion. Nechui, like many realists, liked to work from a tangible, particular sensory experience in recreating physical space and other aspects of his fiction. The link to the personal was always near. He even mentioned (though he did not describe) the town of Siedlce where he worked as a schoolteacher from 1867 to 1873 in his semi-fictional travel narrative, "Zhyvtsem pokhovani."

The benefit of personal geography in the hands of a realist writer is, of course, the appearance of authenticity that this familiarity allows the author to achieve in his works. Nechui certainly takes advantage of this opportunity. In reference to the geography of *Mykola Dzheria*, Oleksander Bilets'kyi asserted that the entire path traversed by the escaped serfs could be traced accurately on a map even in the twentieth century.[4] Even more significant than coordinates on a map are the specific details of local scenery, society, and economy. Nechui's beloved Stebliv, for example, was in fact the site of both a sugar refinery and a textile mill in the nineteenth century. These industrial enterprises appear (with considerable accuracy,[5] if we take the word of Stebliv's own Serhii Khavrus', director of the Nechui museum in Stebliv and an untiring promoter of both the writer and the town) in *Mykola Dzheria*, whose protagonist works in the sugar refinery, and in *Burlachka*, which features the textile factory. Something similar, albeit on a smaller scale, is true of Nechui's Kyiv. In *Khmary*, Nechui's close personal knowledge of the city is evident in a number of descriptions: the broad dramatic landscape from the left bank of the Dnipro as the pilgrims from Russia approach (2:6); the Brotherhood Monastery (2:8–9) and the adjacent home of the merchant Sukhobrus (2:20); the panorama of urban views around the monument to St Volodymyr (2:113–14); and the depiction of recreational activity in the Tsar's Orchard and the Chateau de Fleur café, that is, in the parks on the high bank above the Dnipro, where the Dynamo-Lobanovs'kyi stadium stands today (2:116–18, 2:223–4); the view of the Institute for Noble Girls, which Nechui describes as a prison (2:119), as if anticipating its role under the NKVD in Soviet times. The Chateau de Fleur appears again with additional details in *Neodnakovymy stezhkamy* (8:443). In *Nad Chornym Morem* and *Navizhena*, Nechui places his characters in the vicinity of prominent landmarks in Kishinev and Odessa. In the former, it is the Pushkin Alley (now the Alley of the Classics of Moldovan Literature in Stephen the Great Park in Chişinău) (5:100). In the latter, it is the famous stairs (now called the Potemkin Stairs) with a view of the harbour (5:130), Derybasivs'ka street and the tram line to Malyi Fontan (5:145), and various oceanfront and resort locations at the Malyi and Velykyi Fontan. Nechui also offers descriptions of smaller towns that he knew well, particularly the Jewish quarter and riverfront of Bohuslav in "Rybalka Panas Krut'" and the railroad station and town square of Bila Tserkva in "Zhyvtsem pokhovani."

Nechui's use of personal geography has a predominantly urban character. Of course, scenes from large cities have more currency as significant landmarks (as they would for a tourist) and are more likely to be recognizable to readers. But Nechui uses personal geography for more than just familiarity. As a general rule, setting is not a major concern in his technique, but when he focuses his narrative stream on location, the emphasis is usually on three factors: aesthetic wonder, symbolic meaning, and a relation of place to characters that can be called rootedness. These qualities are visible in his descriptions of both Kyiv and Odessa.

Khmary is essentially a novel about the denationalizing role of misguided education and the social and intellectual attitudes that such an education fosters. The most appropriate setting for such a theme is Kyiv, which not only had a historical tradition of education but was an important centre of education in Nechui's own time. The depiction of the tree-lined alleys on the grounds of the Orthodox academy, the erstwhile home of the illustrious Mohyla School, reflects not only the pleasant beauty of the location but also a special relationship between the setting and the theme. Nechui drives home this point in a very simple manner:

> Всі студенти говорили московським язиком, і рідко траплялося почути співучу, м'яку розмову українську. Серед самого монастиря стояла велика гарна Богоявленська церква. На полуденній стіні церкви була залізна дошка з написом над могилою гетьмана Конашевича-Сагайдачного. Самий монастир з академією стояв на Мазепиному дворі. І, невважаючи на те, в академії Петра Могили, св. Димитрія Туптала й інших не було й духу, й сліду тих давніх діячів України, тих Сагайдачних, Могил. (2:9)

> [All the students spoke in the Russian language and only rarely did one hear a song-like, soft Ukrainian conversation. Within the grounds of the school stood the beautiful large church of the Epiphany. On the south wall of the church hung an iron plaque with an inscription above the grave of Hetman Konashevych-Sahaidachnyi. The entire monastery with the academy stood on the grounds of the Mazepa court. Regardless of that, in the academy of Petro Mohyla, St Dymytrii Tuptalo, and others there was no trace of either the spirit or the presence of these old Ukrainian champions, these Sahaidachnyis, Mohylas.]

The spirit of patriotism and excellence that had characterized the Mohyla Academy in the seventeenth and eighteenth centuries is evoked through the names of its famous patrons and scholars: Sahaidachnyi, Mazepa, Tuptalo, and, of course, Mohyla himself. These are deliberately contrasted, both in the brief description itself and in the general outline of the novel, with the sorry state, both intellectually and nationally, of the academy in the mid-nineteenth century.

Another, perhaps even more revealing, descriptive element is found in the scene of urban entertainment on the terrace of the Chateau in chapter 7. Nechui follows Ol'ha and Kateryna, the spoiled denationalized children of academy professors, as they and their mothers enjoy an evening out on the town. The description of the event emphasizes its popularity and exotic flavour:

> В Шато була велика гулянка. На афішах було оповіщено, що того вечора співатимуть в садку тірольці, потім пускатимуть шар, а в кінці всього будуть запалені бенґальські вогні й фейєрверк. Народу зібралось велика сила! Все Шато на долині було залите масою публіки. Дармова публіка так завзято лізла в Шато через частокіл, що поліцейські москалі ледве встигали стягувать її за ноги. (2:117)

> [There was great exuberance at the Chateau. Posters announced that tonight a Tyrolean choir would sing in the garden, then there would be a balloon launching, and finally Bengal lights and a firework display. A large crowd had assembled. The entire valley of the Chateau was drowning in a mass of spectators. Gatecrashers were so energetically climbing the palisade to get into the Chateau that the police could barely keep up pulling them down by their legs.]

With characteristic humour, Nechui describes the spectacle as less than entirely successful:

> Вийшли тірольці й почали співать більше чудно, ніж гарно, нагадуючи своїми дуже довгими трелями неестетичне ревіння альпійських коров або перегукування людей, що заблудились в горах і згукувались. Публіка давала браво, а студенти сміялися і свистали. Тірольці зійшли з підмосток; там з'явивсь якийсь німець і почав лагодити свій шар з помагачами. Шар прив'язали вірьовками як слід і почали сповнять його газом. Вже шар надувся й почав блищать в темноті. Публіка ждала, що він от-от здійметься й полетить, але шар почав сплющуваться так, що його боки позападали, як у самого німця. Шар луснув з одного боку. Публіка почала сміяться. (2:117)

[The Tyroleans came out and began to sing, in a manner strange rather than beautiful, their very long trills sounding like the unaesthetic bellowing of alpine cattle or the yelling of people who have got lost in the mountains and are calling out to each other. The audience applauded while the students laughed and whistled. The Tyroleans stepped off of the stage, and in their place appeared a German who began preparing his balloon along with his assistants. The balloon was tied down properly with cords and they began to fill it with gas. The balloon was filling up and began to gleam in the twilight. The audience expected the balloon to take off any minute now, but it began to deflate: its sides were collapsing, as was the German himself. The balloon had burst on one side. The audience began to laugh.]

Eventually, the German fixes his balloon and takes off, but it does not stay aloft for long and descends directly on the spectators, forcing the girls and their mothers to flee in a panic, directly into the path of a group of students that includes the handsome Pavlo Radiuk, with whom Ol'ha is immediately smitten.

While the immediate function of this episode is to produce a first meeting between the hopeful lovers Ol'ha and Pavlo, Nechui carefully emphasizes the foreign, dislocated character of the amusements. He describes the Austrian yodellers (if that is what they are) with extraordinary scorn. Both the yodellers and the German balloonist have a misplaced, ungrounded quality, although they are very popular with the local audience: they are without roots in the local culture. The balloon, in particular, becomes a symbol of the desire to ascend above the limits of the indigenous. But for Nechui, this is a dangerous illusion. The Daskkovych and Vozdvyzhens'kyi ladies are nearly crushed by the failure of the ambitious hot-air contrivance. Like General Turman's widow or her sister, the Marquise de Pourverser (2:102–3), the pretentious francophone administrators of the Institute for Noble Girls, the yodellers and balloonist have no cultural authenticity. They are representatives of a deracinated urbanity that Nechui sees as a major problem for Ukrainian culture.

At the opposite end of the spectrum is the description of the home of the old Kyiv artist and merchant of kitsch religious art, Sydor Petrovych Sukhobrus. In keeping with his surname, which means "dry beam," his home is a relic of the past: "Старий мурований будинок стояв не на вулицю, а серед двора проти воріт. Він був так збудований, як будували доми в старовину: з ґанком, з довгими сіньми через цілий дім, з другими дверима в садок" (2:20) [The old masonry building did not face the street but stood in the courtyard, across from the gate. It was built the way buildings were built in the old times, with a porch, a long hallway through the whole building, and a second door out into the orchard]. The ancient character of the establishment is further reflected on the interior walls, where, besides some very old-fashioned religious paintings hang cheap paper portraits of Tsar Paul I (reigned 1796–1801) and General Kutuzov, the hero of the Napoleonic Wars. For the 1840s, when the novel begins, these are figures from a previous generation. An even earlier tradition is reflected in other decorative paintings:

> На одних дверях був намальований вусатий і чубатий запорожець, котрий танцював козачка, держачи в руках пляшку й чарку, – сцена, може, прямо перенесена маляром з Братського плацу, де колись гуляли запорожці по дорозі до Межигірського монастиря й до чернечої ряси. (2:21)

> [On one door there was a painting of a Zaporozhian cossack, with moustache and scalp lock, dancing while holding a bottle and glass in his hands. This scene was, perhaps, directly reproduced by the painter from Brats'kyi Square, where Zaporozhians once danced on the way to the Mezhyhirs'kyi Monastery and the black gown of a monk.]

Nechui summarizes the significance of these home decorations with characteristic directness: "На стінах світлиці можна було читать історію нещасного Києва, котрого шарпали й перекидали з рук у руки сусіди" (2:21) [On the walls of the living room you could read the history of unfortunate Kyiv, which was snatched and tossed from one to another by its neighbours]. Unlike the Chateau, which is foreign, exotic, and anything but indigenous in its character, Sukhobrus's home is, for better or worse, a reflection of local history, traditions, and culture, even where that means foreign conquests and shifting loyalties.

If Kyiv embodies history and education, Odessa is the queen of cosmopolitanism. Naturally, when Nechui set out to write a novel specifically addressing his understanding of the conflict between national identity and European internationalism, he could find no more appropriate setting than the thriving young metropolis on the Black Sea. But his description of that city in *Nad Chornym Morem* emphasizes its steamy, earthy atmosphere and its colourful, expansive views:

> Комашко та Мавродін скупались в морі і йшли побережною вулицею, що вилася понад морем кругом заливу. Од складів вугілля піднімалась чорна

легка курява й обсипала политу, мокру вулицю. Мостова з тесаного каміння чорніла од чорного пороху, неначе рілля. Повітря було гаряче, наче в натопленій хаті. Тхнуло духом порту: важким духом теплої морської води, смоли, земляного вугілля, диму од паровиків залізної побережної дороги. З политої мокрої мостової піднімавсь опар. Паничі дійшли до широких кам'яних сходів, що спускаються з спадистої невисокої гори, неначе широке розстелене полотнище. Всюди по сходах вештались пани з простирадлами в руках, обвитих ремінцями, панії з гарненькими плетеними кошиками в руках, з котрих витикались вишивані рушники та тонкі простирадла. На верхніх східцях вгорі сиділи густими рядками няньки з дітьми, мамки та усякі міщани, неначе кури на сідалі. [...]

Комашко та Мавродін мовчки дивились на широку картину заливу та моря. Сонце впало в степ за плискуватою Пересиппю. Небо горіло. Вода в заливі черв̀оніла. Між червоним небом та водою чорніла довга смужка невисокого берега, що десь далеко-далеко тонула в імлі й була неначе намальована пензлем на червоному прозорому склі. Була година й суша. Надворі було тихо. На морі стояв великий корабель, спустивши білі вітрила, неначе крила, й ніби дрімав, мов лебідь на воді, а за ним на обрії видно було смугу сизого туману, в котрому ворушився пароход, а над пароходом пасмо чорного диму ніби плуталось в тому тумані, неначе чорна нитка в білій тканці ... Залив, порти, рядки кораблів в портах ніби дрімали й засипали, вкриті синім шатром неба, облиті червоним гарячим одлиском од неба та води. (5:129–30)

[Komashko and Mavrodin bathed in the sea and were walking along the seaside street that wound around the bay. A light black powder rose above the stacks of coal and gently fell on the wet, washed street. The polished stone pavement glistened from the black dust like a newly plowed field. The air was hot, as in a well-heated house. The air was heavy with the smell of the port: the heavy scent of warm seawater, tar, coal, the smoke from the steam engines of the coastal railroad. Steam rose from the wet pavement. The gentlemen reached the wide stone steps that descend from the small steep hill like a wide outspread canvas. Everywhere on the steps were gentlemen with tablecloths in their hands, girt in leather belts, and women with wicker baskets in their hands, from which embroidered towels and thin tablecloths were hanging. On the upper steps sat nannies with children in thick rows, governesses, and other city women, like chickens on a perch ...

Komashko and Mavrodin silently watched the landscape of the bay and the sea. The sun had set into the steppe behind the flat Peresyp spit. The sky was aflame. The water in the bay was crimson. Between the red sky and water was the long black line of the low shoreline, which faded far, far away into the distant haze and seemed as if painted on the red transparent glass. It was clear and dry. Outside it was quiet. There was a large ship on the water with its white sails down like wings and it seemed to be dreaming, like a swan on the water. Beyond it, in a strip of distant haze, was a steamship, and a ribbon of black smoke seemed to get lost in the haze, like a black thread on a white cloth. The bay, the port, the rows of ships in the harbor all seemed to be dreaming and falling asleep, covered by the blue tent of the sky, sprayed with the hot red reflection from the sky and the water.]

A similar colourful description of the square next to the cathedral near Derybasivs'ka Street occurs in the next chapter (5:145). Odessa (Nechui calls it Odes, using a masculine gender noun) is not a foreign or an exotic place for Nechui. For him, it is not the city but its inhabitants that are multicultural, as evidenced by Sania's description of a Jewish merchant woman:

Пописана й помальована, неначе індійський ідол. Я на її постаті налічила вісім кольорів! Подумайте собі: сукня ясно-червона, накидка темно-зелена, на шиї разок товстих круглих коралів і золотий здоровий медальйон на товстому золотому ланцюжку, ще й зверху рожева стрічка з довгими кінцями до пояса; на грудях синя стьожка: через усі груди до пояса теліпається золотий ланцюжок, а серед грудей зверху на ґудзику вона причепила золотий годинник, неначе орден якогось індуського лева або тигра. На голові чорний парик з начосами, а на парику копиця жовтих та червоних рож, а зверху стримить чорне перо. Прикиньте до того білі черевики з срібними застібками – і вийде американський парадовий індієць! Ну і вподоба в убранні в тутешніх дам! неначе в Константинополі. (5:135–6)

[Made up and painted like an Indian idol. I counted eight colours on her. Just think, a bright red skirt, a dark green jacket, on her neck a string of thick beads with a large gold medallion on a thick gold chain, and a pink ribbon with long ends hanging down to her waist. A blue kerchief on her breast, a gold chain dangling across her breast down to her waist, and in the middle of her chest, attached with a button on top, is a large watch, like a medal of an Indian lion or tiger. On her head is a black hairpiece with an elaborate design, with yellow and red roses and a black feather sticking out of the top. Add to this white shoes with silver buckles and

> you get a circus American Indian. You wouldn't believe what these local women wear! Like in Constantinople!]

A few paragraphs later Sania offers a similar description of Arystyd Selabros, the Greek bank clerk who is an ardent admirer of her friend Nadezhda Murashkova. To paint his portrait, she says:

> Я поставила б на столі з вісім чорнильниць, з усякими фарбами, – сказала Саня, – почала б писати зверху, цебто з голови, чорним, потім жовтим, потім червоним, далі золотим, далі синім, ще далі зеленим, а на споді намалювала б червоні панчохи в срібних черевиках і підписала б: "Це індійсько-одеська благородно рождена маркиза од кукурудзи, вівса та ріпаку!" (5:137)
>
> ["I'd put eight inkpots on the table with various colours," said Sania. "I'd begin at the top, that is, from the head, with black, then yellow, then red, and on to gold, then blue, then some green, and at the bottom I'd paint red stockings in silver shoes and I'd sign it: 'This is an India-Odessa noble-born marquise de corn, oats, and rape-seed.'"]

The colourful Odessa landscapes and street scenes are a hospitable venue for the equally colourful multinational residents and visitors. At every step Nechui emphasizes the serene beauty of the location, both in the city itself and at the oceanside resorts, the Malyi (5:153) and Velykyi (5:194) Fontan. Everywhere there is warm humid sunshine, cool ocean breezes, and an impressive variety of tropical vegetation. The rows of acacias, bountiful orchards, and scenic villas help to evoke the holiday spirit, the easy carelessness, the languorous indolence for which Odessa is justly famed. For Nechui, however, this easy idleness extends to the mind and the spirit, as well as the body. The relaxation Odessa offers to the weary becomes an excuse for intellectual laziness, spiritual cowardice, and ethical complacency. These qualities appear in some measure in all of the characters in this novel, but most obviously in the ditzy party girl Khrystyna Melashkevych, her friends the Borodavkins, the cowering bureaucrat Kharyton Navrots'kyi, and the misguided liberals Murashkova and Selabros. The qualities of the place are reflected in the character of its inhabitants, even if they are mostly vacationing tourists from Kishinev.

In Nechui's works this quality of rootedness, of traits shared between a place and its inhabitants, is not limited to urban space. The majority of his works are set in rural space, and here too Nechui emphasizes the relationship between location and people. The place and its inhabitants are mutually shaped by each other. The description of the Derkachivka estate in *Neodnakovymy stezhkamy* shows such a relationship (8:303–4; quoted below). Another example occurs in the opening paragraphs of *Mykola Dzheria*, where Nechui's narrative eye swoops down into the valley of the Rastavytsia River to discover a village called Verbivka – "Willow-ville" – flooded by a green sea of willows (3:34–5). Like the willow fence posts that have taken root and grown into mature trees, defining the outline of every street and property, the people of this village have sunk their roots into the soil as well. The lives and customs of the villagers are bound up with the land and the location (including the master who owns both the land and the people). So when Dzheria and his colleagues abandon their village, they are not merely runaway serfs who have become refugees from an oppressive social system built on slavery, but they are also culturally and psychologically uprooted from the land that nurtured and shaped them. Their travels cut them off from their native place, and when they finally return, they are no longer at home in their own village.

As an expression of personal geography, the most conspicuous location in Nechui's works is, as already noted, the valley of the Ros' River. That river and the surrounding countryside are noted for their natural beauty, and Nechui's attachment to the area is well known and frequently mentioned by his readers and critics. Descriptions of the area occur both in works where the location is explicitly defined (as mentioned above) and in works where the location is deliberately pseudonymous or anonymous, for instance, in the "Gastroli," where the Kyiv opera singer's country cottage, on the outskirts of a "substantial town on the Ros' in Kyiv province" (8:130; presumably Bohuslav or Bila Tserkva, but with a close resemblance to Stebliv), offers magnificent natural landscapes (8:134–5) that soothe the tired and jaded spirits of its urbanized visitors.

For all of the certainty with which literary historians depict Nechui as the champion of the ethnographic village, the chronicler of the daily lives of the common people (літописець побуту) as Iefremov calls him,[6] his presentation of rural geography has more of the aesthetic delight of the vacationing opera singer than the practical appreciation of a lifelong tiller of the soil. Nechui's Ukraine has plenty of scenic vistas but very few fields of grain. The rural setting ends at the perimeter of the village, and the village itself is only a vague combination of homes and a church. There's much more of *Homes and Gardens* and *Country Living* than *Farm Journal* or *Progressive Farmer* in Nechui's outlook, and there is always more landscape than land in Nechui's works. Even in the novel *Kaidasheva sim'ia,* one of the very few of Nechui's works where we can encounter an actual peasant who works on the land, the descriptions of a farm and farming are minimal. The opening scene, where the brothers Karpo and Lavrin discuss who is the least ugly of all the village girls, takes place on the threshing floor beside the barn, but the narrator gives no description of this place – it could just as well be a Hollywood sound stage expressly built for the comic conversation between the brothers. Their father is sitting on a stool just inside the open doors of the barn. Nechui's description inadvertently reveals the aesthetic origins of this image: "Густа тінь в воротях повітки, при ясному сонці, здавалась чорною. Ніби намальований на чорному полі картини, сидів Кайдаш в білій сорочці з широкими рукавами" (3:301) [The thick shadows in the doorway of the barn seemed black in the bright sunlight. Kaidash sat in his white shirt with wide sleeves as if painted against the black background of a painting]. No doubt the cinematographer took a few light readings before he found the perfect placement for the lamp reflectors, bounce board, and Kaidash's stool, which would highlight the old man's features and white clothing perfectly framed by the open barn doors and the dark interior as backdrop. The description of the Dovbysh home, where Karpo hangs out waiting to meet Motria, is also stageworthy. The ravine lot with cherry blossoms and a pond make an ideal setting for a romantic duet. But the famously uneven road on the hill behind the Kaidash home – the one that Karpo and Lavrin lazily refuse to dig out no matter how many times they overturn the hay wagon there – is never actually described. There is nothing particularly colourful or scenic about potholes. The anecdote's humour is behavioural, not visual.

This predilection for scenic landscapes informs the geographic descriptions in all of Nechui's works. In *Nad Chornym Morem,* for example, beyond the various panoramas in and around Odessa, there is a description of a particularly poetic evening on the shores of the Black Sea at the Dnister River estuary. A romantic sunset followed by an expansive night sky reflected on the smooth surface of the sea evoke dreamy visions of biblical Egypt and landscapes from the novels of Thomas Mayne Reid in the young Komashko (5:165–6). Komashko narrates this recollection from his youth to Sania in an unusual and elaborate scene (5:165–74) that underscores Nechui's understanding of the relation between geography and people, between the dramatic and colourful landscapes and the emotional life of his characters. The entire monologue, as Sania understands, is a declaration of Komashko's love for her, an unveiling of his soul before her (5:166). Komashko's declaration is also an attestation of his commitment to the Ukrainian national question and a plea for Sania's conversion to this cause. But it is more than an attestation, it is a description of his conversion to the cause. The beauty of the night sky, the joy of the conversation with the old fisherman Khtodos', the colourful sunrise reflected in the estuary – these aesthetic perceptions evoke a mystical, almost religious appreciation for sensual beauty in the young Komashko, and he equates this natural beauty and the joy it brings with the simple people among whom he has experienced it. Ukraine and the *narod* are thus cemented as the primary virtues in the young boy's heart. His national sentiment is rooted in the experience of this particular place. And yet it is not merely its aesthetic and esoteric qualities that attract him. After all, his first associations were with exotic places from his readings, whether the Bible or Mayne Reid. It is the human presence, both here and now as well as in the past, that cements the tie to Ukraine and Ukrainians. The estuary and the Dnister River that flows into it are the historic scene of many cossack battles and other events from Ukrainian history. The young boy's imagination extends this association to Gonta and Zalizniak, to Taras Bul'ba and his sons, to Sava Chalyi. The imagined historical watershed spreads to Smila, Uman', Dubno, and the scenes of historical battles between Ukrainian cossacks and Poles (5:169–70). For Komashko, as for Nechui, geography is history, geography is beauty, and geography is people. All three form a nation, and the mystical emotional power of a place creates a rational permanent attachment to the nation.

For Nechui himself, the power of place has yet another dimension. In his enchantment with the beauty of the Dnister estuary, Komashko observes old Khtodos' reciting his morning prayers:

> Дивлюся – дід Ходось стоїть над кручею, наче кам'яний, облитий червоним світом, молиться богу, хреститься й кланяється до зорі. Я хочу й собі молитись, шепочу слова молитви, але я їх не розумію. Молитва не йде мені на душу. Темна ніч говорила мені за феваїдські печери, за молитви, за чорну одежу, говорила за рай. Пишний, веселий ранок говорить мені не те, а щось інше. За що він мені говорив, я й сам гаразд не розумів. Щось неясне, неомежоване ворушилось в серці; але воно було радісне, як те веселе небо. Радість, веселість ворушилась в серці; серце грало, як риба в воді.

Не молитва, а пісня йшла на душу. Я неначе чув музику в своїй молодій душі. Якісь пишні очі з довгими чорними віями манили мене. Я почував серцем, що хочу любити; але що й кого любити? ... Якісь музичні мелодії лунали в моїй душі, неначе вони лилися з неба, розкішного, розмальованого рожевими, жовтими та червоними смугами, неначе вони піднімались з блискучого пофарбованого лиману.

"Буду вчитись співати або грати; я люблю музику, – ворушилось в моїй думці. – Або вивчусь лучче малярства, буду малювати; змалюю ту красу, що в небі, що на лимані, – думав я, – або … буду писати вірші, складу віршами книжку, таку, як "Катерина"… Напишу про діда Хтодося … про безщасних, прибитих бідою … Про їх, про їх!" – ворушиться в мене далі думка. Я почував, що когось люблю … Люблю чиїсь пишні карі очі; десь я либонь бачив ті очі, – пригадую я собі. Люблю діда Хтодося, люблю рибалок й усіх людей, люблю оте розмальоване небо, отой блискучий, квітчастий лиман … Чую рай в своїй душі, хочу, щоб і для всіх був рай. (5:173–4)

[I look – Grandpa Khtodos' is standing on the cliff as if he were made of stone, washed over with red daylight, praying to God, making the sign of the cross and bowing to the sunrise. I too want to pray, I whisper the words of the prayer, but I don't understand them. The prayer doesn't enter my soul. The dark night had spoken to me of the Fevaid caves, of prayers, of black clothing – it spoke of paradise. The luxuriant, happy morning spoke to me of something else, not that. What it spoke of, I did not understand very well myself. Something unclear, undefined was stirring in my heart, but it was joyful, like the happy sky. Happiness, joy were stirring in my heart; the heart was jumping like a fish in the river. Not prayer but song was entering my soul. It was as if I could hear music in my young soul. Beautiful eyes with long black lashes were beckoning me. My heart felt that it wanted to love, but to love what? Love whom? Musical melodies were echoing in my heart as if they were pouring down from a bountiful heaven, painted in pink, yellow, and red bands that seemed to rise from the shining, painted estuary.

"I will learn how to sing or play an instrument. I love music," stirred in my soul. "Or, better yet, I will learn to paint, I will paint, I will paint this beauty that's in the heavens, in the estuary," I thought, "or … I will write poetry, I will collect a book of poems, like 'Kateryna.' I will write about Grandpa Khtodos', about the unfortunate, about those who are crushed by poverty. Yes, about them! About them!" continues the thought within me. I felt that I love someone. "I love someone's rich brown eyes, I must have seen them somewhere," I remember. I love Grandpa Khtodos', I love

> the fishermen and all people, I love this painted sky, this shining, flower-coloured estuary. I feel the paradise within my soul, I want this paradise to extend to all people.]

The mystical, emotional experience of beauty is a direct stimulus of the creative drive. The prayer becomes a song, the song a painting, and the painting a work of literature. Komashko's ecstatic urge to sing the beauty of paradise for all transcends the confines of this novel and becomes Nechui's life's work as a writer. For him geography has a special place in the creative process. The beauty, history, and symbolism of place have a deep significance.

The importance in Nechui's personal geography of the Dnister estuary is confirmed by the fact that it appears again in another novel. In a passage that mirrors in some ways the emotional power of Komashko's recollection in *Nad Chornym Morem*, Nechui describes a fishing expedition in the same place in *Mykola Dzheria*. Like Komashko, but without the youthful exuberance, Dzheria and his fellow fugitives from serfdom find on the estuary's shores a corner of paradise that allows them to forget the miseries they are running away from. Nechui describes a scene of fishing from the beach that parallels the description in *Nad Chornym Morem* both in its content and in its emotional impact (3:100–4). Evidently the author himself had witnessed such a scene and experienced its emotional power.

The power of natural landscapes to create a personal geography of aesthetic panoramas is also evident in some of the short descriptive sketches that Nechui produced in the later years of his life. Two such works deserve particular attention. The first, actually published during Nechui's lifetime, is entitled "Nich na Dnipri" (A night on the Dnipro). It recounts a celebratory expedition in June 1877 by members of the Kyiv Hromada to Vyshhorod, a historical village eighteen kilometres north of Kyiv. The expedition sailed up the Dnipro in three small boats for an afternoon and evening in Vyshhorod, and then returned during the night to arrive in Kyiv at sunrise. Nechui describes this excursion with rapture and ecstasy; indeed, no description in any of Nechui's works displays more passion and emotional involvement. The author is simply beside himself with wonder, admiration, and joy. "Яка далеч! Яка широчінь простору і в небі, і на землі! Яка велична картина! Які дивні кольори! Скрізь надзвичайний простір, скрізь розлита краса – і в небі, і на землі" (8:198) [What an expanse of space both in the heavens and on the ground! What an impressive image! What strange colours! Everywhere an unusual landscape, everywhere beauty poured out in the sky and on the earth]. The view from Vyshhorod to Kyiv at sunset, across the wide expanse of the Dnipro and the Obolon' meadow, offers Nechui the tableau he likes most: a wide panorama including land and water, stark contrasts at twilight or during the night, dramatic colours, flowers, and long shadows:

> На південь сизіли гори, а на горах було видно Київ, що неначе потопав в легкій прозорій імлі. Забудування неясно мріли в сизій далечі, а над ними були розкидані ніби золоті букети: то лисніли позолочені бані та хрести на монастирях та церквах. Та далека картина здавалась якимсь квітником з золотими маківками та золотими квітками, за які розказують тільки в казках. І високе та глибоке синє іюньське небо, і ті далекі сизі шпилі й гори з Андріївським собором на чолопочку шпиля, і золоті букети з бань та хрестів – усе це було схоже на ті вигляди, що часом сняться у сні, що за їх розказують в казках. Вік проживеш – і не забудеш за цю пишну картину, як часом ніколи не забувається дивно гарний сон.
>
> Сонце вдарило з-за лісу червоним промінням на київські гори. Широка зелена Оболонь і Поділ вкрились тінню й потемнішали. Виразніше виступили високі смужки київських гір під ясним чистим небом, обсипані збоку червонястим промінням. Тисячі вікон в домах, позолочені хрести та бані на церквах ніби зайнялись і запалали.
>
> Од їх посипались наче пучки золотих стрілок. На дзвіницях неначе горіли червоним золотом хрести та маківки, наче плавали високо-високо понад горами в синьому небі, ніби линули якісь казкові золоті птиці. Вигляд на Київ став якийсь фантастичний. Здавалось, ніби на горах з'явивсь і мрів пишний міраж, сплетений з чудових тонів, з блиску, з золота, з рожевої імли та сонячного проміння. Передо мною неначе з'явились палаци й садки Паризади з "Тисячі й однієї ночі."
>
> Сонце спустилось ще нижче над лісом і почало ніби ховаться десь в сизих борах. Оболонь, луки й Поділ ніби тонули в тінь ще глибше. Київські сизі гори стали фіолетові. Золоті бані й хрести ніби жевріли, як погасаючий жар, горіли без проміння. Усе облилось делікатними фіолетовими одлисками. За Києвом і за Дніпром небо од низу темнішало, посинішало й лисніло легеньким фіолетовим одлиском. Сонце неначе впало десь у бір. Кольори на Києві згасали. Огонь на вікнах та на золотих банях потроху щезав. Надворі сутеніло й поночіло. Ніч впала на Дніпро, на гори, – і зникли й потонули в темряві усі чуда дивного міражу. (8:189–90)

[To the south, hills appeared in the distance and atop the hills you could see Kyiv, which seemed to sink in the light transparent mist. Buildings were shrouded in a dreamy haze and above them were scattered bouquets of gold – the shining gold-covered domes and crosses on the monasteries and churches. This distant image resembled a flowerbed with the golden poppy bulbs and gold flowers that are spoken of only in fairy tales. The high and deep blue June sky, the distant grey peaks and hills with St Andrew's Church on the crown of the peak, and the golden bouquets of domes and crosses – all this was similar to those visions that appear in a dream and are described in fairy tales. You'll live your entire life and never forget such a beautiful image, as sometimes you remember a strangely beautiful dream.

The red rays of the sun struck the Kyiv hills from behind the forest. The wide green Obolon and Podil were covered in shadows and grew dark. The outlines of the Kyiv hills, speckled with red rays of sun, grew sharper against the clear bright sky. Thousands of windows, the gold-covered crosses and domes on churches seemed to ignite in flames. Swarms of golden arrows seemed to scatter from them. On the bell towers, crosses and poppy bulbs seemed to burn in a red gold, floating high above the hills in the blue sky as if they were golden birds from fairy tales. The view became somehow fantastical. It seemed a marvellous mirage had appeared atop the hills, dreamily shimmering, woven from marvellous tones, of glimmering colors, of gold, of pink haze and rays of sunlight. Before me there seemed to rise the palaces and orchards of Parizade from the *Thousand and One Nights.*

The sun fell even lower over the forest and began as if to hide somewhere in the distant thicket. Obolon, the meadows, and Podil seemed to sink into even deeper shadows. The grey Kyiv hills turned purple. The golden domes and crosses seemed to glow without casting rays of light like the embers of a dying fire. Everything was covered in delicate violet reflections. Beyond Kyiv and beyond the Dnipro, the sky was darkening from the ground up, turning a deeper blue, shining with a light violet reflection. The sun fell completely into the woods. The colours in Kyiv were extinguishing. The fire in the windows and on the golden domes was slowly going out. Twilight and darkness were falling. Night fell on the Dnipro and on the hills – and all the wonders of the strange mirage disappeared and sank into the darkness.]

Later in the story, Nechui offers a similar image of sunlight reflecting off Kyiv's domes, this time at sunrise (8:197). The entire narrative is structured as a nostalgic recollection of the emotional impact on the author of the sights and sounds of the trip, and the dominant metaphor is that of a fantastic and magical tale. But the actual objects described – Kyiv, the Dnipro, churches, St Vladimir's monument – and the occasion for the trip (an outing of the members of the Kyiv Hromada) combine to give the story a national, a Ukrainian colouring. The majesty of natural images is tied to a sense of local history and development that leave the author aroused and inspired. The exoticism of the beauty and grandeur is seemingly and silently contrasted with the mundane drudgery of the city, much like the description of Stepan Radchenko's approach to Kyiv in Valerian Pidmohyl'nyi's *Misto*, written twenty years later. Magical Kyiv, whose historical legacy shines forth across the wide river and out into the surrounding country, is a powerful magnet for personal and patriotic feelings.

This combination of personal and patriotic feelings finds expression again in Nechui's most detailed description of Kyiv, "Vechir na Vladymyrs'kii hori" (An evening on Vladymyr Hill; 9:70–94). After his move in 1909 to an apartment on Volodymyrs'ka Street, Nechui lived within easy walking distance of St Andrew's Church, the Mykhailivs'kyi Monastery, and the adjacent hill where the famous monument to St Volodymyr (Vladimir) stands. This story recounts one such walk on a Sunday evening, in June 1910, following an afternoon thunderstorm. Serhii Iefremov cites this story as evidence of Nechui's psychological frailty, his withdrawal from active life and social interaction.[7] He is badly mistaken. This is a love song, a public declaration of Nechui's affection for Kyiv. Characteristically, the narrative is full of scenic panoramas and dramatic vistas, starting with an enormous rainbow set against the black sky of the retreating storm and concluding with a night-time view of the lights of the Podil and along the banks of the river. Along the path of his walk, however, Nechui emphasizes people. Everywhere, crowds of Kyivites are enjoying the summer evening. A river of humanity surges onto the paths of Vladymyr Hill (as Nechui calls it). The benches are packed and near the banisters there is hardly any free spot to look out at the views. The restaurants are full and sparkling with light. Everywhere people are having fun, and Nechui delights in their energy and happiness. Of course, everyone is awed and silenced by the aesthetic majesty of the magnificent views:

> І невважаючи на таку силу народу, скрізь поблизу й навіть серед того натовпу панує велика тиша. Обертаюсь я і позад себе бачу предовгий рядок людей на

довгих лавах і ослонах, щільно поставлених. Усі сидять тихо. Знать, що усі одпочивають і усі дивляться на картини природи, на гарні закутки нанизу на першій терасі. Ті люде, що стояли й ніби обнизали низками парапет і вгорі, і на терасі коло пам'ятника, так само не розмовляють, стоять неповорушно; ніхто навіть не ворухнеться. І всі вони втирили очі в дивні вигляди на Дніпро, на небо, то ніби помальоване чудовими кольорами на заході, то сизе, аж чорне за горою Царського садка. На кого не глянеш, до кого не придивишся, у кожного неначе задума в очах і на обличчі, неначе кожний лине думками в вигляди або вникає сам в себе, в свою душу, в свої естетні почування і не може одвести очей от того дива. І ті молоді, що йдуть сюди й туди і часом за щось вряди-годи розмовляють, і ті говорять стиха, сливе ніби нишком, неначе вони увійшли в якийсь храм і почувають близькість якоїсь Вищої Сили й Розуму, котрий сповняє усе небо й землю й утворив несподівано в той час ті картини високого штучництва, недосяглого для художників усього світу. Я почуваю, і не наздогад, що в цих усіх українських душах, в глибочині цих усіх серців діється те ж саме, що і в моїй душі, і в моєму серці. Ця уся силенна сила натовпу так виразно показує мені, що вона має природжену вдачу великих естетів, коли сливе ніхто не балакає, не розмовляє, не сміється й не жартує. Мені здається й навіть уявляється, що ці усі українці зібрались неначе не на гулянку, а ніби повходили в якийсь напродиво великий та пишний храм, ніби для якоїсь молитви так само, як колись на цих-таки горах в давню давнину, ще за київських князів наші київські предки збирались кругом стародавнього свого бога Перуна на молитву або десь над Почайною та в гаях коло криниць на молитву богам сил природи.

Одродіння поетичної вдачі стародавніх киян, наших українських предків, сучасників князя Святослава та Владимира, я постеріг душею в цих довгих рядках очей сьогочасних українців, задуманих і втуплених в прекрасні вигляди й колоритні дивні картини, так дивно скупчені на небі й на горах. Неначе й вони слухали, як колись дзвеніли й "рокотали" струни в піснях і в "замислах" стародавнього Бояна та творця "Слова о полку Ігоревім." (9:82–3)

[Despite the great mass of people, everywhere near and even within this crowd there is a great quietness. I turn around and behind me I see a first row of people on the plentiful and tightly spaced long benches and shelters. They all sit quietly. You can see they are all resting and looking out at the views of nature, at the graceful landscapes on the first terrace below them. The people who were standing like a necklace around the railing above and around the monument on the terrace below were also quiet, avoiding conversations, standing still, without even moving. And all of them have locked their eyes onto the strange sights on the Dnipro, in the sky, which seemed to be painted in magical colours to the west but are grey, even black, behind the hill of the tsar's orchard. Whomever you look at, whomever you study, each shows thoughtfulness in their eyes and on their faces, as if each were being carried in their thoughts into the landscape or perhaps into themselves, into their own souls, into their own aesthetic sensibilities and thus cannot tear their eyes away from this wonder. And the young people who wander back and forth, sometimes talking about one thing or another – even they speak softly, as if whispering, as if they had entered a place of worship and felt the presence of some Higher Power and Wisdom that fills all the heavens and earth and unexpectedly created at this time these images of high art that worldly artists cannot achieve. I feel, and it's not just speculation, that in all of these Ukrainian souls, in the depths of all of these hearts, the same thing is taking place that is taking place in my own soul and in my heart. This great mass of people clearly shows me that it has the inborn sensibility of great aesthetes, when almost no one talks, converses, laughs, or jokes. It seems to me and I can even imagine that all these Ukrainians have gathered not just for some fun, but have seemingly entered a marvellously large and beautiful place of worship as if to pray, as in the distant past, in the times of the Kyiv princes, our Kyiv ancestors gathered around their ancient god, Perun, for prayer or somewhere along the river Pochaina and in the groves near wells to pray to their gods of natural forces.

In these long rows of eyes belonging to our contemporary Ukrainians, contemplative and mesmerized by the beautiful vistas and colourful strange images that appeared on the sky and on the hills, I observed in my soul a rebirth of the poetic temper of ancient Kyivans, our Ukrainian ancestors, contemporaries of Sviatoslav and Vladimir. As if they too were listening to the ancient strains of the stern lay of Boian and of the author of the *Tale of Igor's Campaign*.]

The beauty of Kyiv is a testament to the innate appreciation of beauty that characterizes Ukrainians. But Kyiv and its Ukrainians both now and in the past are not only masters of the aesthetic – they are creators of the wonderful and the magical. Returning home, Nechui again passes the Kyiv funicular, this time at night:

Дивлюся я, од темної трамвайної станції на самому краєчку кручі простяглося шість широких арок з стовпчиками, закруглених зверху, неначе в широкій галереї. Ці усі арки галереї були помережані ніби взорцями з рам і засклені, і мені здалеки здалось це усе якоюсь оранжереєю, що світилась наскрізь, бо була засклена тахлями в мережаних чудернацьких шибках з обох боків. Ці ясні арки галереї все нахилялись униз одна нижче од другої, висіли навскоси, неначе вони були поставлені не на землі, а збудовані й притулені до крутого покату кручі. Мені здалось, що ця галерея висить в темряві назукіс над безоднею, причеплена до станції, теліпається на повітрі, заглядає в глибоке чорне провалля і, нахилившись та висунувшись над безоднею, заглядає в його. От-от впаде, шубовсне!

Я тільки очі витріщив з дива і сам до себе засміявся. Мені здалось, що цю іграшку почепили незмисленні діти без тями в голові. На мене найшов острах, що ці дурні арки от-от незабаром одчепляться й шубовснуть в чорну глибочінь. Незабаром я побачив, що з дна глибокої чорної безодні ніби котиться потихеньку вгору ясний білий чималий клубок, неначе вирнув з темряви, а далі за ним вигулькнув з темряви вагон, червоно обмальований, з тихим, неясним, неначе потайним світом всередині. Мені уявилось, що якась допотопна летюча звірюка з огняною пащекою плазує вгору та вгору. І без найменшого шуму й навіть шелесту вона всунулась в ясну галерею і в мент спинилась. В одну мить разом одсунулись усі дверці в вагоні, поставлені рядочком назукіс, і звідтіль висипались не люде, а ніби темні силуети в брилях та капелюшах і тихесенько, без шуму пішли врозтіч та все вгору по гранітних сходах. А натомість по другий бік, ніби з-за темної рами сінематографа, висунулись інші силуети постатів, посунулись за вагон і десь зникли й поховались. Те завальне здоровецьке допотопне дивовище знов без стукоту, навіть без шелесту тихо посунулось з галереї наниз, помаленьку покотилось у безодню й зникло, і я тільки вглядів, як докотився круто навскоси, сливе сторч, навздогінці наче здоровий огняний ніби метеор на чорному небі і тихо впав кудись в чорну безодню.

Я задивився на цей нічний пейзажик і довго милувався ним, все кмітив несамохіть, як ніби чиясь небачена рука кидала огняну опуку то вгору, то вниз, і та опука то котилася наниз, то сунулась і плазувала вгору й тягла за морду, залигану ніби налигачем, якусь чудну здоровецьку червоносту животину з куценькими ніжками. (9:92–3)

[I look and see that there are six arcs with the posts curved on top, as in a wide gallery, stretching out from the tram stop on the very edge of the cliff. All these arcs of the gallery were edged as with designs on a frame and glassed in, and they appeared to me from a distance as if this were an orangery that shone throughout, since it was covered in glass panels with whimsical designs from both sides. These bright arcs of the gallery were bending downward, one below the other, hanging at an angle as if they had been set not on the ground but constructed and then leaned up against the uneven angle of the cliff. It seemed to me that this gallery hung at an angle in the dark as if above a sheer drop, was attached to the station, and hung fluttering in the air, peering into the dark abyss, having stretched out into the air above the cliff to look down. Any minute it would fall down.

I could only stare in wonder and laughed to myself. I thought this plaything had been hung by thoughtless children without good sense in their heads. I began to fear that these foolish arcs would break off and fall into the black abyss. After a while, I noticed that out of this black abyss something was quietly rolling uphill, a large, bright white bundle was appearing from the darkness and behind it, a tramcar painted red with a dull secretive light inside. I thought it was a large flying prehistoric monster with a fiery maw slowly crawling up the hill. And without any noise or even sounds it pushed into the gallery and immediately came to a stop. In a moment all the doors of the carriage, arranged at an angle in a row, opened simultaneously and from inside spilled not people, but dark silhouettes in bowlers and bonnets who quietly exited and scattered upward along the granite stairs. On the other side, however, as if from the dark side of a cinema screen, appeared another group of silhouetted figures who went behind the tramcar and disappeared somewhere. This massive prehistoric creature again quietly, without any noise, thrust itself out of the gallery downward, slowly rolled down into the abyss and disappeared. I could only just make it out as it rolled down, almost vertically, like a fiery meteor on a black sky, silently falling somewhere into the black nothingness.

I got caught up watching this night-time spectacle and enjoyed it for a long time, unwittingly noting, as someone's invisible hand was seemingly throwing a fiery ball first up then down the hill, and this ball first rolled down then climbed and crawled up the hill, pulling with a leather strap tied around the snout a large, mysterious, red creature on stubby legs.]

The magic of this Kyiv evening eventually culminates in the arrival of an actual streetcar, described in a Baudelairian urban image of fantastic horror and exotic wonder:

Але десь за стіною почувся далекий стукіт та гуркіт, неясний, неначе одляски глухого далекого грому. Гуркіт наближався, ставав дужчий і чутніший. А далі за стіною за углом загуркотіло й застукотіло так, що аж гора застугоніла й задвигтіла. Дивлюся я в темний куток на крутій поворотці за стіну, а звідтіль

> неначе посипався з-за угла стіни ґвалт та скрипіння, рипіння та стогін, неначе, як кажуть в казці, "стукотить, гуркотить – сто коней біжить". І несподівано з-за угла стіни з вузького Святополк-Михайлівського переулочка висунулась ніби огняна пащека, закручувався освічений тулуб якоїсь звірюки або змія, усього в огні. Звір з'явився увесь, затріщав, залущав, загуркотів і раптом, в одну мить спинився коло маленької станції. Станція од одлиску з вагона ніби зайнялась одразу. А з вагона посипались люде, бігцем побігли й поховались у веранді коло станції. (9:94)
>
> [From behind the wall a distant rumble and clanging arose, like the sound of distant thunder. The clanging was approaching, becoming louder and clearer. And then, behind the wall in the corner, there was such a rumble and clatter that the hill itself groaned and trembled. I looked at the dark corner at the turn behind the wall, and from there poured forth a clanging and banging, moaning and groaning, crying and yelling, as if all the fairy-tale armies were advancing against us. Then, unexpectedly, from behind the corner into the narrow Sviatopolk-Mykhailivs'kyi alley came a fiery snout, with a twisting illuminated torso behind it, the whole dragon covered in fire. The monster appeared in its entirety, roaring, belching, grinding, until suddenly it stopped at the small station. The station was immediately illuminated by the lights from the carriage. People streamed out the doors of the streetcar and ran onto the veranda near the station.]

Another description of Kyiv in exotic colours can be found in Nechui's 1910 sketch entitled "Apokalipsychna kartyna v Kyievi" (An apocalyptic vision in Kyiv), which describes a fire along the wharves and in the Podil district of Kyiv. Nechui explicitly finds beauty in this tragic event. Before he reaches a vantage point that allows him to see the fire itself, he describes the beauty of the majestic St Andrew's Church framed against the red clouds beyond it, reflecting the fire below. When he reaches the terrace below the church and views the fire spreading from the riverbanks across the residential areas of the Podil, he draws a comparison between the valley of flames in front of him and the blood-covered grounds of Lysa Hora (Bald Mountain) just south of the city, which at that time was the site of executions by hanging. This unusually stark and jarring connection is made on the basis of an aesthetic feature – the blood-red colour of the flames.

Nechui's personal aesthetics animate many of his geographic descriptions, but this personal aesthetic is usually tied, as we have seen, to historical events and national symbols. A key text in this regard is the 1880 travelogue of Nechui's visit to the gravesite of Taras Shevchenko near Kaniv on the banks of the Dnipro entitled "Shevchenkova mohyla" (Shevchenko's grave-mound). This description has the features typical of Nechui's personal geography: a heavy dose of colourful flowers and vegetation, sweeping expansive views down onto the river and the surrounding countryside, and comparisons to exotic places – in this case, Mounts Pilatus and Rigi in the Swiss Alps near Lucerne (4:9). History is embodied in Shevchenko himself as well as the reference to the eminent scholar and friend of Shevckenko's, Mykhailo Maksymovych, whose estate lies across the river from the gravesite. Nechui structures the description with theatrical metaphors. The hills around the gravesite, taller than the one on which Shevchenko is buried, create the illusion of an amphitheatre. The forests and vegetation form a natural curtain. The arcs of the tree-covered hills form a proscenium arch above the stage where the "great man," as Nechui calls him, is buried. But the views in this theatre are reversed. It opens up onto the river, and the panoramas it provides, north, east, and south, encompass the better part of Ukraine. Nechui, for whom Shevchenko was a personal inspiration in his career as a Ukrainian writer, describes both a sacred pilgrimage and a tourist adventure. Comparing what he calls Shevchenko Hill (traditionally known as Chernecha or Tarasova Hora) and the surrounding hills of right-bank Dnipro with the infinitely larger Swiss Alps (which he had visited), Nechui emphasizes the symbolic grandeur of this site and its significance as a destination for tourists. But at the same time he also describes the oxen grazing on its sides, the village homes and fishermen's huts nearby, and the topographic features that surround and protect the hill. Shevchenko's resting place is almost a native element of the geography here. It is grounded in this place with natural, national, and historical roots.[8]

The Ros' River area, where Nechui was born, is but a short distance from Shevchenko's gravesite. In his travelogue Nechui mentions that the Ros' flows into the Dnipro, just a little south of Shevchenko Hill. Furthermore, Shevchenko was born and raised in the area just south of Stebliv, Nechui's own birthplace. Thus Shevchenko's presence was deeply felt in this area. But the Ros' River area in a wider sense was also the setting for many important events in Ukrainian history, including those connected with the Khmel'nyts'kyi revolution of 1648 and the Haidamak uprising of 1768. This is the heart of Right-Bank Ukraine, a territory marked by strong Ukrainian identity and a long history of Polish-Ukrainian conflict. These links to local history find expression in

Shevchenko's poetry and they are also significant in Nechui's frequent return to this area in his fictional works. It embodied – historically, naturally, personally, and symbolically – the essential Ukrainianness that Nechui kept at the centre of his authorial attention. Even when his writing occasionally strayed beyond the narrower bounds of what he usually considered Ukraine – as it does in two travel narratives, "U Karpatakh" (In the Carpathians; 4:355–88 – about his visit to Szczawnica in 1884) and "Drehochyn ta Ostrih: Pomershi ukrainski horody" (Drogichyn and Ostrih: defunct Ukrainian towns; 5:14–23) – his focus is on uncovering the Ukrainian elements that inform a particular area, whether they be the presence of ethnic Ukrainians, moments from Ukrainian history, or contacts with Ukrainian culture. Nechui's geography always remained personal, national, and symbolic.

Territory acquires national particularity only when it is inhabited. Nechui's Ukraine was undoubtedly a place, but it was first and foremost people. For Nechui, this meant the people whose national identity was Ukrainian. But in the typically circuitous logic of national identity constructions it also meant all the inhabitants of Ukraine, no matter what their nationality, as evidenced by the Ukrainianness of all the Kyivites he depicts on Vladymyr Hill in the story cited above. Just as Nechui in his works deliberately encompassed a wide swathe of Ukrainian geography, so too, with equivalent deliberation, he depicted as wide an array of Ukrainians as he could. This included people of diverse nationality, social class, profession, intelligence, appearance, character, and almost any other characteristic by which people are distinguished.

Nothing is more central in Nechui's technique as a writer than the depiction of character. Like many realist authors, Nechui generally builds his characters as exemplars of a personality type. Their characteristic features are mostly external, visible, and derived from a particular feature or trait that subsumes their being under a single dominant attribute: the vengeful slave owner, the irresponsible materialist, the foolish simpleton, etc. In Nechui's fiction, these character types are spread over a very wide array of people, distinguished by social and personal categories. Of course, the most important category is nationality. But since nationality is such a major factor in Nechui's works, that topic will be dealt with separately, in the next chapter. So, too, will the depiction of conflict between social classes. Nechui's depiction of class conflict, however, is often interwoven with other forms of conflict, and issues of social class are not always the dominant consideration.

Nechui's reputation as an ethnographic realist implies that his works are predominantly about peasants and their village customs. Actually, peasants are not nearly so plentiful among Nechui's characters. And the peasants that do appear in his works are often endowed with qualities or biographies that distance them from an agricultural environment. The hero of *Mykola Dzheria* is certainly a peasant. He and his family are serfs working on the land for the landowner and Nechui depicts them harvesting and threshing grain. He also depicts some of the customs and ceremonies involved in a village wedding. But at the close of chapter 2, Mykola runs away from his village and does not return until the very end of the novel. In the intervening chapters he is an itinerant worker at various mills or a fisherman on the Black Sea coast, and is not involved in agricultural work or in the social and cultural life of a Ukrainian village.

The works that contribute most to Nechui's reputation for ethnographic portraits of Ukrainian peasants are the novel *Kaidasheva sim'ia* and its short-story predecessors and sequels about the two village hags, Paraska and Palazhka. Here we are certainly in the presence of peasants, even if Omel'ko Kaidash is also a skilled wheelwright, an occupation that might enhance his farm income and raise him and his family slightly on the social scale if he were not also a drunkard. His wife prides herself on her former service in the home of a gentryman and thus considers herself superior to her neighbours. Both of them, as well as the hags Paraska and Palazhka, are relatively flat satiric characters and thus hardly the robust examples of Ukrainian peasants that readers might expect from a presumed paragon of ethnographic realism. However, two other features of Nechui's depiction of peasants manifest the qualities associated with this stereotype.

The first of these is Nechui's frequent use of idealized visual images. Among the legacies of Taras Shevchenko's poetry was an idealized image of the Ukrainian village as a quiet, beautiful, and idyllic setting. Nechui, like all Ukrainian writers in the post-Shevchenko era, worked under the powerful influence of the great romantic poet, and some of the images in his prose recall or resemble those in Shevchenko's poetry. But in Nechui's works these idyllic images are often problematic – as, indeed, they were in Shevchenko's works as well. In the second chapter of *Kaidasheva sim'ia,* for example, Karpo Kaidash visits the Dovbysh home to meet his sweetheart, Motria. Nechui describes the home from the perspective of the approaching young lover:

> Довбиш був багатий чоловік; він жив на самому кінці села, там, де глибокий яр входив у ліс вузьким клином. В самому кутку того яру блищав маленький Довбишів ставочок. Над ставком стояла Довбишева хата, вся в черешнях. Од вулиці було видко тільки край білої стіни з сінешніми дверима. Густі високі вишні зовсім закривали од вулиці вікна й стіни, наче густий ліс.
>
> Карпо йшов помаленьку, скоса поглядаючи на Довбишів двір. Перед ним блиснув вугол білої стіни, підперезаний внизу червоною призьбою; зачорніли чорною плямою одчинені двері з одвірками, помальованими ясно-синьою фарбою з червоною вузькою смужкою навкруги. Довбишева хата була нова, велика, добре вшита, з чималими вікнами. Коло вікон висіли віконниці, помальовані ясно-синьою фарбою. (3:309)
>
> [Dovbysh was a wealthy man; he lived at the very edge of the village, where a deep gorge entered the forest in a narrow wedge. In a corner of that gorge shone Dovbysh's little pond. The Dovbysh home stood beside that pond, surrounded by cherry trees. From the street only a portion of the white wall with the door was visible. The thick tall cherry trees completely blocked the windows and walls from the street.
>
> Karpo walked slowly, glancing cautiously at the Dovbysh yard. A corner of the white wall appeared, belted below with a red *pryzba* [mound of earth around a peasant house]. The black spot of the open door stood out, with the hinges painted light blue and a thin red line around them. The Dovbysh home was new, large, and well-constructed, with large windows. By the windows hung shutters, painted light blue.]

With all those cherry trees around the home, a reader cannot help but think of Shevchenko's best known idyllic image, "Садок вишневий коло хати!" [The cherry orchard by the house]. But Nechui's propensity for verdant natural growth and lush colour in his descriptions obscures the craft in this depiction. It is Saturday afternoon and Motria's parents are at the market – she's alone at home. The scene has just a hint of an illicit meeting between lovers. The house is barely visible through all the vegetation. But what is visible has familiar features: a white corner, red footings, and a dark spot where the door opens. This is the image of a woman in a white blouse, red boots, black eyes and hair, and blue ribbons or sash. She's hidden from Karpo, they're both hidden from passersby and parents, and the domestic life of one and all is hidden behind a veneer of idyllic bliss.

Nechui frequently uses the contrast between idyllic village stereotypes and the reality hidden beneath them as an essential feature of his descriptions of Ukrainian peasants and their villages. The satiric portraits of the Kaidashes and the hags Paraska and Palazhka are built on this principle. The ideologically inspired presumption that Ukrainian villagers are noble creatures – an outgrowth of Herderian romanticism coupled with the political populism that dominated liberal thought in the late nineteenth-century Russian Empire, particularly Ukraine – are satirically deflated in the portraits of lazy, foolish, stupid, immature, pompous, egotistical, and malicious peasants. Occasionally Nechui even uses this contrast for more than mere satire. In the novel *Khmary* there are two episodes where intellectual townsfolk return to their native rural setting. In chapter 6 Professor Dashkovych visits his father, a village priest, and discovers a variety of social ills. After a walk by the pond where he encounters a textbook example of pastoral young lovers, Dashkovych returns to the village, where he hears heart-rending screams. He enters the house to discover a man he knows, Ostap Dubovii, mercilessly whipping his wife and his children. When Dashkovych addresses the man to bring him to his senses, Dubovii threatens to whip him too. Dashkovych hastily retreats, having at least given the wife and children an opportunity to run out of the home and hide in the bushes (2:92). He ponders the contrast between the young lovers courting by the pond and the mature married couple. The actual peasants who inhabit the romantic village hardly live up to Herderian ideals.

A similar sentiment arises from a scene in chapter 9 of the same novel. The young idealistic student Pavlo Radiuk returns to his home village to find many of the same problems that Dashkovych found in his – more taverns than schools, more poverty than natural bounty, more stubborn foolishness than common sense. But the university student is intent on establishing his own link to the common people. He goes out to the melon patch with his father, where they encounter the old watchman, Onys'ko, who treats them to a juicy ripe watermelon that cools them off in the midday heat. When Onys'ko eventually excuses himself to get back to work, Radiuk reads him a quick lesson in social equality and offers to join him. Despite the old watchman's protestations, Radiuk starts picking cucumbers. But after a short while Radiuk is sweating profusely and can barely endure the heavy strap eating into his shoulders. Onys'ko, who has followed in Radiuk's footsteps, has gathered a full bag of vegetables that Radiuk missed. The old man sends the student off for a rest: "Lie down over there and read a book" (2:192), he tells him. A peasant's work is much more back-breaking than the romantic poets and populist intellectuals imagine, and Nechui enjoys indulging his pragmatic anti-intellectualism with mild satiric barbs aimed at the hopeless ineptitude of bookish men in practical mattters.

The description of cucumber picking in *Khmary* points to another important characteristic of Nechui's peasants: an abundance of details. Nechui was clearly familiar with rural life. Although his works do not contain the kind of details that only an actual peasant labourer would know, he is certainly familiar with the culture, work, setting, and objects that make up the lives of peasants. While some of this familiarity was no doubt the common inheritance of any Ukrainian in the mid-nineteenth century whether or not they had any connection to the village, the authenticity of Nechui's details suggests more than merely a general acquaintance. In any event, Nechui enhances the reader's image of peasants and their lives with generous brushstrokes depicting a variety of details including outdoor agricultural work, domestic chores, the implements of farming, husbandry, and daily life, social and religious rituals, and other matters. The old hags Paraska and Palazhka can be seen reaping in their adjoining and contested fields (3:6), arguing over a piglet that has gotten into the vegetable garden (3:9), and fighting over the use of a well (3:12). The Kaidash family also works on the fields and even earns money by working for the rich landowner (3:334), since slavery has now been abolished, but Nechui shows us little of the outdoors in this novel: there's Lavrin's visit to the mill, the Kaidash family drive to the Balash home in chapter 5, and Melashka's trip to Kyiv in chapter 6. The balance of the work is a domestic drama staged mostly indoors. The major actors are the women: the menfolk have little to do indoors besides eat and sleep. The women argue over cooking, baking, washing, spinning, weaving, sewing, and all manner of domestic chores. But Nechui does not give lengthy descriptions of these activities. On the contrary, they appear entirely as pretexts for the various quarrels between Kaidash's wife ("Kaidashykha") and her daughters-in-law. Many critics have long pointed out that Nechui's descriptions of village life have a strong folkloric flavour. The family arguments in *Kaidasheva sim'ia* are the traditional tales of village gossip. Here is the proud and lazy mother-in-law who abuses her son's wives as if they were domestic help and the precocious young women who haven't yet acquired much experience in domestic management. These are not characters from Nechui's realist imagination, even if they are given enough personality to make them interesting individuals. They may indeed have come from folklore, but they could just as soon have come from Molière or Aristophanes or any of a long list of satirists and comic writers who have created and embellished such stock characters for as long as comic writing has been practised. Nechui's indebtedness to folklore in the creation of his village characters is not particularly clear or significant.

Indeed, in examining Nechui's depiction of village life, it is very apparent that he is deliberately avoiding indulgent descriptiveness for its own sake. He also steers clear of popular ethnographic elements that were often included in other works. For example, when the Kaidash sons fall in love with village girls and send matchmakers to arrange the weddings, Nechui merely tells us that this happened. He completely and deliberately skips the traditional description of matchmaking and replaces it with a family visit that allows the Kaidash parents to display all their comic traits and prejudices in front of the in-laws to be. Here, as in all the other domestic scenes, Nechui is not motivated either by a realist's penchant for meticulous description or by an ethnographic urge to share the colourful elements of culture. The text is structured by the demands of comic writing. The details of village life that Nechui offers are sooner the props of slapstick comedy than the background and setting of a realist painting.

This functional quality of village descriptions is further evidenced in those of Nechui's works that are set in the village but do not focus on typical peasants. Here the village sights and rituals may not be comic, but they are nevertheless tied to thematic rather than descriptive functions. The opening paragraphs of the short novel *Ne toi stav* (He's not the same) focus on two women, Zin'ka and her daughter Nastia, who are engaged in a decorative ritual chore – whitewashing their domestic clay stove, the centrepiece of every village home:

> Домазавши припічок, Настя вмочила віхоть в глиняник з білою глиною і помалесеньку підводила зверху на грубі на карнизі смугу взорців, вималюваних зовсім такими червоними та синіми зірками та хрестиками, якими вишивають рукави сорочок. Ті квітки вималювала Настя з своїм братом Романом.
>
> Незабаром у хату увійшов Роман, високий білявий парубок з ясними очима. Він приніс здоровий пучок ласкавцю, гвоздиків та крокосу, котрий вже зацвів жовтогарячими патлатими квітками.
>
> – А що, сину, нарвав бадилля свиням? – спитала мати в сина. (6:301)

[Having finished whitewashing the front area of the oven, Nastia dipped the brush into the jug with the white clay and slowly began tracing the

> outline of the designs on the cornice of the oven, which were styled in the same kind of red and blue stars and crosses as the embroidered arms of a shirt. These flowers had been painted by Nastia with her brother Roman.
>
> Roman soon entered the house, a tall and pale young man with bright eyes. He carried a large bunch of lanceleaf, carnations, and safflower blooming in orange shaggy flowers.
>
> "Did you pull up some stalks for the pigs?" his mother asked him.]

The detail regarding the outlining in white clay of the coloured designs on the top of the stove could well be a rare gem of realist description, except for the immediate juxtaposition with Roman's entry into the home with flowers in his hands. Nechui tells us that Roman is partially responsible for the decoration of the stove, a domestic function generally considered women's work, as reflected in the comparison to embroidery and also as it was depicted in *Kaidasheva sim'ia*. His entry at this moment casts his gender identity into doubt. He is associated with aesthetic functions, such as decorating the stove, and he is carrying flowers. The description of a domestic chore serves to characterize Roman as an unusual male. The language of the description, which includes the architectural term "cornice," distances this passage from the peasant milieu. With his usual redundancy, Nechui explains that the exceptionally self-reliant Zin'ka smiled at the thought that her grown son was still taking on women's work (6:302) and further tells the story of how Roman painted the decorations on the stove and elsewhere in the house.

Roman in *Ne toi stav* is a misfit peasant. He does not properly belong in the village, but then the women in this novel are also quite unusual, as we shall see in a later chapter. Roman cares more for the romantic side of nature than the actual environment in which a peasant works for his living. Solomiia follows him into the forest one day and finds him communing with nature, delighting in birdsong and experiencing a religious joy in the beauty of the natural surroundings (6:385). This is not the comportment of an industrious peasant! Roman is a dreamy intellectual captivated by existential and religious questions that arise from his contemplation of nature. Peasants, of course, seldom become philosophical at the sight of a tree.

Another set of intellectual interlopers in the village appears in Nechui's *Na gastroliakh v Mykytianakh*, about an opera singer and his wife who spend a summer vacation in the village. This is, of course, a story about the contrasts between urban and rural characters. A similar plot involving the same opera singer and his wife can be found in the story "Gastroli," but in that instance, they are in a country home outside a small town rather than in a village. In the village of Mykytiany the somewhat phlegmatic singer, Flegont, descends on the home of his brother, the village priest. There he encounters Leonid Lahodzins'kyi, the brother of the priest's wife and a painter who serves as something of an alter ego to Flegont. Leonid, like his new friend the singer, delights in the aesthetic pleasures of the village and sets off for the village millpond to paint the delightful landscape. Nechui spares no effort in depicting the scene, the warm sunny day, the clean air, the large stone structure of the mill and residence, and the pond behind the dam with a charming, tree-covered island in the middle (8:64–7) – a tranquil, picturesque corner of a rural paradise:

> В гарячому повітрі було тихо. Усе стояло непорушне, ніби намальоване на полотні. Далеко на ставку понад берегами під лозами було видно на воді сідла рибалок на чотирьох кілках. Рибалки сиділи з удлищами непорушно, неначе вироблені з міді людські постаті. Надворі було тихо, але в тій ніби мертвій зачарованій тиші закипіло світове життя. Веселі гуси ґеґали на ставку, брьохались, ляскали крилами, вигравали по воді; качки безперестану кахкали, пливучи довгими рядочками. Удлища в рибалок вряди-годи ворушились, неначе ті мідні постаті, мов пам'ятники на майданах, вряди-годи оживали. Самий веселий світ вранішнього сонця був ніби живий і ворушив життя в усьому. Над берегом світ дрижав, мов живий. Вода хилиталась і ворушилась, мов жива. (8:65)

> [It was quiet in the hot air. Everything was still, as in a painting. Far away on the pond, on the bank beneath the ferns, the four-legged stools of the fishermen were visible on the water. The fishermen sat motionless with their rods, like human figures cast in copper. It was quiet outdoors, but in this seemingly dead, enchanted stillness natural activity boiled up to the surface. The happy geese were hissing and waddling on the pond, flapping their wings, and playing on the water. The ducks were constantly quacking, swimming in long rows. The fishermen's rods occasionally stirred, as if these copper figures, like statues in the square, sometimes came to life. The very world of morning sunshine seemed to be alive, and living things stirred everywhere. On the banks the earth trembled, as if alive. The water stirred and lapped as if it too were living.]

Inspired by this poetic scene, Leonid sets up his canvas and gives himself over completely to painting, with a song on his lips. Before long, however, he hears a thunderous sound and sees a herd of cows marching towards the water. They are followed by a herd of charging horses, who have also come to drink. The cloud of dust raised by the animals obscures the sun and temporarily spoils the perfect scene Leonid is painting. Then come the sheep:

> Маляр оглянувсь на греблю. Через греблю сунулась густа отара овець на всю ширину. Вівчарі ставили отару на стійлі по другий бік ставка в холодку під вербами, що росли на окопах коло городів. Вівці позбивались докупи, ніби позлипались. Здавалось, що гребля вкрита здоровецьким живим чорним вивернутим кожухом, на котрому подекуди манячіли білі латки та уставки.
>
> Порох душив Леоніда Семеновича. Очі в його запорошились. Він устав, хапком одсунув триноги й картину на самісінький край греблі до низенького тинка, котрим була обрамована гребля од ставка. Живий кожух посунувсь незабаром на місток і пхав маляра з лавки, зачіпаючи його довгі ноги. (8:68)
>
> [The painter glanced at the dam. A herd of sheep was approaching the dam at full width. The shepherds were moving the herd to a pasture on the other side of the pond, in the shade beneath some willows that grew by the ditch near the gardens. The sheep had bunched together, as if glued to each other. It seemed the dam was covered in a large, living, black fur coat turned inside out, with white patches and insertions appearing in places.
>
> The dust choked Leonid Semenovch. His eyes were full of dust. He got up, quickly grabbed his tripod and painting, and moved them to the edge of the dam by a low fence that separated the dam from the pond. The living fur coat moved onto the bridge and was pushing against the painter on his bench, brushing against his long legs.]

Pushed off of his stool by the living fur coat, Leonid abandons the painting and goes home. The Ukrainian village would be easier to paint if it were a little more cooperative! Nechui's descriptions of it are usually designed to illustrate an ironic point.

Another example occurs in chapter 6 of the same work. Flegont and his wife have moved from his brother's house into the more spacious but ramshackle schoolhouse. One night they hear noises in the building. Suspicion first turns to the possibility of a thief, but the problem turns out to be some owls nesting in the attic. The city folk are then shown inspecting the roof thatch and other features of rural construction to discover where the birds might have entered the structure. When the holes are finally repaired, another problem arises: an old window is opened too aggressively and it breaks, leading to another problem. The broken window must now be stuffed with a pillow every night to prevent intruders. Nechui explores these issues of domestic security, particularly weak security compromised by the negligence of the owners, without any specific explanation. But he isn't suggesting that the Ukrainian village is a place where security needs very particular attention. The topic serves to highlight the principal theme of the story, namely, the conditions that lead the opera singer's wife to engage in an affair with one of the young men visiting the village. While taking active steps to keep burglars and birds out of his temporary quarters, the husband does little to protect his marital happiness from intruding lovers. Once again, Nechui presents descriptions and stereotypes of rural life in a manner that undermines the traditional view of the Ukrainian village as a noble, wholesome, and salubrious environment.

The most prominent group of non-peasant village residents in Nechui's works is certainly the clergy. There's a personal logic in this, since Nechui himself came from an old family of village clergymen and had been brought up and educated in a religious environment. But the clergy as a literary topic offers other advantages as well. This was one of the most socially mobile groups in the Russian Empire. Their professional function put them into immediate contact with the lower classes, particularly in rural settings, but they were also accorded a somewhat higher social status than their parishioners and could mingle and interact, if sometimes uncomfortably, with higher social classes. The male children of the clergy would usually receive an education, which further set them off from their surroundings and provided opportunities to escape from both religion and the village. So in choosing to write so often about clergymen, Nechui was not only focusing on what he knew best, but also on a social stratum that allowed him the widest breadth in depicting Ukrainian society. And of course, in nineteenth-century Ukraine religion itself was a very pervasive element in Ukrainian culture, regardless of any personal beliefs.

Nechui's clergymen come in a variety of shapes and sizes. So, too, do the various critical analyses of his depiction of the clergy and religious life in general. Among the most insightful is that of Serhii Iefremov, in part, no doubt, because he too, like Nechui, was the son of a clergyman and a graduate of the Kyiv Theological Academy. In his monograph on Nechui, Iefremov emphasizes questions of the clergy's social position relative to the peasants. Using *Starosvits'ki batiushky ta matushky* as the key text, he first outlines the biographical and then the historical significance of the gradual professionalization of the Orthodox clergy in the Russian Empire and the chasm that this created between the village clergy and the peasants.[9] Nechui's works reflect this transition. The "old-world" priests in the title of his novel are the local men, like Kharytin Mossakovs'kyi, the youngest son of the previous pastor, whom the community elects to be their new pastor after his father's death despite his lack of education, weak character, and low social profile. Their counterparts are the new generation of priests, educated, ambitious, and snobbish, like Father Marko Balabukha, the chief villain of the novel, who was a competitor for both the parish and for Onysia Prokopovych, the woman Kharytin married. Nechui has a sentimental nostalgia for the old ways and the simple men who were at the same time priests but also friends and neighbours to their peasant parishioners. But his comic wit and satiric instinct never abandon him, and the "old-world" priests are by no means idealized. Their simplicity sometimes dissolves into foolishness (if not worse), their friendliness often resembles hedonism, and their helplessness in the face of modernity and social hierarchy undermines their usefulness in the parish. What's more, Nechui almost never depicts priests performing a religious function or ministering to their parishioners, so even those priests to whom he is sympathetic often appear to be indolent and lethargic. The priests of the opposite category are characterized as malicious and materialistic careerists.

Nechui's interest in the "old-world" clergy is evident from his earliest works. The 1869 novel *Prychepa*, which is not particularly concerned with the clergy, except that the young bride is a daughter of a priest, opens with a memorable scene of her very light-hearted father, Reverend Khvedor Chepurnovs'kyi, drinking vodka and smoking cigarettes with his good buddy, Reverend Moisei. The scene is reminiscent of another famous drinking scene involving two priests that occurs in Anatolii Svydnyts'kyi's *Liuborats'ki*, where the two clergymen justify their rounds of drinks with sacred numbers, progressing through the Holy Trinity, the four evangelists, the six days of creation, the twelve apostles, and the fourteen epistles of St Paul until they're approaching the forty saints.[10] While Svydnyts'kyi's novel might have been written earlier than Nechui's, it was not published until much later, in 1886. In any event, there is no question of influence by one author on the other. More likely, both of them, as sons of priests, were using anecdotes about the propensity of the clergy to alcohol that were generally familiar in Ukrainian society, and particularly in clerical families. Nechui's characteristic improvement on the anecdote concerns the role of the priest's wife. In Svydnyts'kyi's version, the priest's wife, or *panimatka*. Liuborats'ka joins her husband. In Nechui's version, Father Khvedor hides his drinking from his wife, Maria Vasylivna, who tries, with little success, to keep him in line. In both novels the anecdote is designed to show the easy-going, provincial camaraderie of the "old-world" clergy. In both novels the children of these comfortable clergymen become the denationalized victims of their own ambition and their parents' desire for a better life for their offspring. What distinguishes Nechui's version, however, is the characterization of the wilful denial of responsibility on the part of the priests. Svydnyts'kyi's version is simply a piece of malicious satire as the drunken friends blabber religious nonsense and screech out drinking songs.

Nechui also satirizes his characters, but he makes a point to characterize – and in a friendly manner – the indulgent self-deception of the two priests. They know they should not be drinking – they discuss the merits of the advice that a doctor has given Father Moisei about the need to stop drinking. But the temptation is great and heaven knows that doctors aren't to be trusted, so the two give in (1:128–9). A similar exchange concerns cigarettes. Moisei firmly refuses to smoke, on doctor's orders, but Khvedir suggests that a gradual reduction is more likely to succeed than a sudden cold-turkey abandonment – so they have a smoke (1:130). When the vodka runs out, Khvedir carefully sneaks into the living quarters of his home, where his wife is sleeping, to get some more. But when he hears his wife stirring in her bed, he quickly runs out and hides the carafe he has just filled from the barrel in case his wife comes out and finds them drinking (1:134). Later in the evening he even sneaks into the living quarters again, to get the whole barrel, but in his haste and fear of waking his wife he brings out the inferior vodka rather than the better one, unable to distinguish them in the darkness (1:138). This stream of slapstick burlesque is interspersed with what is made to appear as the normal chatter of two old friends. Khvedir speaks of the need to marry off his seven daughters, no matter who the suitors turn out to be. He goes on to mention how the local Polish landlord has befriended him and is drawing his children into a Polish cultural world. Finally, he talks about how poorly his son studies at school and compares this to his own studies, which began very poorly but eventually, when he saw the error of his ways, took off so that he became an outstanding student. Nechui deliberately juxtaposes these three topics (marriage, Polish snobbery, and a disinclination to study) with the priests' carefree attitude about their health. Just as they consciously ignore what they know is the reasonable advice of their doctors and their wives, so too, it will turn out, they ignore what they expressly acknowledge as important social problems. "Never mind the doctor, have another drink" is a formula that can be applied not only to personal health but also to social problems, to the abandonment of cultural identity, and to the heedless quest for material possessions. The novel's opening scene has a much firmer connection to the thematic material of the work than might appear on a casual reading focused on the amusingly epicurean clergymen.

In *Starosvits'ki batiushky ta matushky*, clergymen are no longer incidental in the plot: they are at the very centre of attention, both in terms of the plot and the themes of the novel, as Iefremov explains. But the social history of the clergy that Iefremov analyses is not the only theme in this novel. In constructing the psychological profile of his characters, Nechui here, as in other novels, frequently relies on contrasts between traits of personality such as modest vs proud, simple vs educated, sedentary vs active, convivial vs aloof, cheerful vs melancholy. He typically introduces characters with the contrasting trait or traits to help highlight the personality of his protagonists. Perhaps the most notable feature of this model of character depiction is the emphasis Nechui places on friendliness and camaraderie. This is part of his emphasis on joy, a topic explored below, in chapter 5. What is notable here is the association between the "old-world" Ukrainian clergy and this friendly, sociable disposition. The old Ukrainian customs of hospitality and friendliness are important not only because they cement the social bond between the clergy and their peasant neighbours (indeed, they do not always achieve this end), but because they describe a social pattern of behaviour, a culture that Nechui clearly sees as characteristically Ukrainian.

Among the memorable characters in this novel is Father Mel'khyzedek, i.e., Melchisedec. While the presence of biblical names is not unusual for clerical families, Melchisedec is certainly not a common name among Ukrainian priests. The biblical character appears in the book of Hebrews, in the Old Testament, as a somewhat ambiguous figure to whom the patriarch Abraham pays tribute and who is associated with a special order of priesthood that will include Jesus Christ. He is the king of righteousness and the king of Salem, which is either peace or Jerusalem. In giving his character this name, Nechui emphasizes a special status for this person as the embodiment of an old tradition of priesthood. He is not an unconditionally positive character. Father Mel′khyzedek is not particularly sensitive to social injustice – he can calmly bargain about the number of serfs (i.e., slaves) required as part of a dowry to cement a marriage arrangement as if these were not living people whose fate was being decided by the whims of others – but he and his wife are barometers of culturally expected and acceptable friendly relations with neighbours. Nechui deliberately constructs this novel in a series of contrasting events at which Mel′khyzedek and his wife, Marta, play conspicuous roles. The first of these incidents is the engagement of Marko Balabukha to Oleksandra (Olesia) Terlets′ka, in chapter 3 of the novel. Mel′khyzedek, who is Balabukha's uncle, visits the Terlets′kyis as matchmaker for his nephew. Of course, since Kvitka-Osnov′ianenko's *Marusia,* in which the Germans arriving from Turkey recite all the traditional formulas of ceremonial matchmaking, the engagement ceremony had been a staple element of Ukrainian literature. But Nechui again not only avoids an ethnographic description of the traditional ritual, he actually works against it. The traditional observances mask what is, in fact, a potentially delicate negotiation. Mel′khyzedek and his wife skip the niceties and jump right into the negotiations. Nechui subverts the reader's expectations and thereby further satirically characterizes Uncle Mel′khyzedek as an unconventionally direct and straight-talking fellow:

Отець Мельхиседек з жінкою, не довго думаючи, неначе до стіни притиснули Терлецького й Терлецьку й почали говорити за придане.

– А що, отче Петре! Сказати правду, ми оце приїхали сватати вашу дочку, Олесю, – сказав отець Мельхиседек. – Чи оддасте, чи нехай підросте?

– Ми з жінкою ладні оддати. Балабуха чоловік вчений, пригожий, має вже парафію. Не знаю, що дочка скаже, – промовив Терлецький.

– Коли вже, дякувати вам, така ваша воля, то треба й дарити дітей. Що ж ви думаєте дати за дочкою? – сказала просто Мельхиседекова жінка, Марта Тарасівна.

Терлецький глянув на жінку й сказав:

– Дамо сто карбованців.

– Сто карбованців гроші, то правда, – заторохтів отець Мельхиседек, – але, сказати правду, не великі.

– Авжеж не великі, – заторохтіла Мельхиседекова жінка. – Гроші грішми, але треба чогось і до грошей. На господарстві треба й корів, треба й волів, треба й возів, треба коней, треба й до коней. Треба миски й ложки, треба чогось і до ложки. І вже, господи, що то й казати! Ви самі, здоровенькі, знаєте, чого треба на господарстві, та ще й новому та молодому, часом необміркованому...

Терлецька сердито глянула на цю просту, в намітці, сваху, котра жебрала, неначе стара циганка. (4:92)

[Without giving the matter much thought, Father Mel'khyzedek and his wife jumped right into the matter and pinning the Terlets'kyis to the wall, spoke immediately about the size of the dowry.

"What say you, Father Peter? We come to make arrangements for the marriage of your daughter, Olesia," said Father Mel'khyzedek. "Do you consent or do we repent?"

"My wife and I are inclined to let her marry. Balabukha is an educated man, of appropriate stature, and he already has a parish. I'm not sure what my daughter will say, however," spoke Terlets'kyi.

"If such is your will, thank you – then it's time to speak of what the children will have. What are you going to give with your daughter?" said Mel'khyzedek's wife, Marta Tarasivna, simply and plainly.

Terlets'kyi glanced at his wife and said: "We will give one hundred karbovantsi."

"One hundred is real money, that's true," fired back father Mel'khyzedek, "but to speak plainly, that's not a large amount."

"Indeed, it is not large," added Mel'khyzedek's wife. "Money is one thing, but a household needs other things as well. They will need cattle, oxen, horses, and something to go with the horses. They will also need bowls and spoons, and something for the spoons as well. And, good lord, what's there to say? You yourselves know full well what is needed in a new household, for a young, inexperienced, and not always thoughtful young couple."

Mrs Terlets'kyi angrily glanced at this simple peasant woman in a village cap who was to be her in-law but was begging like an old gypsy.]

The reaction of Mrs Terlets'kyi points to the key factor. She comes from a gentry family, and the Terlets'kyis consider themselves socially superior to the simple village priests with whom they associate. So they see nothing but crudeness and provincialism in the behaviour of the matchmakers. When the deal is finally struck and Marko and Olesia exchange rings (rings, not embroidered towels!), Reverend Terlets'kyi attempts a formal oration that would show off his learning before the young priest fresh from the academy, but he gets lost in his words. Marta Tarasivna makes up for it, however, with a traditional wish for happiness and good fortune with lots of children and grandchildren (4:95). At this point, by custom and personal inclination, Mel'khyzedek and his wife are ready for the hearty feast that should celebrate the newly established social ties. Instead, the Terlts'kyis bring out a small, showy carafe of vodka, appropriate for a single drink for each of the participants, and a samovar. The party-loving Mel'khyzedek is deeply disappointed. Needless to say, the wedding that results from this engagement is equally dull, solemn, and meagre. The party ends early, and the guests leave hungry and thirsty.

The contrasting scene appears in the next chapter, where Kharytin Mossakovs'kyi comes to visit the Prokopovyches and their daughter Onysia, whom he wishes to marry. The atmosphere is tense, since the Prokopovyches have heard that Kharytin has not been given the parish his father had held, and Mrs Prokopovych is beside herself, worrying about the diminished prospects for her daughter. But when Kharytin explains that the villagers stood firm and he has been assigned the parish and Balabukha sent elsewhere, the tense atmosphere suddenly explodes in joyful celebration. In contrast to the forbidding engagement scene at the Terlets'kyis, the Prokopovych home is bursting with friendship:

> Прокоповичка кинулась в хижку, в пекарню, гукнула на наймичок. В пекарні затопили в печі. Закиркали під ножем кури. Наймит впіймав порося. В світлицю неначе на крилах влетіли пляшки з наливками та настойками. Десь узялись пироги в сметані, бублики на яйцях, маковники, пундики. Чарка пішла за чаркою. Онися винесла тарілки з горіхами та фігами. Усім стало весело. Моссаковський розговорився, розчервонівся, повеселішав. Прокоповичка любенько дивилась на його делікатне з рум'янцями лице й тепер довідалась, що він схожий не на чехоню, а на хохітвянського пана.
>
> – Тепер хоч і під вінець! – сама прохопилась Прокоповичка, випивши чарку запіканки. – Нема нам чого длятись. Ми тепер зовсім обробились на полі. Робити нема чого, а гуляти маємо доволі часу.
>
> – Про мене, хоч і зараз, – сказав Моссаковський, – справді, нема для чого одкладати діла!
>
> – Шкода, що ви не приїхали з братом! А ми б оце поговорили з ним, як з сватом, – говорила Прокоповичка, любенько заглядаючи Моссаковському в очі. – Ми таки своєї дочки не зобидимо: є в нас, хвалити бога, й худоба, й коні, й воли, й плуги, й пасіка.

"Воно так, а все-таки краще б було привезти з собою повітового свата отця Мельхиседека та повітову сваху Марту, – подумав собі Моссаковський, – бо старі на словах, – як на цимбалах, а на ділі – як на талалайці!" (4:110)

[Mrs Prokopovych ran to the pantry, the kitchen, she yelled at the servants. In the kitchen they lit the oven. The chickens raised a ruckus under the knife. The hired hand captured the piglet. Like winged creatures bottles of clear and flavoured liquors flew into the living room. Pyrogies in sour cream appeared out of nowhere, followed by egg muffins, poppy seed cake, and doughnuts. Glasses had no chance to sit empty. Onysia brought out platters with nuts and figs. Everyone felt their spirits rise. Mossakovs'kyi was talking up a storm, his face flush. He was in good cheer. Mrs Prokopovych looked sympathetically at his delicate features and came to the conclusion that he didn't resemble a carp after all, but sooner the master of Khokhitva.

"All that's left is to put the wedding crowns on them," burst out Mrs Prokopovych, after a glass of distilled spirits. "There's no point in putting this off for a long time. We've just finished all the work in the fields. There's nothing more to do, so let's party!"

"That's fine with me, we can start right now," said Mossakovs'kyi. "Indeed, there's no reason to put this off."

"It's a shame you didn't bring your brother. We'd have a nice talk with our in-laws, then," Mrs Prokopovych went on, lovingly glancing into Mossakovs'kyi's eyes. "We'll do right by our daughter, you can be certain. Thank God we're not lacking for cattle, horses, oxen, plows, or even beehives."

"But it probably would have been even better if I had brought the expert matchmakers, Father Mel'khyzedek and his wife, Marta," thought Mossakovs'kyi to himself. "These old folks are promising a wedding symphony, but in practice it may turn out to be a plain tune on a rusty hurdy-gurdy."]

A week later, they're celebrating the wedding. Nechui gives an elaborate description of the preparations but not the wedding ceremony itself. Indeed, his focus isn't even on the wedding feast *per se* but on the hijinks of Mel'khyzedek and his wife, who are not only good at matchmaking and bargaining but are also inveterate pranksters and party animals. After a long evening of music and dancing, Mel'khyzedek wakes everyone by pulling off their covers. His wife dresses up as a Jewish huckstress (a mildly anti-Semitic stereotype) and accosts her husband (who does not recognize her) with offers of plump chickens and fresh eggs for comic effect. First at the home of the bride's parents and then at the home of the newlyweds, the celebrations go on for a week, almost until Saturday evening, when the mostly clerical guests are, of course, obliged to sober up to serve Saturday vespers and then Sunday mass at their own parishes.

Through the contrast of these two engagements and weddings, Mel'khyzedek and his wife become the symbols of a fun-loving, down-to-earth, friendly spirit among the Ukrainian clergy. The most memorable scene in this regard occurs in chapter 6, as Kharytin and Onysia celebrate their child's birth and christening. Two other children had died within hours of their birth, so this event is a truly joyous one for the family. The party is as warm and happy as the earlier wedding had been, and Mel'khyzedek is again the life of the party, singing songs with guitar in hand, "like an old village kobzar" (4:158), says Nechui. He's still full of pranks and practical jokes. When the women join their husbands for a late-night drink, he replaces the nuts in a bowl with small washed potatoes, provoking a variety of comic reactions (including a learned remark from Balabukha about the different varieties of nuts that are found in Turkey). Then, when everyone finally goes to sleep, he stands outside the window of the women's quarters and frightens the sleeping ladies. Finally, he has some crawfish collected and puts them under the bedrolls of the sleeping guests in order to cause a commotion when they awake in the morning (4:167). All in all, Nechui's "king of righteousness," if that is the correct translation of the Hebrew "Melchisedec," more closely resembles a college sophomore on Halloween than an evangelical Christian preacher in contemporary North America. But when compared to a surly and stolid Balabukha, Mel'khyzedek is the epitome of good cheer. After the jokes resulting from the crawfish subside, the entire company, at Mel'khyzedek's suggestion, pack up to continue the party at the home of whoever lives closest. That turns out to be Balabukha. First, the tipsy Balabukha falls out of his sleigh, so that the company arrives at his home without him. After the nearly frozen priest is retrieved and they eventually enter his home, the atmosphere proves so morose and unfriendly that they quickly decide to go on to another home – this time Mel'khyzedek's own, where they are guaranteed a good time.

In Soviet literary criticism, a good deal of misunderstanding arose from Nechui's inclination to display this carefree, less serious side of the clergy. Soviet ideology encouraged a completely ridiculous reading of Nechui that included such concepts as atheism and anticlericalism.[11] True, Nechui himself contributed to such a reading by a statement in his letter to Oleksander Konys'kyi on 29 December 1880 that Konys'kyi should not be frightened by the title of his new work (*Starosvits'ki batiushky ta matushky*). "The work," he says, "is not clerical, but the opposite" (10:285). But it is a hasty assumption to interpret this sentence to mean that the work is ant-clerical, unless we take anticlericalism to include everything other than pious subservience to the clergy. Nechui's novel certainly pokes fun at the clergy and makes very serious accusations about the development of a social schism between the common people and religious authorities, which eventually included the village clergy. But if the term "anticlericalism" is to be meaningful, it must surely indicate a position hostile to the role of organized religion as a whole, not merely a critical view of various features of the social relations between clergymen and the laity. Nechui can, without doubt, be characterized as a writer who saw various faults in the way orthodoxy was practised in the Russian Empire. But his satiric depiction of these problems is much closer to what one would expect from a religious reformer than from an antireligious crusader. Any mention of atheism is simply preposterous.

What is curious and requires attention is the depiction – or rather, non-depiction – of the clergy in their capacity as religious, spiritual men and ministers of a Christian faith. Nechui's priests are hardly ever seen performing religious duties. There are, of course, references to Sunday mass, but they are infrequent. In all of *Starosvits'ki batiushky ta matushky*, only three masses are directly mentioned: the one Onysia attends in chapter 2, expecting Kharytin will be there (4:70); the one that Balabukha serves, in chapter 3 (4:101–2); and the one Olesia attends to see the officers in chapter 7 (4:186). There is also the outdoor prayer service (*parastas*) that an unnamed priest serves for Kharytin's father in the opening pages of the novel (4:40) and the communion and mass before Onysia and Kharytin's wedding. This communion and mass are dismissed in a single short sentence: "Молоді запричастились і, по давньому звичаю, після служби повінчались" (4:116) [The young couple took communion and, in keeping with the old customs, were married after the mass]. The other services are tied to social rather than religious functions. The mass that Balabukha serves in Vilshany, particularly his homily full of Church Slavonic terms and Latin expressions, is an opportunity for Nechui to show his alienation from the parishioners. The prayer service at the opening of the novel, however, is precisely the opposite, and it is a metaphor for the old ways that are passing, may they be granted eternal remembrance:

Священики встали з-за столів, а за ними разом повставали усі люди на всьому широкому дворі. Гомін стих одразу. Настала така тиша, неначе на всьому дворі не було живої душі. Стало чуть, як щебетали в садку пташки. Старий сивий священик, обернувшись до церкви, почав правити здоровим басом парастас. Його голос розлягався по всьому подвір'ї. Старий батюшка наприкінці парастаса підняв голос і голосніше покликнув "вічную пам'ять" небіжчикові. І все духовенство, яке тут було, заспівало "вічная пам'ять!" А в той час титар, сивий, аж білий, з довгими вусами, тричі навхрест підійняв вгору здоровий полив'яний червоний жбан сити, придержуючи зверху рукою хліб, котрим був накритий жбан. Усі люди, що стояли в дворі і за двором, почали хреститись та кланятись до церкви: сотні рук замахали, сотні голів то нахилялись, то піднімались, сотні уст шепотіли не дуже тихо: "Вічная пам'ять! вічная пам'ять!" І несподівано неначе схопився серед тиші в дворі вітер, і неначе зашелестів на вітрі лист в садку на дереві. І той шелест помаленьку стихав, доки зовсім не стих … і знов в дворі і на причілку стало тихо-тихо, аж мертво. (4:40)

[The clergymen got up from the table and all the people in the wide yard followed suit. The chatter died down immediately. There was such silence, as if there weren't a single person in the yard. The chirping of the birds in the orchard became audible. An old grey priest turned toward the church and began the *parastas* service in his deep bass. His voice spread across the whole yard. At the end of the service, the old clergyman raised his voice and called for *Vichnaia pamiat* [eternal remembrance] for the deceased. And all the assembled clergymen sang *Vichnaia pamiat*. At that point the elderly, white-haired sexton with a long moustache raised a large, red, lacquered jug of mead and, holding down a loaf of bread on top with his hand, thrice made a sign of the cross with it. The people standing in the yard and beyond it began to cross themselves and bow toward the church. Hundreds of hands were waving, hundreds of heads were lowered and raised, hundreds of lips were whispering, not very quietly: *Vichnaia pamiat, vichnaia pamiat*. Suddenly, it seemed, a wind had arisen in the silence of the yard and it sounded like the rustling of leaves on all the trees in the orchard. The rustling gradually died down, ever softer, until again the yard was silent, deathly silent.]

In other novels, too, Nechui depicts priests performing religious rituals mostly as a social function. In *Mykola Dzheria*, the protagonist's father, Petro, famously bargains with a priest over the cost of his son's marriage (3:49). The same priest later tells Petro that, for his own health and with the priest's dispensation, he should ignore the Lenten fast rules and eat more nutritious foods, but Petro is afraid of sin and goes to his grave fasting. Later, after Mykola runs away and his wife, Nymydora, nearly goes insane, Mykola's mother takes Nymydora to the monastery to meet with Father Zenon, who turns out to be a drunkard. But Father Zenon reads the Exordium for Nymydora and other women and they leave the monastery in better spirits after mass and communion (3:120). In chapter 9 of the novel *Pomizh vorohamy* a scene takes place during a mass and the timing of the events is narrated in relation to the parts of the mass (6:285–8). Leonid Pasenko has come to church to get a glimpse of his sweetheart, Valentyna (Vatia) Kremnyts'ka, the daughter of the priest. But the mass is only an ironic backdrop to the hopeless romance of the young couple and the relentless feud between their families. Father Artemii, who is presumably serving the mass, is not mentioned at all. His wife and daughter do not enter the church until long after the mass has begun and only to discover that their mortal enemies are occupying their customary places. This is not a religious event at all, but a version of *Romeo and Juliet* played out in church. Father Artemii is far more concerned about his social standing than he is about spiritual matters. The invitation he receives to bless a newly constructed mill is seen as a romantic outing (6:199). The mill workers assemble around the millstone with candles in their hands, while children climb up into the rafters. The interior of the mill is lit up with candles that cast an intriguing light throughout the building. Leonid compares the spectacle to an ancient secret mass in the Roman catacombs, while his sweetheart, Vatia, says it reminds her of a ballet or opera (6:204). Religious ceremony, it seems, is most effective when it carries strong aesthetic associations.

This absence of spirituality is even more apparent in those satiric portraits that are deliberately aimed at uncovering the faults of religious officials. Among them are the portraits of Kryskent Kharlampiiovych Mlynkovs'kyi, the *stolonachalnyk* (chief administrator), and the bishop in *Starosvits'ki batiushky ta matushky*. In a series of financial, professional, and personal assaults on Kharytin, Nechui presents three visitors to Kharytin's parish. The first is Balabukha, who is angry over an exchange of insults between their respective wives. He comes to inspect the parish, collect his bribes, and lambast Kharytin for the poor management of his parish (4:243). Then comes the local chief administrator, making his annual rounds, collecting his larger share of bribes, and also leaving two of his seven hungry daughters at Kharytin's to save himself the expense of their upkeep (4:243–53). Later, in what turns out, quite literally, to be the *coup de grâce*, the bishop arrives and berates the now elderly priest for his timidity, for his ignorance of Russian, for his lack of education, and for the poor quality of his church bells (4:254–60). He strips Kharytin of his church vestments, a personal insult that quite literally puts Kharytin on his deathbed. In all three episodes, Nechui emphasizes the personal corruption and mercenary and mercantile instincts of these church officers. They are nothing but clerical vultures, exploiting their church office for personal gain and behaving like the shamelessly dissipated gentry with whom they prefer to associate. In another novel, *Afons'kyi proidysvit*, Nechui depicts the black clergy – that is, monks – in a Kyiv monastery as similarly corrupt and shameless materialists. In this case, however, the cunning and dishonest monks (Palladii, Isakii, Ieremiia, and Tarasii) are outwitted by a very smooth swindler, the Athenian tramp of the title, a Greek named Khrystofor Kopronidos.

Not all of Nechui's religious characters are entirely lacking in spiritual values, of course. But devout and kindly clergymen are an exception to the general pattern. One such exception is the metropolitan whom Onysia visits after her husband's death and after she has been chased away by the bishop. The metropolitan, Nechui says, was very old, very good, quiet in disposition, and a great ascetic (4:260). On hearing Onysia's troubles, he orders that the parish be tied to the orphaned daughters (i.e., that a seminarian could only occupy the parish by marrying one of the late priest's daughters). The metropolitan is motivated only by charity and his good-hearted nature, but even he must fend off Onysia's own insistent materialism. When he makes his decision and announces that a third of the parish income would go to the widow, she asks that it be increased to fifty per cent. The meek and kindly metropolitan turns down this request and politely ends the conversation with a recommendation of prayer, something rarely heard from a clergyman in Nechui's works.

In *Pomizh vorohamy*, Father Porfyrii Nerushevych, the widowed priest who lives in town by the train station and whom Father Artemii likes to visit, is a different kind of exception. His primary role in the work is as a foil to Father Artemii, the rather materialistic and hare-brained protagonist of the work. As his name suggests, Porfyrii has the qualities of purple lassitude. He is an intellectual do-gooder who has been jaded by the difficulty of accomplishing any reforms in a Ukrainian village in the Russian Empire. His disenchantment has led to a retreat from social interaction. When he meets Artemii or other priests, Porfyrii's wry, often sarcastic comments usually reflect his disdain and indifference. In characterizing him, Nechui can't resist a swipe at the social conditions in Russia, the benighted state of Ukrainian peasants, and the illusions of quick success that many reformers nurture:

> О. Порфирій вийшов з семінарії одним з перших студентів. Зайнявши парафію, він з завзяттям взявся й за просвіту в школі, і за підняття моральності в селі, щонеділі говорив проповіді, а найбільше проти п'янства, завів братство, товариство тверезості, навчав селян на обідах, вчив в розмовах, але побачив, що його просвітня проповідь не вчинила чуда: не переробила селян на янголів за якийсь десяток років, чого він сподівався, не маючи і втямку про те, що такий психічно-історичний моральний розвиток темних мас не робиться за якийсь десяток років, та ще й тоді, коли нема ні доброї національної школи, ні народних бібліотек, ні читалень, ні піддержання й ініціативи од громади й зверху … І о. Порфирій дійшов до песимізму, зневірився в своєму ділі і … на все махнув рукою, закопавшись в книжки. (6:173–4)
>
> [Father Porfyrii finished the seminary among the best students. On receiving a parish, he enthusiastically took on the cause of spreading education and raising the standards of morality in the village. Every Sunday he preached, usually about the evils of drunkenness. He started a lay brotherhood and a temperance society. He taught the peasants at meals and in conversations, but he saw that his enlightening instructions were not accomplishing miracles. After ten years they did not turn the peasants into angels, as he had expected, since he didn't understand that the psychological-historical moral development of the dark masses does not come about in a mere ten years, particularly when there are no good national schools, nor public libraries, nor reading rooms, nor support and encouragement from the community or from the top. And so, Rev. Pofyrii sank into pessimism, he was disenchanted in his cause, he just gave up on everything and buried himself in his books.]

Porfyrii is certainly not one of the friendly old-world priests that Nechui favours, but he is also not one of the crass careerists whom he sees replacing them. He is not particularly spiritual in his outlook, but his restraint, education, and good sense also distinguish him from the usual qualities that besmirch the new, professional clergy. Thus he represents something of a neutral, middle category among priests: withdrawn from society, but not hostile to it; educated with real benefit, not just for the sake of appearances; sensitive to and conscious of a responsibility to the common people, but alienated and overcome by the enormity of the problem.

This unusual portrait of Father Porfyrii underscores another important factor in Nechui's characterization of the clergy. In a notorious essay about Nechui, Valerian Pidmohyl'nyi, one of the earliest Ukrainian authors to be seriously interested in Freudian psychology, raises some suggestive ideas about Nechui's relation to his father.[12] In this essay Pidmohyl'nyi outlines a case for a peculiar relationship between Nechui and his father, based on various aspects of his personality as reported in Iefremov's biography. A key component of this analysis involves Nechui's recollections of his father in the autobiographical essay that was included in Iefremov's monograph (the only biographical source Pidmohyl'nyi's cites). While Pidmohyl'nyi's larger argument may be questionable, his inclination to use Nechui's relationship with his father as a key to understanding the writer has merit beyond mere Freudian psychoanalysis, particularly in regard to Nechui's depiction of the clergy. Given Nechui's portrait of his father as an austere, bookish man,[13] Porfyrii Nerushevych may well be modelled in part on the author's father. What is very clear, however, is that the clergymen Nechui most often depicts, whether they be old-world sociable hedonists like Khvedor Chepurnovs'kyi in *Prychepa* or new careerists like Balabukha in *Starosvits'ki batiushky ta matushky*, are not based on his father. Of course, they may well be modelled on the many other clergymen the young Nechui would have encountered in his extended family and among his father's friends. But if there is a peculiar psychological component in Nechui's portraits of clergymen, it lies precisely in the abundance among these characters of those qualities that his father lacked. Perhaps the good impression Nechui gives of the friendly old-world clergy is a veiled accusation against a father who showed little parental warmth towards his children. Perhaps even more significant is the consistent pattern of contrasts between friendliness and sociability, on the one hand, and bookishness and learning, on the other. From what Nechui tells us about him, his father was a man who favoured books and learning over social interaction. In the menagerie of Nechui's fictional characters, these qualities are almost universally negative.

Another somewhat unusual clergyman is Father Harasym in the short novel *Ne toi stav*. He is a minor character in the work but plays an important role as a mediator, and we shall meet him again in chapter 5 in the discussion of the role of women. Aside from his interactions with Zin'ka, which are very important in the development of the central theme of this novel, he is also associated with Zin'ka's son, Roman, who turns into a bookish recluse after marrying Solomiia. In both cases, Father Harasym is the obvious source to whom these villagers turn for advice and assistance in spiritual matters. Zin'ka turns to him with a personal wish, founded, as she says, on dreams. In these dreams her mother urges her to organize a celebration honouring the myrrh-bearing women, an Orthodox holiday that falls on the second Sunday after Easter. Although Father Harasym has an intellectual's characteristic suspicion and disdain for spirituality that derives from dreams and visions, he treats Zin'ka with respect and courtesy. He does not hide his disinclination towards her plans, but he eventually helps Zin'ka organize the event. When her devout son, Roman, asks the priest to help him obtain religious books, Father Harasym advises him to read more entertaining books, such as The Lives of Saints, rather than the *Minei*, or Monthlies, which contain canons and troparia (6:381). Later, when Roman has become disillusioned, the priest agrees to buy back the books from him, but advises him to apologize to his wife and mother and bring peace to his family (6:412). Harasym is thus cast in the unenviable role of an intelligent clergyman encouraging religious devotion based at least partially on superstitions and dreams while discouraging the spiritual devotions of a man with a bookish inclination. Nechui does not particularly favour irrational and superstitious spirituality – he makes this abundantly clear in the satiric portrait of Filon Chechot, Roman's foolishly devout father-in-law – but he is also quite consistent in presenting spirituality based on bookish and scholarly sophistry as false and counterproductive. Roman's religious reading is contrasted in the novel with his friend Denys's reading of *Natalka Poltavka*. For Nechui, religious scholasticism is a dead end, whereas real intellectual advantage lies in modern secular thought, and in the newly developing Ukrainian literature.

Religious scholasticism is more common in an urban setting, and Nechui's most important satire on the intellectual failings of orthodoxy in Ukraine and Russia is in the depiction of Kyiv's Theological Academy in *Khmary*. Here the seriousness of the intellectual enterprise is revealed by the exchange between the Kyiv metropolitan and the Russian student and later professor at the academy, Stepan Vozdvyzhens'kyi, at the final exam. The question concerns the German secular philosopher

Hegel. When Vozdvyzhens'kyi stumbles in his reply to the question, the metropolitan helps him with characteristic intellectual percipience: Since Hegel was a heretic, "that means he was a dope" (2:39). Nechui then remarks that the portraits on the walls of the seventeenth- and eighteenth-century scholars who had taught at the school were laughing at the current state of affairs in the former Mohyla Academy. The great intellectual traditions of this institution had been replaced by religious obscurantism.

Nechui's censure of intellectual obtuseness is not limited to the clergy or to religious institutions. Vozdvyzhens'kyi's opposite number in *Khmary*, the Ukrainian Vasyl' Dashkovych, is described as a true scholar and a good teacher. He becomes a professor at Moscow University but later returns to Ukraine and teaches at Kyiv University (2:50). The quality of his scholarly work, however, does not spare him from Nechui's condemnation. Dashkovych is an ivory-tower intellectual with little interest or aptitude for practical and mundane matters. When his wife throws a party he clumsily gets his feet tangled in his dance partner's dress and almost tears it off her (2:54). His wife takes over management of the household, he is completely unaware of what his daughter is doing, and his academic interests isolate him from the reality of life around him. These familiar satirical stereotypes are more than just comic anti-intellectualism: as we shall see in the subsequent chapter, among the practical matters that Dashkovych ignores is the plight of his own nation. In *Khmary, Nad Chornym Morem, Ne toi stav, Neodnakovymy stezhkamy*, and other works where intellectuals and questions of learning are addressed, Nechui typically distinguishes the type of learning that is theoretical and devoid of practical benefit for the Ukrainian people from intellectual pursuits that have a direct bearing on the welfare of Ukrainians, particularly the poorest and least educated among them. Since the difficulties imposed by the Russian imperial government and the prejudice of high society in the late nineteenth century made any intellectual pursuits on behalf of the common people difficult if not impossible or illegal, Nechui finds few if any truly positive figures among Ukraine's intellectual elite. This absence of positive learned characters furthers the impression of a generally anti-intellectual atmosphere in Nechui's works.

There are, however, some minor characters who exemplify Nechui's understanding of the benefits of education and intellectual pursuits for Ukrainian peasants. Denys Odnosumenko, Roman's friend, brother-in-law, and foil in *Ne toi stav*, is a literate peasant with an instinct for rebellious behaviour. He is not an intellectual, but the fact that Nechui has him reading Kotliarevs'kyi rather than the religious books Roman reads puts him in a special category. Over time, he becomes the voice of good sense and good, practical husbandry in the village. In *Neodnakovymy stezhkamy*, a villager named Nykon Kuchma shows an interest first in music and then in books. He becomes the director of a village choir and borrows Ukrainian books from Iakiv Ulasevych, the doctor. Nechui depicts this peasant as a very thoughtful and introspective man. Nykon is a vegetarian by principle, since he doesn't believe man has the right to slaughter animals. Furthermore, he proclaims that all men are brothers and wonders why other people have such disdain for Jews (8:328). But Nykon's village activism ends after the police order him to stop assembling his fellow peasants in his home.

Another important category of characters in Nechui's works is the gentry. In nineteenth-century Ukraine, the gentry comprised a wide variety of different people: Russians, Poles, and Ukrainians; very rich, moderately wealthy, and some even poor; descendants of Russian nobility, descendants of Polish *szlachta*, or nobility, descendants of Ukrainian cossack officers, merchants who had successfully risen in social class, and still other categories. As a general rule, the gentry had no particular association with Ukrainian national identity, although there were certainly those among them who were proud Ukrainians and even worked to advance the Ukrainian national idea. An outstanding characteristic of Nechui's writing is that he includes gentry characters in his stories and novels and embraces them as part of the larger family of Ukrainian society.

Some of Nechui's gentry characters are identified by nationality and appear as enemies of Ukrainian culture and identity as well as of the lower classes. This is particularly true of Polish landowners such as Stanislav Iastshembs'kyi in *Burlachka* and Bzhozovs'kyi in *Mykola Dzheria*, characters who will be examined in the next chapter. But Nechui also depicts gentry characters who are not depicted as enemies or exploiters, at least not primarily so. For example, the parents of Pavlo Radiuk, the student at Kyiv University who is the principal hero in the second half of *Khmary*, are Antin Antonovych Radiuk and Nadezhda Stepanivna Iskra, whom Nechui describes as not very wealthy but comfortably well-off landowners in the Poltava area [Не дуже багаті, але заможні полтавські дідичі (2:124)]. They are, thus, in a middle category of the gentry. Stepanyda Dashkovych, who would be happy to have her daughter Ol'ha marry their son, Pavlo, describes them with almost the same phrase: "They are not upper gentry, but quite comfortable, they own Zhurbani" [Вони люде не з великих панів, але доволі заможні, мають село Журбані (2:229)]. Her daughter, however, immediately asks for details and is disappointed to learn that Zhurbani is a single village, not an estate with a number of villages. Nechui describes both the home and the parents in considerable detail. Zhurbani is a speck of a village surrounded by the vast steppe and the endless sky and defined by rows of squat windmills, tall cranes for raising water buckets from wells, and the church. In the midst of these stands the manor house:

Панський будинок стояв край села, в садку, недалечко од церкви, біля вигону. Будинок був невеликий і невисокий. Навкруги його була галерея попід стріхами, а в садок виступав круглий ґанок, чи тераса, густо обплетена виноградом. Кругом тераси були повироблювані клумби для квіток. Між клумбами і скрізь по садку вились чисті доріжки, посипані жорствою й піском. Перед домом був широкий двір, такий широкий, що вози ледве встигли протерти кругом його вузьку дорогу. Серед самого двора росла трава й степові квітки, наче в лузі. Косарі косили там сіно, як на сіножаті. На тому дворі далеко з другого боку стояли хати для челяді й станя, за хатами були довгі кошари для овець, широкі загороди й повітки для товару. Все те добро Радюків батько взяв за своєю жінкою, Надеждою Степанівною Іскрою.

Старий Радюк, Антін Антонович, вийшов з людей небагатих. Він був син козака, і по смерті батька й матері йому достався батьківський хутір недалечко од Журбанів. Він служив в війську в гусарах, покинув службу й спочивав у своєму хуторі.

Вернувшись у свій хутір, Антін Антонович не думав жениться, бо й не було на кому жениться в цілій околиці. Кругом в хуторах і селах було дуже багацько паннів, але хуторянки не подобались йому. Він дуже багацько на своєму віку бачив усяких людей і не міг вподобать собі хоч і гарних, але трохи простих полтавських хуторянок. Зате ж він сам був ідолом для сусідських паннів.

Радюк був колись дуже гарний з себе! Високий на зріст, рівний станом, з чорними кучерями, чорними бровами, блискучими веселими очима й повним лицем, він був гарний, як чорнобривець, і мав силу причаровувать до себе серце кожної молодої панни. Сміливий, як козак запорожець, трохи причепливий, як москаль, він мав надзвичайний дар розмови й оповідання. Він усе розказував українські народні анекдоти, смішні, повні жарту й юмору, знав їх без ліку, міг розказувать цілий вечір, другий вечір, тиждень і все десь їх набирав, неначе витрушував з якогось безоднього мішка. Пробуваючи на Україні по селах і хуторах, він наслухався їх од народу, між панами й духовними, між селянами й городянами, і знав їх більше, ніж Шехерезада знала казок. Він розказував їх чудовою українською мовою, плавкою, повною квіток поезії, чому позавидував би найкращий оповідач. Він умів так смішно, розказувать, що всі реготались, аж за боки брались. (2:124–5)

[The manor house stood at the edge of the village, in an orchard, near the church and before the pasture lands. The building wasn't large or tall. Around it was a thatch-covered gallery with a circular porch or terrace sticking out into the orchard and covered in thick grapevines. The terrace was surrounded with cultivated flowerbeds. Between the flowerbeds and throughout the orchard were snaking clear pathways, paved with sand and stones. In front of the manor house was a wide yard, so wide that wagons barely managed to carve out a narrow path around it. In the centre of the yard grew grass and wildflowers, as if in a meadow. Mowers actually cut the grass for hay here, as on a hayfield. In the distance, on the far side of the yard, stood the servants' quarters and the barn. Behind those were the long pens for sheep and the wide enclosures for cattle. All of this wealth came to Radiuk as the dowry of his wife, Nadezhda Stepanivna Iskra.

Old Radiuk, Antin Antonovych, came from a family that wasn't wealthy. He was the son of a cossack, and after the death of his father and mother he inherited their farmstead not far from Zhurbani. He had served as a hussar in the army, then left service to retire on his farmstead.

Returning to his farmstead, Antin Antonovych had not been thinking about marriage, because there was no one suitable in the entire area. There were many young ladies in the villages and farmsteads all around, but he did not like the farmstead girls. He had seen a great many people in his day and he just couldn't find anything to like about even the prettiest ones from among the simple farmstead girls of the Poltava region. On the other hand, the local girls all admired him like an idol.

Radiuk had once been a very handsome man! Tall in stature and upright in posture, with black curly hair and black eyebrows, shining cheerful eyes, and a round open face, he was as handsome as any black-browed man can be, and he had the power to captivate the heart of any young maid. Fearless, like a Zaporozhian cossack, a little touchy, like a Russian soldier, he had an unusual gift for conversation and storytelling. He was always telling funny Ukrainian folk anecdotes, full of humour and wit. He knew untold numbers of them and could keep up a constant stream

> of them all evening, as if he were pulling them out of a bottomless sack. The time he had spent in various villages and farmsteads in Ukraine had allowed him to hear very many such stories from the simple folk, the gentry, the clergy, villagers, and city folk. He knew more anecdotes than Scheherazade knew stories. He recited them in a beautiful, supple Ukrainian, full of the flowers of poetry, which the finest storyteller would envy. He could tell stories with such humour that everyone would be roaring with laughter, holding themselves by the sides.]

A number of this description's features deserve attention. A gentry home is not a very common occurence in Ukrainian literature of the late nineteenth century, but this one is almost a natural element in the landscape. The large expanse of grass, the flowers, the vine-covered veranda, all help to tie the home to the natural surroundings described in the preceding paragraph. The overhanging thatch "gallery," the building's small size, and its proximity to the servants' and animals' quarters further associate it with the qualities of a Ukrainian village. The residents are also carefully described. Antin Radiuk comes from a simple cossack family, but he is an orphan who served in the cavalry. He apparently picked up just enough worldliness to beguile all the eligible young ladies of the surrounding countryside, at least until he met up with the wealthy Nadezhda Iskra. He has the gift of entertaining storytelling. Nechui emphasizes that Antin spent time all over Ukraine and that he speaks in a beautifully smooth and poetic Ukrainian. He is, in short, a charming product of the innate virtues of Ukrainian culture, albeit somewhat modified by the experience of service in the military and the absence of his own family to help guide him. His wife, however, is an entirely different creature. The estate, wealth, and social pretensions come from her side of the family, the Iskras. Since the estate is in the vicinity of Poltava, this surname cannot but call out associations with the famous colonel of the Poltava regiment, Ivan Iskra, who, along with Vasyl Kochubei, denounced Hetman Ivan Mazepa to Peter the Great. The name Iskra, thus, can be interpreted as an emblem of Ukrainians who abandon their own nation and its interests to side with the dominant, powerful Russian state. Nadezhda, whose name is given in this Russian form (rather than the Ukrainian Nadia), is a product of the Kharkiv Institute for Girls, an institution that, like its Kyivan equivalent in the novel, produces pretentious and Russified ladies whose accomplishments are measured in their hostility to the lower classes and to all things Ukrainian. Nadezhda Iskra-Radiuk matches this model. When her son returns home from the university wearing an embroidered shirt, speaking Ukrainian, and mouthing liberal democratic ideas, she is horrified by what she sees as the demoralization of her son and his backward, downward movement on the social ladder.

Nechui depicts a very different setting in the home of Ivan Korniiovych and Oleksandra Ostapivna Masiuk, whose daughter, Halia, Pavlo Radiuk will eventually marry. They are old friends of the Radiuks, but they are not in the same category as far as wealth is concerned. They are farmers who live comfortably on their own land and hire labour but also work on their farm themselves. Nechui highlights Ivan Masiuk's good husbandry and simple ways when Pavlo comes to visit. While the young visitor is only interested in seeing Masiuk's daughter, the old farmer is proud to show the young man around his property and even picks up a pitchfork to help his workers stack the wheat on a hot, sunny day (2:164). It is later in this chapter (IX) that Pavlo Radiuk visits a melon patch on his own father's property and discovers the difficulty of agricultural labour. The chief quality of the Masiuk household is its unpretentious Ukrainian friendliness mixed with nostalgia:

> Масюкова світлиця й кімната давно була знайома Радюкові. Не раз і не два він заїжджав з батьком до Масюка, сидів і слухав до півночі їх братерську розмову. Йому давно була знайома трохи європейська й трохи сільська, стародавня обстава Масюкової світлиці й кімнати: ті дві канапи в світлиці, вкриті по спинках гарними килимами, великий образ в шаті в кутку, на котрому висів дорогий вишиваний рушник, скляна шафа коло порога, звідкіль виглядала скляна маслянка, зроблена круторогим бараном, звідкіль колись лякав його великий скляний синій ведмідь, повний настойки; старий годинник коло груби з великим циферблатом, на котрому були намальовані рожі, червоні пташки.
>
> Але більше од усього він любив, як був малим, кімнату й пам'ятав, як там було тепло, гарно, спокійно, привітно зимньої темної ночі. Було, надворі гуде вітер, порощить у вікна метелиця, стукотить віконницями, гуркає десь у загороді недобре причиненими ворітьми, а в кімнаті тихо й тепло; в лежанці горить огонь, обливає двері в світлицю червоним світом, бігає хвилями на помості, на стінах. На лежанці стоїть самовар, а кругом лежанки сидять Масюк, Масючка, його батько та все балакають та балакають. (2:168)

[The living room and family room of the Masiuk home were well known to Radiuk. He had made more than a couple of visits here with his father,

> listening to the friendly conversations between them. So he had long since grown accustomed to the mixture of European and old-fashioned village charm that was found in these rooms: the two sofas in the living room with their backs covered in beautiful kilims, the large decorated painting, which was covered with an embroidered cloth, the glass china cabinet by the entry, where stood a glass creamer in the shape of a ram with curved horns, where also stood a liquor carafe in the shape of a big blue glass bear that had frightened him in his youth. By the fireplace there was also an old clock with a large face on which were painted rosy red birds.
>
> But more than anything, when he was young he loved this room. He remembered how warm it was, how peaceful, friendly, and inviting on a dark, cold, winter night. Outdoors the wind would be howling, a wet snow peppering the windows, the wind banging on the shutters, an unlatched gate in the animal pens creaking and clanging, but in this room it was quiet and warm. A fire burned on the grate, pouring red light onto the door and the living room, and running in waves over the walls and floor. Over the fire was a samovar, and around it sat the Masiuks and his father, talking and talking.]

The Masiuks, along with their foolish, meddlesome old biddy of a neighbour Lekeriia Vysoka, are the lay equivalents of old-world priests. Nechui treats them very sympathetically, but he also drives home their status as the embodiments of an outdated vision of Ukrainian rural paradise when he packs them off to Kyiv, along with the newlyweds Pavlo and Halia, in chapters 13 and 14 of the novel, where the country hicks, particularly the loquacious Vysoka, marvel at the fashions and mores of the big city.

A somewhat similar portrait of old-world landowners (but less indebted to Gogol) is found in *Neodnakovymy stezhkamy*, where Andriian Kyrylovych and Teklia Opanasivna Hukovych live on the Derkachivka estate, passed on through her family. The estate is on the left bank of the Dnipro, close to Kyiv and the railroad. Once again, Nechui emphasizes the age of the estate, its rootedness in the land itself:

> То була держава козацького роду Теклі Опанасівни. Чимала Гуковичева оселя була край села. Дім був чималий, дуже довгий, але стародавній, низький, неначе присадкуватий, з довгим рядком вікон та мальованих, збляклих од сонця віконниць, причеплених по обидва боки кожного вікна. Дім й уся оселя були на невеликому пригорку. А од дому по згористому широкому покаті наниз до течії слався старий парк, насаджений, певно, ще

прадідом старої Гуковичевої. Од самісінького дому до течії тяглась широка липова алея. Столітні липи розрослись густим гіллям і подекуди вгорі позчіплювались гілками докупи. По один бік алеї розрісся старий овощний садок; а по другий бік алеї по зеленій траві були розкидані столітні липи, берести та дуби, що розрослись на волі й розпустили широке гілля і вгору і вшир на всю свою могутню силу. Нанизу в ярку лисніла невеличка течія в зеленій осоці. Проти алеї вода зібралась в довгий ставочок під крутими горбами. А за течією на взгір'ї знов пишались столітні дуби та граби по два й по три рядочком, розкидані нарізно, а подекуди скупчені кружалами. Поміж ними біліли старі гіллясті берези, неначе на пригорки вийшли на прогуляння панянки в білих сукнях. Парк розстелявсь далеко й широко по горбах. А за парком стояв зеленою стіною лісок. В одному кутку в парку білів березник, неначе панни в білих убраннях стовпились докупи десь на балі. Побіч оселі за домом чорніла здоровецька клуня на току. Кругом току на окопах гнались високо вгору рядки старих осокорів. Давнє дідицьке гніздище навкруги обросло й заросло деревом і нагадувало стародавні діброви ще вольної, не дуже залюдненої старої України. (8:303–4)

[This was the property of the old cossack family of Teklia Opanasivna. The large Hukovych estate was at the edge of the village. The house was of considerable size, very long, old-fashioned, low, and stumpy looking, with a long row of windows and painted shutters, faded from the sunlight, attached on both sides of each window. The house and the entire estate were on a small hill. From the house, along a smooth wide incline down to the creek, stretched an old park, planted, no doubt, by the great-grandfather of old Mrs Hukovych. From the house itself down to the river there was an alley of linden trees. The hundred-year-old lindens had grown out in dense crowns of branches that intertwined between the trees. On one side of the alley was an old fruit orchard. On the other side there were large old individual trees scattered freely on the grass, extending their dense branches to the full height and width of their enormous power. Down below, in the ravine, shone a small stream dressed in green sedge. Across from the alley it widened into a long pond with uneven banks. Beyond the stream, on a rise, there were hundred-year-old oaks and elms, sometimes in rows of two or three, sometimes scattered separately, and sometimes bunched together in a circle. From among them peeked out white birches, like ladies in white frocks gone out for a stroll on the hillside. The park stretched far and wide on the hills. Beyond the park was a forest, standing like a great green wall. In one corner of the park there was a copse of birches, as if the ladies in white dresses were all bunched together at a ball. Alongside the estate, behind the house, stood the great black barn on the threshing grounds. Around the threshing grounds, on the outlying edge, a ring of black poplars stretched their trunks into the sky. The ancient family nest was overgrown on all sides with trees and resembled the thick old groves of a sparsely settled, ancient Ukraine.]

This rather remarkable association between gentry estates and old Ukraine becomes the background for a series of transformations and a decline that sees a new, vain, corrupt mercantile economy replacing the virtues, values, and objects of the past. Nechui paints a symbolic image of this transformation in the remodelling and new furniture that come to Derkachivka when Teklia and Melasia return from Kyiv with items like those they saw in the apartment of Taisa and Liuba Svatkvis'ki. Among the items are large floor-to-ceiling mirror panels that need to be trimmed because the old house has low ceilings. But the pièces de résistance are two floor lamps in the shape of life-size, topless black Arab women holding lanterns. The items cause consternation among the servants, who comically mistake the female figure for devils:

– Їй-богу, несуть два чорти! – крикнула куховарка. – Це вже чорти світитимуть в покоях; аж страшно стає.

– Я ввечері боятимусь і по горницях ходить, – сказала горнична.

– Та придивись лишень краще! то не чорти, а чортиці, та ще сливе голісінькі, тільки в самих куценьких спідничках, – обізвавсь лакей.

– А справді чортиці, бо наче молодиці: в спідничках та в золотих сережках, ще й у золотих намистах. Мабуть, ото в пеклі така поведенція в чортиць, що вони так чудно вдягаються, – казав один дід в жарти.

– Ще й білі лопатні повитріщали, мов сміються аж на кутні зуби. Та й ротаті ж та вухаті оті чортиці, – додав один наймит.

– Мабуть, не з біса веселі, – додав другий наймит, – дивись, бра! ще й неначе пританцьовують чи навшпинячки спинаються, мов напідпитку. Мабуть, раденькі, що держать оті каганці в руках.

– От теперечки не буде нам сором вітать женихів в наших покоях! – сказала Текля Опанасівна, походжаючи по горницях та оглядаючи обставу. (8:316)

["I swear to God, they're bringing in two devils," cried the cook. "Now it'll be devils lighting up the rooms – it's scary."

"In the evenings, I'll be scared to go up to the bedrooms," said the chambermaid.

"You take a closer look – those aren't he-devils, they're she-devils, and they're naked, too, with just some flimsy skirts," added the lackey.

"They are she-devils, indeed, they look like young maids, with skirts and gold earrings and gold necklaces, too. Maybe that's the fashion among the she-devils in hell these days, wearing these curious outfits," said an old man, joking.

"And they've bared their white fangs, as if they were laughing with their whole jaw. And what mouths and ears these she-devils have!" added one of the servants.

"And look how devilishly happy they are!" added another. "Look, they look like they're dancing, or maybe they're on their toes 'cause they're drunk. No doubt they're happy to be holding those lanterns in their hands."

"Now we won't be embarrassed to welcome matchmakers in our home!" said Teklia Opanasivna, surveying the rooms and scrutinizing the new items.]

Nechui's satiric juxtaposition of the servants' amazement and Teklia's smug pride as a consumer and mother of a marriageable daughter captures the ambiguity of his presentation. The chambermaid's superstitions are just as foolish as Teklia's confidence in the aesthetics of these items. The old furniture really was primitive and worn. The new items really are too expensive for the family to afford.

This model of the changing economics of the gentry is a central feature of *Neodnakovymy stezhkamy*. The old money and traditional, if not very successful or loving (8:312–13), marriage of the Hukovyches is compared to new money and new forms of marital partnerships. The first comparison is with the family of Teklia's old friend Taisa Svatkivs'ka, a widow who has sold off her estate to live with her daughter in circumstances more opulent than their income will allow. Her daughter Liuba lives with her second husband, Elpidyfor Vanatovych, director of prisons in Kyiv gubernia – except he is not actually her husband, since his current wife refuses to give him a divorce. This family triangle functions as a paradigm of wasteful materialism, vanity, and insincerity. Despite his high social position, Elpidyfor does not substantially contribute to the family finances and indeed keeps Liuba and Taisa at a distance from his own self-adoring person. He considers old-world Ukrainian landowners beneath his dignity and seeks approbation only in the highest circles of Russian imperial society. He is the recipient of the Order of St Stanislav, a significant imperial award, a fact Nechui even mentions twice, perhaps by mistake (8:372, 8:421), but he is also a vain and mean-spirited individual. Liuba is something of a social climber and gold-digger, attaching herself to Elpidyfor's rising star but actually turning to her foolish, bored, materialistic, and extremely religious mother to bankroll the adventure. They live in the lap of urban luxury, which Nechui delights in describing (8:268–71).

Another set of contrasts links together the brothers Ulasevych – Iakiv and Mykhailo – with the sisters Hukovych – Lida and Melasia. Iakiv, the younger brother, is a doctor. He worked as an assistant to a famous Kyiv doctor, Ivan Hurkovenko, but when the older doctor died and Iakiv's private practice did not prove lucrative, Iakiv was forced to take up a position as a country doctor in Dryzhypil', a Left-Bank town near Kyiv and not very far from the Hukovyches' Derkachivka (8:317), where he will fall in love with Lida, the younger daughter of Teklia and Andrian. Lida is a quiet girl whose views have been shaped by the constant bickering of her parents and the foolish materialism of her mother and sister, both situations from which she often tries to escape. Iakiv's older brother Mykhailo, nicknamed Myshka, is an urban dandy and ne'er-do-well who lies about anything if that gives him any advantage. He even reads some poetry he claims to have written himself, which his uncultured companions do not recognize as Pushkin's (8:289–96). He is looking for a "good" marriage, i.e., one that will give him enough wealth to continue doing nothing other than amusing himself in style. Melasia, foolish and naive, suits him perfectly, and her parents are, moreover, very eager to have her married. In a development that seems too mechanical and contrived (because such customs were not in fact widely practised in Ukraine), once Melasia and Mykhailo are married, Nechui invokes a secondary affinity incest taboo (a person may not marry the sibling of his or her sibling's spouse, i.e., two sisters cannot marry two brothers) that now prevents Iakiv and Lida from also marrying. Thus he achieves another contrast: a well-matched and loving couple are forced to live without the blessing of institutional marriage, while their very reckless, irresponsible, and foolish siblings Melasia and Mykhailo enjoy the benefits of legal marriage.

Beyond the classes of characters already mentioned, Nechui's works also contain a variety of other characters. Among them are representatives of middle social strata, ranging from Hlikeria, the woman hired to seduce Father Tarasii in *Afons'kyi proidysvit*, to Marta Karalaieva, the middle-aged husband-hunting Kishinev socialite in *Navizhena*. And there is also the exquisitely named Madam Pozatorits'ka (Mrs From-the-Year-Before) (8:276). Women are a particularly important category in Nechui's works, one examined separately in chapter 5. So too with Jews and other characters whose nationality is a matter of specific concern, examined in chapter 3. With only a few exceptions – in works such as *Skryvdzheni i neskryvdzheni*, subtitled "A Hindu legend," which takes place in a fairy-tale variant of India – Nechui's works are set in Ukraine and populated with Ukrainians. The Poles, Russians, Greeks, and Jews in Nechui's works are also Ukrainian: they are part of Ukrainian society, no matter what their ethnicity. What binds them all is a shared culture.

No comprehensive account of the contents of Nechui's works can avoid the notoriously inscrutable concept of culture. What makes Ukrainian geography and the Ukrainian nation Ukrainian? For Nechui, the answer is Ukrainian culture. But what, for him, is Ukrainian culture? The simple answer is tautological: Ukrainian culture is what makes Ukrainian territory and the people who inhabit it Ukrainian. It includes their beliefs, values, behaviour, habits, customs, history, language, aesthetic tastes, material constructs, and creative inventions. All these elements are the essential ingredients of Nechui's writing.

Nechui himself took an interest in culture and developed his views on the subject in a variety of publications. His ethnographic study of the mythological beliefs of prehistoric Ukrainians[14] may not always meet the high standards of twenty-first-century anthropology, but it clearly shows his own interest in exploring national culture as myth, superstition, ritual, and custom. His description of early Ukrainian culture includes not only spiritual issues concerning gods and the origins of the world, but also includes more mundane matters such as holiday rituals, games, songs, and various superstitions, from witches and omens of good luck and demons. Similar ideas are expressed in his essay "Nepotribnist' velykorus'koi literatury dlia Ukrainy i dlia Slavianshchyny," where Nechui discusses the three leading principles of literature in his own times: realism, national character, and the quality of *narodnist'*, that is, the quality of pertaining to the common people, the *narod*. The political aspect of Nechui's view of national character will be examined in the next chapter. What is important here are the qualities of culture he sees as the basis of this national character. National character, he says, has an extrinsic property, which is the language, and a set of immanent properties. Among these immanent properties he emphasizes three specific qualities of the Ukrainian national character: (1) its psychic character, which consists of a broad, torrid imagination, deep tender feelings, quiet contemplation, laugher mixed with tears, and humour [Широку гарячу фантазію, глибоке ніжне серце, тиху задуму, сміх зі слізьми, гумор]; (2) its social character, that is, its deeply embedded democratic outlook; and (3) its own community and family character [Власний народний громадський та сім'яний характер], which Nechui equates with individualism and the unwillingness to bend before personal (rather than collective) authority.[15]

Nechui's faith in these immanent properties of national culture is a predilection he shared with many other thinkers in the nineteenth century, both in the Russian eEmpire and in Europe. In his essay he specifically mentions Hippolyte Taine, whose attempt at a scientific account of literature, based on the categories of race, milieu, and moment, is clearly one of the models for Nechui's own ideas. Even more important as a source of Nechui's arguments are the historical and social essays of Mykola Kostomarov, from whom Nechui borrows not only the general concept of national cultural qualities but also many of the specific details he presents as arguments in his essay. But these ideas and specific qualities are not merely intellectual fodder for anthropological essays; Nechui implements these principles on the pages of his works as well. Both the general principal of national cultural features and the specific features he mentions in the essay are abundantly represented in his novels.

The psychological qualities that Nechui calls the psychic character of Ukrainians are a universal component and a fundamental principle in his writing, but they are not specifically identified as Ukrainian qualities. Nechui peoples his works with characters who display these qualities, but he does not, of course, stop his narrative to explain that the reason, for example, that Father Mel'khyzedek is a fun-loving man with a wild imagination is because Nechui wants to endow this character with this typically Ukrainian quality. The meeting between Valentyna Kremnyts'ka and Leonid Pasenko in *Pomizh vorohamy*, the recollections Panas Krut' has of Odarka in "Rybalka Panas Krut'," and Ivan Mykhalchevs'kyi's rescue of Vasylyna Palianyk in *Burlachka* are not marked with Post-It notes to call attention to the fact that tender emotions are typically Ukrainian. There are no footnotes alongside Lavrin Kaidash's first view of Melashka and Roman Mysan's communing with nature in the forests of *Ne toi stav* to remind readers that quiet contemplation is also a Ukrainian characteristic. The "Ukrainianness" of these general human qualities is, of course, completely subjective. Nevertheless, Nechui deliberately endows his positive characters with these qualities, rather than others such as intelligence, grace, humility, fortitude, temperance, or prudence. In his fiction he is creating a composite image of Ukrainian character types. Unlike Balzac, who in his *La Comédie humaine* sets out to catalogue all human character types, Nechui narrows his ambition to those features he considers specifically Ukrainian.

The idea that Nechui deliberately endows his characters with what he considers Ukrainian qualities may be objectively undemonstrable, but it is likely to be intuitively obvious to readers of his works. The topic of national cultural qualities is explicitly addressed in *Khmary* and *Nad Chornym Morem*, where Russian and Greek characters, among others, are described as behaving in a manner typical of their specific national culture. Jews are also presented mostly in terms of a cultural stereotype, and since the stereotype focuses on negative qualities the presentation is often indistinguishable from anti-Semitism. And, of course, the very principle of national cultural qualities invites accusations of racism. Whether or not Nechui is to be tarred with this epithet, it is important to understand that he accepts national culture as a justified intellectual construct. The overwhelming bulk of his efforts in depicting national culture is aimed at describing and defining Ukrainian culture. Other national cultures are presented in contrast to Ukrainian culture, and they all necessarily come out losers in the comparison. In most cases this should be understood as patriotism rather than something else. Ukraine and Ukrainians are not only the objects of Nechui's interest, they are the objects of his sympathy as well. But Ukrainian culture, positive as it may be, is not the model and measure for other cultures. Nechui knows its faults and shortcomings. The portrait of Ukrainian culture that Nechui depicts is not unequivocally flattering.

Another factor that gives evidence of Nechui's intention to focus on specifically Ukrainian cultural traits can be seen in an unusual work of his that is titled *Ukrains'ki humorysty ta shtukari*. This is not a work of fiction, but, as a subtitle explains, an ethnographic description of various humorists. The fact that Nechui compiled such a work already shows his interest in establishing the cultural specificity of Ukrainians, at least as far as humour is concerned. The nature and style of the humour and comic behaviour he describes is very specifically identified as Ukrainian:

> Усі вони були виявцями народного національного гумору, котрий затаївся в усіх звиках розуму й фантазії щирого українця, гумору природженого, сказати б, непочатого, суцільного, ще не стертого й не переінакшеного втиском та впливом міської цивілізації, бо в наших городах цей національний гумор виявляється в українців хіба тільки в розмові та в мигах. (5:356–7)
>
> [They were all examples of Ukrainian national humour that has hidden itself in all the turns of wisdom and imagination of a sincere Ukrainian; of a humour that is natural, inborn, you might say, immaculate, of one piece, not yet worn down by the pressure and influence of urban civilization, because in our cities, this national humour is evident among Ukrainians only in their conversations and gestures.]

This characterization of humour as being specifically national in character finds particular expression in Nechui's description of the chief character in this ethnographic study:

> Антін Радивиловський – це тип нервового українця, яких у нас чимало трапляється по селах. В кожній жилі цього цупкого, еластичного організму неначе б'є й ворушиться живе джерело самої живої натури. І прориваються ті збитки живоття наверх через нерви, через рушіння, через миги та жести. Антін пригадує мені в своїх скажених танцях зручних і в'юнких чорноморських козаків-пластунів, їх дивовижну джигітовку й танці-козачки, котрі мені й доводилось бачить. Він тип нервово-ворушливого надзвичайно жвавого степового українця. Цей тип виглядів, викохав, вигодував широкий сухий вольний степ, потайний, небезпечний, повний бродячого народу, дикої татарви, повний потаємних пригод та притичин, як те синє вольне море викохало сміливих піратів норманців; той степ, де колись треба було залягати в траві, в тирсі, як залягає лев в бенгальських очеретах, де треба було щогодини стерегтися ворога, підстерегать, закрадатись нечуйною тихою котячою ходою, плазувать на животі по-гадючому, як плазують і тепер чорноморські кубанські пластуни, кидаться на ворога одним скоком лева та тигра й хапать за шию ворога пальцями, як обценьками. Українець цього типу жилавий, нервовний, прудкий, проворний, говорючий, красномовний, навіть трохи крикливий і лепетливий, мов провансалець або араб, цей син далекого Сходу. (5:389–90)

[Antin Radyvylovs'kyi is a type of nervous Ukrainian, of which you can find many examples in our villages. In every vein of this tough, elastic organism flows, you might say, the very wellspring of a vivacious character. And these particles of vivacity come to the surface through the nerves, through actions, through gestures, through pantomime. Antin reminds me in his wild dances of the dextrous and agile Black Sea cossacks, the *plastuny*, their unusual *dzhyhit* [trick riding]and cossack dances, which I have been fortunate to witness. He is of the nervous-active, unusually animated type of steppe Ukrainian. This type was raised and nurtured by the wide, dry, free steppe with its secrets, dangers, marauding outlaws, wild Tatars, its secret adventures and accidents, just as the free blue ocean raised and nurtured the Norman pirates. The steppe, where it was necessary to hide in the grass like the Bengal tiger hides, where it was necessary every day to stay on guard against the enemy, and to sneak up and slither away with the silent motions of a cat, to crawl on your stomach like a snake (as the Black Sea *plastuny* still do), to throw yourself at the enemy in one jump, like a lion or tiger, and to grab your enemy's neck in your fingers, as in a vice. The Ukrainian of this type is muscular, nervous, quick, agile, talkative, well-spoken, even somewhat loud and chattering, like a Provençal or an Arab, this son of the distant east.]

Nechui's evident delight in the antics of Antin Radyvylovs'kyi – crude and offensive as they sometimes are – is a symptom of his engagement with the idea of a national cultural model of behaviour. So too is the similarity between the characters in this ethnographic essay and those in his belletristic works; while no specific detail is repeated, there is a general similarity between some scenes and characters in *Starosvits'ki batiushky ta matushky* and this essay. This general similarity is enhanced by the autobiographical flavour of both Nechui's fiction and his ethnographical writing. For example, the description of Father Vasylii Ielys...'s and his wife's relations with his Polish landlord and the travelling bishop in *Ukrains'ki humorysty ta shtukari* (5:370–4) is obviously paralleled by the relationship between Kharytin and Onysia Mossakovs'kyi and the Polish landlord and visiting bishop in chapter 9 of that novel (4:253–61). It seems likely, as he suggests in the essay, that Nechui copies these characters from a real-life experience. In any event, they demonstrate the smooth transition between ethnographic and fictional material in Nechui's writing. What's more, Nechui even structures his ethnographic essay as if it were a work of fiction, creating the illusion of a sequence of events and describing the characters and their actions with comparisons, similes, and colourful turns of phrase that are typical of narrative fiction. His approach to the specifically ethnographic assignment is no different from his approach to fiction because the same purpose informs both kinds of writing. Whether in a work of fiction or in an explicitly culturological work, Nechui is always focused on character types and behavioural patterns that he sees as national cultural characteristics.

This predilection for ethnographic, culturological portraiture is, of course, a major factor in Nechui's reputation as an ethnographic realist. We have already seen that he is not primarily focused on peasants and their colourful customs. Nechui does not describe traditional ethnographic weddings, betrothals, christenings, and other staple events of ethnographic literature. His ethnographic bent, to the degree that it is discernible, lies in his persistently evident notion that elements of behaviour such as friendliness, warmth, humour, independence, dignity, and sociability are national characteristics fostered by a common history and social circumstances. One particularly important result of this view is the extraordinary focus on joy that informs so much of Nechui's writing.[16]

Ukrainian culture is not limited to behavioural characteristics. In Nechui's works, culture is addressed or presented as four other elements: language, history, creative arts (high culture), and material culture. Language is, of course, a basic consideration for any writer, but for Nechui it is not only the instrument of his craft – it is often the subject of his narrative, particularly where conflicts arise between Russian and Ukrainian, as they do in schools where only Russian is taught, and in the urban prejudice against Ukrainian. Language is thus one of the principal elements in Nechui's depiction of national conflicts, as discussed in the next chapter. History is another important component of Nechui's understanding of Ukrainian culture, but it plays a rather small role in his fiction, outside of his specifically historical works, which are discussed in chapter 6, below. There are, of course, occasional references to historical events in the conversations of his characters or in narrative comments, but these are infrequent and usually connected with a specific situation, for example, the discussion of the Sviklits'kyis' family history in "Zhyvtsem pokhovani" (7:272), the beginnings of SukhobRus's art business (2:21), or references to illustrious scholars of the former Mohyla Academy in the novel *Khmary* (2:37, 2:331). Where historical events are mentioned, however, they are specifically linked to Ukraine.

References to works of high culture are also infrequent, but they follow a different pattern. We have already noted that Denys Odnosumenko in *Ne toi stav* reads Kotliarevs'kyi (6:354–5) and that Nykon Kuchma in *Neodnakovymy stezhkamy* reads recent publications by Ukrainian authors, especially Shevchenko (8:327–8). Shevchenko and Soshenko are mentioned in "Zhyvtsem pokhovani" (7:274–5). Shevchenko and Gogol are mentioned in *Nad Chornym Morem* (5:261). Shevchenko's name is also invoked in explaining why Narkys Nazariv is called Nazar Stodolia in *Na gastroliakh v Mykytianakh* (8:75). For Nechui, reading books is generally a good thing, but the value of this cultural activity has its limits. In chapter 5 of *Starosvits'ki batiushky ta matushky*, Nechui deliberately juxtaposes his two antagonists reading to their wives. Kharytin Mossakovs'kyi reads aloud a hagiography of St Barbara, but his wife Onysia's mind is elsewhere and she keeps interrupting him to run to the kitchen and attend to household matters (4:132). Balabukha, on the other hand, finds his own religious reading interrupted by his wife, who is singing and playing a guitar and insists that her husband listen to her. Captivated by his reading, he pays no heed to his wife's singing. When she reproaches him, he says that he could read aloud for her from a historical chronicle about Ukraine and Bohdan Khmel'nyts'kyi. "What's Ukraine?" and "Who is Bohdan Khmel'nyts'kyi?" responds Olesia, and she recommends instead a novel entitled *Volshebnytsia Rahi-Muina and Prince Ibrahim* (The enchantress Rahi-Muina and Prince Ibrahim; 4:139–40). The title is meant to accent Olesia's frivolous nature and her desire for mindless diversions. Nechui even gives a snippet of the novel's plot to drive home the point. The entire scene ends with husband and wife mutually throwing each other's book out of reach.

In both families, reading and high culture separate men and women, husbands and wives. Balabukha may be something of a villain in relation to Kharytin, but he is at least a well-read villain, and one that knows not only European culture but Ukrainian history as well. This idea is further advanced later in the text when the philandering Olesia's naive romantic flirtations with Hanush, the handsome, young, and blonde music teacher, run headlong into the reality of his actual musical knowledge. Where she had merely wanted his presence in her private music lessons, he delivers a concert of serious European music, playing Beethoven and Mozart on the piano and then singing Schubert's "Der Erlkönig." Schubert's lieder and Goethe's text show her a deeper meaning of love and of culture:

Балабушиха вперше на віку почула справдішню артистичну музику, артистичний спів. Її душа ніби прокинулась; вона ніби побачила очима дивний ліс при місяці, ввесь укритий інеєм, залитий синюватим фантастичним світом. А з гущавини того лісу, з глибокої долини, закиданої деревом в інії, вона ніби почула чаруючий, як кохання, якийсь потаємний голос, побачила пишний чийсь вид. З очей її скотилось дві сльози.

Ґануш скінчив. Балабушиха схопилась з крісла, простягла руки, як простягають на молитві. Її очі блищали. Вона швидко перебігла залу й крикнула:

– Боже мій! Чом мене не вчили грати й співати? Я була б цілий вік щаслива, щаслива!

Вона трохи не крикнула, щоб Гануш вчив її співати, але схаменулась і чогось засоромилась. Їй тепер одразу стало сором за все те, що вона трохи не призналась в коханні, що вона чіплялась до молодого хлопця. Їй хотілось просити, щоб Гануш вибачив її за всі слова, які вона сказала йому колись в саду; їй стало сором, що вона задумала брати уроки музики на старість. Кров кинулась в її лице. Вона ходила по залі та все слухала, як Гануш перегравав п'єсу за п'єсою, доки не втомилась і впала на крісло, затуливши очі долонею. В її вроді прокинулась не тільки романтична, а може, й справді артистична душа, закинута в сільську глушину, загублений вищий дар божий, заглушений сільською мертвотою.

Од того часу Балабушиха часто просила Гануша грати й співати, й любила слухати його, сидячи в кріслі. Вона покинула свої уроки музики й годила йому вже за його артистичну музику та пісні. (4:296)

[For the first time in her life, Mrs Balabukha heard real artistic music and artistic songs. Her soul seemed to come alive. It was as if she had seen a strange forest in moonlight, all covered in dew, flooded with fantastic blue light. From the depths of that forest, from a deep ravine tangled in fallen trees with dew, she heard a magical, secret voice, enchanting like love itself. She had seen a vision. Two tears rolled down from her eyes.

Hanush finished. Mrs Balabukha jumped up from her chair and extended her arms, as if in prayer. Her eyes were shining. She quickly ran across the room and yelled:

"My God, why didn't they teach me to play and sing? I would be happy my whole life!"

She almost yelled out that Hanush should teach her to sing, but she caught a hold of herself and felt shame for some reason. She immediately felt ashamed for all this: she had almost declared her love to him, she had tried to capture a young man. She wanted to beg Hanush to forgive her for all the words she had once said to him in the orchard. She felt ashamed that she had conceived of studying music in her old age. Blood rushed to her face. She walked around in the room and listened as Hanush played one piece after another, until she finally got tired and fell into a chair, covering her eyes with her palm. In her spirit there arose not only a romantic but perhaps even an artistic soul, buried in the village obscurity, a lost higher Divine sensibility crushed by the deadening village.

After that Mrs Balabukha often asked Hanush to play and sing and she liked to sit in a chair and listen to him. She abandoned her music lessons and looked up to him now for his music and singing.]

As the example of Schubert's song demonstrates, Nechui uses a different scale to measure verbal and non-verbal culture. While living in Kyiv Nechui had a piano in his apartment, and apparently he enjoyed music all his life. Classical European music is not often mentioned in his works; he is careful to maintain social verisimilitude and mentions works of music and art only where they would be socially appropriate. But when he does mention European music or visual art, they are set in a paradigm that distinguishes high or true art from kitsch and poor taste, rather than the national paradigm of Ukrainian vs foreign. In *Prychepa*, the poor Lemishkovs'kyis try to impress the visiting Seredyns'kyis with their presumed cultural sophistication by mentioning their travels to Warsaw and Paris, rattling off in one sentence the names Beethoven, Rossini, and Bellini, and then mentioning performances of Verdi's *Traviata* and Bellini's *Norma* (1:187). While the false pretensions of the Lemishkovs'kyis are being satirized, the value of these European cultural giants is not put in question. A similar musical judgment is expressed in "Gastroli," when the opera singer Flegont Litoshevs'kyi comes home to a vision of his wife on the veranda set off against the dark background of the night. Nechui compares the image to a Rembrandt painting and says that the husband thought she looked like a figure from *The Thousand and One Nights*. With his feelings stirred by this vision, Flegont begins singing Faust's love song to Marguerite from Gounod's opera (8:142). His feelings for her are genuine and sincere. But Sofiia Leonivna has tired of her husband and is captivated by her neighbour Nikolaidos. In her faithless heart, her husband's operatic aria elicits a very different song, a Ukrainian folk song with the words: "На городі бузина, – в неї листу нема: одчепися, препоганий! в тебе хисту нема" [There's a lilac in the garden – but it has no leaves; go away, you ugly wretch – you have no talent] (8:143). Flegont's sincere feelings are embodied in a famous work of European music.[17] The Ukrainian folk song – ironically, recalled by a woman who is not even Ukrainian but Russian – expresses rather crude sentiments driven by lust and loathing. Surprisingly, Nechui allows a Ukrainian cultural work to compare unfavourably to a work of sophisticated European culture, but the scale here is artistic value rather than national culture.

Artistic and national values more often coincide where Nechui depicts low artistic value, or kitsch. In *Starosvits'ki batiushky ta matushky*, for example, we have the following description of Balabukha's home decor:

> В покоях було по-міському, з претензією на панство … Коло вікон висіли портрети Кутузова та інші й дві нові картини, куплені в Києві на контрактах: на одній – панна з голими плічми держала на руках кота, на другій картині – панна з заслоненими плічми, але з голими руками держала на пальці канарейку й годувала її з своїх червоних уст. На вікнах стояли вазони герані. (4:137–8)
>
> [The rooms were adorned in the urban fashion, with pretensions of aristocratic taste. The unpainted floor was smoothed with sand and freshly washed. By the windows hung portraits of Kutuzov and others, as well as two new paintings purchased at the Kontrakty market in Kyiv: one was of a woman with bare shoulders holding a cat, the other, of a woman with covered shoulders but bare hands holding a canary on her finger and feeding it from her own red lips. On the windowsills there were vases with geraniums.]

Portraits of General Kutuzov, the Russian hero of the war against Napoleon, generally signify an absence of good taste, and an excess of imperial patriotism, but they are, at most, innocuous holdovers from a previous era. The two new paintings the couple has hung are symptoms of severely crippled aesthetic sensibilities. Furthermore, since this is the home of an Orthodox priest, they are rather inappropriate, perhaps even indicating a blindness to his spiritual obligations. Even the geraniums suggest unsophisticated taste. Pretentious and kitschy urban tastelessness compares poorly with the simple and natural beauty of the village, even if the villagers themselves are sometimes judged to be crude and aesthetically blind. Examples of this urban tastelessness can be found throughout Nechui's works. We have already mentioned the floor lamps shaped as topless black Arab women in *Neodnakovymy stezhkamy*. There are also the portraits of cupids and a half-naked Hercules fighting a lion that adorn the living room of Reverend Terlets'kyi, Balabukha's father-in-law, where there is also a portrait of Christ with the less-than-appropriate caption: Ecce Homo (4:75).

Nechui's presentation of cultural values thus generally has two parallel scales, one national and the other aesthetic. Ukrainian culture represents a core value, but so, too, does refined art. As a general rule, Nechui avoids juxtaposing European artistic values against Ukrainian ones. As he emphasizes in his culturological essays, European art is an abiding, true achievement of civilization. Ukrainian culture, in his view, can participate in this universal cultural achievement, it can become a participant in the achievements of European civilization, so long as it does not abandon its own national character in the process. In other words, his vision of Ukrainian culture, the third aspect in his conception of what Ukraine consists of, is contingent in its valuation on the fourth aspect of this conception, national identity. The value of Ukrainian culture depends on its Ukrainianness.

In Nechui's works, national identity appears in two specific manifestations. The first of these is embodied in his writings on Ukrainian history, which specifically address questions of the formation and development of a Ukrainian national identity. The second manifestation of national identity is found in the numerous examples throughout his works where Nechui presents the persistent burdens, challenges, and conflicts that Ukrainians endure on the level of national identity in Ukraine. It is to this topic that we now turn.

3 Defending Ukraine

The centrality of Ukraine in Nechui's writing is not exhausted by its role as the primary object of his descriptive observation. Ukraine is also the principal thematic interest in his works. Nechui writes about Ukraine both in the sense that descriptions of Ukraine fill the pages of his works and in the sense that the idea of Ukraine is the organizing principle in them and informs his very purpose in writing. Ukraine is the intellectual as well as the material subject of his works. Just as his writing was deliberately shaped by the desire to describe Ukraine, so it was equally influenced by the need to nurture and protect it – to defend Ukraine and Ukrainianness from any forces, circumstances, and ideas that undermined the material or spiritual existence and comfort of the Ukrainian nation.

While the dangers that faced Ukraine were many and various, Nechui's defence of Ukraine takes the general form of exposing three specific enemies: social conditions and government policy, national intolerance and persecution leading to denationalization, and wilful abandonment of national identity. The first and most pernicious danger faced by the Ukrainian nation was the state and its government – the Russian Empire and the social conditions it supported. In his efforts to expose the problems that resulted from government decrees or from social conditions, Nechui resembled many other realist authors of the late nineteenth century who focused on social ills. What distinguishes his approach is its often backward-looking historical context and its distinctly Ukrainian focus. The second area in which Nechui sought to defend Ukraine was the strictly national arena. Social, political, cultural, and interpersonal pressures often resulted in the denationalization of Ukrainians, particularly those inclined towards social advancement.

This pressure could be a result of social conditions, but it also came directly from both Russians and Poles. Nechui produced a number of works in which he focuses on the mechanisms and consequences of this denationalization. Finally, the loss of national identity could be a result of intellectual positions that Nechui felt were detrimental to underdeveloped nations, particularly Ukrainians. Specifically, he felt that cosmopolitanism, as advanced by left-leaning Ukrainian thinkers such as Drahomanov and Franko, was a suicidal idea for Ukrainians whose negative consequences were comparable to those of official imperial policies of denationalization. All three of these dangers are addressed in Nechui's novels, where fictional characters become emblems of the dangers from which the author hopes to defend Ukraine.

Social Issues

Although Ukrainian literary scholars of the Soviet era depicted Nechui as a committed and active fighter for the rights and freedoms of the lower social classes, the truth of the matter is much more nuanced than ideologically motivated critics could admit. Nechui was certainly a defender of the interests of the Ukrainian lower classes, who were mostly peasants. He sympathized with the injustices they endured, and his works depict numerous forces and social ills that impinged on their freedom, welfare, and happiness. But he was far from any ideas that suggested a radical social reorganization would be desirable. Indeed, Nechui often addresses social problems and their consequences but only rarely focuses on the specific mechanisms – whether institutional, interpersonal, or cultural – that operate in these circumstances. With the exception of such universally accepted and ambiguous notions as the abolition of serfdom, Nechui never actually advocates any specific solutions to the problems he exposes. Thus, while Nechui is certainly an important figure in describing and uncovering various social problems in nineteenth-century Ukraine, unlike many of his contemporaries he is not a reformer. He does not advocate change, and he does not analyse the problems he describes. His goal is to highlight those social ills that threaten Ukraine. These ills receive considerably more attention in his earlier works than they do in his later ones.

Nechui's earliest work, "Dvi moskovky," offers an instructive example. The story tells the familiar woeful tale of peasant families whose lives are destroyed by military conscription as practised in imperial Russia in the nineteenth century. Since the term of conscription was twenty-five years (fifteen after 1859), the young man who went into military service (often unwillingly) was effectively lost to his family and community. If he ever returned, he would likely be a very different person from the one that had been conscripted. Meanwhile, his family was not only deprived of a son or a husband, but also of the labour and potential income of a young man. Although there were rules to avoid the most obvious hardships, military conscription could potentially lead to very serious financial difficulties for a soldier's family. On the other hand, for a serf conscription meant freedom. The conscripted serf became a free man, with the caveat that his serf obligations were now exchanged for military duty. An enserfed woman married to a conscript also acquired freedom. The official policy of quartering soldiers in rural areas made uniformed soldiers a familiar presence throughout the country and, for better or worse, insured contact between them and village women and girls.

The great mass of peasants in the Russian Empire viewed military service as a great evil. Before Nechui, this topic had already appeared in the works of Taras Shevchenko and Marko Vovchok in two specific dimensions. First, conscription into the military was a blight that tore young men from their families and communities. Second, the presence of soldiers, particularly officers, among the rural civilian population put at risk the virtue and socially acceptable behaviour of village women. For Ukrainians, fear and resentment of this social institution became crystalized in the very term by which it was named. A soldier was called a "*moskal'*." The word itself derives from the name of the city and river Moskva (Moscow) and means Muscovite, an inhabitant of Moscow or Muscovy. Used in the meaning "soldier," the word thus carries a double pejorative. It embodies the negative view of soldiering itself and then further associates this soldiering with foreignness. The word itself suggests how this institution was to be portrayed, and so it was in various literary works.

For all of his indebtedness to both Shevchenko and Marko Vovchok, Nechui takes this topic in a new and somewhat unexpected direction. Nechui's story does not examine the institution of military service. His plot does not even encompass an episode of conscription. The story "Dvi moskovky" involves two women, Hanna and Maryna, both of whom fall in love with the same soldier, Vasyl', who spends a few years in his own village with his mother while on leave from the military.[1] Hanna marries Vasyl' and spends a few happy years with him before he is called up for active service again. Gradually, contact with her husband ceases. Alone with their son, Ivas', Hanna cannot earn enough to survive and slips into poverty. As the son of a soldier, Ivas' is enrolled in a military academy in Kyiv, where his education and change in social status distance him from his mother and his village. He puts further financial burdens on his impoverished mother and eventually asks her to sell her home and property to provide him with the inheritance he needs to pursue an advantageous marriage to a woman in Tula. Hanna refuses the request but nevertheless dies impoverished and alienated from her son. This half of Nechui's plot resembles the traditional anti-military narrative. The absence of the soldier-husband destroys the family financially while the institution itself destroys the character of the son. But Nechui has very deliberately altered a crucial element of the traditional story. Hanna's husband was a soldier before she married him, and thus her happiness was not destroyed by an unpredictable and unjust process of conscription. Vasyl''s return to active duty was a foregone conclusion. Hanna entered into this marriage with eyes open. In the story Nechui makes a point of describing the messenger who brings news of Vasyl''s call-up and his son's enrolment in the military academy as the same person who would give serfs instructions about their duties to the landowner. Thus, by comparing military service to serfdom, Nechui characterizes both as evils that beset peasants from some higher authority. But in Hanna's case, the choice was made freely.

By allowing Hanna to choose her own terrible fate, Nechui effectively combines the two dimensions of the military scourge: Hanna is seduced by the good qualities of Vasyl' just as Shevchenko's Kateryna is seduced by the good looks of her handsome but irresponsible lover. But where Shevchenko depicts his *moskal'* as a wastrel and moral bankrupt, Nechui's Vasyl' is a model citizen, a devoted husband, and an industrious peasant. Shevchenko's Kateryna chose a morally despicable man and paid a terrible price for what can be seen as a moral transgression. Nechui's Hanna makes an excellent choice on moral grounds. She marries an outstanding man whose only fault is that he is a soldier. Since no moral fault is involved, the fate she suffers is, in its logic, purely a matter of social injustice. Shevchenko's Kateryna is punished by her parents, by society, and by fate for trusting a man unworthy of her love. The fact that he is a soldier makes his untrustworthiness all the more predictable. Nechui's Hanna, on the other hand, would seem to be the poster girl for an indictment of the Russian imperial program of military service. But Nechui does not focus on this social problem. Instead, he builds a moral comparison between two women.

As the title suggests, "Dvi moskovky" is built around the juxtaposition of two soldiers' wives. The "other woman," Maryna, is severely disappointed to "lose" Vasyl' to Hanna. She tries to mitigate her loss by marrying another soldier, Mykyta, but the marriage is loveless and Maryna is not displeased to see her husband called back to active duty. Indeed, Maryna longs not for her husband but for the man she did not marry, Hanna's Vasyl'. Grudgingly resigned to her fate, Maryna becomes the village party girl, acquiring a reputation for loose behaviour yet maintaining a generally cheerful disposition. Her good cheer even extends to comforting Hanna. But Hanna will not stoop to debauchery and will not be cheered by Maryna's insistence that her own fate is even worse than Hanna's. Hanna had at least loved and lost, while Maryna had never found any true happiness. But whatever their outlook, both women are doomed to an unhappy fate. Hanna dies alone, without husband or son, in poverty and misery. Maryna eventually tires of her life in the village, sells her possessions, and moves to the city, where she continues her dissolute life and drinks and parties herself to death, with the tavern-keeper quietly carrying her corpse out onto the street to avoid unnecessary disruption in his place of business.

By structuring his story as a contrast of these two women, Nechui achieves unexpected results. Although he is obviously writing about a common social problem, he avoids – as he will throughout his career – turning the story into direct social commentary. It is a work of fiction focusing on the personalities of two women and on how these very different women deal with the problems of being a soldier's wife. But in the contrasting reactions of Hanna and Maryna, the reader finds a common lesson: the fate of a soldier's wife is miserable, no matter how she responds to her fate. The institution itself is the problem. By moving the focus away from social issues and onto personalities, Nechui, surprisingly, clarifies and sharpens the social commentary.

The focus on two women in this story can also be understood as Nechui's response to a potential weakness of Shevchenko's "Kateryna." Many readers are surprised by the strict and unforgiving response to Kateryna's transgression on the part of her parents and fellow villagers. This lack of sympathy and understanding seems to belie the opening verse of the poem, where Shevchenko pretends to accommodate a woman's right to happiness: "Кохайтеся чорнобриві, та не з москалями" [Love whom you will, my black-browed beauties, but not a *moskal'*][2]. Kateryna is so overwhelmingly ostracized in Shevchenko's poem that the memorable phrase "love whom you will" is made meaningless. "Love only those your parents and the community approve of" is much less poetic, but apparently more in keeping with the social justice Shevchenko presents in the poem. Nechui, whose debt to Shevchenko was enormous, divides the role of Kateryna in two and absolves the soldier of any wrongdoing, as if to clarify the role of the tsarist military service in society. In Nechui's hands the evil of the military institution is not a result of the moral depravity of soldiers – Vasyl' is a wonderfully decent man. Nor, more importantly, is the social harm caused by the military a result of the moral vagary of women. Nechui is careful to present both possibilities: an honest, reliable woman, and a carefree, licentious one. But the outcome is identical in both cases. Shevchenko's thesis needs clarification. The woman is not at fault. Indeed, as we shall see in a later chapter, the happy-go-lucky woman who ignores society's restrictions on her happiness is no more to blame than the righteous, socially conforming one. For Nechui, Shevchenko's harsh judgment needed tempering.

The tendency to respond to Shevchenko's poetry is also evident in other early works of Nechui's, particularly the short novel *Burlachka*. The debt to Shevchenko is very explicit here – the text opens with references to the poet and the area where he was born. The plot of the novel is a modified composite version of a number of familiar plot lines about abused women. *Burlachka* can be understood as combining elements of Shevchenko's many depictions of the *pokrytka* (the fallen woman, i.e., an unmarried woman who has given birth to a child). Such women appear in Shevchenko's poems "Vid'ma," "Kateryna," "Naimychka," and other works, among them his Russian-language story "Varnak." But the plot of Nechui's novel holds no specific similarities to Shevchenko's characters. The relationship between the works lies precisely in the different treatment Nechui gives this subject. For Shevchenko, the *pokrytka* is an instance of moral transgression. Although these women are victims, they suffer social condemnation and often lose their moral bearings, committing further iniquities in despair or revenge. At best, they are suffering misfits and outcasts, like Shevchenko's version of Maria, the mother of Christ. Nechui's version of the *pokrytka*, Vasylyna, the protagonist of *Burlachka*, is an elaboration and expansion of Shevchenko's stereotype. She is also an attempt to move the focus from a moral plane to a social one. Nechui's Vasylyna is a somewhat naive character who is smitten with her master's good looks and gracious attention and easily gets pulled into his dissolute life. When the inevitable happens, she is genuinely surprised, offended, and embarrassed (despite the many warnings she had been given). Nechui signals her confusion in a passage where she sees her surroundings in the master's house in a new, fantastic, and ghastly image: the piano seems to be a wild beast on short legs, the chair legs look like a human skeleton, the sofa resembles a coffin, and terrible vampires stare back at her from the giant mirrors.[3] This confusion does not absolve Vasylyna of responsibility for her own actions; her embarrassment and flight from her parents indicate she understands this. But it does show Nechui's understanding of a social divide between the worlds of the aristocratic Iastshembs'kyi and the peasant girl. The accoutrements of high society – the furniture that would be out of place in a peasant household – show their true, frightening, and ghoulish character once Cupid's blinders are lifted from her eyes.

Later in the novel this demonization of the upper classes in the eyes of peasants has an industrial correlative. Vasylyna runs away from her aristocratic lover and from her parents and, after killing her baby, takes up employment at a textile mill. In one of the earliest descriptions of an industrial setting in Ukrainian literature, Nechui follows Vasylyna through the napping shop[4] of the factory to her station in the shearing area, where defects are removed from the finished cloth (3:221–2). The hot, loud, and dangerous machines in the napping shop, including one called a "wolf," frighten Vasylyna and give her nightmares. Although her real difficulties are with people rather than machines, Vasylyna gives Nechui an opportunity to paint a negative image of the relationship between people and industrial machinery. Vasylyna's room-mate, Maria, tells a similar story a few pages later about the sugar refinery. Although this time the focus is less on machines than on the work environment, that factory, too, is seen as a dangerous place where the health, safety, happiness, and moral character of employees are endangered.

The greatest social evil in Nechui's novel, however, is not the factory that dehumanizes its workers or even the aristocrats who abuse the naive, unsuspecting peasants. Nechui reserves his strongest indictment for the most nefarious villains – the merchants of evil, who are, invariably, Jewish businessmen. In *Burlachka* there are two such characters, Leiba (= Leyb, no surname indicated) and Leizor (= Eliezer) Rabynenko. Nechui depicts them as the embodiment of mercantile exploitation. Leiba is an expert at enticing workers (recently liberated peasant serfs) to work for the aristocratic landowners. Nechui introduces him at the very outset of the novel, immediately following a scene-setting introduction of the village and the Palianyk family. Vasylyna hears music coming from a wagon entering the village and runs out to see what is going on. Leiba has come to solicit young men and women to work for the aristocrat Stanislav Iastshembs'kyi (= Stanisław Jastrzembski, a Polish name):

> Жид обернувся до Паляникових воріт і почав викликати якраз так, як викликають діди на ярмарках.
>
> – Мир хрещений, усі люди добрі! послухайте, що маю казати. Пан Ястшембський, журавський посесор, закликає вас до себе на роботу, на буряки, дає по восьмигривенику на день на його харчах; для дівчат та хлопців гратимуть двічі на день музики, ще й фургонами привезуть назад до господи! – викликав Лейба такою чистою українською мовою, що, заплющивши очі, можна було б подумати, нібито викликає на ярмарку якийсь дід. (3:147)

> [The Jew turned to the Palianyk gate and began calling out just like the old-timers do at the markets.
>
> "Christian people, good folks, listen to what I have to say. Mr Iastshembs'kyi, the Zhuravka leaseholder, is calling you out to work on his sugar beet fields. He's giving an eighty kopeck coin per day and will provide food. There will be music for the boys and girls twice a day and the wagons will even bring you back to your homes." Leiba spoke in such pure Ukrainian that with eyes closed it would be easy to imagine that it was an old-timer calling out at the market.]

In this passage Leiba's qualities are ambiguously signalled. He is an intermediary between the aristocrat and the Ukrainian peasants, sufficiently close to the peasants culturally to speak to them in their own language, both literally and figuratively. But this cultural similarity is something of a deception. As Nechui's narration specifies, the similarity requires a closing of the eyes. Leiba simulates his affinity to the peasants just as he pretends to serve Iastshembs'kyi's interests. In fact, Nechui tells us a few pages later, Leiba dreams of taking over the leasehold (3:159), and at the end of the novel he will indeed displace the foolhardy aristocrat in that position. But in the meantime, Leiba performs his function of procuring workers for the leaseholder, and that procurement is not limited to field hands for agriculture. Leiba knows Iastshembs'kyi's inclinations, so when he notices Vasylyna's good looks, he makes a point of telling the leaseholder about her, which will eventually lead to her employment as a domestic in his home and thus her drift into a dissolute life. When Vasylyna is eventually dismissed and flees from her parents to avoid shame and dishonour, Leiba once again steps into his role as intermediary. He counsels the helpless girl to return for her possessions and then sends her to the factories in Stebliv, where his colleague will place her in a job.

Although Leiba does nothing more than help Vasylyna formulate her own plans for escape, this time Nechui leaves no ambiguity in his judgment of this character. Since his earlier appearance in the novel, Leiba has moved up in the world:

> Він вмів підлизатись до посесора так, що посесор оддав йому два журавські шинки. Лейба пішов угору, вже не їздив по селах на фургонах з музиками за робітниками, сидів собі у шинку й торгував горілкою. На своє місце він постановив своїх родичів, Гершка й Шулима, виписавши їх з другої губернії. Гершко й Шулим оселились у Журавці, притулившись коло Лейби в шинках з цілими гніздами жиденят. Вони стали його помагачами й агентами. Сам Лейба залежав од свого вищого начальника, стеблівського жида, Лейзора Рабиненка, що держав у Стеблеві підряд у заводах на робітників. Лейзор Рабиненко розпустив свої потаємні сітки на цілі губернії, мав своїх підручників на Волині, на Поділлі, в Могилівщині й Мінщині. Всі вони були повинні настачати йому робітників за плату од голови. Всі вони держали у своїх руках мужиків за довги й висилали безщасних людей на стеблівський й інші заводи. Це було потаємне жидівське товариство з цілою ватагою агентів, більших, менших і найменших, котрі забирали мужиків в свої руки й вертіли ними, як хотіли.
>
> Лейба знав, як важко доводилось Василині, знав, що посесор прожене її од себе, знав, що вона вже не може вернутись до батька у Комарівку. Він знав усю Журавку й близькі села, знав, що лежить у кожного мужика у кишені, знав кожного вдачу, душу й заводив свою жидівську павутину на цілу околицю. Василина попалась у ту павутину несподівано. (3:208–9)

[He knew how to suck up to the leaseholder so that the latter had given him [the concession for] two taverns in Zhuravka. Leiba had gone up in the world, he no longer travelled around the villages with musicians looking for labourers. In his place he had installed two relatives, Hersh [Hirsch] and Shulym [Shalom], whom he had transferred from a neighbouring gubernia. Hersh and Shulym settled in Zhuravka, squeezing in beside Leiba at the taverns with their nests full of little Jews. They became his assistants and agents. Leiba himself was dependent on his own boss, Leizor Rabynenko, who held a concession to supply workers for the factories in Stebliv. Leizor Rabynenko had spread his secret nets over entire gubernias, he had his associates in Volyn, in Podillia, in the Mohyliv area,

> and in the Minsk area. All of them were obliged to provide workers for him for a payment per head. All of them controlled peasants through debts and sent the unfortunate people to work in the factories of Stebliv or elsewhere. This was a secret Jewish fraternity with an entire army of agents, great, middling, and small, who took the peasants into their own hands and did with them whatever they wished.
>
> Leiba knew how hard it was for Vasylyna, he knew the leaseholder would chase her away, he knew that she would no longer be able to return to her father's home in Komarivka. He knew all of Zhuravka and the surrounding villages, knew what every peasant had in his pocket, knew everyone's temperament and soul, and spread his Jewish spider web over the entire area. Vasylyna had fallen into this web unexpectedly.]

This passage and another about Leizor Rabynenko at the opening of chapter 5 (3:219–20) paint a very bleak portrait of labour conditions at the Stebliv factory. Nechui's instinct for realism prompts him to give an unusually detailed account of this contractual arrangement. Rabynenko has a concession to provide labour to the factory at a fixed price. The contract stipulates that if he fails, the factory managers can hire labour at his (Rabynenko's) expense for up to twice the price Rabynenko himself is paid in the contract. Rabynenko himself, of course, hires labourers as cheaply as he can with lodging and meals as part of the agreement. To find the necessary workers and avoid the contractual penalties, he maintains a wide network of agents (e.g., Leiba) who send him workers. To maximize his profit he offers low wages and provides substandard food and lodging. The only people willing to work under these conditions are helpless or desperate peasants like Vasylyna.

Nechui's depiction of the industrial proletariat and the economic conditions under which the labour market functions are an important part of his achievement as a writer, as are the descriptions of the factory. Although they occupy a relatively small portion of the text in this work, they clearly signal his understanding of the changing economic landscape in Ukraine in the second half of the nineteenth century. Nechui takes Shevchenko's (and not only Shevchenko's) story of a seduced woman and advances it onto a social and economic plane. Vasylyna is paraphrasing Shevchenko's "Prychynna" when she says "За що ж ти боже так караєш мене" (3:203) [Why, Lord, do you punish me so!], but Nechui's focus is not on the general moral injustice of forsaken unwed mothers. Rather, his focus is on the specific social conditions into which this condition throws them. Nechui, like Ivan Franko, depicts the introduction of industrial labour opportunities in the Ukrainian countryside as an unqualified disaster for the peasants. There is no mention of the growing wealth of the villages around factories or the opportunities industrial labour offered for improved income, higher skills, or even personal freedom. In the flight from exploitation by aristocrats, Ukrainian peasants who turn to industrial labour fall prey to a morally and socially destructive force.

Furthermore, in *Burlachka* the dangers represented in the exploitation by an aristocrat and the exploitation of industrial labour are not equal. Iastshembs'kyi's exploitation of Vasylyna is presented as the natural consequence of poor morals, sexual desire, beauty, and naivety. Although the aristocrat's ethical failings are not diminished, no particular evil or malicious purpose is imputed to his actions. Nechui shows him as a womanizing scoundrel, but with Vasylyna he is genuinely confused about his own motives. Only when his feelings for her are put in conflict with his other values does he abandon her. Before Iastshembs'kyi meets Vasylyna, Nechui offers a positive evaluation of him that absolves him of serious responsibility because his faults are inherited from his parents, his class, and his nationality:

> Невважаючи на поганий вплив татка, і найбільше мами, в молодого Стася була добра душа і добрий розум. В його синіх ясних очах світилась душа добра, а на білому гарному лиці була розлита така симпатичність, що проти волі притягувала до його душу в кожного. Це була натура добра зроду, але зовсім попсована фамільними традиціями панства та панування над мужиком, над Україною, попсована розкішшю, збитками всякого добра, при чому ні праця, ні розумовий розвиток, ні наука, ні вищі європейські ідеї не були можливим ділом.
>
> З такою просвітою в голові, з традиціями панства, Стась вийшов чваньковитим, гордим перед народом, перед усім, що звалось українським. Він ставив себе без міри вище за кожного українця, хоч би українець був вчена людина. (3:157)

[Despite the bad influence of his father and especially his mother, the young Stas' had a good soul and a good mind. In his bright blue eyes shone a good soul, and his handsome white face was flooded with such charm that it attracted everyone to him despite their wilful inclinations. His was a naturally good character but one completely spoiled by family traditions of aristocratic lording over the peasants, over Ukraine, spoiled by the opulence and wastefulness of their wealth, which did not allow

> work, intellectual development, scholarship, nor higher European ideas to capture their attention.
>
> With such an upbringing in his head, with these aristocratic traditions, Stas' turned out to be a conceited individual, proud before the common people, before everything that seemed Ukrainian. He considered himself immeasurably higher than any Ukrainian, even if that Ukrainian was an educated person.]

Nowhere is this positive evaluation of the Polish aristocrat matched by any exoneration of the Jewish merchants. Their cultural proximity to the Ukrainian peasants turns into a wicked trick, allowing them to better exploit their quarry. Where the Polish aristocrat is judged lightly, his sins dismissed as the result of bad influences from family and class, the Jewish businessmen are judged very harshly. Their crimes are those of self-interested greed. They are deliberate in their exploitation of Ukrainian peasants. The role they assume in the new economic system is based on a malicious exploitation of the weaknesses of mankind.

In this broad condemnation of the injustice modern industrial capitalism brings to the workers it exploits, Nechui is not very different from a number of other European realists, most notably Zola, who depict the evils of industrialization in stark and somewhat exaggerated terms. True, Nechui focuses on the labour managers rather than the owners of the enterprise, but this may reflect the realities of complex ownership structure in Ukraine. Nechui mentions only a Jewish leaseholder as the representative of ownership interests in the factories. The actual owners of such enterprises in Ukraine in the late nineteenth century may have been foreign and invisible to the local workers. Or perhaps Nechui's generally conservative political instincts deliberately shield the owners from criticism while laying blame at the feet of the holders of the contract to provide labour. In any event, the depiction of these businessmen in the darkest of melodramatic colours, as greedy exploiters totally inconsiderate of the plight of their suffering workers, is a tactic well established among realist writers describing the exploitation of the industrial proletariat. But Nechui's entrepreneurial villains are not merely greedy monsters: they're Jewish greedy monsters.

The national identity of characters in Nechui's works is, as we have seen, a fundamentally important issue. So there is nothing surprising in the fact that he identifies his villains by nationality as well. Since Nechui is an advocate for the Ukrainian nation, his villains are generally foreigners, that is, Russians, Poles, and Jews.[5] As we shall see below, his Russian and Polish villains are generally depicted in roles that focus on the denationalization of Ukrainians. Thus their national identity is intrinsically tied to their role as villains. Foreigners who undermine or displace Ukrainian culture in Ukraine are invariably villains in Nechui's works. In *Burlachka*, Iastshembs'kyi's disdain for Ukrainian culture is emphasized, but since he abandons Vasylyna and does not threaten her national identity, the issue of denationalization *per se* does not arise. Perhaps that contributes to the portrayal of this aristocrat as something less than a complete villain. But the status of Jewish villains is different from that of Russians and Poles.

In Nechui's works, Jews are not instruments of Ukrainian denationalization. On the contrary, as we have seen, in *Burlachka* Leiba has absorbed the language and culture of his Ukrainian neighbours. His villainy lies in his economic activity and the impact that activity has on Ukrainian peasants, not in his national identity. Thus, the fact that he is a Jew is not inherently tied to his iniquity. He is identified as a Jew for at least two reasons. In nineteenth-century Ukraine Jews could be found in a variety of occupations and social strata. One of these was precisely as intermediaries between the lower classes of the population, Ukrainian peasants, and the wealthy upper classes, who might be of any nationality but would not likely identify themselves as Ukrainians. Jews had played such a role in Eastern European society, particularly in Ukraine, for a couple of centuries, and a realist author like Nechui could readily copy such characters from real life, with a few extra-heavy melodramatic brushstrokes added to highlight their villainy. An author intent on depicting every aspect of Ukrainian society would naturally include such a character. But there is, of course, another reason he is identified as a Jew. In Ukrainian society in the nineteenth century, Jews were a poorly regarded minority. National and religious antipathy along with social resentment of the mediating role that some Jews played led to the prevalence of a negative stereotype of Jews as exploiters, not fundamentally very different from the negative stereotypes of Jews that existed elsewhere in Europe. In depicting Jewish exploiters such as Leiba and Leizor Rabynenko, Nechui is taking advantage of well-established negative stereotypes that were very common among Ukrainians. Thus, Nechui's readers would readily accept these national stereotypes either because they were indeed familiar to them, or because their national and religious prejudice led them to believe they were familiar figures.

Nechui's characterization of these businessmen as Jews and as exploiters clearly indicates that these two qualities – national and economic – have been welded together in an image of intolerant prejudice. After Leiba and his associate, Srul' (= Yisrael), deliver the workers to Iastshembs'kyi's fields early in the novel, Nechui paints a scene of the two middlemen, who have brought the workers and provided them with a meal, lying down to sleep in the shade under the wagon while the peasants work: "'Чи не лукаві тобі жиди!' гукнув один парубок. 'Повивертались як кабани. Лейбо! А йди лишень буряків полоть" (3:149) ["Aren't those Jews crafty," says one of the fellows. "They've rolled over like wild boars. Leiba, come on over and help weed the sugar beets!"]. The resentment may be understandable, since the peasants naturally feel that they are doing the hard work while the intermediaries make a profit sleeping under the wagon (although the intermediaries have not been hired to do the argicultural work). But the description then goes on to a caricaturish image of the sleeping men, clearly aimed at diminishing their human dignity:

> Дівчата й хлопці сапали буряки, а жиди спали, аж роти пороззявляли. Мухи обсіли Лейбу, обліпили йому очі, чорніли під очима, неначе другі брови, обліпили кругом рот, лазили й вилазили з рота, неначе бджоли з улика. Лейба крізь сон клацнув зубами, перекусив з десяток мух, половину ковтнув, половину виплював і знов роззявив свою вершу. А дівчата сапали та сапали, ще й веселих пісень співали. (3:149–50)

> [The girls and boys weeded the sugar beets, while the Jews slept, their mouths gaping. A swarm of flies alighted on Leiba, covering his eyes, forming a dark streak beneath his eyes like a second pair of eyebrows. They surrounded his mouth and crawled in and out, like bees from a hive. Leiba clenched his teeth in his dream, cutting a dozen or so flies in half, swallowing half and spitting out the rest, and then again opened the cavity. And the girls hoed and hoed, even singing happy songs.]

While this dehumanizing caricature focuses on the presumed exploitation of the peasants rather than the national identity of the putatively lazy intermediaries, a similar confrontation between the Ukrainian workers and Leizor Rabynenko shows more of a religious prejudice. Nechui describes the labour provider's inclination to save money by providing substandard food, particularly pork:

> Сам Лейзор важив на терезах сало, у котрому вже ворушились черви. Лейзор не дуже гидував тією харчею, забороненою законом Мойсея: він скуповував сало по селах і посилав цілі хури в Одесу, у жидівські контори.

– Ей, стережися, Лейзоре, бо оскоромишся, – жартували люди.

– Що вам до того! То я оскоромлюсь, а не ви, – обізвався Лейзор.

– Чи вже ж ти не боїшся свині?

– Чого її боятись? Хіба вона мене покусає, чи що, – говорив Лейзор, але все-таки одвертав носа од того сала, у котрому вже кишіли черви.

Зате ж сало було куплене дешево, а Лейзорові тільки того було треба. (3:220)

[Leizor himself weighed the pork, in which the maggots were already visible. Leizor was not particularly averse to this food, forbidden by Mosaic law. He bought up pork in the villages and sent whole wagonloads of it to Odessa, to the Jewish merchants.

"Be careful, Leizor, or you'll break the dietary laws," the people jested.

"That's none of your business. I'm the one who will be breaking the dietary laws, not you," Leizor answered.

"So you're not scared of a pig?"

"Why should I be scared of a pig? Will it bite me or what?" said Leizor. Nevertheless he turned his nose from the pork where the maggots were pulsing in whole colonies.

But the pork was bought cheaply, and that's all that was important to Leizor.]

The image of feeding industrial workers with rotten meat is a staple caricature in works depicting labour struggles against greedy and heartless industrialists. But the specific accusation here – that Leizor ignores his own religious dietary prohibitions – is largely a matter of religious animosity. Of course, in depicting the growing secularization of Jews, particularly Jewish businessmen who no longer practise all the customs of Jewish tradition, Nechui is perhaps merely being a realist. This was certainly an important social phenomenon within the Jewish community in Ukraine at the time. But Leizor's secularization is tied to his greedy exploitation of the workers in a manner that suggests a causal rather than an accidental connection. Leizor might have simply been a Jew and an exploiter, but it seems he is an exploiter because he is a Jew.

Nechui's reliance on images of Jewish exploiters makes obvious connections with widely held negative stereotypes of Jews. Whatever its causes and origins, the famous enmity of Ukrainian peasants to Jews in the nineteenth century is an ugly and widespread phenomenon. The depiction of Jews in *Burlachka* and other works by Nechui relies on this prejudice and participates in its propagation. The depiction of Jewish characters in Ukrainian literature has recently attracted serious scholarly attention, particularly in the work of Myroslav Shkandrij specifically devoted to this subject.[6] But Shkandrij's approach, as I have made clear elsewhere,[7] is narrowly conceived as an answer to the question of whether Ukrainian literature (and individual writers and works) can be considered anti-Semitic or not. This approach certainly needs no justification and leads to important results, but it is not particularly suited to an understanding of the national dimension of Nechui's depiction of Jewish characters. Realist writers such as Nechui often invoke common stereotypes, including anti-Semitic ones, that offer shortcuts to character depiction. Such are the portraits of Jewish exploiters in Nechui's works. In Nechui's works, as in the works of many Ukrainian realist writers, the mere presence of these images does not in itself offer a sufficient answer to the question of a writer's attitude towards Jews. Ivan Franko, for example, famously depicts Jewish capitalists as exploiters in his novels about industrial conditions in Boryslav, but he also compares Ukrainians and Jews as parallel examples of oppressed nations in other works, particularly his poem *Moses*. Moreover, if anti- or philo-Semitism is the only angle from which a Jewish image is measured, many of its other qualities may be lost, even if these qualities turn out to be equally significant in the overall structure of the work.

Nechui certainly uses anti-Semitic stereotypes in his works, but he also depicts the prejudice itself, although he takes no particular pains to highlight its presence and his narrator does not comment on it, as he does about the presumed faults of the Jews. The remarks addressed to Leiba and Leizor by peasants in the novel are disrespectful and inappropriate. Leiba and Srul' were not hired to work in the fields and there is no reason for them to join the peasants. As Leizor himself points out, whatever dietary laws he may be breaking, they do not apply to the Christians who are rudely badgering him about them. Nechui does not hide the animosity Ukrainian peasants feel towards the Jews. He does, however, expand the antipathy from a prejudice against individual Jews, or even Jews as a national and religious minority, to an understanding of Jewish exploitation as a social institution. He deliberately introduces the terminology of government and repression to describe the operation of the commercial network that Leizor Rabynenko manages. In describing the three Jewish families that live beside his home, he calls them Leizor's police. Leizor himself is the boss (начальник), but he is himself a mere cog in a larger government-like administrative institution: "В Лейзора в Одесі були свої ще вищі начальники: жидівські губернатори і міністри, котрим він подавав звістку за все і приставляв їм пашню. То були міністри пшениці, жита, міністри гречки й проса й навіть міністри свинячого сала, олії й дьогтю: то були взагалі українські губернатори мужицького поту та сліз, міністри людської кривавиці" (3:220–1) [In Odessa, Leizor had higher bosses: Jewish governors and ministers, to whom he reported and to whom he sent fodder. There were ministers of wheat and rye, ministers of buckwheat and millet, and there were even ministers of pork saltback, grease, and oil. They were indeed the governors of peasant sweat and tears, the ministers of human blood]. Leizor himself is characterized as a man who has not yet developed aristocratic habits but is moving up in his career: "По лиці було вже видно, що йому небагато зосталось дослужувати до уряду жидівського губернатора України" (3:221) [From his face it was evident that he would not need to serve much longer to reach the office of the Jewish governor of Ukraine].

The correlation Nechui draws between economic exploitation, modern commercial enterprise, government, and Jewish identity represents one of the greatest threats against the welfare and comfort of the Ukrainian peasant. But the various elements of this threat are not always deployed in the same arrangement. In Nechui's world, some Jews are exploiters, others are victims. The opening chapter of his very early story "Rybalka Panas Krut'" (Panas Krut', the fisherman; 1868) consists of an idyllic description of the town of Bohuslav along the Ros' River (an area Nechui knew well, since he went to school there) sharply contrasted with an equally heartfelt description of the misery and squalour of the Jewish ghetto in that town.[8] Although Nechui does blame some of the ghetto's terrible appearance on the Jewish merchants themselves, who are unwilling to spend money on gardens or flowers, which do not contribute to their profits, the focus of this passage is on the poverty and filth in which the Jews are living. Their destitute children play halfnaked in the streets, their wives tramp like herons through the mud, and their rows of kiosks resemble nothing so much as the markers in a Jewish cemetery. Despite annual fires that ravage their crowded, ramshackle homes, despite their filth and poverty, they endure like the Isrealites of the Old Testament: "Невгамовані, живучі діти Ізраїля. І в воді не тонуть, і в огні не горять" (1:104) [The unrestrained, living children of Israel. They don't sink in water, they don't burn in fire]. While this passage is not quite an example of effusive philo-Semitism, on the whole it is a sympathetic depiction of the difficult lives of the Bohuslav Jews.[9] The emphasis on their perseverance and endurance is meant to highlight the qualities of the protagonist of the story, Panas Krut'.

Panas is one of Nechui's more enigmatic characters. The life story he tells his younger friend, Pan'ko, at night on the river is neither an inspirational story of hard-fought success nor a woeful tale of oppression and injustice. Panas considers himself unfortunate but cannot understand the causes of his misfortune. He is smart and skilful. His father passed on to him the skills and small business of a tailor and furrier. But Panas could never turn these into financial success. Taxes and payments to the local landowner were greater than his earnings. So he borrowed some money from the Jewish moneylender to buy hides and make a wagonful of furs and hats. He took these goods to a distant, large market in Kherson province. But at the market, as he tells it, the Jewish furriers in the stalls next to his were craftier and more cunning in their sales techniques. They aggressively accosted potential customers, inordinately praised the quality of their own wares, and complimented the customers on how becoming they looked in the furs and hats. Panas, on the other hand, followed what he considered a more honest approach:

> А я стою та стою. Прийде хто, скажу свою, справдешню ціну як слід, щоб бога не гнівить і людей не кривдить; не правлю по-жидівській, як за батька. Завгодно бери, а не завгодно, як хоч! Ніхто не силує. (1:113)

> [And I just stood there and stood there. When someone came by, I would tell them my honest, actual price as it should be so as not to anger God or offend people, without bargaining like a Jew, as my late father had done. If you're satisfied, take it, otherwise don't – it's your choice. No one is forcing you.]

Naturally, with such a lethargic approach to sales, Panas failed to sell his goods. He paid off the principal of the loan but could not make the interest payments. There was nothing left to pay his rents to the landlord. So he changed occupations and took up shoemaking, but that wasn't much better and finally, when his wife died, he sold off everything and bought a boat, and has now been fishing for the last twenty-three years.

The financial woes of Panas Krut' are a good example of the complexity of Nechui's views on social issues. Krut' is not a victim of any particular social ills, unless commerce itself is deemed evil. He is not a lazy man, and he even had the entrepreneurial savvy to understand that borrowed capital would allow him to grow his business. But he is unfit for business itself. Significantly, Nechui allows him to pay off the borrowed capital, but not the interest. Panas Krut' and, by symbolic extension, the traditional Ukrainian villager is psychologically, culturally, and ethically unprepared for a world that requires commercial skills. For Krut', the only honest work is work done with the hands. Selling, advertising, negotiating, taxes, rents, interest payments are all beyond his cultural understanding. Taxes, rents, and interest are described as oppressive not because of their size: they are debilitating because they exist at all. This commercial world is the world of the Jewish businessmen of Bohuslav, described in the first chapter of the story. But they are, in fact, no better off than Krut'. In the traditionalist view this story reflects, no one is better off because of the existence of commerce. The Jewish merchants and the Ukrainian fisherman are all losers. But at least the merchants survive, they endure. With a bottle of liquor to further dull his already lethargic disposition, Panas can't control his boat in the spring floods and drowns in the river. And here, ironically, Nechui finally finds the only real villains in the story: "Оддячила там своєму ворогові риба!" (1:125) [The fish took revenge on their enemy!]. The reversal of roles between the fish and the fisherman along with the cheerful, quiescent fatalism of this conclusion neutralize any attempt to find social antagonisms in this story.

Among Nechui's works the one with the strongest claim to social commentary is *Mykola Dzheria*, a novel he published in 1878 after having worked on it for many years. In Soviet times, this was certainly the most praised of Nechui's works. It was included in the school curriculum, attracted a good deal of scholarly attention, and was even translated into English.[10] Given all the difficulties Soviet scholarship had with Nechui because of his unshakeable conviction that Russian culture and identity were undesirable in Ukraine, here at last was a text that Nechui's admirers among Ukrainian readers and scholars could praise without twisting their analysis into ludicrous ideological constraints. Here was simple and unambiguous proof that Nechui was a champion of the working classes who struggled against the class-based exploitation of the Ukrainian peasants. While the thesis is doubtless true, there are at least two serious difficulties associated with it.

Nechui's *Mykola Dzheria* is certainly a broadly sketched indictment of serfdom and the attendant social regulations as they were practised in the Russian Empire. But the social commentary in the novel is an anachronism. Serfdom was abolished in the empire in 1861, before Nechui had started his career as a writer. Condemning serfdom after it was already abolished, no matter how sincere and heartfelt the compassion and outrage, hardly gives Nechui any serious credentials as a Marxist-Leninist revolutionary. Furthermore, the central plot motif of this novel concerns how one particular individual reacts to the injustices he encounters. The novel is named for its protagonist not only because he is the central character but also because his character and his personality are a major concern in the novel. Mykola Dzheria is a victim of the evil social system of serfdom and of many callous and greedy exploiters. But he is also a hothead, a man easily pushed to extremes, a rebellious individualist who can quickly escalate any offence into a major confrontation. Nechui certainly sympathizes with Mykola's angry responses to the terrible abuse that he and his family endure at the hands of a variety of oppressors, and there is no suggestion in the novel that Mykola's cruel fate is in any way justified by his own behaviour. But Nechui does nothing to disguise the angry, violent side of Mykola's personality, which does not help him find happiness. Eventually, he will return to his village after the abolition of serfdom to discover that his wife has died, his married daughter is a stranger to him, and the social conditions in the village still favour the wealthy and the greedy.

In *Mykola Dzheria* Nechui throws light on a variety of different forms of social injustice. Serfdom is shown to be a completely barbaric system, particularly when it is in the hands of a cruel and vindictive man like Bzhozovs'kyi (= Brzozowski), the Polish landholder and master of the village of Verbivka. Abuse of the serfs goes beyond the mere fact that they are forced to work for their "master." They are denied even the meagre rights that this inhumane system guarantees them: they are forced to work more days than required and at times when their own survival depends on tending to their own fields; women are forced back to work very quickly after childbirth; the serfs, men and women, are physically beaten; the men are constantly under threat of being conscripted into the army (and thus separated from their families); and they are even subject to petty thievery by the "master" and his underlings. The opening chapters of Nechui's novel show Dzheria's attempts to defend the very limited rights that serfs do have, thus provoking Bzhozovs'kyi's rage and setting in motion the sequence of events that the novel presents. In his portrayal of the evils of serfdom Nechui is not very different from previous writers who wrote on this subject, particularly Marko Vovchok. Serfdom in the Russian Empire was almost equivalent to slavery, and its obvious injustices lend themselves to melodramatic depictions of suffering. The first two chapters of *Mykola Dzheria* follow such a pattern. What distinguishes Nechui's approach is the focus on rebellion, on a struggle to defend human dignity and personal rights in a barbaric environment. Mykola's struggle soon takes him beyond his village and thus outside the bounds of traditional serfdom in the Russian Empire.

As in *Burlachka,* so in *Mykola Dzheria* Nechui depicts industrial settings where the escaped serfs find employment. Specifically, he sketches two sugar refineries. The first, in Stebliv, is in a beautiful rural setting, with the neat, cheerful homes of the German director and engineers in a meadow at some distance from the industrial works. The second, in Cherkasy, resembles a fortress: it is surrounded by a moat and a wall with sentries and there's a factory with a very urban topography inside the gates. This second site gets considerably more attention in the novel. As in *Burlachka,* the leaseholder in *Mykola Dzheria* is a Jew, Abram Moiseievych Brodovs'kyi – a man Nechui paints with very broad brushstrokes as a stereotypical Eastern European aspiring industrial baron. From his name (Abram Moiseievych = Abraham, son of Moses) to his corpulent figure attired in a dirty black velvet vest with a gold chain and trinkets hung across his chest, Abram is nothing if not the caricatured image of a Jewish industrial manager. Robber barons of industrial capitalism should be pleased to be so exquisitely lampooned. But this caricature focuses on the fact that the character is Jewish. The images of Brodovs'kyi can also be interpreted from the perspective of anti-Semitic propaganda. Social satire is always a dangerous device, because it reveals as much about its author and audience as it does about its victim. Here again, Nechui's realism makes him an extraordinarily useful mirror of the social and cultural situation in Ukraine in the second half of the nineteenth century.

The satiric portrait of the industrial enterprise in *Mykola Dzheria,* as earlier in *Burlachka,* includes an indictment of commerce, seen as a Jewish conspiracy. Abram Brodovs'kyi borrowed the money to buy his leasehold from a rich colleague in Lebedyn named Shmul' (Shmuel) Kaplun. The loan was conditional. For the duration of the loan, Kaplun was to feed the workers in the factory at a fixed price (3:83). It was in Kaplun's interest to reduce costs, so when a stock of rotten fish went begging for a buyer, the workers in Brodovs'kyi's factory suffered the consequences. Once again, Nechui presents the world of commercial contracts as a conspiracy to exploit the working man. In this instance, however, there is no specifically Jewish subtext to the exploitation beyond the identity of the exploiters. What's more, Nechui allows Brodovs'kyi if not dignity, then at least a modicum of respect. When the Verbivka serfs arrive at his factory looking for employment, Nechui describes their instinctive disrespect for the Jewish manager. Nechui shows this in Mykola's first conversation with the leaseholder manager who will be his boss and on whom his employment depends:

> – Ми хочемо стать на роботу в сахарні, – обізвався Микола згорда.
>
> – Ну, коли хочете, то ставайте, – сказав Бродовський.
>
> – А хіба ти приймаєш тут на роботу? – спитав Микола якось з осміхом і гордо.
>
> Бродовський зобидився. Всі робітники осміхнулись.
>
> – Коли хочеш ставать на роботу в мене, то не тикай на мене! Ну, що це таке з цими мужиками! Я тут хазяїн, хіба ти не знаєш, чи що?
>
> – Авжеж не знаю! Хто тебе знає, що ти таке, – сказав Микола якось сердито, як звичайно селяни говорять. (3:79)
>
> ["We're looking to get jobs here," Mykola said arrogantly.
>
> "Well, if you want, then you can go to work," Brodovsky said.
>
> "Do you mean you do the hiring here?" Mykola said with a disdainful grin.
>
> Brodovsky took offence. All the workers smiled.
>
> "If you want to work for me, you should at least try to speak to me properly [i.e., don't use the familiar "thou" form with me]. What's the matter with these peasants! I'm the boss here, don't you know?"
>
> "Well, I didn't! Who knows what you are around here," Mykola snapped roughly, the way peasants usually speak.][11]

Nechui uses this passage to underscore the manager's pretensions – he wants to have the same respect the peasants would normally show to their landholder, the "master." But the use of the second person singular in addressing a complete stranger is not customary. Mykola's use of this form is clearly tied to the fact that the leaseholder is a Jew whom Mykola and the other men hold in contempt. Mykola uses the polite form when he asks for work from the fisherman Kovbanenko, who is not Jewish (3:96). Such disrespect for Jews may have been common among Ukrainian peasants in the nineteenth century, but Nechui understands that it is deliberately disrespectful. He puts both qualities – pretentiousness and disrespect – in play again a few paragraphs later, when Mykola addresses Brodovs'kyi's wife as churlishly as he did her husband (3:82). A bedraggled and desperate escaped serf who deliberately insults his employer's wife is hardly a great champion of social justice, even if her reaction is pretentious and uncharitable. Nechui is not advocating deference to Jewish industrial exploiters and their wives, but he is systematically accenting his protagonist's belligerent character.

Mykola's irascibility is highlighted by a number of incidents in the novel. While still in Verbivka, he responds angrily to various injustices despite his father's warnings about the consequences. On the evening that the Verbivka men run away, Bzhozovs'kyi's fields go up in flames. Nechui does not explain who set the fire, but there is an implication that it may have been Mykola. Kavun says that the arsonist will be revealed by his soul flying above the flames, and Nymydora imagines seeing Mykola burning and rising to the heavens through the flames (3:68–9). In chapter 3, the midnight beating Mykola and the other Verbivka men inflict on Bzhozovs'kyi and his administrator at the inn near the sugar refinery may be an act of justified vengeance, but it is motivated by anger without good sense. Even later in Bessarabia, where he lives relatively well and is given greater responsibilities, Mykola flies into a violent rage and all but kills Kovbanenko when the latter divides their earnings unfairly. This episode, which some commentators cite to show that Nechui also depicted Ukrainians as exploiters, not just Jews and Poles, is mostly an illustration of Mykola's temper, not Kovbanenko's crooked dealings. This is the only instance of Kovbanenko cheating his workers. He has otherwise treated his workers well. Mykola's anger eventually subsides. Although at first he walks out and joins a different crew of fishermen, a year later, after Kovbanenko apologizes and makes amends, Mykola rejoins his former employer and continues to work for him right up to his arrest.

For Nechui, Mykola's character is a combination of pride and irritability. He clearly admires his protagonist's courage in standing up to injustice and exploitation. But, at the same time, Nechui is somewhat fatalistic about these social problems, and he certainly doesn't feel that Mykola's angry rebellions do him any good. The final chapter of the novel is most telling in this regard. Although serfdom has been abolished, there are still many injustices facing the villagers. The former "master" is still in a position of authority and abuses it, as do the Jewish tavern-owners, the elected village officials, and the priest. Mykola leads his fellow villagers in forcing Bzhozovs'kyi to pay better wages, securing a more just distribution of land, removing corrupt officials, and driving the Jews out of the village. But he himself is no happier or better off for these efforts. The final image of the novel, old Dzheria among his beehives telling stories of big fish and faraway places to his grandchildren, is deliberately ambiguous. The simple pleasures he finally enjoys come at a very high price. Like the bees that buzz around him, he is but a small player in his social setting, and the injustices of the society he lives in are not easily undone.

Nechui's early works, examined above, contain the bulk of his social commentary. In later years, Nechui's attention was less often, or at least less directly, focused on socio-economic problems. In these later works social ills are still quite prominent, but they are presented in a general context among many other factors, both good and bad, that affect his characters. Over the course of his career, Nechui moved away from broad attacks on large socio-economic problems towards a narrower depiction of the foibles, vices, and crimes of specific individuals. In his earlier works Nechui had also personified social ills in specific characters, but the wicked and evil characters in his later works will more often represent personal qualities such as corruption, greed, venality, or stupidity than the institutional social ills depicted in his earlier works. This is not to say that social ills disappear from his works; they merely become part of a general background. In line with this widening perspective, the dimensions of social problems also expand. In addition to such ills as serfdom, military service, and the commercial and industrial exploitation of workers, Nechui also exposes a variety of issues tied to specific social orders or institutions. Foremost among these is the Orthodox Church.

As the son of a clergyman and the product of a religious education from elementary school to theological academy, Nechui had a very good understanding of the function and dysfunction of the Orthodox Church in Ukraine in the nineteenth century. In the Soviet era, as noted above,[12] many critics wrongly described him as anticlerical. Nechui was certainly no champion of the Orthodox Church. In Ukraine it was an agent of Russification, and as such it shall be examined below along with similar institutions. But Nechui was not particularly hostile to religion *per se*, nor was he ill disposed to the clergy as a whole. He had a rationalist's modern view of religion. He found much hypocrisy and many human failings among the people who represented religion – the clergy, monks, and the higher orders of the Orthodox Church. But he was certainly no atheist, and he did not portray any characters who were. He understood that Christianity and the Orthodox Church had a mixed history that did not always live up to institutional ideals,[13] but he also understood that religion was a basic element of Ukrainian culture, particularly among the Ukrainian peasants. The fact that he agreed to complete the translation of the Bible begun by Panteleimon Kulish indicates clearly that he had a very high opinion of the importance of Christianity. But respect for Christianity does not automatically entail respect for the clergy. If anticlericalism is understood as opposition to the role of organized religion in society, Nechui was not anticlerical. But if it is defined as a view that challenges and exposes the many problems of the Church, particularly the ineffectual, undereducated, vice-ridden, venal, and foolish clergy, then Nechui certainly fits the bill.

He took great relish in poking fun at the confused religiosity of many simple peasants, who had very little understanding of the difference between pagan superstitions and Christian faith. He also enjoyed sketching portraits of clergymen with all of their human foibles. In some cases these foibles are merely the weaknesses that all men are subject to, but in other cases he savagely satirizes the greed, gluttony, and sloth that he so often finds among the members, particularly the higher ranks, of religious orders. On a lower social level, Nechui's fictional village clergymen are as likely to be good-hearted, friendly fellows as they are to be drunkards and hen-pecked husbands. Others have more serious faults. Some are greedy and take advantage of their flock. Such is the case in *Mykola Dzheria*, in which Mykola's father must negotiate the fee for his son's marriage with a young priest who has already doubled the previous rates. Although Nechui does not minimize the hardship such behaviour brings to Ukrainian peasants, the way he describes old Dzheria's ritualistic bargaining with the priest emphasizes an age-old cultural stereotype rather than an opportunistic exploitation. Like death and taxes, the inflationary spiral in pastoral services is met stoically, with a bottle of vodka, a loaf of bread, and some hard bargaining. After all, when Dzheria tells the priest that he really can't afford the five *karbovantsi* and further adds that his original offer, four *karbovantsi*, was the rate that "God Himself had willed," the young priest concedes and they drink to seal the deal at four (3:49). And it is this same priest who tells old Dzheria to stop fasting during Lent when the old man weakens and is close to dying. It is the old man who refuses and keeps to the religious rules, despite the priest's friendly advice. After his father's death, Mykola's mother urges him to make a pilgrimage to Kyiv to pray for better fortune. Mykola refuses, telling his mother "Коли є той бог на світі, то він бог панський, а не мужицький" (3:59) [If there is a God in this world, he is the God of aristocrats, not peasants], a sentiment that echoes Shevchenko. When Mykola returns to his village twenty years later, Nechui once again mentions that there was a new young priest who had raised the rates (3:140). Nevertheless, Mykola does not abandon religion, and at the close of his life he sometimes prays in his apiary, kneeling to face the rising sun (3:140).

Religion has both good and bad features for Nechui, but it is not among the root causes of the injustice the peasants suffer. It is the individuals in religious orders and the hierarchical structure of the church that causes problems, not the faith itself. As Mykola's outburst indicates, the problem is that religion offers no help or remedy for social injustice. The likelihood that religious institutions or individuals were implicated in social problems was directly proportional to their social status and the personal desire for social advancement. Some social problems surround religious institutions but are not an essential component of religion or the religious establishment. In *Kyivs'ki prokhachi* Nechui examines the world of professional mendicants, whom he portrays as cynical and corrupt individuals who live in relative comfort but put on rags and a destitute appearance to elicit compassion from the hordes of religious tourists and pilgrims visiting Kyiv. The begging is tied to religious shrines, specifically the Pechers'ka Lavra (Monastery of the Caves) and the Mykhailivs'kyi (St Michael's) church and monastery, two of the most important tourist destinations for religious pilgrims in Kyiv. But there is no formal connection between the church and these beggars. Some churchmen give them alms, others do not. It's the beggars, among whom there are drunk soldiers and officers, bankrupt aristocrats, bureaucrats looking to improve their income, and an assortment of cheats and lazy bums – besides some real cripples and social outcasts – whom Nechui sees as miscreants. They feign poverty, disability, and distress while bullying or literally fighting each other for prime locations and denouncing the wealthier passers-by as heartless, callous wretches. Of course, the mere fact that Nechui wrote such a story reveals something about his conservative social views. While he was certainly a defender of the downtrodden peasant, his empathy for the suffering of the lower classes was not absolute.

Another work, *Afons'kyi proidysvit*, tells the story of a cunning cozener who enters a monastery in order to bilk the rich monks out of their money. The monks are portrayed as fools and hypocrites, vain men who seek a comfortable life and their own advancement, materially and socially. The flimflam man, purportedly a Greek named Kopronidos (or is it really Kipra, as he told his landlady?), plays on the vanity, greed, stupidity, and self-indulgence of the monks to con them into loaning him money at the incredible rate of 50 per cent interest per anum. Once the money is in his hands, the swindler refuses to make the interest payments or return the capital, brazenly telling them that monks are forbidden to engage in moneylending and that a scandal would do them even greater harm than the financial loss they have suffered. Only in the case of Monk Tarasii, a powerfully built dandy and former soldier whom he had won over with the help of a woman of loose morals, does Kopronidos actually take steps to protect himself, and finally he flees Kyiv with the money, leaving the monks to quietly lick their financial wounds.

Yet another example of Nechui's negative portrayal of Orthodox religious institutions occurs in the novel *Khmary,* in which the Kyiv Theological Academy, the school where Nechui himself studied, is ridiculed as anything but a serious educational organization. Nechui was critical of most schooling in the Russian Empire (although the universities are outside his field of vision), and his views of the Kyiv Academy fit in with his general argument about the state's failure to provide modern, purposeful, effective, and goal-oriented schooling for its citizens. The academy was indeed an old-fashioned religious school at that time, and Nechui does not hesitate to editorialize on this topic in the first chapter of the novel:

> Київська академія того часу стояла дуже низько і не давала нічого для мислі … Академія зосталася дуже позаду од свого часу: в ній панувала схоластика, од котрої висихала всяка мисль в головах студентів. Світські науки були закутані в дух теології. Тільки одна філософія стояла усе дуже добре. Академія випускала тоді в семінарії професорів, котрі були темні, як темна ніч, і нічому не вчили, бо й самі нічого не тямили – тільки з горя горілку пили. Од темноти, од п'янства, од бідності вони сходили з ума, дуріли, бігали по вулицях в одних сорочках, тонули темної ночі де-небудь в калюжах, у канавах. (2:13–14)

> [At that time the Kyiv Academy was academically very weak and gave nothing for the mind … The academy was very far behind the times and still governed by scholasticism, which dried up any thinking in the minds of the students. Lay subjects were embalmed in the spirit of theology. Only philosophy was on solid ground. The academy graduated professors for the seminaries, who were as benighted as the darkest night and could not teach anyone anything because they did not understand anything themselves. In despair they could only turn to drink. From their benighted state, their drinking, and their poverty, they lost their minds, went crazy, and ran around the streets half-dressed, wallowing at night in puddles and sewers.]

His scathing appraisal of the academy (matched by a similar assessment in his memoirs) is augmented by one of the best-known scenes from this novel, an excerpt Nechui himself published separately in Lviv's *Pravda* (the full text of the novel first appeared in Kyiv) under the title "Ekzamen" (Examination). It is the final public exam for the students and is held in the presence of the Kyiv metropolitan (archbishop). When Vozdvyzhens'kyi gets confused in his answer to a question about Hegel, the metropolitan reassures him that Hegel was an idiot.

Later in the same scene, the rector of the academy asks for the text to follow a student's recitation in Greek, but he can't make out the words because, it turns out, he is holding the book upside down. According to Nechui, the religious authorities who control the Orthodox schools are poorly educated fools, and the quality of the education reflects their incompetence. But this is not a blanket indictment of religion or even religious education. Nechui's narrator observes that the portrait of Feofan Prokopovych, one of the academy's great scholars from the past and a major figure in Orthodox reforms in the eighteenth century, seemed to be laughing at the proceedings, while in his portrait the school's founder, Metropolitan Petro Mohyla, was sternly worried. The failures of education are the result of modern carelessness and the abandonment of the old, traditional principles of what had once been the leading educational institution in Orthodox Europe.

The idea of diminishing standards coupled with a nostalgic view of the past often informs Nechui's views of modernity. This is also true of his depiction of the country clergy, about whom he wrote two novels, *Starosvits'ki batiushky ta matushky* and *Pomizh vorohamy*. The first of these is an expansive panorama of the way things were for village clergymen in Ukraine during the times of Nechui's grandfather and father. It focuses on two clergymen and their families, Kharytin Petrovych Mossakovs'kyi and Marko Pavlovych Balabukha. It opens in the 1820s with their competition for the same girl (a clergyman's daughter) and the same parish (formerly held by Mossakovs'kyi's father). Although Balabukha studied (but did not finish) at the Theological Academy, he loses both the girl and the parish and ends up marrying a different girl, one with aristocratic pretensions, and receives a parish in town and the position of archpriest, with supervisory authority over Mossakovs'kyi's parish. The novel follows the two into old age and Mossakovs'kyi's death. The more successful and ambitious Balabukha is a most unhappy man, whose wife manipulates him, spoils his daughters, spends his income, and cheats on him. Mossakovs'kyi, a simpler, friendlier, and easy-going man, is happier, mostly because he is closer in spirit and culture to the peasant parishioners who elected him as their pastor, although he, too, is blessed with a commandeering and materialistic wife. None of the clergymen depicted in the novel is a truly virtuous man. They are all schemers who do what they can and must to pursue their goals, please their wives, marry off their children, and generally keep body and home in order. They are not spiritual men in any particular sense; they are merely individuals who perform religious functions, whether directly for the laity or in a higher church office. It is in their resemblance and proximity to their parishioners that Nechui sees positive qualities in these men.

This point is driven home by the visit of the bishop to the aging Mossakovs'kyi's parish. The arrogant bishop, who cannot even understand Ukrainian very well, browbeats the old priest, calling him an uneducated dope and a village simpleton in front of the assembled parishioners (4:256). The very notion of a priest chosen by his parishioners displeases the bishop, who exemplifies the new face of the Orthodox Church in Russia in the second half of the nineteenth century. The bishop turns down the priest's invitation and has his dinner with the local Polish magnate. The already sickly Mossakovs'kyi is so frightened and overwrought by the bishop's visit and unkind words that he falls ill and dies. To avoid losing the roof over her own and her daughter's heads, Mossakovs'kyi's widow convinces the metropolitan to assign the parish to her daughters by claiming that the bishop's behaviour killed her husband. The materialistic and domineering widow gets to keep control over the household, provoking a whole new round of conflicts between her and her son-in-law. The new era in church appointments, replacing the custom of locally elected clergy and favouring educated men who no longer feel any social bond to the parishioners, is depicted in Nechui's novel as a step away from effective and humane religious care for Ukrainian peasants. What Nechui depicts in his novel is the disappearing world of simple peasant priests that characterized Ukrainian Orthodoxy in the first half of the nineteenth century. Because his yardstick is the culture of the Ukrainian village, the new clergy are a failure. But the old clergy weren't very religious either. Their chief virtues (and their chief vices as well) were tied to their simple humanity. The markers of this humanity were just two: they liked people and they enjoyed life.

Nechui sketched many scenes in his various works that show good-natured clergymen enjoying themselves. In *Starosvits'ki batiushky ta matushky*, father Mel'khyzedek, whom we discussed in the previous chapter, is a prime example. His antics lead to a commotion that results in a pillow fight. "Дурієш, як малий хлопець" (4:165) [You're going nuts, like a little boy], says one of the older priests, throwing a pillow at Mel'khyzedek. This may not be the dignified behaviour serious and pious Christians expect from a clergyman, but it is not evil or immoral either. In Nechui's time, Orthodox religious censors in Russia did not allow the publication of anything that portrayed the clergy in a bad light, and he often had trouble with specific passages, including parts of this novel. Nechui even allows faults to appear as positive characteristics, as in the scenes of clergymen drinking to excess.

Although Nechui apparently did not drink himself, the very frequent use of alcohol by his various characters is not necessarily meant as a grievous fault of the individuals involved. In general, Nechui tends to excuse human peccadilloes when they derive from goodwill and fellowship with others. What he does not excuse is arrogance, pride, and ill will. When the 1847 reforms of serfdom known as "inventories" are decreed, obligating serfs to perform feudal obligations not only to the landlord but to the parish priest as well, Kharytin Mossakovs'kyi is genuinely embarrassed and confused before his parishioners (4:234). In the uprising that follows these "reforms," he and his wife hide the leaders of the uprising from the soldiers sent in to pacify the village.

No such camaraderie is to be found in *Pomizh vorohamy*, the second novel Nechui wrote about the life of the clergy. The title itself carries the message. Artemii Kremnyts'kyi and his wife Susana are far removed from any direct relations with peasants and they can't abide the village elders either, particularly the secretary and his wife. But their arrogance is in conflict with their material interests, since the only hope for marrying off their daughter is the secretary's brother-in-law. The mercenary self-interest of all concerned shows a very different breed of clergy than what had obtained in the earlier novel. Where the old-world Mossakovs'kyi's parishioners had helped him willingly (4:151–2), Kremnyts'kyi must fool his parishioners into working for the church by setting out large bottles of water and pretending they are full of vodka (6:298–9).

Nechui knew the life of the Ukrainian Orthodox clergy very well and depicted it often. Most characters in his works are depicted in a humorous, satirical context, with their faults generally more prominent than their virtues. Priests and religious leaders are not an exception, so the clergy as a whole, whether judged by the standards of Soviet Marxism's holier-than-thou atheism or twenty-first-century evangelical zealotry, seem to be regarded in terms that are universally negative. But Nechui measures all his characters by human, not religious or ideological, standards. Yet even here there are caveats. Nechui allows for some doubt even in the one area of religious life where his judgments seemed clearly formulated – his favourable view of the less pretentious and less educated old clergy that had been elected by their parishioners in relation to the more educated new clergy with their pretensions to aristocratic status. Education is not a vice, except that it drives a wedge between the parishioners and their clergy on both a social and a national level. The old-world priests, and particularly their wives, had dreams of social advancement too, but they were culturally and nationally in sync with their flock. Nechui condemns education and social advancement when they lead to denationalization and an abandonment of cultural traditions. This view applies to the laity as much as to the clergy.

In his novel *Neodnakovymy stezhkamy*, Nechui depicts the family of a Ukrainian aristocrat, a landowner whose wife and children insist on living beyond their means. It is a familiar plot line among Nechui's works, where lesser aristocratic families frequently end up bankrupt because of their pretensions to a lifestyle beyond their means. The novel is structured around a series of character juxtapositions. The friendly and industrious old-world landowner, Andrian Kyrylovych Hukovych, will eventually lose his property to a bank foreclosure. Yes, Nechui does see him as an ineffectual man, a penny-pinching bumbler unable to control the foolish spending of his wife and daughter, but he also emphasizes that Hukovych has his feet firmly planted, both socially and culturally, in the land he lives on. This old-world landowner is the last Mohican of a traditional rural agricultural society, the lay equivalent of Father Mossakovs'kyi. Across the Dnipro from Hukovych is the director of prisons in the Kyiv gubernia, a local bureaucrat's son who advanced his career by moving to the capital and has now returned with high office and an even higher notion of his own worth. This Elpidyfor Petrovych Vanatovych (his given name means "hopeful" in Greek) is a callous and narcissistic wastrel who will not stoop to speak with his spouse's lifelong friends, but takes bribes and physically beats his subordinates at the prison administration. It is precisely in these cases, where social inequality leads to the abuse of power and cruelty to socially subordinate individuals, that Nechui is most anxious to defend Ukraine against the dangers of social injustice. These dangers can be found in the commercial, administrative, and religious spheres, but their seriousness pales in comparison to what Nechui considers the greatest peril facing Ukraine: denationalization.

National Identity

Beyond any doubt, the national question is at the heart of Nechui's lifelong activity as a writer. Nechui was not merely a writer who wished to depict his beloved Ukraine: he was an activist whose purpose was to protect Ukrainian culture from the dangers it faced and indeed, despite these dangers and obstacles, to advance Ukrainian cultural development. Of course, the national question and the promotion of Ukrainian culture meant different things to different people. For Nechui, two elements were central: the great mass of the Ukrainian nation, who were peasants, and the language. Although Nechui was not a theorist or scholar and thus was not inclined to provide very clear formulations of his views, his ideas on the national question are not only reflected in his fictional works but are also discussed directly in his essays and, to a lesser degree, in his correspondence. The most important statements of his views on the centrality of Ukrainian identity and culture for Ukrainians are in two of his essays: "Nepotribnist' velykorus'koi literatury dlia Ukrainy i dlia slovianshchyny" and "Ukrainstvo na literaturnykh pozvakh z Moskovshchynoiu."

The first of these essays was, as we have seen above,[14] a long-winded emotional response to the Ems Ukaz. Nechui's general argument in the essay is a simple one. The literature of Russia and the literature of Ukraine are not and cannot be identical. Before the seventeenth century, a congruence was possible because in that period all literature was in a foreign language (that is, in Old Church Slavonic, or, as Nechui calls it, Bulgarian) and it was the exclusive domain of an elite social class. From the sixteenth century onward, the situation changed and the two nations no longer completely shared one literature. The change, argues Nechui, culminates in the nineteenth century, in the present, as a new literary "school" develops. Three principles characterize the new literature: realism, *natsional'nist'* (national character or, in North American usage, ethnicity), and *narodnist'* (the quality of being of the common people, the opposite of elitism). Using these three principles as a measure, Nechui shows that Ukrainian and Russian literature are not only different, but that modern Ukrainian literature, which adopted all three principles from the very start, does not benefit from the presence or the example of Russian literature for two reasons: (1) Russian literature is slow in adopting the third principle, *narodnist'*, and (2) it reflects Russian instead of Ukrainian *natsional'nist'*. Most of the essay is devoted to detailed examples of these two points. Much of the essay, particularly its second part, deals with Russian rather than Ukrainian literature. Nechui examines a number of Russian writers, among them Tolstoy, Goncharov, Gogol, Uspenskii, Turgenev, and others. In every case he shows that the characters, the setting, the style, and every other quality of these works is quintessentially Russian, not Ukrainian.

From a twenty-first-century perspective, Nechui's argument amounts to a tautology. Russian literature is not suitable for Ukrainians, because it is Russian rather than Ukrainian. But in arguing that Russians, their literature, and their culture are distinct and separate from Ukrainians and their literature and culture, Nechui embellishes his presentation with some gems of Russophobia. For example, "Недостача елеґантности, естетичности, фантазії й глибокого серця зразу дає впізнати великоруські поетичні твори" [Insufficiencies of elegance, aesthetic taste, inventiveness, and sympathetic feeling immediately allow one to identify Russian poetic works].[15] After quoting a Russian song in which "великоруська дівчина малює собі мрію про свій ідеал, про кохання парубка, котрий подививсь на неї по-звіриному так, що в неї одежа попоролась, розтопилось золото й намисто й перли потріскались" [a Russian girl imagines a dream about her ideal – the love of a young man who gazes at her with such an animal-like look that her clothes split at the seams, her gold jewellery melts, and her necklace and pearls break],[16] he offers this analysis:

> Нічого похожого на такий великоруський деспотизм в поезії не можна знайти в українських піснях, бо вони вилились з інших народних психічних основ. В великоруській сім'ї панує деспотизм батька над цілою сім'єю, над жінкою, над дітьми, і натурально, що той деспотизм виявляється і в піснях, де тільки виступають на сцену стосунки чоловіка до жінки.[17]

> [Nothing similar to this Russian despotism in poetry can be found in Ukrainian songs, because they flow from different national psychic foundations. In the Russian family there reigns a despotism of the father over the whole family, over the wife, over the children, and it is natural that this despotism manifests itself also in songs, wherever the relationship of men to women appears on stage. In the composition of the Ukrainian and Belorussian family there is no such despotism, and therefore it does not appear in poetry when the subject is the relationship of a boy to a girl or a man to a woman.]

In cataloguing the perversities of Russian national character, Nechui's examples can be seen as deliberately insulting, but he is merely following in the footsteps of a respected historian, Mykola Kostomarov. In the essay "Dve russkija narodnosti," published in *Osnova* in 1861, Kostomarov makes both of the arguments cited from Nechui above: the less-than-idealized presentation of young Russian women in folk songs, and the pervasive despotism (Kostomarov uses the same word) of Russian fathers within their extended families. Like Kostomarov, Nechui sees distinctions between Russian and Ukrainian identities, but, unlike the historian, he does not see them in a hierarchical relationship to each other. For Nechui, Ukrainian culture is simply a different culture from Russian – separate but equal. It is the culture of a different nation and thus has the same right to exist and develop as any other culture. It is not a provincial variant or a minor subset of some other culture. This argument is made even more explicitly in the second essay, which also relies heavily on Kostomarov, by challenging a Russian review of a history of Ukrainian literature.

This essay, marking Nechui's second attempt at defining his views on national culture, is an extended critique of a review by Aleksandr Pypin of Omelian Ohonovs'kyi's *Istoriia literatury ruskoi* (History of Rus'ian literature). Ohonovs'kyi was professor of Ukrainian literature at Lviv University and an outspoken champion of Ukrainian cultural distinctiveness. Aleksandr Nikolaevich Pypin was a noted Russian scholar, author of a history of Russian literature, cousin of Nikolai Chernyshevskii, and an advocate of moderate, liberal views. His review of Ohonovs'kyi's *History* appeared in *Vestnik Evropy* (Herald of Europe) in the September issue of 1890. Nechui's response, under the militant title "Ukrainstvo na literaturnykh pozvakh z Moskovshchynoiu" (Ukrainianness in a literary duel with Muscovy), appeared in the Lviv journal *Dilo* in 1891.

In the spectrum of Russian political opinion, Aleksandr Pypin, who wrote on Shevchenko's poetry and Ukrainian folklore and was a member of the Shevchenko Scientific Society, was hardly an enemy of Ukrainian national aspirations. Nechui was well aware of this.[18] Pypin's review of Ohonovs'kyi's history is certainly not completely one-sided criticism – he does see some virtues in the work. But Nechui takes Pypin to task for his suggestion that Ukrainian literature is essentially provincial and not entirely separate from Russian literature. Nechui's essay is poorly organized in six sections. In the first section he supports the unity of Ukrainian cultural identity. Pypin had argued that western Ukraine, where Ohonovs'kyi's history was published and whose peculiarities it reflected, cannot represent a general Ukrainian culture: it cannot be held up as a model by an advocate for Ukrainian culture because it has had a separate and different historical and cultural development than the part of Ukraine that is in the Russian Empire. Nechui's response is to explain that under conditions of extraordinary repressions against the Ukrainian language in Russia, western Ukraine has acquired this role by default. Furthermore, western Ukraine is no provincial backwater, cut off from a knowledge of developments in the Slavic, particularly Russian, cultural world. It is the Russian provinces that are cultural backwaters, argues Nechui, not Ukraine; and he uses a breakdown by province for subscriptions to *Vestnik Evropy* to show that Ukraine is more familiar with developments in Russian culture and scholarship than are other areas of Russia.

In the second section of his essay, Nechui turns to the origin of the name *Rus'*. Pypin had charged that Ohonovs'kyi's claim regarding the Ukrainian origin of this name was lifted from the Polish historian Franciszek Duchiński,[19] regarded by Pypin and others as something of a racist, rather than from Kostomarov, as Ohonovs'kyi had claimed. Nechui demonstrates that Kostomarov, particularly in his essay "Dve russkiia narodnosti," did in fact make very similar claims to what Ohonovs'kyi is advancing.

The third section focuses on the historical development of the Ukrainian language. Ohonovs'kyi, arguing against the notion that Ukrainian can be compared to Low German, compares the development of Russian and Ukrainian to the parallel development of nations and languages in Western Europe. Pypin dismisses this comparison as unsuitable, since the European cultures in question did not derive from a single culture and state. Nechui argues for a historical separation of the Russian and Ukrainian languages from the earliest times, comparing the relation between them to that between French and Provençal.

In the fourth and fifth sections Nechui addresses Pypin's frequent reliance on the historical determinacy of a single Rus' state, which, argues Pypin, played a vital role in creating a unified culture and ethnicity among its Slavic inhabitants. Nechui counters by introducing Hippolyte Taine's ideas of the central importance of race, milieu, and moment in shaping cultural development, and by stressing the negative influence of state interference in culture, particularly in an imperial setting. The sixth and final section, the longest in the work, is devoted to Chinese culture. Nechui takes aim at the notion that Russian literature represents a separate historical cultural type, whereas Ukrainian literature does not. At great length, using commonplaces from the *Vseobshchaia istoriia literatury* (Universal history of literature) edited by

Valentin Korsh, Nechui highlights various qualities of Chinese literature and culture, concluding his analysis with the simple assertion that here, in Chinese literature, we see a distinct cultural type, while Russian literature does not offer such a clear and distinct pattern.

The essay is certainly not one of Nechui's finest literary products. As the description here shows, it rambles through what seem at times to be endless and pointless analogies to demonstrate minor points. In a general sense, it is an attempt to show that Slavophile conservative views have penetrated every level of Russian intellectual thought surrounding Ukrainian culture and national aspirations. On a practical level, however, it is an attempt to diminish the stature and significance of Russian culture and to enhance the appearance of Ukrainian culture. There is little of the negative stereotype that was evident in the earlier works, but the entire essay is driven by an animus towards Russia and an insistence that Pypin's views are exclusively the product of a chauvinist blindness and a mistaken judgment of the glory of Russia and its cultural achievements. Ohonovs'kyi's reputation and Ukraine's glory are defended and enhanced not in their own right, but by a diminution of the stature of Russia.

Nechui's views of Russian culture are neither logical nor systematic. The various symptoms of animus that can be found in his works cannot be easily categorized or explained with a ready formula. Furthermore, the hostility we have seen must be tempered with examples of his admiration. After all, Nechui spent half of his adult years as a teacher of Russian literature. He translated some of Saltykov-Shchedrin's stories into Ukrainian and he spoke favourably of many Russian writers. When Borys Hrinchenko, as an aspiring writer, turned to him for literary advice, Nechui advised him, among other things, to read Russian literature.[20] On the other hand, however, he is unusual among Ukrainian writers of his time for the clarity and frequency with which he shows his hostility to Russian culture. Furthermore, his hostility is not accompanied by a political agenda. The combination of anti-Russian sentiments with a specific Ukrainian political agenda is a historical development that has not yet taken place in Nechui's time.

Historically, Nechui's views need to be situated among the familiar currents in Ukrainian-Russian relations in the nineteenth century. Unlike his younger colleagues, for whom Ukrainian identity will become an explicitly political issue, Nechui still sees this as a cultural matter. His energies are focused on establishing the dignity and reputation of a distinct Ukrainian literature, culture, and nation. Among his younger contemporaries, these sentiments were either taken for granted or reformulated as specific proposals for political action, whether in the domain of education policy, lifting censorship rules, or allowing for local autonomy. Nechui, very pointedly, does not formulate any political demands in his essays. At the same time, Nechui is no longer searching for a formula that will accommodate Ukrainian identity within some larger framework. Despite his enthusiasm for the works of Kostomarov, Nechui does not embrace – indeed he never even mentions – Kostomarov's view of Ukrainian identity as a harmoniously reconcilable subset of a larger Russian nationality. Nechui's position is in a narrow chronological space between those for whom identity was still ambiguous and those for whom it was an overtly political issue.

With an allowance for the complexities of expressing such ideas in a work of fiction, Nechui's belletristic works generally exemplify the ideas he voiced in his culturological essays, but with one important exception. Nechui hardly ever writes about Russians. The energy he devoted in his essays to examining Russian literature and culture is simply absent in his fiction. There are hardly any Russians, there is no geographical Russia, and there are barely any allusions to Russian culture. A passionate hostility to Russian culture is nowhere to be found in his fiction. There are plenty of references to the destructive role of Russian education, Russian bureaucratic restrictions on Ukrainian culture, and the Russian language, but these are almost always abstractions and offstage developments. Nechui's anti-Russian sentiment is expressed by ignoring Russia. What makes this absence even more curious is that he treats Polish national identity differently.

Even the few Russians who do appear in Nechui's works are not treated equally. In the novel *Na gastroliakh v Mykytianakh*, Sofiia Leonivna, the wife of the opera singer Flehont Petrovych Litoshevs'kyi, is a Russian from St Petersburg. She ends up betraying her husband in an affair with a university student named Narkys (Narcissus), but Nechui does not tie her faults to her nationality. Indeed, she is shown to be receptive to Ukrainian culture. She actually learns the language and reads Ukrainian books (8:13)! That's a very strong commendation from Nechui, for whom the Ukrainian language and Ukrainian literature were the chief abiding values that outweighed all others. In the novel she is held up as a paragon of liberal democratic values and national tolerance. It's her servants and her husband who earn Nechui's scorn. The entire novel is structured as a moral lesson in what happens when individuals try to rise above their social class and nationality. Flehont Petrovych is a Ukrainian who has risen to high social station as a successful opera singer. He has married a sophisticated urban Russian girl who symbolizes the abandonment of his social and national roots. When this worldly couple decide to spend a summer in the country at the home of Flehont's brother, a village priest in Mykytiany, all signs point to impending conflict. The country mice are apprehensive about the manners and tastes of their urban siblings. The city mice are enticed by a romanticized and sanitized image of life in the country. In a plot line parallel to the Flehont-Sofiia marriage, Nechui presents Leonid Semenovych Lahodzins'kyi, the brother of the village priest's wife. He too, like Flehont, married a Russian woman, a coddled beauty, as Nechui calls her, who relished her youth and beauty and conducted one affair after another, yet would not agree to a divorce from her husband. Lahodzins'kyi's life, says the narrator, was ruined by his aesthetic sense, by his inborn attraction to all that was beautiful (8:45). The urban, artistic lifestyle is inherently self-destructive because it invites epicurean self-indulgence. Both marriages disintegrate, both Ukrainian husbands suffer miserable consequences not because their wives are Russian but because they married women who do not share their values, who seek only to gratify their desires, whether these desires be carnal or aesthetic. Of course, by marking both women as Russians, Nechui emphasizes the difference in culture and values between husbands and wives. They do not share the same culture. But the implication that Russian women are unfaithful to their husbands because they are Russians is nowhere suggested in the text.

In *Na gastroliakh v Mykytianakh*, it is not nationality itself that makes Russian culture a destructive force – it is the urban excess and aristocratic pretensions associated with it. If she were not an unfaithful wife, Sofiia could be a very positive character. Not so Masha Dudarets'ka, her servant, cook, and nanny, Ukrainian urban snob from Kyiv who turns up her nose at everything from the village, which for her means everything Ukrainian. Flehont himself laughs at this ostentation and explains that these urban upstarts now call villagers *khokhlushky* and *khokhly* (top-knots), Russian derogatory terms for Ukrainians. His brother, no doubt speaking for the author, replies:

> – А як я вчився в школах, то тоді міщани й крамарі ще не дражнили такими прізвищами селян: певно, тоді й себе ще залічували до хохлів та хохлушок. Цікаво б знати, за кого ж то вони тепер мають самих себе, коли нехтують селян і навіть українську мову, мов справжні пани, – говорив о. Зіновій.
>
> – Мабуть, вже й міщани, і крамарі, і навіть самі куховарки й горничні, що недавнечко самі поскидали очіпки, і вважають на себе, як на панів, котрі не повинні ні в чому єднаться з мужиками, навіть у мові. (8:13)

["When I was a student, the city folk and merchants didn't yet call villagers such names. They probably even counted themselves among the *khokhly* and *khokhlushky*. I wonder what they now consider themselves, if they have such disrespect for villagers and even the Ukrainian language, as if they were genuine aristocrats," said Rev. Zinovii.

"The city folk and merchants, even the very cooks and chambermaids who only recently took off their own kerchiefs, now probably consider themselves real aristocrats who dare not share any similarities with the peasants, even in language."]

Masha is just such a social and national quisling. Unlike the actual Russian, Sofiia, who is friendly and speaks Ukrainian as best she can with her hosts, Masha scorns her fellow servants in the priest's home. She feels contempt for everything Ukrainian and everything in the village. She speaks to the village servants contemptuously and in broken Russian. Her first words on entering the kitchen are "Ой, какое ж тут у вас свинство в кухне!" (8:21) [What a pigsty you have in this kitchen!], a rare case of Nechui using Russian words in his works. Nechui even allows himself some of his favourite linguistic jokes, where Russian words are misunderstood by Ukrainians. When Masha complains that the kitchen in the village home has no wooden floor (пола нет), the cook interprets the Russian word for floor as the Ukrainian word for a type of bench (піл, gen. = пола) and contradicts her (8:22).

Masha is a minor character whom Nechui uses for comic relief, but she is also an emblematic example of Nechui's basic understanding of the national question. The desire for social advancement coupled with the perception that Ukrainian language and culture are inherently inferior produces a very dangerous situation for Ukrainian identity. In order to demonstrate their social advancement, Ukrainians themselves abandon their language and culture. They look down on their own culture and attempt to replace it with Russian culture, which they do not firmly command. It is a prescription for national suicide. Masha, the Ukrainian, disdains her own language and speaks in a Russian-Ukrainian *surzhyk*, while Sofiia, a Russian, treats Ukrainian with respect. It is not the fault of the Russians in this novel that Ukrainians are losing their national identity. It's the Ukrainians themselves who give it up. By extension this applies to the two cuckolded husbands as well. Had Flehont and Leonid not sought trophy brides for beauty or social standing but married women of their own cultural milieu, perhaps their marriages would not have disintegrated.

The most notorious Russian in Nechui's works is Stepan Ivanovych Vozdvyzhens'kyi, one of the foreign students at the Kyiv Theological Academy in the novel *Khmary* . He is the leader of a group of Russian seminarians travelling from Tula, a city 193 kilometres south of Moscow. Their first stop is to visit the metropolitan, also from Tula, whom we have already met as the examiner who is content to know that Hegel was a heretic. Struck by Vozdvyzhens'kyi's large, burly appearance, the metropolitan characterizes him thus: "Бравий хлопець! зовсім богатир Ілля Муромець!" (2:8) [A strapping lad! A regular bogatyr Illia Muromets!]. The comparison to this legendary knight of superhuman strength is decidedly double-edged. In size, strength, and distant origin, Vozdvyzhens'kyi is indeed similar to Muromets, but are size and strength the optimal qualities for a student at the Theological Academy? The novel is structured around a comparison of two of the academy's students, later professors, the Russian Vozdvyzhens'kyi and the Ukrainian Dashkovych. In this juxtaposition, the Russian is everything crude, rough, uncouth, and abrasive. He is somewhat dim-witted and lacks all social graces. He is boorish towards women, drinks in excess, and seeks material wealth and social position. But Nechui doesn't just construct Vozdvyzhens'kyi as a crude character, he defines him as a crude character because he is Russian. In the first chapter of the novel, where the arriving students settle in at the academy, all of the characters are defined by their nationality. The Bulgarian sits like a Turk. The Serb wears Turkish slippers and a fez. The Laplander is morose and silent. The Greek is lively and soon opens a tobacco shop. The Ukrainian is studious and spends his time writing. Everyone but the Laplander and the Russian is neat and clean. Vozdvyzhens'kyi's character is deemed "despotic." True to his basic understanding, Nechui sees everyone in national terms and their characters are defined by stereotypical national qualities (as we observed with Jews above). Vozdvyzhens'kyi thus embodies the negative qualities that Nechui associates with Russians. His success is attributable, at least in part, to the good graces of other Russians in Kyiv, such as the metropolitan, who naturally favour one of their own.

No matter how savagely Nechui caricatures Russian characters, it is not their mere presence that lies at the heart of Ukraine's national problem. Two other characters in *Khmary* illustrate this situation. The oldest daughters of Vozdvyzhens'kyi and Dashkovych are both enrolled at the "Institute blahorodnykh divyts'" (The institute for noble girls), the famous women's school in Kyiv, located on the hill diagonally across from what is today Independence Square, commonly called Maidan, the scene of recent political turmoil. In the novel the school is under the care of two aging sisters, daughters of the late Marquis de Pourverser, who moved from Provence to St. Petersburg, where he was received in high society. The older daughter married a German who was a general in the army and died young; afterwards the widow, Madame Turman, and her sister, Mademoiselle Pourverser, were installed in this school so that they might educate the young ladies of "Southern Russia." Nechui is merciless in satirizing the pretentious manners of these ladies, whose perverse function is to pour the poison of effete snobbery into the hearts of the young ladies entrusted to their care, and to insure that they acquire no practical modern skills. The girls they graduate become the carriers of that materialistic, pretentious Russian culture that Nechui sees as the greatest enemy of Ukrainian identity. They disdain everything that is Ukrainian, everything that would be familiar to the common man. When Ol'ha's suitor, Radiuk, declares his interest in the Ukrainian question and reads Shevchenko to her, their courtship is over. Radiuk's mother, also a product of the same kind of finishing schools, has similar views. But in Nechui's repertoire of characters, the Pourverser sisters are sooner the objects of pity and derision than incarnations of an evil menace. The real blame for the denationalization of the professors' daughters lies with their foolish, pretentious mothers and their careless fathers, not with the comic Franco-Russian peacocks.

As this example demonstrates, the dangers of Russian culture in Ukraine do not require the presence of Russians. The real culprits in the denationalization of Ukrainians are the Ukrainians themselves, particularly their negative assessment of their own culture. Ukrainians who aspire to the finer things in life – material comforts, wealth, education, employment, social status, fame – often believe that the first step towards their goals must necessarily be the abandonment of the Ukrainian language and identity. It's a problem that is very familiar in twentieth- and twenty-first- century Ukraine as well. The perception of Ukrainian as a lower-class provincial language and culture that are inherently and necessarily inferior to Russian has led to a massive abandonment of Ukrainian identity in Ukraine and continues to cause problems for cultural development in the country today. Indeed, the problem is not unique to Ukraine's modern history in the Russian Empire. Something similar obtained among Ukraine's nobility in relation to Polish Catholic culture in the sixteenth and seventeenth centuries. Most nineteenth-century Ukrainian writers express their dismay with this phenomenon in one way or another – including Shevchenko. But Nechui is unique for the frequency and clarity of his depiction of this issue, and for the central role it plays in his works and in his thinking.

The views Nechui held on this issue put him in a very complex predicament regarding a number of social problems faced by Ukrainians in the nineteenth century. Foremost among these was education, which was sorely neglected both in Ukraine and in the rest of the Russian Empire. A schoolteacher by profession, Nechui was certainly a strong advocate for wider and better education. But in his works education generally appears as a negative phenomenon, at least as far as national identity is concerned. The more education a character has experienced, the more likely that character is to abandon Ukrainian identity. Much the same is true of wealth and social advancement. Nechui's works are full of minor characters who have given up their Ukrainian identity as a result of education and advancement. Education is also tied to social class, a correlation that remains important in the minds of many characters, both high and low, in Nechui's works. Thus arises, in Nechui's world, the irreconcilable conflict between the desire to see the misery and poverty of the Ukrainian village eradicated and the fear that the forces that could effectuate such a change would inevitably lead to the denationalization of Ukraine. Education, social mobility, capital investment, and industrial development – these are the forces that could enlighten the village and sweep away the dark clouds covering the Ukrainian sky, but they are also the forces that systematically undermine the Ukrainianness of Ukraine, that dissolve the national identity of the nation. Unlike modern historians and theorists of national identity, Nechui does not see Ukrainian identity as a historical development of his own time. Ukrainian identity, for him, was not struggling to get established in the second half of the nineteenth century, it was a clearly established fact that needed protection from dangerous social forces. Since the forces that attacked it were, like education, socially desirable and historically inevitable, Nechui's unshakeable faith in the value of maintaining national identity leaves him only a slim and crumbling ideological foothold, looking backwards at a socially undesirable past with nostalgia for its traditional and nationally determined culture. The view in the opposite direction is almost invariably bleak. The future holds very little promise for Nechui.

A cultural transition of the kind that Nechui fears necessarily involves forces of both attraction and repulsion. The culture perceived to be superior has the attractive power of prestige, modernity, and popularity. The inferior culture, of course, repels by the mere perception of its inferiority. No one chooses the less desirable. In the case of Ukrainian culture in the late nineteenth century, this inferiority was tied to the peasantry and the village. These factors were understood both as a social class (the lowest) and as a cultural paradigm. The village was backward, dirty, physical, and traditional in its values, rather than modern, progressive, intellectual, sophisticated, industrial, or creative. In order to combat these perceptions, Nechui consistently chooses to highlight the false pretentiousness of the urban, its ignorance, its shallow and materialistic culture, and its shameful prejudice against anything Ukrainian. The rural, on the other hand, is poetic, authentic, and honest. But Nechui, as we have seen, is not a blinkered supporter of peasant backwardness. Thus his prescription for change characteristically lacks conviction. His heroes are few, and even these are ambiguous. He is much more effective satirizing urban hypocrisy than he is in advancing a prescription for the restoration of Ukrainian culture.

The best-known instance of this predicament occurs in *Khmary*, where the presumed hero of the work, Pavlo Antonovych Radiuk, tries and fails to make a dent in the acceptance of Ukrainian culture among the urban elites. Radiuk is a student at Kyiv University where the influence of European ideas (2:131) has sparked his interest in the common people, the *narod*, and particularly in their culture and language. In one of the most famous scenes in all of Nechui's works, Radiuk comes back to his parents' home after a year at the university wearing the embroidered finery of Ukrainian peasants. His parents, who expect the university to produce the opposite effect, are very surprised. His mother, who is a graduate of a girls' finishing institute not unlike the one attended by the professors' daughters in Kyiv, is horrified and tells him to take off the coarse outfit, which might even injure him (2:135).

Beyond wearing the national costume, speaking Ukrainian, and reading Ukrainian books, Radiuk does not really engage in any particularly meaningful activity on behalf of Ukrainian culture and language. He urges everyone to treat the Ukrainian peasants and their culture with respect, but aside from some planned but unrealized publications and short-lived Sunday schools to educate the masses, these good intentions are not channelled into an actual program of action. Radiuk dreams of great achievements in wiping away the dark clouds of national and social oppression in Ukraine (2:319–20), but he doesn't really do anything other than speak out on the need to do something.

This characteristic inertia on the part of Nechui's hero generated considerable criticism from the time of the novel's first publication onward. Drahomanov noted it in a review in *Kievsii telegraf*[21] and later called Radiuk "just a laughable idiot."[22] Konys'kyi published an extended essay analysing this phenomenon in *Pravda*.[23] Iefremov discusses it in his biography,[24] and in his introduction to the 1926 edition of Nechui's works Iurii Mezhenko observes: "Even the most active of Levyts'kyi's heroes does not go beyond passionate speeches and theoretical discussions."[25] In Soviet times, critics were quick to point out this quality, which they could ascribe to Nechui's presumed failure to understand Marxist principles of revolutionary activism.

There is certainly justice in criticizing the passivity of Nechui's national heroes. We can make such an assertion unequivocally because the first criticism came from Nechui himself, or, rather, one of his characters. Kyrylo Petrovych Kovan'ko is one of Radiuk's friends and a fellow university student. He is characteristically iconoclastic, making fun of everything and anything. He plays practical jokes and says irreverent things, no matter how politically incorrect. His values are not corrupted or skewed, he merely takes nothing seriously. Thus, Nechui can safely let Kovan'ko paint a satiric portrait of Radiuk. In a scene where they are competing to make a favourable impression on a young lady, Kovan'ko sarcastically tells the girl that Radiuk will force his feminist and nationalist ideas on her, make her get a job in an office, learn Ukrainian, speak it, and write poetry in it:

> Чи ви пак знаєте, що наші студенти тільки й думають, як вони житимуть в курінях на баштанах і як їх жінкиноситимуть їм обіди з дому, як вони будуть орать однією рукою, а другою книжку держать, а третьою писати докторські дисертації. (2:214)
>
> [And do you know that our students think of nothing else but how they will live in shacks in the melon patches and how their wives will bring out their lunches into the fields, where they will hold the plough in one hand while holding a book in their other hand and using the third to write a dissertation.]

By having Kovan'ko refer to the melon patch, that is, by making an allusion to the incident with Radiuk picking cucumbers with the old watchman, Onys'ko – an incident in the story that Kovan'ko did not witness – Nechui signals direct authorial involvement in this caricature. Radiuk may be Nechui's hero, but the author is well aware of his ambivalent qualities. Indeed, Radiuk is very much like Nechui himself. The period depicted in the novel is evidently the late 1850s and early 1860s, when Nechui himself faced the question of whether his involvement in the Ukrainian cause should be active or passive. Kovan'ko's cynical comments, set, no less, in a context of masculine sexual competition, make perfectly clear that Nechui is well aware of the limitations of his hero. Of course, Kovan'ko's cynical comments are easy to dismiss; he himself does nothing but poke fun at serious issues, although his judgment of the situation is no different from Radiuk's. But the failure of the generation of activists that Radiuk represents to achieve concrete results in the defence of Ukrainian culture is, like so much of Ukrainian life in the nineteenth century, depicted very accurately by Nechui. Some of the failures were due to repression. Radiuk faces extraordinary opposition and oppression for his views. He can't even rent an apartment without trouble resulting from rumours about his dangerous views. But Nechui is also honest enough in his depiction to show that the activists themselves, to the degree that Radiuk represents a large segment of Ukrainian intellectuals, were confused and ambiguous in their willingness to implement a strategy of open confrontation with the status quo. When the goal is cultural dignity but not political rights, the opposition of a repressive state will make all efforts ineffectual until the means are transformed. Nechui, inherently conservative in his politics, was never in favour of revolution, whether social or political. Thus his hope for cultural change is always dampened by a realization that such change is not achievable. The next generation of Ukrainian activists made the transition to political goals, not just cultural ones, and thus no longer understood Nechui's reticence. For those who want to walk on the moon, the ambitions of those who merely wanted to fly into space were timid and risible. But Nechui's and Radiuk's clear statement of cultural goals was a major accomplishment for Ukrainians in the nineteenth century. It was a pioneering effort. Without their shoulders to stand on, their later critics would not have been able to conceive their own larger goals. As Oleksander Konys'kyi argues in his essay about Nechui's *Khmary*, Radiuk represents the limits of what was possible at the time.[26] For radicals, it was obviously not enough. For most of the country, it was far too much.

Nechui, however, saw his goals in a different context. In the novel Radiuk's faults are noted, as we have seen, in Kovan'ko's derisive remarks, but the real contrast is not with Kovan'ko but with Dashkovych. Yes,

Radiuk must actually discover that he does not like the village and does not want to be a gentleman farmer. But he is firm in his national principles. Despite his temptation in the form of a girlfriend who feels no sympathy for the national cause, Radiuk stays true to his values, finds a different girl to marry, and keeps his vision focused on the Ukrainian cause. Not so Dashkovych, who studies national cultures but cannot see the one closest to him. His visits to his father's village do nothing to remind him of his own origins. He sympathizes with the plight of an oppressed people and culture, but sees this as a universal phenomenon. When he finally chooses a culture to study in detail, it is Japanese, not Ukrainian. Nechui's point, of course, is not that Japanese culture does not deserve attention, but that Dashkovych's scholarly blinders obscure what is closest and most pressing in favour of an esoteric and bookish topic that does not require emotional commitment. In this context – and this is the context that Nechui is working to establish in the novel – Radiuk may still seem a weak hero, but at least he is true. In the end he is defeated not by his own timidity but by a government willing to repress the slightest signs of dissent, and by an urban materialistic society that cannot see or overcome its prejudice against the local culture.

The basic outlines of this formula are repeated in Nechui's later novel *Nad Chornym Morem* (At the Black Sea) in which the protagonist, Komashko, like Radiuk, is an advocate for the Ukrainian nation and for the *narod*. Where *Khmary* was largely focused on a juxtaposition of the city and the village, *Nad Chornym Morem* is entirely urban. Radiuk's infatuation with rural culture eventually dissipates and he realizes that his own role is that of an urban *narodovets*, or populist, who will champion the interests of the rural *narod*, it's culture and welfare, from his own position as an urban intellectual. Komashko begins where Radiuk left off. There is no longer any talk of visiting villages or adopting the quaint customs of the countryside, whether they be wearing folk costumes or lying in melon patches. The scene of the action is now Odessa, the atmosphere is one of leisure and sophistication. The various characters in the story sip tea by the famous stairs, ride the tram to the outlying beaches, and play cards to pass the time. As we shall see below, Nechui's focus in this work is specifically on the relationship between the Ukrainian question as the populists see it, and the importance of sophisticated European civilization and culture. But the weakness and uncertainty of the activists is still an important factor, as it was in *Khmary*. This timidity is emblematically shown in a scene where Kharyton Kyrylovych Navrots'kyi speaks with his wife, Raisa Mykhailivna, who is worried about the behaviour of their daughter, Sania, who is Komashko's girlfriend. Raisa scolds her husband and argues that he should do more to control their daughter, who is behaving altogether too independently and is apt to infect her younger sister with her free-thinking spirit. Sania has no respect for her elders, says her mother. Relax, says Navrots'kyi, sometimes it's better not to respect elders, to which Raisa responds with amazement and indignation. Navrots'kyi's reply is significant:

> – Та ми ж дома: можемо, здається, зняти машкару з лиця, котру надіваємо при людях та перед начальством, – промовив Навроцький.
>
> – Знімай вже ти, коли вбрався в машкару. Я завсіди ходжу без машкари. Про начальство говори, та й міру знай. Он сидиш та й сидиш товаришем предсідателя. І бог зна, коли будеш предсідателем. Частіше надівай машкару на лице, коли вже тобі припала охота часами скидати її. (5:196)

> ["But we're at home! We can, it seems, take off the masks from our faces that we put on before others and those in authority," declared Navrots'kyi.
>
> "You take yours off – if you've put on a mask. I always appear without a mask. You can talk about those in authority, but be careful. Here you are stuck for years as assistant chairman. And heaven only knows when you're to become chairman. If you're sometimes feeling an urge to take off your mask, you should put it on your face more often."]

The difficulty their daughter's boyfriend Komashko faces in promoting Ukrainian language and education lies in the general intellectual climate of stasis, apprehension, and falsity. The possibility of social change disturbs the comfort level of the middle class. There is no intellectual courage in society, and no willingness to encourage debate. New ideas are a threat to the status quo. This timidity infects Nechui's activists as well, and thus neither Komashko nor Radiuk can find the certainty and conviction to embark on a program of radical change. But Nechui does not judge them very harshly. They are too much like their author. And moreover, their timidity may be well justified. In both novels, the eventual defeat of the Ukrainian program is not a matter of insufficient effort or courage on the part of the activists. Heavy-handed government repressions doom the protagonists of both novels. The Sunday school movement Radiuk had helped create in *Khmary* (much like the actual Sunday school movement in Ukraine in 1859–60) was abolished by government decree. Komashko is charged with seditious activity (as were many Ukrainophiles in the 1870s) and sent to Siberia. Even the unambiguously positive peasant Nykon Kuchma, a minor character in the novel *Neodnakovymy stezhkamy* who organizes his fellow peasants into a reading society, endures a police search of his home and is ordered to stop conducting meetings (8:414–15). The Ukrainian cultural cause that Nechui so passionately advocated had many ideological and organizational weaknesses, but its real problem was not insufficient motivation but the repression of an authoritarian government committed to exterminating this activity. Nechui understood full well the weaknesses of the Ukrainophile position that Alexei Miller gleefully reports.[27] But in Nechui's mind, there was no question that the failures of this cause were due to the deliberate anti-Ukrainian policies of the government of the Russian Empire, which had chosen Russian identity, Russian language, and Russian culture as the paradigm for Ukrainians and enforced this choice with punishment and repression.

In history and in practice, however, Ukrainians had another choice, and it was one to which Nechui objected just as vigorously. From the fifteenth century onward Ukrainians, at least those in Right-Bank Ukraine, where Nechui was born and lived most of his life, were exposed to Polish culture and to the presence of Poles among them. This Polish presence was not consistent throughout Ukrainian territory, but in the areas Nechui was most familiar with, it had the character of a dominant foreign social class, reflecting the history of Ukrainian subordination to the Polish Commonwealth from the sixteenth to the eighteenth century. In Nechui's own lifetime, this meant that Right-Bank Ukraine under the Russian Empire had a substantial number of inhabitants who considered themselves Poles, were largely descendants of the free, landowning class, and who distinguished themselves from both the Ukrainian lower classes and the Russian governing elite. In the nineteenth century, this distinct patriotism led to occasional Polish uprisings against Russian rule, particularly in 1863. For the Ukrainian inhabitants of the Russian Empire, the Polish presence represented yet another challenge to their own identity and welfare. Polish aristocrats formed another layer of social and national oppression for Ukrainian peasants, who were in financial dependence to Polish landlords who in turn held the Ukrainian peasants in contempt both socially and nationally. Alternatively, socially mobile Ukrainians were just as likely to abandon their national identity in favour of a Polish identity as they were for a Russian identity. But unlike the Russians, who are few in Nechui's works, the Poles are many, reflecting their actual historical presence.

Polish landowners can be found in a number of Nechui's works. We have already seen Mr Bzhozovs'kyi in *Mykola Dzheria*, a character whom Nechui does not describe or even give a Christian name, but one who is identified only as an evil Polish landowner. Another exploitative Polish aristocrat is described in the story "Zhyvtsem pokhovani," where the author relates his conversation with a carriage driver, Vasyl' Skvilits'kyi, whose family were once small landowners in the area. Recounting his family history, the impoverished Skvilits'kyi describes the wealth of the Branits'kyi (= Branicki) family, now the major landowners in the area. According to Nechui, Franciszek Ksawery Branicki (1730–1819), an actual historical figure who later became crown hetman of the Polish-Lithuanian Commonwealth in 1774–94, was given enormous landholdings in the area of Bila Tserkva by the last king of Poland, Stanisław August Poniatowski, as a reward for his brutal suppression of the 1768 Ukrainian Haidamak uprising (7:270). As we have seen, Nechui felt a strong historical connection between the Koliivshchyna uprising and the area where he was born, and he saw the enrichment of Polish noble families for the slaughter of Ukrainian rebels (at the cost of Ukrainian landowners, whom Branits'kyi cheated out of their possessions) as a historical injustice. Although Branits'kyi's Ukrainian wife, Oleksandra von Engelhardt, supported Orthodox churches and set aside money for a peasant school and a band, the hetman himself was a systematic Polonizer, introducing Catholicism and Polish culture into the area and discriminating against Ukrainian Orthodox landowners. Nechui underscores the exploitation of the Polish aristocrats by narrating a description of the lavish lifestyle of the old hetman, who loved hunting and kept a stable of dogs. The poor peasants, says Nechui, would all but weep at the wastefulness, when told to slaughter an ox every day for the German kennel keepers to cook a broth for the dogs (7:281–2).

Branits'kyi is one of many larger or smaller Polish landowners who exploit, demean, and ridicule Ukrainian peasants, priests, and village authorities in a variety of Nechui's works. But Nechui also focuses his attention on another aspect of the Polish presence in Right-Bank Ukraine: Ukrainians who convert to Catholicism and adopt a Polish identity. In "Zhyvtsem pokhovani," the owner of the carriage Skvilits'kyi drives is a man named Hnidys'kyi, a former leaseholder on Branits'kyi's estate. Hnidys'kyi's social background is uncertain – perhaps he was a small landowner, perhaps even just a peasant. But his nationality was Ukrainian until his father converted to Catholicism and began to kowtow to the Polish aristocrats. Then, abruptly, his prospects changed (7:280).

Now this denationalized Ukrainian family lives like aristocrats in a fine home in the city and has its carriage driver, Skvilits'kyi, earn extra money using the carriage as a cab for hire when they don't need it. To avoid discrimination and to achieve social position, Ukrainians on the Right Bank could pass themselves off as Poles. Among the Poles in the Russian Empire, a very considerable number were from formerly Ukrainian families who had made such a conversion. For Nechui, this was another serious threat to Ukrainian identity.

The novel *Prychepa*, one of Nechui's earliest works, is an extended lesson in the dangers of overreaching in social position. The story line focuses on two young families, the Seredyns'kyis and the Lemishkas. Both husbands are denationalized Ukrainians. The Seredas were an old cossack family. A few generations back, one of their sons had been brought in to serve in the home of a Polish landowner; eventually he converted to Catholicism, changed his name to Seredyns'kyi, and became Polish. The current Seredyns'kyi, Ias', a man with more ambition than good sense, marries Hania Chepurnovs'ka, one of seven daughters of the local Orthodox priest. With so many girls to marry off, Father Khvedor, a somewhat careless man, is not about to object to any son-in-law, even if he is a pretentious Catholic. The Lemishka family has different roots. Iakym Lemishka's father was a wealthy merchant who wanted to give his son an education, despite the boy's obvious distaste for learning. Schooling turns Iakym into a pretentious, Russian-speaking, but still foolish young man who now calls himself Lemishkovs'kyi. His hard-working parents, particularly his mother, push him into higher society, where he meets Zosia Pshepshyns'ka (= Przeprzinska), the spoiled, dreamy-eyed youngest daughter of the local police chief, a Pole, like most of the town officials. As if to disprove Tolstoy's witty jibe at the Karenins, Nechui's two families are very similar in their unhappiness. The mixture of Polish gentry culture with simple Ukrainian values is universally a failure in Nechui's world. Nechui depicts the Poles in these two marriages as unrestrained hedonists, uncontrolled and immoral pleasure-seekers who believe that the world owes them material comforts and pleasures because they are Polish gentry. Their Ukrainian spouses are alienated, and the two Poles, Ias' and Zosia, have an affair. Everything concludes badly when the prince on whose estate Seredyns'kyi serves as administrator finally has enough of his employee's dissolute lifestyle and fires him. Both families end up in dire circumstances, their pretentious lifestyle gone for good – misery and hard times their constant companions.

Without the Polish cultural element, this novel might be little more than a moral lesson on the dangers of a debauched lifestyle. But Nechui makes a point of emphasizing the national element in the equation. It is the Poles who are licentious party animals. The Ukrainians are not saints – they, too, enjoy hedonist pleasures. That is why the novel opens with a scene of two Orthodox priests engaged in excessive drinking. But the two priests know their place in society. Ias' and Zosia do not. They believe themselves entitled to material comforts and pleasures, despite, or perhaps because, they have no other values. But in the aftermath of their affair, it is not only the Polish pair who suffer, but their Ukrainian spouses as well. Hania eventually dies, as do her parents. Iakym is left with a broken marriage and few if any prospects for himself. For Nechui, this is the inevitable result of "mixed marriages" between individuals of different nationality. Nechui sees Hania and Iakym's abandonment of their Ukrainian identity as a transgression, whether it be in pursuit of higher social status or merely to resolve the difficulties of finding a suitable match for seven daughters.

There are many similarities here to Anatolii Svydnyts'kyi *Liuborats'ki*. Both authors portray the threat of denationalization into a Polish identity motivated by a desire for social advancement. The families of clergymen are particularly susceptible for they stand one rung higher in society than their peasant parishioners, but lower than the Polish gentry whose social prestige they wish to share. The steps they take in that direction lead inevitably to the collapse of an entire social order and pose a serious danger to Ukrainian national identity. The combination of Polish discrimination against Ukrainians and the desire of these Ukrainians to gain social acceptability presents the same risk of denationalization in the rural setting that Russian cultural identity presents in the urban environment. Nechui used his satiric pen in defence of Ukraine against both these forces. But the Ukrainian cause was threatened not only by these external enemies, Poles and Russians, but by internal enemies as well. The threat arose not only from those ambitious Ukrainians who lacked the European sophistication to resist the lure of foreign cultures, but also from those who believed that this European sophistication itself was more important than national identity. Foremost among them was Mykhailo Drahomanov.

Cosmopolitanism

The Ukrainian cause in the second half of the nineteenth century was not a simple, unified idea. A number of different cultural, social, and political programs shared the general goal of advancing Ukrainian culture, but they differed in the specific details of what should be done and how. The differences between these programs stemmed from various factors, including tactics, circumstances, and primary values. The intellectual relationship between Nechui and Mykhailo Drahomanov was an instance of a conflict resulting from such differences.

The very notion of an intellectual relationship between Nechui and Drahomanov is problematical. The two parties in it were certainly incompatible. Drahomanov, born in 1841, was only a few years younger than Nechui, but his inclination and upbringing pointed to an academic future. He studied at Kyiv University and worked as a docent there until he was expelled. In fact, however, Drahomanov was a natural politician and civic leader. From his early days as a student he became heavily involved in a variety of Ukrainian movements and causes. Drahomanov was among the organizers of the Sunday schools in Kyiv in the early 1860s and was one of the founders of the Kyiv Hromada. He became a vital link in the growing ties between Ukrainians in Galicia and those in the Russian Empire. Drahomanov was also an important political thinker. He not only stimulated and organized various activities, but also grounded his efforts in carefully considered and well-constructed political ideas, which he expressed in publications both within and outside the Russian Empire to justify his projects and to convince others. In all these qualities – his scholarly intellectualism, his social orientation, his political inclination, and his philosophical acumen – Drahomanov was very different from Nechui. Our schoolteacher from Stebliv was not an ivory-tower intellectual with scholarly inclinations: he was a solitary man with no ambitions to organize civic movements or to get involved in political action. And Nechui never argued from philosophical principle, but from practical experience. Nechui and Drahomanov were not of the same cloth and thus it is hardly surprising that they did not see eye to eye on issues of tactics or strategy. Yet they certainly agreed on the overall cause: Ukrainians and Ukrainian culture were unjustifiably oppressed and deserved a better future than what was in store for them. But these two men were not likely to have similar views on what was to be done to advance the Ukrainian cause.

Nechui and Drahomanov were not close colleagues, although they certainly knew each other and no doubt met on more than one occasion. A photograph of Kyiv Hromada members from August 1874 includes both of them, so they certainly met at least once. But they were not friends, and there is no record of direct correspondence between them. Their respective careers moved them both geographically and organizationally away from each other, making contact unlikely. In a letter to Hrushevs'kyi from 1905 Nechui says that it was Drahomanov who asked him to write a local description for Élisée Reclus's monumental *Nouvelle Géographie universelle* (10:449), and the initial idea of writing an opera about Marusia Bohuslavka, a project Nechui and Lysenko worked on, came from Drahomanov.[28] Nevertheless, there was likely little direct contact between the two men. Indirectly, however, there was considerably more.

In Drahomanov's voluminous published correspondence, Nechui's name occurs infrequently but with some regularity, although never as a direct addressee.[29] Drahomanov kept a very keen eye on developments in Ukrainian literature and publishing, frequently commenting in his letters on the appearance of various items he found interesting. The bulk of his references to Nechui are simply factual. They begin shortly after Nechui's first publications in Galician periodicals. Not long afterward, however, Drahomanov's references to Nechui become critical. On 18 January 1873 Drahomanov writes a very long letter to Buchyns'kyi from Florence in which he discusses, among other matters, the works of Panas Myrnyi, whose real name was Panas (Afanasii) Rudchenko. Although at this point Nechui had published only a few works, Drahomanov finds sufficient grounds to draw a negative comparison between him and Myrnyi. Drahomanov, often a harsh critic, begins by criticizing Myrnyi, who is, as Drahomanov has discovered, the author of a tale entitled "Lykho" (actually "Lykhyi poputav," published in *Pravda* in 1872):

> Автор "Лихого," як узнав я з пісьма Ив. Рудч., єсть брать іого Афанасій Яковлевич у Полтаві, – которого я було прочитавши у Правді віршу про вічну „ниву" записав було у мертвяки (я ще з роду нігде такого тупоумія не бачив, як у наших віршемазів: як таки 40 чоловік слово у слово 30 год одно і тоже пишуть, та ще кожний разів по 5, що було вже раз на свій час не погано сказано Шевченком! Чі вони сонні віршують, чі пьяні?) Аж ні, – возстав з мертвих, та ще й добре. Знаєте, я Вам скажу, що хотя „рівноваги" ще мало у Аф. Р – ка, але я надіюсь з іого більш, ніж з Нечуя, бо не бачу

ніякого узколобія тенденціозности, яка бье очі у Нечуя у Причепі (у Горіславскій Ночі, котора пахне Тургеневим, і у Двох Московках меньше і рівноваги). Чі то може на час Куліш так заклепав іому голову, – та тільки поет, що сходить з обьективизму і міша ідею з тенденціозностью, стоіть на краю могили, у котору попадали і не такі сили, як Нечуй, а і такі, як Гоголь, як попавсь у бондарню славянофілів. Да хранить бог наших беллетристів і од бондарні украйнофилів, – бо все, що зроблено було доси живого у нашій беллетристиці і поезіи, було зроблено людьми, которі були влекомі або поетичною интуіцією, або обще-чоловічим соціальним, або гуманним идеалом, – Квітка, Шевченко у лучшому і М. Вовчок у 1 части оповіданій, – де вони стояли за народ, а не за народність традіціонну. Треба признатись, що той, имже превозиесохомся, був батьком и нашоі мертвячини, хомяковщини украінскоі, – т. е. Шевченко. Але він не винуват, що іого переходяще і не головне, а то і слабе – другі приняли за суть і затягай безконечне хникане і фразеологію, б ..., котора довела і беллетрістів молодих до чистого богомазія, а не живописанія.[30]

[The author of "Lykho," as I have learned in a letter from Iv[an] Rudch[enko], is his brother, Afanasii Iakovlevych in Poltava, whom I had listed among the dead after reading his poem in *Pravda* about eternally toiling in the field (I have never in my life encountered such boneheadedness as we find in our so-called poets: these forty people have spent the last thirty years writing the same thing word for word, and each of them writes it at least five times, even though Shevchenko in his time already said it not badly; do they write poetry while asleep? or drunk?). But no, this one rose from the dead and did it nicely. You know, let me tell you, although there is still little balance in Af[anasii] R[udchen]ko, I still have higher hopes for him than I do for Nechui, because I don't see any narrow-mindedness or tendentiousness in him, qualities that simply jump out at you in Nechui's *Prychepa* (in "Horyslavs'ka nich," which smacks of Turgenev, and in "Dvi moskovky," where there's also less balance). Can it be that Kulish has temporarily hammered his head shut? But the poet who has fallen away from objectivity and confuses ideas with tendentiousness stands on the edge of a grave into which have fallen far more capable men than Nechui, even such as Gogol, who was caught in the cooperage of the Slavophiles. May god protect our writers from the cooperage of the Ukrainophiles! Everything that's alive in our literature has been done by people who were pulled either by poetic intuition or by an all-human social or humane ideal – Kvitka, Shevchenko at his best, and M. Vovchok in the first part of her stories – where they stood for the *narod* rather than for traditional *narodnist'*. We must admit, that He Who Was the First of those Called, i.e., Shevchenko, was also the father of our lifelessness, our Khomiakov-inspired [= Alexei Khomiakov, prominent Russian Slavophile] Ukrainian status. But he is not to blame that those qualities that were transitional, not central to his work, and therefore weak were accepted as the essence and generated endless whining and phraseology, which led young writers to pure iconography instead of literature.]

The very complex sentiments Drahomanov expresses in this paragraph regarding questions of literary judgment, national cultural preoccupations, and the importance of universal social values are far from unique. They appear frequently in his letters and in his publicistic writing. For example, not much later, on 7 May 1873, while still in Florence, Drahomanov writes about Radiuk, one of the central characters in Nechui's *Khmary*, and criticizes both Nechui's writing and his thinking. Specifically, he complains about this passage in the novel that describes a change in Pavlo Radiuk's thinking, his turn towards a nation-oriented program of social action:

Одпочивши добре на волі, молодий Радюк почав думи думати молодою головою. Наймилішим місцем його молодих дум був старий садок. Наниз од дому Радюка колись давно була посаджена алея з лип та дубів, але натура давно попсувала діло людських рук. Старі липи та дуби росли вже давно по своїй волі; деякі виступили за алею й широко розкидали своє гілля на всі боки. Два дуби вигнались вище за липи серед самої алеї. Колишнясь алея стала вже лабіринтом старого дерева, під котрим росла зелена трава, рівна й гладенька, як килим, а за алеєю на низині блищала ясно-зелена осока, така зелена й ясна, що в найсумнішу негоду здавалось, неначе на неї світило сонце. Молодий Радюк любив ходить поміж тим старим деревом, між липами та дубами, любив саму гущавину, де серед сонячного дня було сливе поночі.

[Радюк побув рік в університеті і вже скинув з себе той космополітизм або великорущину, якою надаряє нашу молодіж великоруська гімназія.]

Європейські ідеї й наука показали йому новий світ, нове живоття. Його давні дитячі літа в Журбанях, з українською мовою й піснею, між челяддю й селянами, тепер неначе вертались знов. (2:148–9)

[Having rested well out in the open, the young Radiuk began to turn his young mind to serious thoughts. The most pleasant location for his young musing was the old orchard. Down from the Radiuk home there was an alley of lindens and oaks, planted a long time ago, but nature had long since spoiled the work of human hands. The old lindens and oaks had long since found their own freedom, spreading their branches widely in all directions. Two oaks had pushed well above the lindens in the alley itself. What had once been an alley had become a labyrinth of old trees beneath which grew green grass, soft and even like a carpet. Behind the alley, in the hollow, shone bright green sedge, so green and bright that it seemed the sun was shining on it even in the worst of weather. The young Radiuk liked to walk amid the old trees, among the lindens and oaks; he liked the very thickest growth, where even during the brightest day it was as dark as night.

[Radiuk has spent a year at the University and abandoned that cosmopolitanism or Great-Russianness which Great Russian high schools bequeath to our youngsters.]

European ideas and scholarship had shown him a new world, a new life. His old childhood year in Zhurbany, where Ukrainian was spoken and sung among the servants and the peasants, now seemed to be returning to him.]

In this early novel, written before his active engagement with the intellectuals of the Kyiv Hromada, Nechui already signalled an important cornerstone of his position on the advancement of Ukrainian culture. Cosmopolitanism is equated with Russian nationalism, and the pernicious mechanism that promotes these twin ideas is the Russian-language high school. Furthermore, European ideas are tied to national, not cosmopolitan, ideals. In a gesture very characteristic of Nechui's writing, the judgment concerning cosmopolitanism is set against the metaphorical background of an overgrown element of planned landscaping. Nechui is consistently inclined to see carefully planned ideas undermined by the natural course of affairs. The lindens and oaks in the alley will revert to their natural condition, no matter how many gardeners try to shape them into a more desirable appearance. Nechui's understanding of Ukrainian culture as the deeply rooted natural product of the land itself informs his view of the desirability of any foreign cultural meddling by cosmopolitan gardeners with new ideas about social landscaping.

For many readers, particularly those born in the second half of the twentieth century and raised on the primacy of modernist aesthetics, this may sound preposterous. For them literature is an anti-traditional, playful, highbrow Art, and Europe is often the primary source of wisdom, beauty, and artistic credibility. In our modern and post-modern sensibility, Europe and cosmopolitanism are two hypostases of the same deity. For many, it is simply impossible to separate the two and to equate cosmopolitanism with Russia while tying Europe to Ukraine. But this is precisely what Nechui does. Although he does not explain this association anywhere, the logic of what he is doing is neither incomprehensible nor absurd, only unusual and somewhat anachronistic.

In analysing Nechui's view of Ukrainian cultural development, the major difficulty is that he never gives this matter sufficient attention to develop his views fully. His two culturological essays, although very long and involved, are much too diffuse and poorly argued to give a clear and consistent exposition of the underlying ideas he applies to this issue; however, the essays do give any number of hints, the chief of which is the reliance on Taine's notion of the influence of race, milieu, and moment. Unlike Drahomanov, Nechui is not very adept in constructing a logical argument or conducting a rational intellectual debate. Thus his fundamental ideas and principles need to be inferred from various declarations on cultural topics in his fiction, his essays, and his correspondence.

The first principle in Nechui's understanding of culture is that it is fundamentally national in character and that nations are eternal and immutable objects. In an intellectual world dominated by Benedict Anderson's descriptions of nations as constructed myths, as imagined communities, Nechui's view may seem hopelessly misguided, but he was certainly not alone in his belief that nations are absolute. Many Western Europeans thought so as well. The fact that Drahomanov clearly understood the constructed character of nations and compared the Ukrainian struggle for national recognition to the situation of the Welsh, Scots, and Irish in England and to the Provençal, Breton, and Flemish under French rule speaks very clearly to his modern understanding of the concept of nationhood. But in the 1870s a "modern" understanding of the constructedness of the Ukrainian nation was precisely the logic behind the Ems Ukaz. If nations need to be created in the public imagination, then prohibitions against efforts to promote national identity will be effective. Under these circumstances, from the point of view of "national awakeners" (a category that includes both Drahomanov and Nechui) the "modern" compromising, realpolitik positions of moderate cosmopolitans might prove less effective and less successful than the totalizing, extremist position of a nativist patriot. Ironically, it was Drahomanov who was expelled from his position at

Kyiv University and left Ukraine, while Nechui stayed in the Russian Empire and even returned to Kyiv to continue his intemperate struggle against Russian culture. Drahomanov's cosmopolitan, moderate view of the national question was not the reason for his dismissal from the university – quite the contrary, he was punished for being a staunch Ukrainophile – but it did not win him any friends in the Russian camp, and it eventually contributed to the frictions that distanced him from his erstwhile friends at the Kyiv Hromada.

All this is not to suggest that there is a right and wrong in the debate between nativists and cosmopolitans. It is merely to underscore that the cosmopolitan position, despite its appeal to modern readers, has its own inherent weaknesses. In any event, Drahomanov's reaction to Radiuk, as expressed in the lettter of 7 May 1873, is one of wonder and amazement at Nechui's inability to grasp the fundamental postulates of Drahomanov's position. After calling Nechui's novel laughable from an artistic point of view, Drahomanov paraphrases the passage concerning Radiuk's turn away from cosmopolitanism on the basis of European ideas and then throws up his hands in exasperation:

> Що ж таке космополитизм, – як не евр. наука? А відкіля він узяв іі, – як не з великор. гимназіи и университета? Відкіля набрав Радюк литогр. Бюхнера и т. д., – як не по части з Москви, – з города на ріццi Москва? Хто був Герцен? и т. д. Чогож тут плутать и других морочити, ставлючи якось у роздвій космополитизм и укр. народовство, великорущину, … т. є. тенденцій молодіжі и литератури великор. з нашими?[31]

> [What is cosmopolitanism, if not Eur[opean] learning? Where did he get it, if not from Great R[ussian] high schools and universities? Where did Radiuk get the lithographs of Büchner and so on, if not in part from Moscow, from the city on the Moscow River? Who was Herzen? What's the point of confusing the issue and muddling others by putting up an opposition between cosmopolitanism and Ukr[ainian] populism … that is, between the direction followed by the youth and the literature of Great R[ussia] and our own?]

He then goes on to predict that such a presentation of the issue will only cause Ukrainian youth to gravitate "од українізму одбігатиме и перебігатиме не тільки до російщини, – (ми й сами усе таки россіяне), але й до велико-рущини и почасти, – бо великоруська по части молодіж справди одрізняется своїм логичним космополитизмом и соціальною демократією"[32] [not only toward Russianness (because after all, we, too, are Russians [i.e., citizens of the Russian State]) but also in some measure to Great Russianness, since Great Russian youth has such a clear orientation on cosmopolitanism and social democracy]. As this argument makes clear, both Drahomanov's and Nechui's position share one common characteristic – they are both based on the circular logic of absolute faith. Nechui believes in the primacy of Ukrainian cultural values, Drahomanov in the primacy of cosmopolitan, social principles.

In the novel *Khmary*, cosmopolitanism is presented in images that are true to Nechui's view of the issue, which is to say in the depiction of incidents that show whether contact with a transnational community of values or people tends to denationalize Ukrainians or to solidify their culture and identity. The chief answer to this question is, of course, negative. The swarms of foreigners who attend the Kyiv Theological Academy in the novel are not converts to a Ukraine-centric cultural world. On the contrary, they enforce the foreign, Russian, cultural spirit of the school and thus help to seduce Ukrainians away from their own national identity and remove them from the ranks of those who might do something for the betterment of Ukrainian culture or Ukrainian peasants. Vasyl' Petrovych Dashkovych, first a student and then a professor at the academy, epitomizes this loss of Ukrainian spirit. Under pressure from the academy, from his materialist wife, and from his scholarly temperament and instinctive aversion to mundane affairs, Dashkovych turns, as we have seen, into an ivory-tower intellectual, who, while not quite denationalized, is nevertheless lost to the cultural needs of his nation, preferring to study Japanese culture rather than his own.

Radiuk's position in the novel stands in contrast to Dashkovych. While the old professor loses contact with his own family and culture, Radiuk keeps his ties to both and marries a village girl after a failed romance with Ol'ha Dashkovych, the professor's daughter, who graduated from the Institute for Noble Girls, another Russificatory school with inauthentic cosmopolitan pretensions. Although Nechui unambiguously favours Radiuk's position and condemns cosmopolitan pretentiousness, this judgment does not immediately translate into a universally flattering depiction of either the young activist or of the village and villagers he tries to help. Radiuk is not a particularly forceful or energetic man, and Nechui shows him rather easily dispirited by the myriad faults he finds in the village and the repressive public atmosphere that treats his Ukrainophile initiatives as a criminal activity. But even with these caveats attached, Radiuk quite naturally attracts the scorn of Drahomanov.

Although cosmopolitanism is not a matter of specific concern in Nechui's culturological essays, he does, as I have noted, consistently emphasize the national qualities of various European and Asian literatures in these essays. Thus, the pursuit of foreign models, in his view, leads back to a focus on the national. There is nothing wrong with the human species as a whole, but culture exists only on the level of nations, and Nechui is fundamentally interested in the preservation of culture, Ukrainian culture in particular. Cosmopolitanism, for him, did not mean a feeling of communion with all of mankind; it meant an abandonment of one's own culture. But this is not how the issue was understood by Ivan Franko, who had learned much from his association with Drahomanov. In his review of Nechui's "S'ohochasne literaturne priamuvannia," Franko questions the idea that Ukrainian literature should be totally independent and isolated from Russian literature:

> Для кого має бути ся відрубна література? Чи для самої інтелігенції? Очевидки, ні, бо інтелігенція, вже коли хоче бути інтелігенцією, не може замкнутися в тіснім кружку одної літератури, але мусить студіювати, читати і порівнювати й твори других літератур – московської, німецької, французької і проч. Значить, тут відрубності не заведеш, бо тут головна ціль – іменно якнайбільшеий космопоітизм думки і научної праці.[33]

> [For whom is this isolated literature supposed to be written? Is it for the intelligentsia? Obviously not, because if the intelligentsia wants to be the intelligentsia, it cannot lock itself up in the tight circle of a single literature, but rather must study, read, and compare the works of other literatures – Russian, German, French, and others. Which means you cannot introduce isolation here, because the main goal here is precisely the widest cosmopolitanism of thinking and scholarship.]

Although there is no specific evidence indicating that Nechui was seeking to answer either Franko's or Drahomanov's criticism, he may well have felt a need to illuminate his views of nationality and offer a rebuttal to the ideology of cosmopolitanism. This is the program that informs the first novel Nechui wrote after his retirement to Kyiv, *Nad Chornym Morem*.

The plot is built on parallel love stories: a central one between two Ukrainians, Sania Navrots'ka and Viktor Komashko; and a secondary one between Nadezhda Murashkova, daughter of a mixed Greek-Ukrainian marriage, and Arystyd Selabros, a Greek. Although the principals are from Kishinev, most of the story takes place in Odessa, where they have all travelled on holiday. The tone and setting of the novel are similar to Khvyl'ovyi's unfinished *Val'dshnepy* (The woodcocks), where a holiday setting and romantic trysts frame a search for personal and national values. The languorous, exotic seaside setting and the carefree, flirtatious behaviour of the company of vacationing friends provide a backdrop for an intellectual drama concerning the role of the Ukrainian intelligentsia. Komashko, in many ways the author's idealized self-portrait, is a schoolteacher passionately dedicated to the realization of his ideas, "а найбільше ідея за національну самостійність, за українське письменство та добробут українського народу" (5:132) [most of all the idea of national independence, Ukrainian literature, and the prosperity of the Ukrainian people]. Sania is also a schoolteacher, but, unlike Komashko, she teaches in a school for Jewish girls "не для заробітку, а ради принципу космополітизму, щоб допомогти найбільше пригнобленій нації, найбільше пригніченій женщині" (5:100) [not for the income, but on account of the principle of cosmopolitanism, to help the most persecuted nation and the most oppressed woman]. She and her friend Nadezhda are attuned to the most recent social ideas, particularly feminism. But for Nechui, their values have a serious flaw:

> В принципах вони були космополітки, як люде без національності. На цю стежку потягла їх мішанина в національностях в місті, незнання народу, великоруська школа з некраєвою, великоруською мовою й теоретичність їх пересвідченнів, ще неприложених до будлі-якого доброго, путнього діла на практиці. (5:101)
>
> [In their principles they were cosmopolitans, people without a nationality. They were pulled onto this path by the mixture of nationalities in the city, ignorance of the common people, their Great Russian schooling with its foreign Great Russian language, and by the theoreticalness of their views, which were not yet applied to any useful, good cause in practice.]

The arguments Nechui specifically makes against cosmopolitanism take on the appearance of direct rebuttals to Drahomanov's ideas. The debates between Komashko and Sania (= Oleksandra) attack the issue head-on. Komashko begins:

> Людина без національності, як дерево без коріння: воно зачучверіє й всохне.
>
> – Я поважаю ваш погляд, але знаю, що націоналізм часом доводить до темних проявків, до воєнщини, до бісмарковщини, – сказала Саня.
>
> – Як у кого. Не думайте, Олександре Харитонівно, що я встоюю за такий націоналізм. Наш націоналізм – то свобода, прогрес, гуманність:

це націоналізм новий, а не націоналізм давнього старотгя; він виступає з великою толерантністю до інших народів та до усякої віри, стає за маси, за народ. А щоб служити чимсь народові, треба доконечне промовляти до його його ж мовою, бо як же він нас зрозуміє? Ви стоїте за народ? – спитав Комашко в Сані.

– За народ повинна стати … хоч я за це якось мало думала, бо мало свідома в цій справі: але я встоюю й за вічні ідеї добра, правди, просвіти. Ці принципи вселюдські й всесвітні! – аж крикнула Саня. – Тим-то я й космополітка.

– Авжеж всесвітні, їх зрозуміє кожний народ, де б і коли б він не животів, – обізвалась Мурашкова.

– Невже ви думаєте, що я держусь інших принципів, що я йду проти свободи, добра, честі, просвіти? – сказав Комашко. – В цих принципах і я космополіт.

– Я вже доволі знаю вас і цього не думаю, але мені здається, що націоналізм – діло давнє, старе, що через його повстає тільки колотнеча між народами й державами, – говорила з досадою Саня.

– Ні! Не через те. Націоналізм – то вічна форма, в якій з'являтиметься й ростиме людське живоття на землі; це грядка, де сходять і ростуть усякові високі космополітичні ідеї, але народи вже й тепереньки не змагаються і не будуть змагатись через те, що вони належаться до іншої національності. Б'ються тепер не народи, а королі, дипломати та генерали. (5:157–8)

["A person without nationality is like a tree without roots. It will wither and die."

"I respect your opinion but I also know that nationalism sometimes leads to dark manifestations, to militarism, to Bismarkism," said Sania.

"It depends where. Do not think, Oleksandra Xarytonivna, that I support that kind of nationalism. Our nationalism is liberty, progress, humanity. It is a new nationalism, not the ancient nationalism of old. It manifests great tolerance for other nations and for all faiths, it stands up for the masses, for the common people. And to serve the common people, you certainly have to speak to them in their own language. How will they understand us otherwise? You're for the common people, aren't you?" Komashko asked Sania.

"I guess I am for the people … although I have not given this much thought, because I am not well informed on this issue. But I'm for the eternal ideas of goodness, truth, enlightenment. These are universal principles!" Sania said, almost yelling. "That's why I'm a cosmopolitan."

"Indeed they are universal. Every nation understands them, whenever and wherever they live," added Murashkova.

"Do you actually think, that I hold to different principles, that I'm against freedom, goodness, honour, and enlightenment?" said Komashko. "In these principles I'm cosmopolitan too!"

"I know you well enough by now and I don't think this, but it seems to me that nationalism is an old idea from the past. It only leads to conflicts among peoples [*narods*] and nations," said Sania with anger.

"No. Not because of that. Nationalism is an eternal form in which human life on earth appears and develops. It's a field on which various high cosmopolitan ideas germinate and grow. But people [*narods*] already don't engage in conflicts amongst each other merely because they are of different nationalities. It's not people who engage in conflicts, it's kings, diplomats, and generals."]

Nechui lets his point of view triumph in the novel: Komashko gets the better of the argument, and eventually Sania will change her mind and agree to marry him. But, characteristically for Nechui, the triumph of the idea of nationalism in the novel does not lead to a victory for the protagonist. Komashko and Sania are stymied by government repression and the ill will of envious and malicious cosmopolitans. After Komashko and Sania are married Komashko is dismissed from his job as a teacher, arrested, and sent to Siberia. This gives Sania a chance to pursue her feminist ideal of self-fulfilment: she enrols at the university. When Komashko returns she opens a school for girls in a city on the Black Sea.

Nechui's arguments against cosmopolitanism in this novel may or may not be specifically intended to answer Franko and Drahomanov. But the latter likely understood it that way, to judge by the rather harsh review of *Nad Chornym Morem* he published in *Narod* in 1891. In this review, Drahomanov says that "the whole novel is written to defeat cosmopolitanism,"[34] but that Nechui's distorted definition of cosmopolitanism makes this task too easy, since it amounts to having the woman make the right romantic choice between an honest man and a spy. He accuses Nechui of confusing cosmopolitanism as an idea with the negative qualities of some individuals who disguise their faults with the trappings of cosmopolitan virtues. And then Drahomanov continues: "На світі є ознаки національні як результат обставин географічних і історичних, процесів біологічних. Всяка розумна людина, котра хоче щось працювати для громади, мусить застосуватись для краєвих обставин, в тім числі й до національних. Тільки ж вона зовсім не обов'язана бути рабом тих обставин як яких-небудь святощів, а мусить навіть перероблювати їх відповідно до свого ідеалу, котрий давно вже на світі став вироблятись процесом інтернаціональним, космополітичним"[35] [National qualities exist in the world as a result of geographic and historical circumstances as well as biological processes. Every intelligent person who wants to work for the good of the community must adapt to these local conditions, including the national characteristics. But this person needn't be a slave to these characteristics, as if they were something sacred, but must even transform them according to his or her own ideals, which have long since been formulated in the world by international, cosmopolitan processes]. And then he adds: "Націоналізм же д. Ів. Левицького не дає нам гарантій, що він буде завше вільним і прогресивним" [The nationalism of Ivan Levyts'kyi gives us no guarantees that it will always be free and progressive] and further goes on to say that Nechui's admirer Barvins'kyi is a Catholic reactionary trying to impose Greek Catholicism on all Ukrainians, which would lead to abuses like the efforts of Catholic bishops in Western Europe to remove Rome (only recently added in 1870) from the Italian unified state.[36] Drahomanov is certainly right in accusing Nechui of using dramatic and exaggerated personal traits to paint his fictional supporters of cosmopolitanism in the darkest of colours. But Drahomanov is doing much the same thing himself in this review, accusing Nechui of being somehow complicit in Catholic plots to dismember Italy. The logic of this assertion is best left unexamined. It's a wonder Drahomanov had the temerity to make such an accusation.

Drahomanov's review of Nechui's *Nad Chornym Morem* is most noteworthy not for the occasionally dubious logic of its argumentation or even the essential statement of principles it contains (which Drahomanov elucidates more clearly elsewhere), but for the almost visceral antipathy he displays for Nechui, his writing, and his ideas. The review is dismissive in tone, arguing essentially that Nechui does not really understand the concept of cosmopolitanism and, indeed, does not really know how to write or think very well. The review ends with a famously dismissive quotation from someone whom Drahomanov refers to as "з України одна особа, котра дала безспорні докази активної прихильності до української нації" [a person from Ukraine who has given direct evidence of an active sympathy for the Ukrainian nation].[37] This mysterious person turns out to be his niece, Lesia Ukrainka, another intellectual giant in Ukrainian cultural history, like her uncle. The words he quotes are from a letter she wrote to him on 22 August (September 3) 1891, reprinted in her collected works:[38]

> Бога ради, не судіть нас по романах Нечуя, бо прийдеться засудити нас навіки безневинно. Принаймні я не знаю ні одної розумної людини в Нечуєвих романах, якби вірити йому, то вся Україна здалась би дурною. У нас тільки сміються з того "Чорного моря," а прочитавши його, можна тільки подумати, чи не час би вже Нечуєві залишити писати романи, бо вже як такі романи писати, то краще пір'я дерти. А пожалься боже того пера й чорнила! Мені тільки жаль, що наша бідна українська література отак поневіряється через різних … "корифеїв."

> [For God's sake, don't judge us by Nechui's novels or we will be forever condemned unjustly. I for one don't know of a single intelligent person in Nechui's novels. If we were to believe him, then all Ukraine would seem to be stupid. Among our friends, they only laugh at his "Black Sea," and after reading it you can only figure that perhaps it's high time Nechui abandoned writing novels, because if you write novels like that, it's better to pluck chickens. Have mercy on the pens and ink! I can only feel pity for our poor Ukrainian literature that suffers so at the hands of these various … corypheuses.][39]

It hardly helps to know that the ellipsis in the last sentence expands in the original letter to the names of Nechui, Konys'kyi, Chaichenko, and "etc." With the self-confident bluster characteristic of a twenty-year-old child prodigy, Lesia joins her uncle in dismissing a whole school of realist writers, a whole generation of nativist activists, and anyone who does not see the wisdom and promise of cosmopolitanism. For her, they're nothing but a bunch of dopes. No wonder Nechui defended his nativist position so vehemently! His views were certainly not as sophisticated intellectually as those of Drahomanov and his wunderkind niece, but they did not include any contempt for shredding feathers, tending watermelon patches, or any other activity practised by over 90 per cent of the population of his country. Most of all, he assumed that a Ukrainian peasant's dignity, honour, and political rights did not derive from the possibility that this peasant might become a Paris philosopher or a London statesman but from what that person already was, a Ukrainian peasant. These Ukrainian peasants may have needed help in the form of education and freedom, but they did not need to aspire to be something other than what they were.

For all of his respect for the dignity of peasants, Nechui's works are not, as we have seen, an unmitigated encomium to the lower classes. He is often satirical, sometimes even strongly critical (as in the depiction of a husband's abuse of his wife in *Khmary*) in his depictions of them. But for readers inclined to see the lower classes in a negative light, Nechui's friendly and mild satire, coupled with his unmistakable goodwill towards peasants, appear as undiluted praise, as mindless, knee-jerk support for the worst characteristics of the Ukrainian *narod*. In an overview of Ukrainian writing in the period 1866–73 that was meant to appear in Russian in the *Vestnik Evropy* (but was stopped by the censors), Drahomanov argues that Nechui's naive populism buries liberty and human dignity in the mud of dilettante ethnographism by glorifying the *narod's* most primitive characteristics – its ignorance, its superstitions, and its materialism. Focusing on Nechui's comic novel *Kaidasheva sim'ia*, he sees nothing but a sermon on the true ethnographic faith (propovid' etnohrafichnoho pravovirstva).[40] What is needed, he says, is to leave ethnography to anthropologists and to use the ethnographic qualities of the common folk only as an instrument to assist in "вживаючи їх яко ключки або форми при подаванні суспільності й масам народу знання й ідей, що повиннні розвити в них поняття про людську гідність і подати їм способи задля боротьби за нього з природою та з останками понять, які нагнітають чоловіка" [bringing to society and the masses the knowledge and ideas that should develop in them a sense of human dignity, and to offer them the means to struggle for this dignity against the forces of nature and the legacy of ideas that oppress mankind].[41] For Drahomanov, the ultimate success will occur when this educated peasant, instead of putting *kutia* on the hay (a folk tradition) to benefit his cattle, will write a textbook in zoology and veterinary science for the common people.[42]

The image of Drahomanov's exemplary peasant zoologist underscores one area in which he and Nechui found common cause, namely, education. The high school teacher and the university professor both frequently addressed the need for general education among the masses, an area of social policy in which the Russian Empire was particularly remiss and one that very many activists from that era could agree on. But while the need to offer education to the masses was generally accepted by all reformers, the specifics of such a policy elicited passionate debate. For Ukrainians the first point of contention, of course, was the language of instruction. A group of Ukrainian activists in Kyiv had founded Ukrainian Sunday schools in 1859. These schools were eventually outlawed by the government, but even before then they elicited arguments among the activists who had created them. The first of these schools (there were eventually three schools for men and two for women) was founded in the Podil district of Kyiv, and Mykhailo Drahomanov, then a student at Kyiv University, was among the teachers there. There were 149 pupils of various ages. Since these schools were a new venture without any official support from the government, numerous practical questions of pedagogical significance arose immediately. While everyone involved agreed that Ukrainians should be taught in Ukrainian, there were disagreements on the use of Russian in these schools. Drahomanov relates this in his "Avstro-Rus'ki spomyny (1867–1877)" [Memoirs from Austrian Rus']:

Зараз поступивши в університет (1859 р.), я пристав з усім нашим полтавським кружком до "воскресных школ" … Тут практика поставила перед нами перше з українських питань: на якій мові вчити в школах? Ми вирішили це питання тим, що вчили на обох: на російській і на українській, тілько, звісно, більше на першій, бо на ній було більше книг. Згодом, окрім нашої школи, склалась друга (новостроєнська) … Скоро наших, подолян, новостроєнці стали звати космополітами, а себе українцями, хоч на ділі й вони не більше наших вчили своїх учеників по-українському. Суперечка виходила проміж нас більш теоретична, бо коли гарячіші новостроєнці казали нам, що школа неукраїнська більш деморалізує, ніж учить народ, ми признавали, що наука все-таки наука, та що поки українського письменства, а надто учебного, майже нема, то треба користуватись хоч російським. З таких спорів доходило до спору про вагу національного й народно-традиційного елементу і всесвітнього, наукового. Ми вище ставили останній, новостроєнці – перший. Ми їх за те ставили вряд з московськими слов'янофілами.

[Immediately after enrolling at the university (1859), along with the entire Poltava circle, I joined the "Sunday schools" … Practical reality put before us the primary Ukrainian question: In which language should we teach in the schools? We answered this question thus: we taught in both languages – in Russian and in Ukrainian – except, of course, that we used the former more, because there were more books in that language. Eventually, in addition to our school, another one was founded (in the Novostroienia district [of Kyiv]). Soon, the Novostroienians started calling us, in the Podil school, cosmopolitans, while they called themselves Ukrainians, although in practice they taught their students in Ukrainian no more than we did. The dispute was more of a theoretical one. While the

> Novostroienians told us that a school that was not in Ukrainian did more to demoralize than to teach the students, we claimed that learning was after all learning, and that as long as there was hardly any Ukrainian writing, especially of the pedagogical variety, we would need to use Russian materials. From these arguments flowed further arguments about the relative value of national and common-traditional values vs universal and scholarly values. We put a higher value on the latter, while the Novostroeinia group preferred the former. For this, we put them in the same category as the Muscovite Slavophiles.

In this unusually temperate account of the differences between the cosmopolitans and the nativists, Drahomanov makes clear that he actually understands the issue very well. Although he cannot resist the urge to compare the nativists to the despised Slavophiles (a comparison that is not wholly appropriate), he nevertheless admits that the real difference is simply in different priorities. Cosmopolitans like Drahomanov see education as the path to personal advancement for every individual. If such advancement requires foreign inputs because the extrinsic elements are at a more advanced level of civilization, then Drahomanov supports these foreign elements in education. Indeed, his ideal world is one in which all national differences are equally respected but hardly significant, because every individual has advanced to a higher level of civilization where national distinctions are less important. Of course, cosmopolitans are unwilling to admit that this plan puts national identity at risk and in practice produces a gradation of national cultures, those at a more advanced level and those at a less advanced one. The less advanced cultures are unlikely to develop, since development is tied to the individual, who is free and is indeed encouraged to adopt the national identity of a more advanced culture.[43] Drahomanov's idealized peasant zoologist is likely to speak and write in Russian, since that is the language in which he learned his subject. His neighbour, who has less intellectual potential, either failed to learn to read at all, since his schooling was in a foreign language that he understood poorly, or adopted Russian as the more sophisticated language in a bilingual world where languages are unequal in status.

Nativists like Nechui, on the other hand, hold national culture to be the primary value. The goal of education in an oppressed and underdeveloped culture is to provide the masses with rudimentary skills in their own language that reinforce their own cultural identity. Primary attention is not lavished on the intellectually gifted, since they will find their own way in the world by using the tools available in the dominant, more developed culture. The masses will be given a reinforced sense of their own dignity, one that does not invite them to look down on their own culture. The results of this learning will gradually raise the level of civilization not only of the individuals who receive the education, but of the society and culture as a whole, thus providing for national as well as personal advances in civilization. Of course, nativists are also unwilling to acknowledge the risks inherent in their view. By relying on an underdeveloped culture, they risk tying this culture to primitive models and forever condemning it to second-class status, turning the benefits of civilization on their head by denying all values other than national ones. This is precisely the fault that Drahomanov finds in Nechui. He assumes that Nechui is an uncritical champion of the actual culture of the masses and thus finds him quite literally stupid, mired in the primitive and uncivilized depths of rural boorish culture.

All his life Nechui, the high school teacher of Russian language and literature, insisted that schools for Ukrainians must be in Ukrainian. It's as if he were trying to undo the damage he watched himself inflicting as a cog in the empire's scheme of Russifying the non-Russian masses. At every opportunity – in his novels, in his essays, in his letters – he insisted on the importance of teaching Ukrainians in Ukrainian. But he and the other Ukrainian nativists of the second half of the nineteenth century were fighting a losing battle against modernity in its three essential manifestations: culture, politics, and civilization. In the positivist philosophical climate of the late nineteenth century, the gap between the civilized world and the backwater of Ukrainian peasants was growing. The attraction of cosmopolitanism was becoming harder to resist. Culturally, a new generation of Ukrainian writers was losing its commitment to nativist cultural forms. Modernism in culture, particularly in literature, meant an abandonment of the lower classes, both as an object of description and a target for consumption of the cultural product. Ukrainian society had moved up the ladder of civilization just enough to give modernist Ukrainian culture an audience sufficient to maintain the illusion that they were creating culture for a sophisticated readership. Politically, the intransigence of the government meant that pressure for social change was growing faster than the pressure for national autonomy. Eventually, the explosion of social forces that changed the face of Ukraine proved both the cosmopolitans and the nativists equally right and equally wrong. Drahomanov turned out to be right that social considerations and cosmopolitan ideas about humanity as a whole trumped the national interests of Ukrainians: the forces that promised social justice triumphed over those that fought for national identity. But Nechui's position was also affirmed to some extent. After a brief honeymoon motivated by political expediency, the cosmopolitan forces abandoned any notion of the equality of national cultures and returned to a system of cultural values that provided for superior and inferior cultures. The Ukrainian lower classes were abandoned to an assimilatory process that did not leave room for cultural arguments against the cosmopolitan ideal. Nativist ideas were tolerated only as long as they did not challenge the cosmopolitan ideals.

In his lifetime Nechui felt the need to defend Ukraine against various enemies. The chief enemy was the Russian Empire with its brutal social and political regime. Russian cultural hegemony and penetration into Ukraine was also an important opponent, as was – though on a different order of magnitude – Polish culture and Polish social dominance in Right-Bank Ukraine. The list of enemies against which Nechui felt he needed to defend Ukraine also included the cosmopolitan internationalists, among whom were many prominent Ukrainian intellectuals, including Drahomanov and Franko. For Nechui, any force that challenged Ukrainian culture was to be resisted. Cosmopolitanism was, for him, precisely such a force. But, much like today's opponent of cultural and commercial globalization, Nechui was in an uneven struggle that he was doomed to lose. Victors write history, and Nechui's nativist, anti-cosmopolitan views were ridiculed by his opponents and by succeeding generations of Ukrainian intellectuals. In his own day, however, these views were neither ridiculous nor obviously flawed. The challenge to Drahomanov that Nechui raised is merely another instance in a long history of Ukrainian cultural challenges to foreign influences. These same ideas still have their place in Ukrainian cultural debates today.

4 Realism, Rhetoric, and Repetition

Viewed from the perspective of technique, Nechui's writing is both characteristic of the time and place in which he wrote and somewhat peculiar. In the 1860s, when Nechui was beginning to write, Ukrainian prose was not very well developed or established. Among his predecessors in creating Ukrainian belletristic prose only a few were of any significance. Hryhorii Kvitka-Osnovianenko is generally credited with laying the foundations of Ukrainian prose. His stories and tales from the 1830s are a mixture of folk customs, peasant humour, and religious sentiment. His works do not delve into social issues and their plots are not much more than expanded anecdotes. His direct influence on Nechui is negligible. The second major figure was Panteleimon Kulish. He introduced historical subjects, social issues, and European, particularly Scottian, traditions into his stories and novels in the 1840s. But for Kulish belletristic prose was a sidelight he largely abandoned later in his career. His influence on Nechui's early works was direct and significant – as an editor, mentor, and intermediary with publishers – but the importance of his own prose as a model for Nechui is not very large. Kulish wrote in a formal manner and with serious purpose rather than as an expression of an aesthetic sensibility. His prose would never get confused with Nechui's. Their second point of contact lies in the Ukrainian translation of the Bible, an endeavour that Kulish began and that was completed after his death by Nechui. Of course, this project had no impact on either writer's stories or novels – in both cases the translating was undertaken long after the bulk of their belletristic work had been completed. The third major figure preceding Nechui in Ukrainian prose was Maria Vilins'ka, better known by her pseudonym, Marko Vovchok. The abolitionist stories she wrote and published in the 1850s introduced a new vitality into Ukrainian writing – the voice of the common Ukrainian peasant. Wrapping timely themes of social injustice in an aesthetically stylized but nonetheless authentic and vibrant language, Marko Vovchok raised the standard for Ukrainian prose in three distinct categories: social engagement, linguistic vitality, and popularity with readers. These are lessons that Nechui took to heart. In particular, his first published work, "Dvi moskovky," focused on the plight of women, as did Vovchok's stories, and showed similar descriptive devices derived from folkloric models.[1] But aside from this first work, a larger, specific debt to Marko Vovchok is difficult to identify.

Aside from these three, there were, of course, other Ukrainian prose writers in the years before Nechui began his career, but these were minor figures. One near contemporary of Nechui's already mentioned is Anatolii Svydnyts'kyi, whose writing, particularly his novel *Liuborats'ki* (The Liuboratski family), represents something of a transition between Kulish and Vovchok, on the one hand, and Nechui on the other. However, that novel, written in 1861–2 was not published until 1886 and thus could not have influenced Nechui's early works. The writer who did influence Nechui was Taras Shevchenko; in fact, Shevchenko's influence extends across the entire range of Ukrainian culture from the 1840s onward. Among Nechui's works there are many, including "Dvi moskovky" and *Burlachka*, that show the influence of Shevchenko's themes and plots. Nechui also shares with Shevchenko a genuine solicitude for the plight of the poor and oppressed. But these are very general issues that do not illustrate anything more specific than the enormity of Shevchenko's legacy. There is likewise a general similarity in the language of the two writers: both rely heavily on vibrant and expressive vocabulary, idioms, and syntax that derive from both folklore and the common speech of the times. Nechui's debt to Shevchenko is important and he specifically acknowledged this in his writing, but the finer points of Nechui's prose technique are not the result of the poet's influence.

Another source of influence, but once again only in a diffuse manner, is found in the Russian prose of the mid-nineteenth century. Mykola Hohol', the Ukrainian who as Nikolai Gogol changed the course of Russian prose, was a major influence on all Ukrainian prose writers of the second half of the nineteenth century, including Nechui. Perhaps the most important aspect of this influence was a detached, ironic, and often humorous depiction of Ukrainian peasants. Nechui, like most other Ukrainian realists, did not adopt a special narrative persona as

Gogol had, but the light-hearted, sometimes carnivalesque temper that characterizes the setting in *Kaidasheva sim'ia, Starosvits'ki batiushky ta matushky*, and the Paraska and Palazhka stories owes its origin to Gogolian precedents. Indeed, this detached, sometimes condescending manner can also be found in the presentations of Nechui's urban and semi-urban characters, who resemble in this regard some of the characters from Gogol's later works in which the setting is no longer specifically Ukrainian. Gogol's humour reflected an important element of the Ukrainian collective psyche that Nechui was happy to adopt, despite his explicit support for the principles of realism in literature, which should have precluded such a stance, on the grounds of its abandonment of narrative objectivity and its potential to dilute the sympathetic portrayal of the downtrodden. This Gogolian influence is thus potentially at odds with the influence of Marko Vovchok, for whom uncompromising compassion with her subjects was an immutable law. In this regard, Nechui differs from some of his Ukrainian contemporaries, such as Ivan Franko or Panas Myrnyi, for whom ideological sentiments and realist principles ruled out a light-hearted tone.

Beyond Gogol, the impact of Russian literature on Nechui can only be measured in the general commonality of literary themes and approaches that characterized the early period of realist prose in the Russian Empire. It is customary to compare Nechui to both Ivan Turgenev and Mikhail Saltykov-Shchedrin. Radiuk, the young hero of Nechui's *Khmary*, evokes some obvious juxtapositions (though not real similarity) with Turgenev's Bazarov in *Fathers and Sons*, and Nechui even mentions Turgenev and that novel in his memoirs. Nechui's contact with Shchedrin was more direct still. He translated the latter's "How One Muzhik Fed Two Generals" and "Wild Landowner," satiric stories about social inequality. But when it comes to the actual properties of their writing, the relationships between Nechui and these two writers prove to be too general to withstand a detailed analysis.[2] What ties Nechui to Russian realism of the 1860s and 1870s is a general tendency towards the depiction of contemporary social mores in a narrow, usually familial, and rural setting. Like many Russian novelists before the changes brought on by Dostoevsky and Tolstoy, Nechui focuses on local settings and local issues, rather than universal human themes and ideas. And psychology is not a major element in his repertoire of devices and approaches. Yes, Nechui was certainly another player in the cultural universe of the Russian Empire in the second half of the nineteenth century, and he shares ideas, social concerns, and aesthetic values with a whole generation of Russian (and not only Russian) writers from this era. But no, despite his professional occupation as a high school teacher of Russian language and culture, Nechui was not a conduit for the transposition of Russian cultural influences into Ukrainian literature. As his memoirs clearly assert, he read both Russian and Western European literature with great interest and admiration. But neither had a very profound impact on his personal approach to writing. For better or for worse (and both tendencies are manifest in large measure), Nechui was largely a singular and peculiar writer who reacted to a variety of cultural stimuli but did not particularly follow any but his own models.

Nechui's singular approach to writing is evident in a number of his authorial predilections: plot construction, character depiction, phraseology, idioms, and repetition. But for all the eccentricity of his writing, its qualities are neither inadvertent nor incidental. Although Nechui was not an incisive literary theorist, he did write occasionally about literary matters, usually in a patriotic, Ukrainian context. In the most famous of these essays, first published in 1878 under the title "S'ohochasne literaturne priamuvannia," Nechui, at that time just beginning his career as a writer, enunciates his view of the leading ideas that were guiding European literature at that time. They were realism, nationality, and *narodnist*. Not surprisingly, these ideas offer a useful yardstick for assessing his approach to literary creativity and surveying his technique as a writer. Nechui begins with definitions:

> Реалізм чи натуралізм в літературі потребує, щоб література була одкидом правдивої, реальної жизни, похожим па одкид берега в воді, з городом, чи з селом, з лісами, горами і всіми предметами, котрі знаходяться на землі. Реальна література повинна бути дзеркалом, в котрому б одсвічувалась правдива жизнь, хоч і тонка, похожа на мрію, як самий одсвіт. Ми далеко стоїмо од того ультрареального погляду на літературу, котрий запанував недавно в великоруській літературі, од часу критичних творів Писарева, що література повинна бути простою копією натури, простою фотографією, та й годі. Такий погляд довів великоруських писальників, як напр. двох Глебових, до коротеньких фотографій з народного бита, в котрих нема й кришки художности ні штучности. Тут винен реальний аж меркантильний дух нашого часу і такий самий національний дух Великоросії. Ультрареальні фотографії, як і абстрактні філософські образи або ідеали, дуже однобічні, дуже прозаїчні, буденні, черстві й тверді, як недобре вварена страва, і такі самі на смак, як сира страва; од їх не дише пишним духом ідеалізму,

фантазії, серця, пишним духом щирої поезії. Сей вищий дух поезії вносить у звичайну людську жизнь, в мертву природу геній писальника, що переварює в своїй душі, в свойому серці всі факти буденного життя, звичайно дуже прозаїчного, всі образи, взяті з натури; надихає своїм духом, нагріває своїм серцем, наливає своєю горячою кров'ю або наливає злістю, жовчею та ненавистю, обсипає сміхом сатани і запечатує печаттю свого прокльону. Поетичні образи в реальній поезії – то результат обидводіяння натури й художника, то спільна праця сили натури й сили художника, котрий надаряє своїм духом образи, перепущені через свою душу, додає натурі ніби куті свого меду. Людська жизнь, в більшій частці, то – вода, а вари воду, вода й буде, як каже приказка. Художник засипає ту юшку своїми крупами, часом такими, яких не дасть вся згорнутість, вся купність живої людської громади, бо він буває і продуктом тієї громади, і воздіячем на неї, вищим од неї. Тим-то художник повинен бути в своїх творах дзеркалом громади, але дзеркалом високої ціни, в котрому б одбивалась жизнь правдива, але обчищена й гарна в естетичному погляді, добре спорядкована й згрупована, освічена вищою ідеєю, і щоб була при тому жива, як сама жизнь.[3]

[Realism, or naturalism, requires that literature be an image of true, actual life, like the reflected image of a [river] bank in the water with a city or a village, with forests, mountains, and all the things that are found on land. Realistic literature should be a mirror in which real life shines forth, though it be fine, like a dream, like light itself. We are far from the ultra-realist view of literature that has recently begun to dominate in Great Russian literature, following the critical works of Pisarev, that literature should simply be a copy of nature, a photograph and nothing more. Such a view has led Great Russian writers – for example, the two Glebovs – to short photographs of the mores of the common people in which there is not a crumb of beauty or artistry. The fault lies with the realist, even mercantilist, spirit of our times and the national spirit of Great Russia. Ultra-realist photographs, like abstract philosophical images or ideals, are very one-sided, very prosaic, ordinary, crusty, and hard, like a poorly cooked meal, and their taste is that of raw food. They do not convey the sumptuous spirit of idealism, fantasy, and emotion – the sumptuous spirit of sincere poetry. This higher spirit of poetry is introduced into ordinary human life, into dead nature by the genius of the writer, in whose soul, in whose heart simmer the facts of daily life, usually so prosaic. All of these images taken from nature are infused by the writer with his own spirit, warmed by his own heart, filled with his own warm blood or soaked in anger, bile, and hatred, sprinkled with satanic laugher and sealed with his own curse. Poetic images in realist poetry are the result of the interaction of nature and the artist, they are the joint effort of the power of nature and the power of the artist, who endows with his spirit these images, filtered through his soul, as if adding honey to nature's cereal. Human life, for the most part, is like water – cook it all you will, it'll still taste like water, as the saying goes. The artist adds his own grains to this broth, sometimes of a kind that could not be found in the entire collective of the human community, because he, the artist, is both a product of that community and an influence on it, higher than it is. Therefore, the writer should strive in his works to be a mirror of his community, but a mirror of high quality, which reflects real life, but cleansed and beautiful, in an aesthetic appearance, well-ordered and grouped, illuminated by a higher idea, and at the same time, alive, like life itself.]

The ideas Nechui expresses here are familiar. Realism is the style that allows an artist to give a true reflection of reality, to abandon artistic stereotypes, social ideals, and thematic moralizing in favour of a direct presentation of the unadorned truth of human existence. But Nechui is not an artistic revolutionary, and his interest in the relatively new ideas of realism is tempered by his allegiance to the old ideas of beauty. His definition of realism includes what seem to be self-contradictory elements. On the one hand, realism is a mirror held up to nature, that is, a direct, objective reflection of the actual world. But on the other hand, Nechui believes it is the author's task to impose his own subjective interpretation on the raw facts of human existence. Keeping to his own metaphor, the writer must add substance and flavour to the plain broth of material facts in order to create a work of art. These two views of artistic creation are largely self-contradictory. They conform roughly to the familiar definition of realism in the first case and romanticism in the second. Of course, the degree of "objectivity" in realism is a matter of considerable controversy in all theoretical discussions of realism, but Nechui is clearly expressing a limited acceptance of the principles of realism as a departure from romanticism, and this transitional understanding of the matter is also evident in the characteristic features of his writing. The important caveat in Nechui's understanding of realism is the role of beauty and artistry. The persistent culinary metaphor in his definition offers an important clue about Nechui's understanding of realism and his implementation of it. The author's role in a work of realist literature, as he understood it, is similar to a chef's. The ingredients must be carefully chosen, masterfully prepared, and pleasantly presented. Nechui devotes a great deal of attention to the artistry of his texts. Unlike many of his fellow Ukrainian realists, notably Myrnyi, Franko, and Konys'kyi, he implements a whole array of devices and techniques to spice up his text, to add flavour to his writing. These techniques distinguish his writing from that of his contemporaries, and they give his texts a particular savour that readers associate with his prose.

No matter which variant of the culinary arts a writer may favour, the essential ingredients are always the same: they are words. The "spices," available to the literary chef – other than the content, the raw food itself – that can enhance the "flavour" of a text are fundamentally only two: selection and arrangement. But since these "spices" can be variously applied with different effects within the body of the text, to a single word or to groupings of words of various lengths, the size of the spice rack seems, effectively, almost limitless. Nechui, like most writers, generally relies on a particular subset of these seasonings. The "usual spices" for Nechui are mostly two: a colourful and idiomatic phraseology that is related to folk literature, and a deliberate duplication of verbal elements in the text.

For a writer who is both admired and maligned for his use of language, there is little in the way of good scholarship that examines the language of Nechui's works.[4] Many of the authors who do write on this subject concentrate on the linguistic prejudices expressed in his publicistic writing, rather than the actual practice in his own texts. As Shevelov and others have noted,[5] in his belletristic prose Nechui did not always follow the linguistic prejudices of his later years. In any event, it is not spelling rules or the etymological provenance of various lexical items that distinguish Nechui's language as an artist, but rather its clarity, transparency, and simplicity, as well as its reliance on expressions that are similar to or borrowed from folklore. Scholars have noted that Nechui introduces into the Ukrainian literary language previously unfamiliar terms tied to agricultural, industrial, and commercial activities, and religious life.[6] These are a direct result of his depiction of rural activities and industrial settings in such works as *Mykola Dzheria*, *Burlachka*, and *Kaidasheva sim'ia*. The vocabulary of intellectual discourse, on the other hand, has a much smaller presence, although in works such as *Khmary* and *Nad Chornym Morem* it does appear to some extent. But on the whole, it is the ordinary and the familiar that dominate Nechui's language. Ivan Franko emphasized this point in his remarks for Nechui's thirty-fifth jubilee in 1904:

> В тіснім зв'язку з характером творчості Ів. Левицького стоїть його мова. Се вже не та поетична, декуди аж переборщено поетична та квітчаста мова

Марка Вовчка, не штучна, силувана, академічно неповертлива мова Куліша, – се переважно буденна мова українського простолюддя, проста, без сліду афектації, але проте багата, колоритна і повна тої природної грації, якою вона визначається в устах людей з багатим життєвим змістом. Левицький ніде не ганяється за язиковими ефектами, не стає на котурни, а коли де й попадаються у нього чисто язиково ефектовні місця (пор. відомий опис невдалого фейерверка: "Тріснуло, блиснуло, і показався синенький димок"), то вони приходять якось так ненароком, самі собою, немов без волі автора, мов граціозні рухи у вродливої, здорової людини.[7]

[Iv[an] Levyts'kyi's language has a close relationship to the character of his writing. This is no longer the poetic, sometimes excessively poetic and flowery language of Marko Vovchok. It is not the artificial, forced, and academically rigid language of [Panteleimon] Kulish. It is mostly the everyday language of the Ukrainian common man – simple, without a trace of affectation, but rich, colourful, and full of that natural grace that distinguishes it on the lips of those with a rich experience of life. Levyts'kyi does not chase purely verbal effects, he does not put on tragic airs, and when occasionally a passage of purely verbal effect does occur in his works (for example, the well-known scene of the failed firework "тріснуло, блиснуло, і показався синенький димок"),[8] they appear seemingly inadvertently, of their own accord, as if beyond the author's will, like the graceful gestures of a handsome, healthy person.]

Franko's comment confirms the correlation between Nechui's practice as a writer and his programmatic claim, expressed in the 1878 essay "Siohochasne literaturne priamuvannia," that "для літератури взірцем книжного язика повинен бути именно язик сільської баби"[9] [for literature, the model of formal language should be the language of a village hag]. This remark, often misused to characterize Nechui as an inveterate enemy of sophistication in culture, is an important measure of Nechui's appreciation for the aesthetic role of language in a literary work. Franko's view of the unadulterated simplicity and ordinariness of Nechui's language makes an important point, but as his own example shows, this "natural" grace does not come without the author's deliberate intervention. The key to Nechui's language, the factor that distinguishes both his language and his writing technique in general, is the attention he gives to aesthetic considerations.

In the notorious passage just cited, Nechui particularly praises the language of the village hag for its syntax, which he describes as "шашкований, повний викрикників, нерозвитий граматично, але живий, іскряний"[10] [checkered, full of exclamations, grammatically undeveloped, but alive and full of sparks]. Nechui's own syntax shares some of these qualities. Halyna Izhakevych claims that his writing is characterized by short sentences with direct word order.[11] He uses simple and compound sentences of an ordinary, familiar type. But Nechui's understanding of the aesthetics of prose goes beyond simple syntax. In keeping with his own prescription for literature, beauty and artistry are qualities the writer deliberately adds to his works. From among the three leading principles of literature[12] that Nechui advocates – realism, national character, and the quality of *narodnist'*, that is, the quality of pertaining to the common people – it is the principle of *narodnist'* that most conspicuously informs his understanding of the role of language in a literary work.

The vocabulary and syntax of his works exemplify this quality – they are the reproductions of the language of the village hag. But so, too, do the frequent interjections of epithets, verbal constructions, phrases, and expressions whose purpose – Franko's comment about the relative absence of purely verbal effects notwithstanding – is to assert beauty, to add artistry to the verbal texture of the work. These interjections frequently take the form of expressions that are characteristic of Ukrainian folk creativity. For example, Nechui often makes comparisons that use a familiar folk negative construction: "It's not this, it's actually that." Such expressions are evident among Nechui's earlier works, among them "Dvi moskovky," where we find: "То не зозуля прилинула в Хомишин садочок, то Ганна перескочила через перелаз в свій огород" (1:66) [It was not a cuckoo that flew into Khoma's orchard, it was Anna who jumped over the gate into her own garden]. Among other similar expressions, some are simply folk sayings. In *Mykola Dzheria* the narrator declares "Любка росла, як у садку вишня" (3:121) [Liubka grew, like a cherry in the orchard]. Nechui interweaves a variety of proverbs, sayings, and aphorisms, usually of folk origin, into his works. They occur in the narrative portions of his text, but most often they are found in the speech of his characters, where they are an important element in the author's arsenal of character-building tools. In *Kaidasheva sim'ia* especially, the characters often speak in the style of folk aphorism. Melashka's mother dismisses her daughter's complaints about her mother-in-law with traditional folk misogyny: "дівка, як верба: де посади, то прийметься" (3:370) [A girl is like a willow, wherever you plant it, it will take root].

Nechui's deliberate use of folk expressions is most evident in rudimentary verbal and syntactic elements, epithets, and similes. As many observers have noted, Nechui frequently uses simple epithets (usually just adjectives) or extended comparisons that derive, as Izhakevych notes, "primarily from the sphere of village customs, agricultural life, and nature. Objects are depicted by the author in the manner that they are directly apprehended by the organs of sight, sound, etc."[13] Furthermore, these descriptive passages often rely on the familiar qualities of beauty as they are understood in folk poetry. Vasyl' Vlasenko explains: "Expressions from [folk] songs, sayings, and aphorisms are not just quoted in the text, they penetrate deeply into the foundations of the author's language."[14] The girls are all black-browed and red-lipped. The men have moustaches the colour of tar. Serhii Iefremov puts it more callously: "Like folk poetry, Levyts'kyi does not know any artistic device other than comparison."[15] After quoting the description of Vasyl' Khomenko from "Dvi moskovky," which ends with "Khomenko was handsome, fresh, and young," Iefremov adds with irritation: "Of course he was handsome, so handsome you want to disarrange him a little, ruffle his clothes, dishevel his hair, reduce his beauty … Mannerism, manipulation, artificiality, monotony, and wordiness are in evidence here." Iefremov sees Nechui as a disloyal realist who allows too much romantic idealism, too much deliberate beauty to enter into what is supposed to be a depiction of bleak social conditions. He also sees Nechui as a poor stylist. Because Nechui adhered to his own aesthetic and stylistic ideas so thoroughly and so consistently, Iefremov sees in him an immovable, unchanging, repetitive, and therefore boring writer. The "verbal decoration" that Nechui adds to his text is, in Iefremov's words, applied "without limit, fastidiously, and completely mechanically."[16] Iefremov sees the appearance of the phrase "сонце на вечірньому прузі" [the sun on its evening arc], which he claims can be found in every one of Nechui's works,[17] as a symptom of this carelessness and lack of imagination. For Iefremov, of course, this Homeric-sounding phrase, like the more numerous folkloric ones, does not belong in a realist work of fiction.

Iefremov's criticism has had a very large influence in shaping the scholarly appreciation of Nechui's writing. His observations have been explicitly or silently (in Soviet times Iefremov was unmentionable) repeated by almost every author who writes on the topic. Many of

Iefremov's judgments get repeated, but even more significant is the impact of his choice of issues. Most discussion of Nechui revolves around the ideas that Iefremov raised in his monograph: the relation between biography and writing, the impact of folklore, the problematic writing technique, the peculiar version of realism, the national idea, and the personality of the anachronistic old curmudgeon. Another of Iefremov's influential gambits is the overall tone of many appreciations of Nechui. Authors often follow Iefremov in focusing on Nechui's weaknesses only to end up praising him for his overall accomplishment. Perhaps the most exemplary among these is Valerian Pidmohyl'nyi in his introduction to the 1927 edition of Nechui's *Selected Works*. This little-known essay is a masterpiece of misdirection. As an introduction to a reprint of a classic author, it should fall naturally into a well-worn genre that includes biographical and bibliographical information as well as a summary of those qualities that make the reprinted author deserving of the reader's attention. Not so in Pidmohyl'nyi's essay, which concentrates almost entirely on two of Nechui's major failings as a writer, only to end up praising the final product nonetheless.

In the Ukrainian literary discourse of the 1920s there was a great deal of writing on the question of literary plots, or, more specifically, on the importance of plot in prose fiction. Essentially, this was a debate between elitists and populists – between, on the one hand, intellectual modernists who felt that literature does not need to serve social functions or meet the expectations of the average reader, and on the other hand, conservative Marxist ideologues who assumed that a work of prose should be driven by plot so that the reader could orient the text within a familiar world. Pidmohyl'nyi would naturally have subscribed to the elitist and modernist position, although like all intellectuals he exercised caution to avoid the more dire consequences of too gleefully disagreeing with Stalinist Bolsheviks. Nechui, however, was a problematic figure as far as plots are concerned. As we shall see below, Nechui's works are not particularly well constructed in their plots. Pidmohyl'nyi, explicitly following Iefremov's lead, discusses Nechui's "feeble dramaticality,"[18] by which he means "a poorly defined plot and a diffuse composition with a tendency to morph into descriptive genealogy."[19] Pidmohyl'nyi argues that Nechui's "first sin," his inadequate attention to composition and the lack of any narrative emotion, is, in fact, no sin at all. "It may, of course, be painful for us to read such an author, but that does not mean it is illegal to write that way,"[20]

Pidmohyl'nyi reassures his readers with a judgment that does not sound like a compliment to Nechui. Anatole France, too, writes without emotion and without plot, he continues. But the author of the introduction then denies that there is any similarity between Nechui and France. "Plotlessness and emotionlessness are not faults at all,"[21] concludes Pidmohyl'nyi, using his views in the 1920s debates about literary construction to "absolve" Nechui of "faults" not because Nechui does not commit them, but because they should not be considered faults.

Having condemned his subject with this feigned praise, Pidmohyl'nyi then goes on to his most damning remarks: "Перший із справжніх гріхів нашого автора єсть необробленість його фрази. Його твори справляють таке враження, ніби автор їх ніколи, написавши, не перечитував – так вдирається в очі кострубатість, неохайність його речень"[22] [The first true sin of our author is the uncultivated shape of his expression. His works give the impression, as if once having written them, he never read them over. The rough and untidy character of his sentences hurts the eye]. As an example, Pidmohyl'nyi then goes on to quote a passage from *Kaidasheva sim'ia* emphasizing in boldface particular words that get repeated in it:

> "Всі люди, що сиділи коло церкви, повставали **й почали христитись**. Кайдашеві було видко увесь шпиль, на котрому стояла **церква**, всіх людей коло **церкви**. Він зняв шапку й **почав христитись**." Навіть не-письменник зміркував-би висловитись так: "Всі люди, що сиділи коло церкви, повставали й почали христитись. Кайдашеві було видко увесь шпиль, на котрому стояла церква, і всіх людей коло **неї**. Він зняв шапку й **теж** почав христитись" (3:314–15). Вживати займенників та сполучників – це-ж перший, дитячий крок в організації, не то художньої, просто пристойної фрази!

> ["All the people who sat by the church got up and **began to cross themselves**. Kaidash could see the entire hill on which the **church** stood, all the people who stoood beside the **church**. He took off his hat and **began to cross himself**." Even an illiterate would figure out to say it this way: "All the people who sat by the church got up and began to cross themselves. Kaidash could see the the entire hill on which the church stood and all the people beside **it**. He took off his hat and **also** began to cross himself. The use of pronouns and adverbs is an elementary, a childish step in the organization of an expression, not just a literary one, but any decent expression.][23]

While the sin of poor plot construction could be dismissed with an appeal to modernist aesthetics (even if they did not properly apply to Nechui), this "first true sin" is a very serious indictment. There can be no such thing as a decent writer who fails an elementary test of clear writing. Although Pidmohyl'nyi goes on to argue that Nechui's works deserve our attention despite these elementary writing flaws, on account of the entirety of the image he creates in them, this argument, this second round of forgiveness, lacks any logic or conviction. There really can be some absolution for a writer's inattention to plot. There certainly cannot be any forgiveness for inattention to words and sentences. If Pidmohyl'nyi's charge that Nechui simply cannot write is true, then surely Nechui does not deserve the attention of successive generations of readers.

Yet, just as surely, Nechui deserves our attention. Even Pidmohyl'nyi, and Iefremov before him, conclude that Nechui is an important author, despite their misgivings about his style and technique. Other critics enthusiastically praise Nechui, and generations of readers have found him worthwhile and memorable (though, to be fair, generations of schoolchildren forced to read his works in the school curriculum have found him boring and too old-fashioned to be of any interest). Is Pidmohyl'nyi wrong in his assessment? Many critics and readers, particularly those enamoured of modernist literature, see Nechui as a hopelessly weak and outdated writer and would, no doubt, be ready to accept Pidmohyl'nyi's evaluation of his skill as a writer. But a careful review of the evidence Pidmohyl'nyi himself provides leads to a different conclusion.

In the example quoted above and in a few of the other examples he gives, the basic issue is repetition. In another set of examples, Pidmohyl'nyi demonstrates that sometimes Nechui makes no particular effort to smooth out the narrative flow from one sentence to another. One short sentence follows another without the familiar conjunctions, adverbs, or other connecting devices that facilitate the reader's comprehension. In a third and final set of examples, Pidmohyl'nyi complains that Nechui relies too heavily on comparisons that lose their vitality because they are repetitious and annoyingly familiar. What's clear in all of this is that Pidmohyl'nyi is responding to a particular style that is evident in Nechui's writing. The key ingredients of this style, in the context of Pidmohyl'nyi's criticism, are a very deliberate, slow pacing and repetition. Pidmohyl'nyi assumes that these are symptoms of poor writing. Perhaps they are in fact merely elements of a style that Pidmohyl'nyi (and many a like-minded reader) doesn't like. Whatever the verdict, they are not accidents from the pen of a careless and inattentive writer. They are very deliberate and conscious choices that Nechui makes to enhance the flavour of his literary feast.

As a term used in reference to artistic works, repetition covers a very diverse range of phenomena. It can apply to any reference or allusion within a single work of art, or to an element within another work of art, or even to an element beyond any work of art. Among the elements that can be repeated are ideas, images, constructions, subjects, objects, motifs, themes, characters, places, actions, etc. Anything that constitutes an element of a work of art can potentially be a repetition. This very wide field of aesthetic and philosophical interest has attracted considerable scholarly attention and represents a very fruitful area for research and exploration. The notions advanced in Gilles Deleuze's *Difference and Repetition* (1968) open a world of fresh new possibilities in the exploration of repetition in literature. No doubt, this approach might be applied to Nechui's works with very interesting results. But that is not the kind of repetition that concerns us here, nor does the understanding of repetition as an accumulation of intertextual allusions. The kind of repetition that is most evident in Nechui's works needs to be addressed with the tools of rhetorical and narrative description, rather than philosophical or historical analysis.

One of the most revealing examples of rhetorical repetition in Nechui's works occurs on the opening page of his novel *Mykola Dzheria*:

> Широкою долиною між двома рядками розложистих гір тихо тече по Васильківщині невеличка річка Раставиця. Серед долини зеленіють розкішні густі та високі верби, там ніби потонуло в вербах село Вербівка. Між вербами дуже виразно й ясно блищить проти сонця висока біла церква з трьома банями, а коло неї невеличка дзвіниця неначе заплуталась в зеленому гіллі старих груш. Подекуди з-поміж верб та садків виринають білі хати та чорніють покрівлі високих клунь.
>
> По обидва береги Раставиці через усю Вербівку стеляться сукупні городи та левади, неодгороджені тинами. Один город одділяється од другого тільки рядком верб або межами. Понад самим берегом в'ється в траві стежка через усе село. Підеш тією стежкою, глянеш кругом себе, і скрізь бачиш зелене-зелене море верб, садків, конопель, соняшників, кукурудзи та густої осоки. (3:34)

[Near the town of Vasylkiv, the small Rastavytsia River quietly flowed across a wide valley between two rows of gently sloping hills. Clumps

> of lush, tall willows dotted the valley where the village of Verbivka lay engulfed in their greenery. A high, white-walled, three-domed church was clearly visible in the sun, and beside it a small bell tower seemed entangled in the green branches of old pear trees. Here and there, whitewashed cottages and black roofs of big barns peeped out from among the willows and orchards.
>
> Communal vegetable fields and meadows stretched across the village on either side of the river. There were no fences; plots were separated only by boundaries or rows of willows. A footpath wound its way through Verbivka along the grassy riverbank. Looking around from that path, one could only see a green, green sea of willows, orchards, hemp, sunflowers, corn and thick-growing sedge.][24]

In this opening landscape of the novel, within the eight sentences that constitute the first two paragraphs, the words "verba" and "Verbivka" (Willow-ville) occur a total of eight times.[25] Perhaps Pidmohyl'nyi would find this excessive and objectionable, but the passage is aesthetically effective and the repetition of a keyword helps create a particular effect on the reader. Nechui is attempting something similar to the famous repetition of the word "fog" in the second paragraph of the first chapter of Charles Dickens's *Bleak House*. Just as Dickens's fog describes both the actual weather in London and the metaphorical lack of clarity in the High Courts of Chancery, so, too, Nechui's willows are more than just the predominant tree in this central Ukrainian village. They are a symbol of the qualities of this place – verdant, luxurious, healthy. They are also, as the village name indicates, a symbolic component of its human dimensions. They stand as metaphorical surrogates of the inhabitants to whom the natural qualities are thus ascribed. This becomes particularly evident in the second paragraph, where the gardens and meadows are described as being without fences, divided only by the willows themselves. Of course, Nechui wants to emphasize the harmony that characterizes village residents in their relations. Unlike Robert Frost's twentieth-century unfriendly New Englander,[26] they don't need fences. But the willows that do separate these garden plots are not there accidently. As Nechui explains on the next page: "Усі вулиці в Вербівці ніби зумисне обсаджені високими вербами: то поросли вербові кілки тинів" (3:35) [All the streets in Verbivka are lined with tall willows that seem to have been planted there on purpose. Actually, they're willow fence poles that have taken root]. As Nechui and most village boys know very well, a willow stick pushed into the ground might easily take root and grow into a tree. It turns out that the willows in Verbivka are not only the natural ornament of this valley; they are also a living monument to human activity, an enduring sign of human civilization. They offer testimony of the naturalness and appropriateness of the human presence in this valley. Like the willows that surround them, the residents of Verbivka have taken root in this place, they belong to it, although it certainly does not belong to them, since they are serfs. Verbivka's willows, its inhabitants, its buildings, and its stream and millpond are all part of a simple natural order

The rootedness of the willows and the peasants is, of course, an important theme in the novel.[27] The story line of the novel depicts Mykola's uprooting, his enforced alienation from his family and the place where he belongs. The repetition of the word "willow" on these opening pages serves to call attention to this natural rootedness. Repetition thus functions as a form of emphasis, which further combines with a metaphorical interpretation of the significance of the repeated image to highlight an important thematic motif in the novel. This emphatic function is, essentially, a product of the reader's awareness of the fact of repetition.[28] This awareness is a form of disturbance in the otherwise smooth flow of a reader's appreciation of the text. Because this disturbance takes place in a temporal dimension, repetition also has a rhythmic function. The reader perceives it as a temporal pattern of events. Even a single recurrence can produce a faint sense of a pattern, but multiple recurrences invariably imprint themselves as a measure of temporal flow that stands in various relations to other temporal measures the reader may be aware of, particularly those of the text itself, its clauses, sentences, paragraphs, pages, chapters, etc. Nechui makes very specific use of this rhythmic function of repetition. He uses it to alter the tempo of his narration and to reinforce the reader's sense of familiarity with the characters and setting of the story.

Unlike a musical rhythm, which sets a basic, underlying pattern, the rhythmic function of rhetorical repetition is a singular phenomenon that the reader perceives against a backdrop of underlying patterns established by other features of the text or the story. However, the first repetition of the word "verba" in *Mykola Dzheria* occurs in the first two paragraphs of the text, before there is much of an opportunity to establish any other rhythm. In what is, by its genre, an introductory, scene-setting landscape description the reader is bombarded with a long sequence of recurrences that highlight and dramatize the passage. The rhetorical rhythm is somewhat at odds with the bucolic languor of the serene river valley. This perception is reinforced by other rhetorical devices, such as the alliteration of the "r" sound in the first sentence. Verbivka and the Ros' River valley get a somewhat surprisingly staccato introduction. In subsequent paragraphs there are fewer recurrences. The reader feels the tempo subside, the tension of the narrative diminishes. The willows still appear in the text, recalling the earlier paragraphs, but their frequency is reduced and they are explicitly referenced as repetitious elements: "На греблі знов у два рядки видивляються в воді дуже старі, товсті, дуплинасті верби" (3:35) [On the dam once again two rows of old, thick, hollow-ridden willows were reflected in the water]. The technique has a curious effect on the reader. The sequence of recurrences is apparently not finished, but its character has changed. The repetition itself now seems familiar, the emphatic effect is therefore reduced. The tempo is diminished. The passage suggests an incompleteness. Something is missing. The reader expects either an abandonment of the repetition – its function is already established – or an elaboration that leads to closure. But in the third and fourth paragraphs, Nechui deliberately holds back, teasing the reader, as it were, with a very unhurried narrative style that draws the reader even further into what will eventually turn out to be a very simple and familiar image of a Ukrainian village. The lethargy and familiarity are, of course, qualities of the village that Nechui thus passes to the reader as a sensation embodied in the text.

Eventually, the author takes pity on the reader and at the beginning of paragraph five, explains the fence-post origins of the willows lining the streets of the village.[29] This recurrence of willows has a different character than the previous ones – it offers a rational explanation of the significance of the image that has been elaborated. Because it explains, this recurrence gives the reader a sense of finality, of closure. After the deliberate delay of the preceding two paragraphs, the rhetorical device and the importance of the image are now complete. But the closure is potentially disappointing. The explanation is so simple. The reader had fully accepted such a reading even before being offered this additional guidance. Nechui's use of repetition is sometimes elaborate, but it is not complicated. The apparent purpose of the device is to give emphasis, but that emphasis is neither surprising nor profound. A more significant function of the device is to control the rhythm of the narration and to enhance the aesthetic qualities of the text. It is a verbal, narrative device used as much for its rhetorical, artistic function in the shaping of the narrative as for its potential to enhance the articulation of thematic material. In this latter recurrence, repetition leads to closure, to a technical break between the opening landscape description and the story that follows. For the most part, however, repetition is decoration, it adds aesthetic qualities to the text. Nechui uses the device constantly. Even as he brings the recurrences of willows to a close, he ends the fifth paragraph with a doubled epanalepsis: "Дивишся й не надивишся, дишеш і не надишешся" (3:35) [You look and you cannot look enough, you breathe in and you cannot breathe in enough]. Nechui repeats, and he cannot repeat enough. It's a central feature of the rhythm and folksy flavour of his prose.

Repetition as an instrument of style controlling the narrative tone and tempo can be found throughout Nechui's works. The examples of poor writing presented by Valerian Pidmohyl'nyi are instructive. The passage quoted above where the word "church" is repeated rather than being replaced by a pronoun is part of the very familiar episode in *Kaidasheva sim'ia* in which Kaidash and his sons break a wagon axle driving down the uneven hillside road that everyone in the village has been too lazy to straighten out and level despite the frequent accidents. So even before any further details are added, the scene depicts the natural anger and frustration of a man who has suffered a road accident and financial loss as a result, at least in part, of his own and his sons' unwillingness to fix the public road. But Nechui wants to build up the comic tension in this scene, so he adds a few elements to the setting. It's Sunday, and Kaidash is an obsessively religious man. In a narrative comment on the previous page, Nechui made clear that peasants honour Sundays and holidays and perform no work on these days, with the exception of bringing in sheaves from the fields. That's what Kaidash and his sons are doing, when the wagons overturn. So Kaidash, not surprisingly for such a devout man, associates the accident with the church as a self-reprimand. If he had gone to church instead of bringing in the sheaves, the accident would not have happened – at least, not today. But the matter does not end there. Kaidash's older son, Karpo, is in love with Motria and expects to meet her in church on Sunday. It is the sight of Motria on her way to church that distracts Karpo on the hill and results in the accident. So when the axle of the first wagon breaks and the second wagon runs on into the first and overturns, for both Kaidash and his older son the church holds a prominent position in their respective self-consciousness: devout repentance for one, and romantic pleasure for the other. The narrator's repetitive mentions of the church mirror Kaidash's mental preoccupation. The church offers him the relief that his guilty, devout conscience is seeking. The recurrence of the word in these sentences flows from a subjective focalization by the narrator on the sensibilities of Kaidash, who wants and needs to express his devotion and contrition, just like the other parishioners whom he observes crossing themselves by the church. Mimicry of the character's feelings is a basic technique of comic narrative, and it is in play here.

Another dimension of this repetition that relates to comedic devices is tempo. Nechui makes every attempt to drag out the scene of the accident into as memorable an experience as he can. This, too, is a basic technique in comedy. The comic hero must squirm in his discomfort for as long as possible – this enhances the power of the joke. Nechui stretches out the narration of the accident with a number of devices, including cuts between the simultaneous events on the hill and Motria's preparations for church. Repetition plays an important role here as well, and it occurs both in the words of the narrator and in the words of the characters. Kaidash alerts his son as the wagons approach the dangerous section of road by instructing him to bear to the right, using the traditional term of Ukrainian peasants for guiding draught animals: "цабе" [tsabe]. Karpo promptly repeats this instruction to the two oxen, separately for each one. A paragraph goes by in which we learn that Karpo is actually watching Motria and his wagon is tipping precariously, and then again we hear Kaidash, now desperately yelling "Держи цабе!" [Keep to the right!] and then again "Карпе, держи-бо цабе!" [Karpo, keep to the right!!]. The comic climax is in the narrator's words, which include an indirect quotation of Kaidash, still yelling "цабе" as the wagon rolls over into the ditch. The repetition of this richly ethnographic word characterizes Kaidash as a comic simpleton and slows down the action, seemingly allowing it to unfold in a repetitious, slow-motion visual and audio presentation in which a brief story time has been stretched into a lengthier narrative time. On the opposite side of the accident, Kaidash twice repeats the phrase "мене покарала свята неділя" (3:314–15) [I have been punished by holy Sunday]. The repetition reflects pious Kaidash's anger and frustration, but it also continues the rhythmic effect of slowing the action by replaying the character's reaction. In a final twist of comic contrivance, Nechui then has Karpo repeat the phrase in ironic mockery of his father, thereby giving closure to the slapstick depiction of Kaidash and turning the reader's attention to Karpo himself, who has lost his chance to meet Motria in church. Repetition has served three purposes: comic irony, narrative pacing, and textual decoration.

Not every instance of repetition in Nechui's works can withstand such a detailed analysis. Iefremov, Pidmohyl'nyi, and many other critics are right to note that the author uses repetition very frequently. And the device is not limited to any particular narrative mode or style. It occurs in the language of the characters. It occurs in the narrator's focalized and unfocalized voice. It occurs between the language of the characters and the language of the narrator. It occurs as a major element in extended passages, and it occurs as a simple oddity in single sentences. The reader is frequently faced with verbal constructions that highlight the recurrence of a word without the elaborate choreography that was shown in the passages analysed above. For example, in the novel *Neodnakovymy stezhkamy* from 1902, Taisa Andriivna, in a moment of self-contentment, consumes "дорогий запашний чай з варенням та крихкими кренделями, до чого ця випещена ласійка була дуже ласа" (8:433) [expensive aromatic tea with jam and crisp pastry, for which this spoiled, craving woman had a strong craving]. A reader with a taste for only the most elegant, lean, and simple linguistic pastry may well find this craving for repetition repetitious, as Pidmohyl'nyi does. But the device occurs with such frequency, regularity, and, occasionally, with such clear purpose, that it is simply impossible to dismiss it as the unconscious product of a careless writer. For better or worse, Nechui employs this device very deliberately throughout his works. Also, its use is tied to a number of other features of his writing, particularly plot development and character delineation.

Another example Pidmohyl'nyi gives speaks directly to the role of repetition in the development and tempo of the story line. He mentions two episodes in *Kaidasheva sim'ia* in which an anticipated repetition is delayed. In the first example between the narrator's announcement that Marusia Kaidash has stepped out of her door to call her family to lunch, using the much-favoured "вечірній пруг" [evening arc] expression, to when she actually calls them in to eat, an entire paragraph intervenes with a lengthy characterization of this pompous woman who served in the master's kitchen when she was young and now behaves as if she were better than the other villagers (3:304–5). When only Lavrin comes to eat, Marusia repeats the invitation and Nechui mentions the arc of the sun again. Late in the afternoon, as Kaidash sets off for church, the sun's position is mentioned once more. Pidmohyl'nyi is apparently annoyed that the narrator does not move directly from Marusia at the door to her calling the men for lunch. The effect here is similar to a cinema flashback: we learn Marusia's biography as she stands in the sunlight, framed by the door of her house. The tableau is not unlike the one that framed Kaidash just inside his barn door on the second page of the novel. Nechui likes to bring his characters on stage and then – slowly, deliberately, expansively, exploringly, exhaustively, annoyingly – to stop the action for a moment while he gives them a character profile. Pidmohyl'nyi, a psychological realist who portrays characters through their actions and words, does not favour this kind of old-fashioned description while the action of the story is arrested. What Pidmohyl'nyi does not note, but might have, is that this scene is not only slowed down by the descriptive digression that delays the act of inviting the men to lunch, its dramatic impact is enhanced by this digression. Through the delay, lunch seems to acquire a greater importance. Actually, of course, Kaidash, who fasts on Fridays, doesn't come home for lunch, only his sons do. Marusia's unusually drawn-out invitation builds a contrast between her pretentious, formal expectations and Kaidash's foolish religious fervour. The day ends with the hungry old zealot wasting his money and his evening at the village tavern, where his day-long fast has finally landed him for some decidedly unhallowed relief. Repetition thus frames a pattern of digression and return that is an important component of Nechui's storytelling.

Something similar occurs in the second example of delay that Pidmohyl'nyi offers. At the beginning of chapter 2 of *Kaidasheva sim'ia* Karpo goes to visit his sweetheart, Melashka, who is engaged in the quintessentially ethnographic activity of whitewashing and decorating her house. Her materials are two jugs of clay, one red and the other white. The girl has the red jug in her hands, and the second jug is on the ground by the doorsill (3:309). Pidmohyl'nyi elaborates: "We read on for a page – there's nothing about this second jug. In the middle of the second page, angry at the author for introducing irrelevant details, we finally forget about the second jug with the white clay, until suddenly, on the third page we see 'Karpo turned around to avoid soiling his boot and struck the second jug with white clay with the heel of his foot.'"[30] What Pidmohyl'nyi doesn't mention is that the jug with the red clay has already spilled. Karpo and Melashka have been engaged in a very familiar scene of slapstick romantic courtship that would not be out of place in a Charlie Chaplin comic film. The fact that the white jug goes unmentioned for three pages while the red jug is at the centre of the comic action is, once again, very basic comic technique. As Pidmohyl'nyi admits, the reader is waiting for the white clay to spill as well as the red clay. Since the joke will end there, the white jug is delayed until the events have played out to their maximum duration. The real issue here is that Nechui's estimate of the maximum length of a comic scene – that is, of the best rhythm for comic material – is different from Pidmohyl'nyi's.

Nechui's use of repetition for narrative rhythm and the framing of narrative digressions is a component of a larger issue concerning the shaping of narrative and the structure of plot in his works. This is a difficult subject in literary studies. The nature of what constitutes an effective plot and, as a corollary, what constitutes an ineffective plot is a highly contentious issue. In the twentieth century, in particular, there has been a great deal of experimentation on this issue leading, seemingly, to the disappearance of any general rules about what makes a good story and how it should be told. Nevertheless, readers have expectations about the shape of a story, particularly when they consider a given work to belong to a specific genre of literature or to represent a particular style of writing. If a murder mystery ends without a solution to the crime, readers will feel disappointed – or, at least, classify the work as an unusual example of the genre. Such reader expectations are, of course, shaped by many factors, including the development of literary forms and the style of a given author or a given work. They are by no means shared by all readers, even in the same time and cultural environment, let alone across generations and cultural boundaries. To a certain degree, they are a matter of personal taste. Yet, there are patterns in these expectations that many readers share. Perhaps it's these differences in personal taste, in the patterns of reader expectations, that have led many readers to regard Nechui's works as poorly constructed stories.

The most damning formulation of this concern occurs in an introduction by Andrii Nikovs'kyi to a popular edition of Nechui's *Mykola Dzheria* published in 1926. In this lengthy essay Nikovs'kyi discusses the difference between works of literature that are based on plot and works that are based on character, and it is this discussion that provoked Pidmohyl'nyi's remarks on plots that were mentioned above. Nikovs'kyi, although not a conservative Marxist ideologue, adopts in this introduction a Marxist position on the value of literary works. He insists that the value of literature is tied to reality, to the depiction of actual issues that affect living people (or those who lived at other times). He distinguishes between two modes of storytelling: one focused on characters, which he terms a portrait approach, and the other focused on events, which he calls a plotted (*siuzhetnyi*) approach. In his view, the portrait or psychological approach is distinctly inferior. It offers the reader only a passing entertainment, although in a great literary tradition the accumulation of these psychological portraits builds up the volume of literary production, which will in turn nurture the growth of true genius. "Only a high level of artistry in developing the fundamental universal plots (and only partially one's own national and local plots) will lead this or that literature out of the limits of domestic usage onto the free expanse of world literature."[31] Nikovs'kyi sees *Mykola Dzheria* as such a psychological type of writing, and he wonders how a European reader, accustomed to the masterpieces of world literature, would respond to this novel. After asserting that such a reader would see the work as a weak variant on the plot of Tristan and Isolde in *Uncle Tom's Cabin*, Nikovs'kyi asserts:

> Пускатися в дальші літературні розумування з цим нашим слухачем европейцем краще не треба, бо нічого доброго окрім непорозуміння з того не вийде: він почне нарікати на малий і кволий драматизм ситуацій або закидатиме Левицькому сірий та безрадісний кінець його героїв, і буде мати рацію, бо тільки те добре в житті і в літературі, що виразно кінчається, – добре або-ж зле, – а тут у нас вийде, що багато чого в повісті (роман з Нимидорою, з Мокриною, відносини з паном, то-що) не кінчається ніяк. Отже покиньмо нашого чужинця з порадою прочитати самому всю повість та познайомитися ширше з українською літературою, погодімось на тому, що якийсь сюжет у повісті Нечуя-Левицького єсть, що він мало розроблений, але все-ж цікавий, що внутрішня діялектика повісти й зовсім слаба, бо не розроблені всі логічні можливості з даної комбінації відносин та психологія втягнутих у сюжет дієвих осіб трактована досить одноманітно, але зате чимало конструктивних дефектів, вад (а не помилок!) можна пояснити самою темою цього твору та свідомою громадською тенденцією цього автора.[32]

[There is no point in continuing a literary debate with our European listener, because, aside from misunderstanding, nothing good will come of it: He will start to complain about the deficient and lame dramatic tension in the scenes or he will admonish Levyts'kyi for the grey and forlorn destiny of his heroes. And he will be right, because in life and in literature, only what ends clearly (whether for better or worse) is good. But here it turns out that plenty of things in the novel (the romance with Nymydora, with Mokryna, relations with the master, etc.) do not end in any way at all. So let's leave our foreigner with the suggestion that he read the entire novel and gain a wider familiarity with Ukrainian literature. Let's agree that there is some kind of plot in Nechui-Levyts'kyi's novel, that it's poorly developed but nevertheless interesting; that the internal dialectic of the novel is very weak because all the logical possibilities that arise from the given combination of relations are not developed, and because the psychology of the characters who are drawn into the plot is treated rather monotonously; but a number of the structural defects, faults (but not mistakes!) can be explained by the theme of the novel and by the conscious political tendencies of this author.]

Despite the confusing and backhanded manner of his presentation, Nikovs'kyi is making a familiar and comprehensible point. Nechui's fictional works generally share two qualities of construction: they are built around a very simple plot that lacks dramatic tension, and they are not built around logical or emotional arguments for a particular thematic idea or position. These qualities of construction are evident on various levels of Nechui's works, from the overall structure of the works to the structure of individual scenes and chapters.

As we have seen in some of the examples of repetition above, Nechui often relies on a circular narrative direction that brings the exposition back to the point from which it started. This circularity is most evident in the large canvas of some of his plots. At the beginning of the novel, Mykola Dzheria gets married and leaves his village. At the end, he returns to his village, but his wife is no longer alive and he is as solitary in his old age as he was during the bulk of his life, which he lived away from his village. The plot has the protagonist actually return to his village and his family, but the chief quality of this plot line, and most of Nechui's plots, is not so much in the actual return to a condition defined at the beginning of the work, but in the absence of any linear progress, the failure (in the development of the plot) to resolve the major issues that were presented at the beginning of the story. This is Nikovs'kyi's major complaint about *Mykola Dzheria*. The novel begins with a manifestation of the horrors of Russian serfdom. It ends with serfdom abolished, but the social situation hardly any better than it was under serfdom. The social rebel who is the protagonist of the work spends his life away from his home and his family, with nothing to show for his suffering and his rebellion at the end. Any revolutionary, and especially a Marxist, would be disappointed with such a plot, since it does not show the benefits of social change. Every reader cannot help but observe that in its plot and in its thematic structure, the novel does not offer an image of progress or redemption, or even heroism. There is no thematic advancement. Whether the action is judged to be circular, repetitive, or simply static, Nechui's plots and thematic constructions generally end up in the same place where they began, or, more precisely, they do not reach any particular dramatic or thematic goal. They are non-purposeful.

In *Mykola Dzheria*, for instance, Nechui does not actually focus on the social problems that critics, particularly Soviet critics, invariably mention as the thematic centre of the novel. As Nikovs'kyi points out,[33] the novel was written a decade and a half after the abolition of serfdom. In 1878 Nechui could no longer adopt the abolitionist tone that characterizes the work of writers such as Marko Vovchok. The novel does indeed depict the inhumanity of serfdom, but these scenes are limited to the first two chapters, a mere quarter of the book as a whole. After that, Mykola and the runaways experience another form of exploitation, industrial labour, but this, too, lasts for only two chapters. The third section of the novel, again two chapters, depicts a life of relative peace and tranquillity, although far from home. Chapter 7 is a digression about the life of Nymydora and those left behind in the village. The suffering here is largely a result of the absence of Mykola, rather than the underlying social conditions. Finally, the last chapter accelerates the action of the plot; events reach a climax but, in an act of apparently divine intervention, serfdom is abolished and Mykola returns home, only to find new loneliness and a new regimen of social inequality. The text ends with the image of an elderly Mykola telling youngsters stories about the adventures he experienced. Beyond any doubt, the work is held together by its titular protagonist rather than an interest in depicting social conditions.

Nechui's novel is often juxtaposed with Panas Myrnyi's *Khiba revut' voly iak iasla povni* (Would the oxen bellow if the mangers were full), a novel that takes a very broad historical survey of both social and family history. But Myrnyi's novel is focused at every turn on the influence of social injustice – historically and in the present – on the behaviour of its protagonist. Nechui's novel is very different. Here, there is hardly any sense of causal relationships. Serfdom is a despicable institution that ruins people's lives, but in the chapters set in Bessarabia, Mykola has in fact escaped its reach, though not very happily. It is the personality of Mykola that is central to the story. He is a rebel, a hothead who responds angrily and violently against injustices of all kinds. But he is not a hero. His rebellions appear sooner as instinct than as purposeful activity. They accomplish very little of value. On the contrary, when he returns his family and his village are suspicious of him and only grudgingly accept him back. Nechui's novel thus never reaches a meaningful thematic statement. Nechui has not produced an exposé of social injustice, he has not produced a portrait of noble suffering, and he has not created a model of heroic struggle. Like Faulkner's Yoknapatawpha County, Nechui's Verbivka and its inhabitants merely endure, but unlike Faulkner's characters, Nechui's do not acquire the stature of exemplary human beings, symbols of the moral and philosophical importance of the human condition. Nechui avoids the elements of plot and structure that would ennoble his characters or provide the reader with abstract ideas that give meaning or explanation to the dilemmas he portrays.

In *Mykola Dzheria*, this avoidance is most apparent in the deliberate unwillingness to explain a key event. In chapter 2, as Mykola and the other serfs are leaving the village, the night sky is illuminated. The master's stackyard and barns have been set ablaze. Nechui depicts the scene in a beautiful, extended passage full of colour and extraordinary detail. But he never explains who was responsible. The men watching on the hillside raise this question and one of them, Kavun, says that the arsonist will be revealed by the image of his soul flying in the sparks of the fire. Mykola rebuffs the superstitious idea, but in the next scene, as noted earlier, Nymydora, losing her rational faculties, sees Mykola in the flames. The matter ends there. As Nikovs'kyi suggests,[34] perhaps Nechui is using this image to reveal who the arsonist is. But there is no certainty here. Nechui clearly does not want to reveal who set the fire. Even without Nymydora's hallucination, readers would consider Mykola a primary suspect. The connection between Kavun's remark and Nymydora's vision is not emphasized, and it is not self-evidently plain. Responsibility for the crime remains uncertain. Analytical readers might suggest various reasons for Nechui's reticence. Perhaps he felt an attribution for the crime would be seen as an endorsement of violent revolt against social order – something censors in both Russia and Austria would view unfavourably. Perhaps he felt an attribution to Mykola would lead readers to turn away from his protagonist and judge him too harshly. But these potential arguments are very weak. Far more likely is the simple fact that such an attribution would clarify what Nechui means to keep vague; it would add rational purpose to what is meant to remain indeterminate, it would alter the character of the fiction he is producing, pointing it towards drama, social significance, and explanation (as in Myrnyi's novel), rather than perception, sensibility, portrait, and landscape – the core elements of Nechui's non-purposeful writing style.

In most of Nechui's other novels, this non-purposeful approach is even more evident. *Starosvits'ki batiushky ta matushky* is unabashedly structured as a chronicle of the way clergymen lived in the first half of the nineteenth century. As already noted, the plot follows the careers of two priests, Kharytin Mossakovs'kyi and Marko Balabukha. The former is a local boy without much education who has been elected parish priest by his community. The latter is a seminary-educated careerist. Nechui switches focus, alternating the two men in their relations with women, their relations with parishioners, their relations with church and secular authorities. In some cases, entire chapters are juxtaposed, each presenting parallel events in the life of one of the priests. Nechui satirizes both men. Balabukha turns out to be more successful, but he is nevertheless unhappy. Kharytin is a hopeless bumpkin, but he is a far more personable and likable man. While Nechui makes no particular effort to suggest any conclusions on the basis of the juxtaposition of these two men, the events in the novel follow a simple logic of comparison. But at the beginning of chapter 9 Kharytin dies and the focus switches to his widow, Onysia. The last two chapters then focus on domestic affairs in the Balabukha household, particularly the role of his wife, Orysia. The balanced comparison of the two priests is thus partially unbalanced in the final pages of the book. The novel concludes with the marriages of the children in both families, that is, it returns to the same issues with which it began, the disposition of parishes and the marriages of clergymen's daughters, which are often one and the same matter. Nechui brings the events full circle to the next generation of characters, with very little purpose other than depicting life, habits, characters, and setting. Nechui's readers would no doubt have recognized that church reforms in mid-century had introduced changes into the life of the rural clergy that brought to an end the manners and customs described here, but this fact is nowhere specifically addressed in the text. The juxtaposition (i.e., repetition highlighting differences) of the two priests is neither an anticlerical satire nor a particular endorsement of the old ways. It is certainly not a justification of the impending institutional reforms intended to professionalize the clergy.

Aside from a nostalgic gratification in witnessing the mundane events in the lives of these characters, Nechui does not convey any special sentiment or judgment regarding the social setting he depicts. The plot is built in a circular pattern with repetition used for contrast. The events with which Nechui builds his plot, both here and in most of his novels, consist of courtship, marriage, and domestic family relations as well as the daily rituals that distinguish people by their professions. Both in its overall structure and in the construction of individual scenes or chapters, the action and the narrative are not designed to convey a particular judgment. For example, Onysia browbeats the metropolitan in Kyiv to assign her late husband's parish to the orphaned children, and her daughters hastily marry young seminarians. But despite keeping the parish in her own hands, Onysia is not particularly fortunate, nor are her daughters. In contrast to this, Balabukha's wife, Orysia, aspires to a great social future for her daughter, Nastia, whom she is matchmaking with the son of the foreign director of the sugar refinery. But the director leaves town after an argument with the local landlord, and Nastia ends up marrying a colourless widower with children who is a local administrative official. Nechui infuses both ends of this comparison with rich satiric details and wonderful comic situations, but there is no larger lesson hiding in the juxtaposition. These are merely fascinating characters with delightful peculiarities in intriguing situations.

The quality of non-purposeful storytelling is evident in the general plot of all of Nechui's novels. *Kaidasheva sim'ia*, like *Starosvits'ki batiushky ta matushky*, is a family chronicle except there is only one family involved (but contrast is developed through juxtaposing the love stories of the two sons). The story begins with discussions of the marriage prospects of the two sons. It ends with the two sons taking over their late father's property and continual quarrels between their two families. The only events along the way are the matrimonial enterprise and foolish domestic quarrels. Of course, this is satire, but the aim of this satire is too broad to have specific targets. Readers generally see this novel as a glorious, rollicking monument to the idiosyncrasies of life in a Ukrainian village. *Kaidasheva sim'ia* is satire without scorn, ridicule without contempt. It's comedy without instructive purpose.

The glue that binds this novel lies in the relations between the characters and in the accumulation (repetition?) of incidents that depict the personalities of the characters in the story. Kaidash is shown to be a weak-willed religious obscurantist. His wife, Marusia, is pretentious and proud. Time and again we see these traits without significant expansion or development. The qualities Marusia Kaidash displays on her visit to the Dovbyshes are no different from the qualities on view during the visit to the Balashes. The jokes may be different, but there is no advancement in the development of her character or in the reader's understanding of it. What there is, however, is a wonderfully colourful interplay of familiar personalities in a slow dance of anecdotal merriment. Works such as *Neodnakovymy stezhkamy*, *Afons'kyi proidysvit*, and *Kyivs'ki prokhachi* have a somewhat sharper focus because they concentrate on a single idea (respectively, social changes resulting from the disappearance of an agricultural economy, the hypocrisy of Orthodox monks, and charity as a corrupt industry). But even here the organization of the episodes and the overall plot do not lead to specific conclusions or to a thematic closure. The ideas presented at the beginning of these works are not significantly elaborated or explored in the course of the presentation.

The most telling examples of Nechui's non-purposeful construction are found in those works that depict the issues with which his writing is intimately concerned: the nationality question and marital relations. Nechui's historical fiction is very noteworthy in this regard, and these works will be explored in a subsequent chapter of this book. Marital relations are an abiding theme of Nechui's writing. The relations between husband and wife – or more generally, between men and women – are surely the most frequently encountered topic in his works. Occasionally, however, this topic assumes a greater significance in his works, as it does in *Ne toi stav*, *Na gastroliakh v Mykytianakh*, and "Gastroli." These works are central in any understanding of Nechui's depiction of women, a topic addressed in the next chapter, but in terms of their structure and plot, they avoid projecting a strong thematic idea. In the first of these, *Ne toi stav*, a woman struggles to find marital happiness with a husband who becomes a fanatically devoted religious scholar and abandons the normal joys and responsibilities of domestic life. Nechui makes clear the dimensions of the problem, but stops short of actually analysing it. His story includes a variety of instruments for comparison and analysis. Solomiia is compared to Zin'ka, Roman is juxtaposed to his friend Denys and his father in law, Fylon, but in the last chapter Nechui has Roman abandon religion and turn to drink, and Solomiia dies helping rescue neighbours from a house fire. The ending seems very contrived and discontinuous. The events and themes of the story lead nowhere, and Solomiia's death simply brings the story to an end, with no thematic closure, no catharsis, no insight. Solomiia is neither heroine nor victim.

Nechui's two variants of the "gastroli" story have a similar structure. In both versions, Sofiia takes a lover while her husband, an opera singer, is away from home. In both works (though more elaborately in the longer *Na gastroliakh v Mykytianakh*) Nechui reveals the incompatibility of the personalities of husband and wife and thus provides motivation for the wife's love affair. In both works, however, the love affair, after developing in a traditional manner that corresponds to the reader's expectations, ends without a morally or dramatically satisfying conclusion. In "Gastroli," the stationmaster, Nykolaidos, is suddenly forced to quit his job. He leaves the area and abandons Sofiia, who moves to Kyiv and finds a new lover. In the other version, Flegont has an angry confrontation with his faithless wife. Her young lover leaves and she returns to her husband. But the story continues for another five paragraphs, detailing the fate of Flegont's cousin, Levko, who also pursues a career as a singer but ends up taking his own life when an unfortunate disease robs him of his voice and his income. The connection between this anticlimactic ending and the events of the story is accidental and thematically obscure. The presumed reconciliation of husband and wife is not elaborated or explored. The melodramatic suicide of a secondary character creates a dramatic coda, but one whose tone seems peculiarly out of sync with the larger plot. Nechui's understanding of the basic form of his story seems disconnected from its plot. Levko's death at the end of the story is neither poetic justice nor tragic irony. Nechui seems explicitly to avoid the expected judgment and its appropriate dramatic exposition around which he has constructed his story.

This non-purposeful approach to storytelling lies at the heart of many readers' disaffection with Nechui's works. Among the earliest negative reactions to Nechui were those provoked by works that focused on what should be his signature theme: the development of Ukrainian national consciousness. As noted earlier, Pavlo Radiuk, the presumed hero of the novel *Khmary*, was criticized by Drahomanov, Konys'kyi, and others for the weakness of his active commitment to the Ukrainian cause, for being merely a spokesperson rather than an activist.[35] But all of these criticisms are built on the highly dubious assumption that Nechui set out to depict an activist hero. In fact, Radiuk – like all of Nechui's heroes from Mykola Dzheria to Andrian Hukovych (*Neodnakovymy stezhkamy*) and including Viktor Komashko, the schoolteacher in *Nad Chornym Morem* – is a product of a non-purposeful approach to story construction that does not presume to offer answers, display essential features, or provide analysis and judgment. Nechui builds his works on a measured, repetitive depiction of Ukrainians and Ukraine, of people and place, of characters and setting. He is not focused on ideas, analysis, or goals. His characters are not heroes, his settings are not metaphors. His writing is meant to offer a reflection of the beauty and reality of Ukraine. It is not directed at a social, political, moral, or even national purpose. In the culinary metaphor that Nechui used to describe his writing, the meal he prepares has no motive beyond good taste.

That meal, the words and images that Nechui assembles into a work of fiction, is nevertheless a reflection of the way things are, a description of the world as it is, a work of realist literature. The non-purposeful mode of storytelling that characterizes Nechui's fiction is not a product of postmodern relativism *avant la lettre*.[36] It is not because he believes that the essential nature of the world cannot be apprehended through the senses that Nechui avoids directing his fiction at particular truths and ideas. He does not subscribe to a postmodernist denial of the possibility of knowing and representing reality. What's more, his realism is not mere empiricism. Nechui's understanding of nationality and his focus on the historical and moral injustice suffered by Ukrainians are ample evidence of his abstract, idealist principles. His realism, like that of many other nineteenth-century novelists in Europe,[37] is focused on character and setting rather than theme.

There are a number of features that exemplify the realist quality of Nechui's writing. Chief among these is the focus on description, on a representation of the qualities of the world around him. As we have already seen, descriptions of setting, whether it be the Ros' River valley, scattered industrial enterprises, or various sites in Kyiv and Odessa, play a very important role in Nechui's writing. His personal geography is a marriage of representational accuracy with a search for beauty. Nechui does not invent settings to accommodate his stories. The places he describes actually exist, and what's more, he had experienced them personally. Like his descriptions of places, Nechui's descriptions of people rely on familiarity. Unlike the settings, though, the characters are, of course, fictitious (except for a few historical works, but even there, the personalities of the historical figures are Nechui's invention). Nechui draws these fictitious persons from the fraternity of his personal familiars, among whom are the families of clergymen, students in Kyiv, simple peasants, and characters from Shevchenko's works. In his later works, urban professionals and the lower gentry are added to the mix. True to realist principles, Nechui's characters are depicted as products of their environment, particularly of its material and financial realities. The description of Petro Dzheria's work-worn hands is a perfect example of realist descriptive practices:

В хату ввійшов старий Джеря, високий, тонкий, з сивуватими довгими вусами, з нужденним блідим лицем та смутними очима. Тяжка праця дуже зарані зігнула його стан. Глибокі зморшки на щоках, на лобі, поморщена темна потилиця од гарячого сонця, грубі руки – все це ніби казало, що йому важко жилося на світі. На його пальцях, навіть на долонях, шкура так поморщилась та порепалась, ніби потріскалась на жару. На лівій руці всі пальці трусились безперестану навіть тоді, як він спав. Скільки він вижав, перемолотив та перевіяв тими руками хліба на панщині за свій довгий вік! (3:40)

[Old Dzheria came inside. He was a lanky man with a pale, worn-out face, a long greyish moustache, and sorrowful eyes. Hard work had bowed his back early in life. Deep furrows running across his cheeks and forehead, his rough hands and the wrinkled, sunburnt back of his neck indicated that living in this world had not been easy for him. The skin on his fingers and even on his palms was so cracked and creased that it looked as if his hands had been burned by fire. The fingers on his left hand shook incessantly, even while he slept. During his long life he had mowed, threshed, and winnowed much of his master's grain with those hands.][38]

The majority of Nechui's characters are products of a less strenuous environment and are more likely to resemble the opera singer Flegont Litoshevs'kyi: "Артист був високенький, плечистий та тілистий, з білим лицем, русявий та з ясними карими очима. По білому виду, по рожевих устах було знать, що цей колишній селюк вже дуже спанів, бо скидався на випещеного панка-дідича" (8:11) [The artist was quite tall, large-shouldered, and fleshy, with a white face, blond hair, and bright brown eyes. The white skin and red lips gave notice that this former village boy had risen in social stature because he looked like a pampered lord and landowner]. The many priests and middle-class characters in Nechui's works are almost universally defined by their apparent leisure. Hardly anyone is ever shown working.

Beyond the important influence of social conditions, Nechui's characters are largely defined by a very limited set of personality traits, chief among which are vanity, greed, and the relations between the sexes. This limited palette is an innate feature of Nechui's writing, and it is not uncommon among realist writers. Furthermore, in keeping with the realist's allegiance to objective depiction, Nechui relies very heavily on self-characterization through dialogue. When combined with his tendency towards repetition, this means that a character might very often be described by the narrator, then have a similar characterization demonstrated in the character's own words, and then finally have these qualities noted by other characters in their speeches. The characters' own words are used to individualize the speakers in a number of ways. As many critics have noted, the peculiar language of the characters is a significant factor in their portrayal. Most of his characters speak in a rich and colourful Ukrainian that corresponds to Nechui's idealized remarks about the speech of a village hag. These qualities are not limited to rural characters – all of Nechui's fictional progeny share this colourful and flexible language. He does not use poor language or local dialects as a device for distinguishing characters. Differentiation is a matter of specific verbal habits, topics, and allusions or comparisons. The quarrelling hags Palazhka and Paraska are particularly adept at malediction, but it is the variety of their venomous invective, not the quality of their language, that makes their utterances memorable.

The directly quoted language of Nechui's characters is part of their individuality, but it does not reflect a concerted effort to reveal the inner workings of their minds. The limited set of personality traits on his character-building palette can produce different combinations that avoid obvious duplication of types, but Nechui is not an assiduous student of the human psyche. Psychology is not part of his toolbox. His characters do not undergo development, and their character is not shaped by events that transpire in the story. Dzheria returns home after a lifetime away with the same rebellious spirit that drove him to run away. Marriages in the Kaidash family open new channels of disagreement, but the principal actors are unchanged. Flegont Litoshevs'kyi watches his wife chase younger men but learns nothing from the experience. This fixed view of human behaviour is apparent in the verbal interaction between characters. These are not actually conversations between people who exchange ideas. Occasionally Nechui even allows the action to develop precisely in the failure of verbal communication, as he does in the love scene in *Pomizh vorohamy*, where Leonid and Vatia discover their feelings for each other through the absence of logic and reason in the words they are uttering:

– Який тут простір на цих рівних луках, між півкругами гір! Яке гарне місце! – говорив Леонід Семенович.

Ватя й не глянула на ті луки, неначе їх і не бачила. Вона тільки чула його голос, дзвінкий, аж трохи різкий, і мовчала.

– Казали ви, що вас нудьга бере на селі. Тепер і я, пробувши два місяці на селі, добре втямив, що ви казали правду. І мене вже нудьга бере, хоч і я зріс на селі, а мій панотець з простих селян. Як зустрінусь з просвіченим чоловіком, то в мене аж душа радіє. Одбився я од села … – говорив Леонід Семенович.

Ватя тепер тільки почала зважливо прислухаться й постерігать тяму в його розмові.

– І я не люблю села. Я по своїй вдачі міська людина. В місті менше клопоту: нема там цього клопотливого сільського господарства, тих поганих полів, овець, свиней, курей, гусей, – сказала Ватя.

– Зате ж в місті коні добрі, хоч нема волів та овець, – сказав Леонід Семенович.

– От коні я люблю, та ще й добрі, прудкі. Я люблю прудку проїздку, так, щоб коні летіли, як птиці, щоб аж дух забивало, – сказала Ватя.

– Панотець оце дав мені, щоб навідаться до сестри, пару робочих шкап, і я насилу допхався до Горобцівки. Од цих коней не заб'є духу, бо вони біжать підтюпцем, – сміявся Леонід Семенович.

– Чи давно бачились з Антосею? Як вам подобається Антося? – спитала Ватя якось несподівано й скоса зирнула на Леоніда Семеновича.

Йому стало ніяково; він замішався й не одразу одповів.

– Так собі … Весела й проворна … і щира людина. Ви любите її? Вона ваша приятелька? – спитав Леонід Семенович.

– Так собі … добра сусіда й знайома, – знехотя обізвалась Ватя, – мені здалось, що вона вам подобається.

– Подобається мені, як усі гарненькі, проворненькі панни, – сказав Леонід Семенович. – От тепер, так я дійсно знаю, що мені гарно з вами отут гуляти.

Ваті стало легше на душі. Вона зраділа й з великою цікавістю ждала, чи не признається він, що її любить. Але Леонід Семенович мовчав. Ватя трохи зобідилась.

– Чи не час нам вертаться назад? Тато й мама, мабуть ждуть мене та сердяться, – помовчавши, обізвалась Ватя. (6:209–10)

["What open space there is on these even meadows, amid the half orbs of the mountains! What a beautiful spot!" exclaimed Leonid Semenovych.

"You said that you were bored in the village. Now, having spent two months in the village, I have come to understand the full truth of what you said. Now I, too, am bored, although I grew up in a village and my father is a simple villager. When I meet an educated person, my spirit is filled with happiness. I have become alienated from the village," said Leonid Semenovych.

Only now did Vatia begin to listen carefully and to detect sense in his conversation.

"I, too, don't like the village. By my nature I am a city person. There is less trouble in the city – you don't have this troubling agriculture, these ugly oxen, sheep, pigs, chickens, geese," said Vatia.

"But there are good horses in the city, although there are no oxen and sheep," said Leonid Semenovych.

"Oh, I do like horses, especially good fast ones. I like a fast ride, with the horses flying like birds, so it takes your breath away," said Vatia.

"My father gave me a pair of his draught nags so I could visit my sister. I could hardly drag them to Horobtsivka. These horses won't take anyone's breath away, because they can barely muster a trot," laughed Leonid Semenovych.

"Has it been long since you saw Antosia? How do you like Antosia?" asked Vatia somewhat unexpectedly and glanced obliquely at Leonid Semenovych.

He felt embarrassed and became confused. He did not answer immediately.

"She's all right. Cheerful and spirited, and a sincere person. Do you like her? Is she a friend of yours?" asked Leonid Semenovych.

"She's all right. A good neighbour and an acquaintance," answered Vatia without thinking. "It seemed to me that maybe you like her?"

"I like her as I like all pretty and cheerful young ladies," said Leonid Semenovych. "At the moment, I know for a fact that it is nice to be walking with you."

Vatia was relieved. Her spirits rose and she was waiting with great excitement to hear if he would declare his love for her. But Leonid Semenovych was silent. Vatia soured.

"Perhaps it's time for us to return? Mom and Dad are probably waiting and angry," Vatia said after a moment's silence.]

From the beauty of the rural countryside we move to the boredom of the village and the quality of draught animals in urban areas. Likewise, a judgment about Vatia's rival, Antosia, cements the allegiance of Leonid to Vatia. This is a well-crafted illogical conversation, somewhat rare in Nechui's works for the irony that permeates its every sentence. It would fit equally well in a novel by Jane Austen or Leo Tolstoy, except that in both those instances, the topic of conversation would need to be more refined and more intellectually coherent. For Nechui, the world as it is, the reality that his works reflect, is eminently comprehensible, familiar, and reasonable. Irony, where it does appear – and that is not very often – is an instrument of satire, a device that allows readers to appreciate the friendly humour of innocent, unselfconscious lovers or long-suffering and long-married spouses. In chapter 7 of *Neodnakovymy stezhkamy*, Iakiv, the serious brother, gets a letter from his frivolous sibling, Myshka, in which the dandy announces his impending marriage to Melashka (8:366–8). The letter itself is mostly ironic, explaining, for example, that one of her better qualities as a marriage candidate is her garrulous nature. But the letter also explains that the inheritance of the estate is tied to the daughters, so he will eventually become a landowner. For the reader and for Iakiv, Myshka's self-ironizing is a symptom of his carefree, jolly disposition. It is not a symptom of an underlying ambiguity in his personality, or in the social order, or in the stable and comprehensible framework of the reality represented in the novel. On the contrary, here irony serves as a device that reinforces the bond of understanding and familiarity between the author, reader, and (at least some of) the characters in the story.

Irony is an important concept in evaluating Nechui's realist position. In his works, the grand cosmic irony of romantic idealism and modernist uncertainty are entirely absent. Mykola Dzheria is not a forlorn plaything of cosmic fate; he is the victim of an unjust human social order. Zin'ka Mysanko and Solomiia Chechit, in *Ne toi stav*, are not crusaders for a revaluation of values; they merely seek their own comforts. Sofiia Litoshevs'ka, the unfaithful wife of the opera singer who is too frequently on tour, is not a symbol of moral ambivalence; she is a product of a bad marriage. Ieremiia Vyshnevets'kyi and Ivan Vyhovs'kyi are not examples of an underlying relativism of national identity. Nechui's reality is coherent, explicit, and intelligible. And it is securely rooted in the most familiar and most fundamental truth of Nechui's creative dogma – the Ukrainian nation, an imagined community whose existence is beyond doubt and beyond reason. His works are a passionate assertion of the existence of such a nation and an artistic representation of its people and the space they inhabit. As we have seen, Nechui's works are an extended enterprise in the representation of the Ukrainian nation and a defence of its legitimacy and right to exist. But these goals and the methods Nechui uses in his fiction are based on emotion and aesthetic appreciation. They do not call for a cognitive, intellectual response. In the universe of modernist and postmodernist literary theory, the synthesis that underlies realism – the notion that a single material world really exists and that human perception is capable of perceiving and comprehending it – is generally held to be naive, simplistic, and intellectually suspect. The synthesis that underlies Nechui's fiction, however, is the national idea, an emotional, imaginative construct that does not rely on intellectual argumentation. In fact, there is very little that can be called intellectual in Nechui's fictional works.

In an oft-quoted letter to her uncle, Lesia Ukrainka, the most rigorously intellectual writer in the entire canon of modern Ukrainian literature, attacks Nechui on precisely this quality. She writes: "For God's sake don't judge us by the novels of Nechui because we will be condemned forever without cause. At least, I do not know of a single intelligent person in Nechui's novels. If you believe him, all of Ukraine would seem to be stupid."[39] The antagonism here is entirely understandable. Lesia Ukrainka and her uncle belong to that caste of Ukrainian cultural activists for whom intellectual issues outrank practically all other matters. Drahomanov even attacked Shevchenko for being insufficiently versed in European intellectual issues (a largely erroneous charge). Lesia Ukrainka, whose primary achievement was the creation of a canon of intellectually complex and argumentative dramas that sought new, modernist forms of expression, would quite naturally find Nechui's old-fashioned, non-purposeful writing disappointing. Many a French modernist thought similarly of Victor Hugo. For Lesia Ukrainka, Nechui no doubt embodied many sins. He was certainly not the European intellectual modernist that she saw as the literary ideal. But he was also not quite the urban, industrial, and politically engaged realist that Western European fiction had established as the previous ideal. His writing was simultaneously simple and unadorned yet also artistic and consciously crafted. This made him a very peculiar realist. Most of all, his aesthetics were derived from traditional folk models of language use, and his realism was not grounded in a socially purposeful and intellectual approach to perceived reality. This made his fiction incompatible with the modernist principles that were gradually establishing a hold on Ukrainian culture even while Nechui was still writing. For some modernists, Nechui became the antithesis of their aesthetic sensibilities. In their assessments of Nechui, today's neomodernist and postmodernist critics still often focus on the qualities that alienate him from modernism, rather than on those that exemplify his own principles.

Ivan Nechui-Levyts'kyi lived long enough to see modernism appear in literature and other arts and to experience the growing realization that his approach to literature was being displaced by a new style. He did not let this new phenomenon pass unobserved or unremarked. On the contrary, Nechui produced both an expository and a literary response to what he perceived as the threat of modernism. Among the unpublished manuscripts that first appeared in the 1968 ten-volume edition of his works is an essay entitled "Ukrains'ka dekadentshchyna" (Ukrainian decadence). This article is conceived as a historical study in the origins and foundation of the new artistic style. Nechui traces decadence and modernism from German romantics to French Parnassians. His list of writers who write in the spirit of the "liberation of the flesh"[40] includes Paul Verlaine, Charles Marie René Leconte de Lisle, Auguste Villiers de l'Isle-Adam, Henri Auguste Barbier, Joséphin Péladan, Joris-Karl Huysmans, Maurice Barrès, Maurice Maeterlinck, Walt Whitman, and Oscar Wilde (10:193). Obviously, this list makes clear that his understanding of the term is very broad. Like many critics of modernism, he finds the focus on individualism, sensation, irrationality, and epicureanism to be morally and aesthetically repulsive.[41] For Nechui, decadence is largely pornography. Despite these moral qualms, Nechui sees a place for decadence: "у великих європейських літературах декадентська література – це неначе розкіш, письменські збитки багатющих літератур, оригінальні й чудернацькі. Ми додамо, що ці збитки часом бувають і поетичні, оригінальні в своїй красі, по своїй доладності і оригніальності картин, які ми часом бачимо в тінях сну або в тінях сінематографа" (10:222) [In the large European literatures," he argues, "decadent literature is something of a luxury, the authorial pranks in these rich literatures are original and strange. We can add that these pranks are sometimes poetic and original in their beauty, in the appropriateness and originality of their images, which we sometimes see in the shadows of dreams or in the shadows of cinematography]. But in Ukrainian and Russian literature, says Nechui, these evils have no redeeming qualities. He sees some of the faults of this method in some works by Ol'ha Kobylians'ka and Natalia Kobryns'ka, but he reserves his most serious and damning criticism for Volodymyr Vynnychenko, Leonid Andreev, and Fyodor Sologub. This response to modernism, particularly of the type practised by Vynnychenko, is hardly surprising for an old-fashioned realist like Nechui. What is noteworthy, however, is his wide familiarity with contemporary French and English literature, even if he doesn't like this new writing and thinks of Whitman as an Englishman. Of greater interest is his literary reaction to the scourge of decadence.

In 1900 Nechui published a satiric story entitled "Bez puttia" (Going nowhere, or Pointless) in the *Literaturno-naukovyi visnyk*, which was still being published in Lviv at that time. The story had a subtitle, "opovidannia po dekadents'komu" (A story in the decadent manner). The plot concerns the romantic relationship between two young Kyivites, Nastusia Samusivna and Pavlus' Malynka. Both are the products of wealthy families whose fortunes have largely disappeared through a profligate lifestyle.

The story is composed of five sections, which somewhat resemble the acts of a play. Act 1 is non-theatrical – it is all scene setting and background. Act 2 depicts the two young lovers engaged in rhetorical lovemaking, expressing their love for each other in a series of ever more colourful, pretentious, ephemeral, abstruse, and confusing metaphors and allusions. Act 3 finds Nastusia in conflict with her father and her aunts, who do not approve of Pavlus'. Her sensitive disposition is deeply distressed by what she perceives as their boorishness and bullying. Act 4 depicts the culmination of Nastusia's and Pavlus''s love in a first kiss, which takes place in the Solomenka district of Kyiv, then a largely working-class neighbourhood characterized by the recently built railroad lines and train station. To the young lovers, however, the industrial landscape is nothing less than idyllic, or at least poetic: they compare the space beneath a railroad trestle to the setting of Offenbach's mock heroic "Orpheus in the Underworld," the show that premiered in Paris in 1858 and made the can-can famous. Act 5 is pure comic denouement. The young lovers flee to Kyiv's Bald Mountain, where they tumble down the hill towards the river in the snow. Peasants heading to market pick them up at the base of the hill and deliver them to a mental asylum, where white-coated doctors allow the lovers to indulge their fantasies and can do little to bring the young couple back to any semblance of reality.

As is often the case with Nechui's satire, the target of his derision is left quite vague. Here, as in most of his satiric works, Nechui is taking general satiric aim at human foibles rather than at any specific social or cultural phenomenon. This is perhaps best shown by Nechui's most famous satiric creations, Baba Paraska and Baba Palazhka, whose satiric portraits do nothing to undermine Nechui's or the reader's general affection for the simple customs of the Ukrainian village. A similar narrowing of satiric focus is seen in Nechui's religious characters, particularly rural parish priests. As we have seen, Nechui shows no general disrespect for religion or for the clergy. In his satiric portraits, Nechui does indeed consistently deflate the pretensions of the rich, the powerful, the educated, and the upper class, but this is hardly a consistent social program or a philosophical view: it is the traditional matter of most satire. But when socially motivated satire turns into aesthetic parody, the situation becomes more complex. There is no "traditional matter" for aesthetic parody. The only way to poke fun at an aesthetic phenomenon is to lampoon the specific features that are associated with it. In the case of Nechui's anti-modernist writing, identifying the aesthetic phenomenon that he's debunking is not such a simple task. The specific targets of his aesthetic scorn are not clearly identified.

The beginning of the story offers an instructive example. It opens with an extended description of the two principals, Nastusia and Pavlus'. The description is built on a series of qualities that both of the young lovers share, one of them having too much of an attribute and the other even more. These qualities are then undermined with seemingly contradictory or inconsistent examples or details. The description of the qualities themselves are also composed of incompatible elements. Thus Pavlus' is beautiful, and Nastusia is, if anything, even more beautiful – but her beauty has the youthful quality of being unwashed. And she's a little pale, and seems tired, and somewhat withered. They were both brought up in wealth, but her father is out of money – and his father has also squandered his wealth. They both spend time in the fashionable and sophisticated cities of Europe, but they do so in a manner resembling gypsies travelling with their tents. Their sleeping habits are a reversal of what is customary. Nastusia actually sleeps at night, the narrator says, but she goes to bed only just before dawn. Pavlus', however, has reversed night and day and in contrast to the sophistication of his dissolute lifestyle, the narrator compares his sleeping habits to those of barnyard creatures: owls and bats. Nastusia is deemed to be an intelligent girl, but one without any sense in her head. Pavlus' is not without good sense – but his head just seems to let it leak out. In both cases, the images are those of poorly made barrels. Throughout the description, there is a consistent juxtaposition of European urban sophistication with rural provinciality. The money that spills from the pockets of the two rich brats in European capitals resembles the flour that spills from a sack on a wagon rolling along a lumpy and cratered road. Eventually, in the fourth paragraph, Nechui reveals the key image: "Його всі звали божевільним; її – навісною" (7:295) [Everyone called him insane, and her crazy]. This is the direction in which the story will move: towards insanity. The final scene will present the young lovers at the Kyrylivs'kyi Psychiatric Hospital still raving about their extraordinary love for each other and mistaking an indulgent and patronizing doctor first for Buddha himself and then for an imprisoned criminal.

In this stream of humorous imagery it is easy to discern a satiric motive. It is far more difficult, however, to identify its particular mode and target. Nechui ridiculed the financial immaturity and wastefulness of upper-class characters in a number of previous works, so these aspects of social satire are readily understood in the context of his familiar outlook on social questions, examined in chapter 3 above. Unlike some of his other efforts in this direction – for example, the novel *Neodnakovymy stezhkamy* – this story ("Bez puttia") does not contain a sympathetic character through whose eyes the irresponsible behaviour is perceived and through whose sensibility the satiric judgment is mitigated. In *Neodnakovymy stezhkamy* Andrian Hukovych is such a touchstone. The reader's judgment of the silly behaviour of his wife and daughter is confirmed (and moderated, too) by the grief Andrian endures in trying to accommodate their spending while still maintaining financial solvency. But there is no such character in "Bez puttia." The fathers of Pavlus" and Nastusia are no better than their children, even if Petro Samus' has a sober estimate of his daughter's foolishness and her boyfriend's dissipation. Nastusia's two aunts, Mania and Sofa, may be well intentioned, but they are silly old biddies. So the only perspective available to the reader is one of exclusionary othering, where the satiric victims are presented as those against whom the reader can measure his or her own identity. If that were all there was to the story, it would be a simple case of crazy spendthrifts presented as crazy spendthrifts, hardly a formula for effective satire.

"Bez puttia," however, has larger ambitions. The subtitle, "opovidannia po dekadents'komu," signals parody. While the target of the parody is not made explicit, the set of possible candidates for this honour is neither infinite nor completely unknowable. The text is saturated with pretentious comparisons and allusions that are atypical of Nechui's style. The young lovers are compared to mythological gods. The narrative emphasizes their imagination and inventiveness in contrast to their diligence and studiousness. The language of the protagonists is deliberately elevated and poetical, full of metaphors, rhetorical flourishes, and extravagant imagery. Along with the subtitle, these are clear signs that Nechui has embarked on the path of aesthetic parody – he is lampooning a literary style. Specifically, he's ridiculing literary modernism, with its pretentious abandonment of socially relevant themes and simple, "objective" aesthetic principles in favour of esoteric intellectual and philosophical concerns and complex, sophisticated artistic methods. As with any parody, the success of the enterprise depends on many factors, not least of which is the reader's ability to recognize the parody in the text and that same reader's sensibility regarding the object of the parodic lampoon. Ivan Franko offers an instructive example.

In 1900, the same year that Nechui published "Bez puttia," Franko published his own anti-modernist poetic declaration as the foreword to his poem "Lisova idyliia." In it he derides Mykola Voronyi's appeal for submissions to an almanac by suggesting the modernist poet and compiler was only interested in works that came without a long list of features, among which were the most important qualities of literature. Today, Franko's witty parody is more often seen as a symptom of his own limited appreciation of the manifold dimensions of literary texts than as an effective comic riposte to modernism. So, too, with Nechui's considerably less witty story. It is unlikely that many readers will respond sympathetically to his humour. Modernism is one of the sacred cows of literary good taste, and a parody of it based on the old-fashioned aesthetics of realism is out of step with twenty-first-century tastes and values. Moreover, Nechui's text suffers from a problem that Franko's does not. The immediate target of Franko's parody is well known: it is the public call for submissions to the almanac *Z nad khmar i dolyn*, which Voronyi eventually published in 1903. Familiarity with the parodied text allows the reader to appreciate the skills, wit, and intention of the parodist, even if the reader does not necessarily share the parodist's judgment. But what is it that is being parodied in Nechui's "Bez puttia?"

Among Nechui's available papers and correspondence there is nothing that identifies the original target of this lampoon. Critics who have written about Nechui have not commented on this question. We are left to our own deductions and speculations. The story itself does not give any obvious hints, at least none that I can recognize. Shortly after the story appeared in the *Literaturno-naukovyi visnyk*, Nechui discusses the story in a letter to Natalia Kobryns'ka, in answer, it would appear, to her question about a particular word used there. After a few remarks on vocabulary, Nechui turns to the story as a whole:

Моє оповідання "Без пуття" – це пародія на декадентство та символізм в письменстві, котрі мені зовсім-таки не припадають до вподоби, і разом з тим це сатира на недоладне й безладне в деяких фамиліях, яке вже трапляється в нас подекуди, та на деяких сучасних киян. Мушу признатися, що ті всі дрібні чудасії, які побачите в оповіданні, всі дочиста нахапані й списані з натури, які вони нібито ні дивовижні, окрім хіба самого кінця, чи закінчення, скомбінованого та стуленого, як умови від усього переднішого ... хоч і тутечки є багато дечого, що мені доводилося бачити на свої очі на своєму віку. (10:367)[42]

[My story "Bez puttia" is a parody of decadence and symbolism in literature, [qualities] that do not find favour with me. At the same time it's a satire on the deformity and disorder in some families, such as now happens here and there among us, and on some of our contemporary Kyivites. I must confess that all these marvellous details that you will find in the story are all collected and copied directly from experience, no matter how strange they may seem, except perhaps the very end, or conclusion, which is constructed and combined as the outgrowth of all the foregoing, although even here there is a great deal that I actually saw with my own eyes in the course of my years.]

Nechui then turns to a discussion of Ibsen, expressing agreement with Kobryns'ka's judgment of Nora (in *A Doll's House*) as a weak, insufficiently motivated character, a product of the author's diluting his usual realism with elements of symbolism. From there he goes on to express his views on symbolism in literature:

Але цей символізм в поезії зовсім мені не до вподоби. Ми, українці і великороси, взагалі не здатні до цих загадок в штучництві та в поезії. По-моєму, ці символи тільки псують та калічать дуже гарні самі по собі утвори. Візьме та закрутить чоловік таку веремію, що тільки очі витріщиш, як корова на нові ворота, бо не впізнає хазяйської оселі ... Цей символізм в нас не прищепиться. Я тому певний. В Європі він в середніх віках був в моді. Символістичний утвір, *Роман Рожі*, Жана-де-Лориса в віршах вийшов в XIII в. і друкувався триста років! Аж до кінця XVI віку! І в *Декамероні* Бокаччіо панни символістичні. І в Англії Драйден пишав вірші про символістичну "Білу серну" та чорну серну, себто про змагання протестанства з католицтвом. Символістична форма в Європі в поетичних творах там і зрозуміла для суспільства і може відродитись. Для нас це все чудасія та й годі! (10:368)

> [But this symbolism in poetry is completely not to my liking. We, Ukrainians and Great Russians, are altogether averse to these riddles in art and poetry. In my view, these symbols only spoil and cripple works that are otherwise beautiful in themselves. A fellow takes and cooks up such a storm of words that you're left staring with your eyes bulging like a cow looking at a new gate, because it cannot recognize its own cow pen. This symbolism is not going to take root among us. I am certain of this. In Europe it was popular in the Middle Ages. The *Roman de la Rose* by Guillaume de Lorris [Nechui has Jean de Lorris], a symbolist work in verse, was first published in the thirteenth century! – and was reprinted for three hundred years! Up until the sixteenth century. And the ladies in Boccaccio's *Decameron* are also symbolic. And in England, Dryden wrote poems about a symbolic "White hind" and a black deer [a panther?], that is, about the conflict between Protestants and Catholics. In Europe, symbolism in poetry is not something new, it is ancient. Perhaps because of this it is understood by the public there and can be rejuvenated. For us it is just a curiosity and that's all.]

These remarks to Kobryns'ka, made not long after the composition of the story, are only partially helpful in analysing the work. Symbolism is an important concept, but Nechui's use of this term is not particularly illuminating. It is easy to place his notion of symbolist writing in the context of early twentieth-century Eastern European writing. It is less obvious how this concept relates medieval Western European religious writing to Ibsen's plays, except in the very basic sense that, like medieval religious writing, early twentieth-century writing is also characterized by elements that are distinctly not realist in their stylistic and intellectual essence. Nechui finds fault with Ibsen only insofar as this usually realistic author abandons these familiar principles in favour of something more modern and less grounded in materialist and rational principles.

By underscoring once again his commitment to realist principles in literature, Nechui's comments in the letter to Kobryns'ka do not add anything particularly new to our understanding of "Bez puttia" or the identity of its satiric targets. A few points, however, deserve attention. Nechui does not cast blame on Western European writers for employing symbolist techniques. He blithely allows them to continue in their own traditions, arguing only that Ukrainian and Russian literature, grounded in a different aesthetic history, should not move in that direction. While this position favours a non-European course of cultural development for Ukraine, it is not an anti-European argument. Indeed, Nechui is using Europe as the touchstone against which aesthetic achievement is measured. Ukrainian aesthetic traditions are measured against those in Western Europe, but that does not mean that Ukrainian writers should immediately adopt them. Another significant point in this letter is Nechui's and Kobryns'ka's focus on Ibsen in discussing the influence of symbolism. This is not an obvious or inevitable choice. Modernist ideas appeared in dramatic works as well as in other genres, but drama was not the primary venue for their introduction. Perhaps Nechui's association of "Bez puttia" with modernist theatre reveals a specific concern that helps to explain the satiric intent? Finally, there may be a hidden allusiveness in the titles of the symbolic works that Nechui mentions, particularly the *Roman de la Rose*. But these hints and allusions, if such they are, are much too subtle to offer convincing evidence that Nechui is thinking about a specific modernist play.

The essay "Ukrains'ka dekadentshchyna" is potentially a source for illuminating this story. Indeed, in the essay itself Nechui mentions that he had earlier written the story "Bez puttia," and he offers the essay as a further effort to show the genesis and beginnings of decadence in literature (10:188). But this language is much too opaque to establish any direct connection. The collection's editors suggest that the essay can be dated to 1911, based on the publication dates of the works cited in the essay (10:521). The ideas and examples in the essay thus might be more closely linked with Nechui's thinking in 1911 than in 1900, when the story appeared. In any event, the essay is divided into three large sections. The first examines the general features of decadence as a phenomenon and traces its development in Western Europe. Nechui mentions and indeed follows the ideas of Max Nordau, presenting much of the rising tide of modernist art as a product of mental degeneration. Individual writers such as Guy de Maupassant, Baudelaire, Nietzsche, and Oscar Wilde – these he simply calls lunatics.

In section 2, Nechui turns to Ukrainian literature and describes a number of authors who mix realist and decadent elements in their works. Among them are Ol'ha Kobylians'ka, Natalia Kobryns'ka, Oleksii Pliushch, and Hnat Khotkevych. While variously condemning particular works and aesthetic features, on the whole Nechui takes a mildly critical view of these authors, in whom he certainly still sees positive traits. He then drifts off into a discussion of his favourite hobby horse, the contamination of the Ukrainian language with western Ukrainian dialectal forms. In the essay's disproportionately lengthy third section, he focuses squarely on the negative qualities of decadent writing. The key culprits here are Volodymyr Vynnychenko and Oleksander Oles'. Nechui references Vynnychenko's third collection of short stories, which, he says, appeared "this year." No doubt he is referring to Vynnychenko's *Tretia knyzhka opovidan'*, which appeared in Kyiv in 1910. In any event, the stories he discusses – "Moment" (A moment), "Zina," "Shchos' bil'she za nas" (Something bigger than us), "Kuplia," "Rabyni spravzhn'oho" (Slaves of reality) – are all from Vynnychenko's second period of creativity, after 1905. Surprisingly, Nechui praises the author for many aspects of these stories, comparing the character types of Vynnychenko's protagonists to the troubled romantic heroes of the Young Germany (Junges Deutschland) movement of the mid-nineteenth century. It is mostly the plays of Volodymyr Vynnychenko that come in for direct criticism. Nechui condemns *Shchabli zhyttia* (Levels of life) and *Chorna pantera i bilyi vedmid'* (The black panther and the white bear) for what he sees as an exclusive and pathological focus on sexuality. So, too, in Nechui's reaction to the poetry of Oleksander Oles', where Nechui finds an excessive concentration on the "dramas of the heart," that is, on relationships between men and women. Nechui ties these trends in Vynnychenko and Oles' to Western European writers, particularly Guy de Maupassant, but he also finds them in Russian literature, especially in the works of Leonid Andreev.

Because it focuses on works from a later period, the essay "Ukrains'ka dekadentshchyna" offers little evidence to illuminate the nature or identity of the satiric target in "Bez puttia." Clues that might help identify the satiric antecedent for "Bez puttia" must be sought in the story itself. In searching for a possible target, the first matters for consideration are the language and nationality of the work being satirized. Judging by the specifically Ukrainian setting, the typically Ukrainian (or, at least, Russian imperial) attitude towards Western Europe, the characters' veneration of Western European comforts and pleasures, and the absence of any foreign allusions or references, it seems likely that "Bez puttia" is a satire targeted at a work or works of Ukrainian literature. Since it appeared in 1900, the universe of possible targets is rather limited – there simply wasn't all that much modernist writing in Ukrainian before the turn of the century. Among the more prominent Ukrainian modernists, only a few had significant publications before 1900. Ol'ha Kobylians'ka had released *Liudyna* (A person) and *Tsarivna* (A princess). Mykhailo Kotsiubyns'kyi's earliest works appeared in the 1890s, but they still mostly reflected a realist aesthetic. Feminist writers like Natalia Kobryns'ka and Liubov Ianovs'ka were active before 1900, but the style of their writings did not reflect modernist values. Volodymyr Vynnychenko's works did not appear until the new century. The popular ethnographic theatre was in full swing, but it certainly could not provoke an anti-modernist reaction. There was one writer whose innovative ideas in both theme and aesthetics might have elicited a reaction from Nechui. Her name was Lesia Ukrainka.

In 1896 Lesia Ukrainka broke her exclusive attachment to lyric poetry and wrote her first play, which she entitled *Blakytna troianda* (The azure rose). Despite her best efforts, it took some time to get the play staged. Eventually it appeared in Kyiv on 17 August 1899, in a production by the theatre company of Marko Kropyvnyts'kyi staged as a benefit for a popular actress named Ratmirova. The performance attracted a sizable audience and very poor reviews.[43]

The plot of *Blakytna troianda* presents love and insanity in an inseparable combination. Roman Weretelnyk offers a summary of the play:

> Orest Hruich, a young writer, is in love with Liubov Hoshchyns'ka, a young woman whose artistic ambitions no one takes seriously. Liubov initially resists Orest's overtures, fearing to become trapped in marriage. Eventually, however, because of her great need to be loved, Liubov succumbs to Orest's protestations of love and agrees to marry him. Their intended union is complicated by everyone's (especially Orest's mother's) belief that Liubov suffers from a hereditary mental illness. They fear that Liubov, like her mother before her, will go mad and will ruin Orest in the process. After professing her love for Orest, Liubov does go mad, but not for the reasons everyone expects. Rather, her action represents a voluntary descent into madness as a viable alternative to her predicament. Liubov leaves for the Crimea to recover, only to be followed there in a year's time by Orest and his mother, who have decided that he cannot live without her. Faced with no option this time, Liubov commits suicide.[44]

The assertion of the voluntary nature of Liubov's descent into madness, it should be noted, is not directly supported by the text of the drama, although it certainly represents a possible interpretation of the events. Contemporary feminist critics including Solomea Pavlychko, Vira Aheieva, Nila Zborovs'ka, Tamara Hundorova, and Lesia Demska-Budzuliak[45] have taken their cue from Weretelnyk's path-breaking work and analyse the play in the context of late nineteenth-century views of feminine hysteria, a condition Lesia Ukrainka personally experienced and for which she underwent treatment. These critics have demonstrated that the play needs to be seen in the context of the early development of feminist ideas and of psychoanalysis. These two fields of developing research did not necessarily mesh well with each other, and this disharmony provoked Lesia Ukrainka and other feminist writers to examine the specifics of women's psychology in a peculiarly fatalistic spirit. Another critic, Lidia Zelins'ka, explains: "this is a play about hysteria, which has been replaced in the plot by the idea of hereditary insanity."[46]

The considerable insight that these literary critics have applied to the play makes it far more interesting and comprehensible, but it does nothing to reduce the obvious faults of the play. Feminist critics from Weretelnyk to Zelins'ka invariably present apologias for this play, but they also admit, for the most part, its theatrical, intellectual, and literary weakness. The play's ideas and issues are not clearly focused, its dialogue is stilted and disconnected, its construction is static and overburdened. These faults reflect features of all of Lesia Ukrainka's dramas, but most significantly, they arise from her inexperience in treating complex intellectual and emotional issues. *Blakytna troianda* was her very first drama. In later works she will find a more appropriate discourse to present her intellectual designs, and she will reduce the psychoanalytical analyses – particularly autobiographical ones – to their cognitive components. That is, she will embody the conflicts she presents in her plays as an intellectual discourse channelled through a rational argument, rather than as an emotional psychodrama presented as the personal feelings of a protagonist. In this play, however, there is ample justification for the viewer or critic who fails to discern the innovative approach to female psychology and perceives instead confusing, disconnected, and pretentious conversations about the inevitability of insanity when emotions are aroused. This was, in fact, the response the play received when it was first staged.[47] In his important essay about the play, Petro Rulin recounts the various reviews that appeared following its premier performance: they were merciless.[48] Of course, some of the critical venom was inappropriate, but as Rulin himself points out, the play has an abundance of flaws that justified the harsh response of critics to the 1899 production and then again to the 1907 production at the Lysenko school.

There is no direct evidence that Nechui actually knew Lesia Ukrainka's play. In terms of chronological possibilities, there is just enough time between the August 1899 staging of *Blakytna troianda* and the publication of "Bez puttia" in late 1900 to allow for the feasibility that

Nechui's own work could have had the play in mind. Indeed, the text of the play was read at meetings in the Staryts'kyi home in 1897,[49] in which Nechui sometimes participated, so he might have been familiar with the text even earlier. It is not my argument that Nechui's "Bez puttia" is necessarily a direct parody of Lesia Ukrainka's play. My point is that Lesia Ukrainka's play could have been part of the modernist wave of materials to which Nechui was reacting. The five-act dramatic structure of Nechui's story and the pretentious language of his protagonists offer small but tangible evidence to support such an argument. Most important, however, is the strange subject itself: love and insanity. Nechui's parodic presentation of a young couple whose love is quite literally depicted as insanity does not ring any particular bells of recognition in the modernist canon, whether Ukrainian or generally European. Moreover, the subject is not particularly associated with modernist themes. It is the particular combination of passionate love and insanity (understood as a metaphorical substitute for hysteria) that makes Ukrainka's text stand out as a possible target of Nechui's parody. The fact that her drama presents this combination very ineffectively, in an illogical and unconvincing manner that would have seemed outright silly to Nechui's eminently rationalist sensibilities, adds more weight to the possibility of a link.

Lesia Ukrainka knew Nechui's story and, naturally enough, reacted negatively to it. There is no indication in her response that she understood the satire in the story to be in any way connected to her, but on the other hand, it seems somewhat unusual that she would react to this story in any way at all. In a letter to Ol'ha Kobylians'ka from December 1900 she says:

> Вертаю до літератури ... і не знаю, чи до речі тут згадувати про "декадентську" повість Лев[ицького], бо то, властиве, не літаратура. Дивно, як-то тепер дехто думає, що тільки треба написати "по-декадентському," то вже це дає право які хочеш дурниці писати. Ліпше б дав собі спокій Лев[ецький] з "новими напрямами" чи там з сатирами на них, бо то зовсім не його діло, досить на нього глянути, щоб зважити, що йому вже до "модерни" ліпше ні сяк ні так не братися... Я тільки дивуюся редакції "В[існика]," що таке надрукувала, могла б пожалувати коли не своїх читачів, то хоч слави ветерана автора і не робити йому такої кепської прислуги.[50]

> [Returning to literature … I do not know if there is any point mentioning here the "decadent" long story by Lev[yts'kyi], because, in fact, it is not

> literature. It is strange how nowadays some people think that merely by inscribing it "in a decadent manner" gives one the right to scribble any old nonsense. It would be better if Lev[yts'kyi] did not take up "the new tendencies" or satires on that subject, because this is completely beyond his ken. It is enough to have a glance at him to see that for him the "modern" is quite out of his reach ... I only wonder that the editors of *V[isnyk]* actually published this thing. They might have taken pity if not on their readership then at least on the reputation of the veteran author and avoid doing him this back-handed honour.]

This reaction does not help establish a connection between Nechui's story and Lesia Ukrainka's play. What's more important than a definite confirmation of such a connection, however, is the possibility that Nechui's aesthetic parody may actually have a real antecedent. In the usual presentation of the conflict between realism and modernism in Ukrainian literature, all the trump cards are in the hands of the modernists, and the aesthetic position of the realists is scarcely given any credit. If Nechui's parody of modernist, decadent aesthetics can be shown to have a real target, albeit a very weak piece that is not really representative of the principal direction and best practices of modernist sensibilities, then the dialogue between realism and modernism in Ukraine acquires new meaning and new life. Thus, Nechui's antagonism to modernist principles, whether it be Vynnychenko's aggressive social commentary or Lesia Ukrainka's intellectual discourse, was a reaction to actual texts – moreover, Ukrainian texts – and not merely a rejection of any new sensibilities.

Nechui's realism was not formulated on a sophisticated and original theoretical understanding of the relationship between reality and human consciousness. His approach is derivative and gleaned largely from European sources. His theoretical and essayistic writing make this abundantly clear. His own input into realist practices consists of two specific elements, the focus on the national question and the recourse to a peculiar personal style based on repetition, comparison, subdued pacing, and a stockpile of folkloric idiom. In this practice, Nechui is consistent throughout his writing career. His later works introduce a wider range of vocabulary and comparisons while searching for new ideas around which to focus his plots, such as they are. But on the whole, Nechui's writing is of a piece, although it is not of uniform quality. Given his sincere and lifelong dedication to realist writing, there is nothing surprising about the negative response to modernism, particularly to the moral laxity and social degeneration that was perceived to lie beneath this decadent trend. In particular, he sees this issue in a national context, allowing that a more developed culture is less threatened by such epicurean entertainments. In one of his little-known late stories, "Vol′ne kokhannia" (Free love), Nechui introduces decadent literature into the plot of the story. Here spoiled aristocrats, luxuriating at their rural mansions after the events of the 1905 revolution have subsided, discuss the "decadent" and "immoral" works of Fyodor Sologub, Leonid Andreev, and Mikhail Artsybashev (9:42). These works become an objective reflection of the moral dissolution of the women in the story, who abandon their husbands to start romances with attractive young lovers, only to abandon these lovers for newer ones soon after. In a characteristic twist of Nechui's humour, however, these decadent works of literature, introduced into the provincial environment by the spoiled young arrivistes from the city, later become the preferred reading of the scandalized rural public. The two old aunts of the cuckolded young husband who had originally been shocked to hear of such writing are seen at the end of the story delighting in the gossip surrounding their nephew's unfaithful wife and ardently devouring the scandalous literature (9:55). Nechui's satiric instinct cannot resist depicting the false modesty of the incorruptible old aunts. For Nechui, however, this issue is not merely a satiric jab at provincial respectability. The question of propriety in human nature, particularly in relation to women, is a constant feature in his fiction. We turn to this question in the next chapter.

5 Nechui's Characters: Women and Joy

The most surprising feature of Nechui's prose oeuvre is the overwhelming primacy of women as a topical focus in his works and the special attention that is ascribed to depicting a woman's pursuit of personal gratification or joy. There is nothing particularly unusual about male writers creating prominent female characters (Lady Macbeth and Anna Karenina immediately come to mind), although most such characters are likely the work of female authors. In Ukrainian literature of the nineteenth century, it was primarily women who brought female characters and women's issues to wider attention. First among them was Maria Vilins'ka, who, very tellingly, wrote under the male pseudonym of Marko Vovchok. It's difficult to supposee that many readers really thought these stories were by a male author, since they are singularly focused on women. What's more, Marko Vovchok's stories always depict strong women, women in control of a particular situation. Whether her characters are female slave owners or female slaves, they are always the dominant personality, controlling their own destiny (to the degree that a slave can have such control), setting a tone for those around them, and making the best of the circumstances they find themselves in. In Marko Vovchok's stories, men are almost exclusively sexual partners or stage decoration to fill in the scenery. Life is experienced primarily by women and their children. Nechui's first story, "Dvi moskovky," has some of these qualities as well. As we have seen above,[1] Nechui's story is something of a response both to Shevchenko's "Kateryna" and to Vovchok's abolitionist stories. What distinguishes it from both antecedents, however, is the deliberate comparison of two women, both of whom are in love with the same man.

Nechui takes the obvious steps to create a comparison between these two women, Hanna and Maryna. First he describes them as identically dressed close friends, and then he contrasts them: one is round-faced, fair-skinned, and demure (Hanna), and the other is long-faced, outgoing, and dark-complexioned (Maryna) (1:57). It is natural to see this juxtaposition in moral terms – Hanna as the good girl and Maryna as the bad girl – and Nechui certainly builds up that aspect of the contrast. Hanna and her husband Vasyl' enjoy the benefits of a happy marriage and hard work, while Maryna engenders gossip and suffers the scorn of morally upright villagers who consider her licentious and unrestrained. Maryna, herself in love with Vasyl', marries another soldier to escape the contempt of her neighbours, but the marriage is loveless and unfullfilling for her. Before long, both husbands are called up again for military service and their wives are left to fend for themselves, a familiar situation in many works of Ukrainian literature in the nineteenth century. This is where Nechui's story finds its central concern: How do these two different women endure the absence of the man they both love?

Even before Vasyl' returns to military service, the story focuses on the sensibilities of women. In the first chapter, the focalizing subject is not the returning soldier but his mother, Khomykha. This is more than an imitation of folklore. Nechui does allow Vasyl' a few words in this chapter, but they do not reveal anything about his character. With the eternal optimism that a mother harbours for her son, Khomykha asks him if life was good in the military: "чи добре було тобі в москалях" (1:54). What a question! It was not, of course, and Vasyl' tells her a story about the physical abuse of recruits. This brings a tear to her eye, but after supper she is again basking in the happiness of having her son at home, even if only for a while, and drifts off into an idealized reverie:

> А тим часом перед сонними очима старої мигнуло свіже лице Василеве, неначе квітка розцвілася од одного разу, а за ним виглянуло десь з кутка лице молодої молодиці. Стара сидить на лежанці та колише малого онучка, а молодиця-невістка порається коло печі. І стало їй легко, дуже легко на серці, неначе вернулись її луччі, молодші літа, неначе вона вдруге народилась на світ. І здається їй в дрімоті, що вона вже сама, молода й хороша, порається в своїй хатині, а покійник її, молодий та гарний, сидить на лаві та говорить до неї. Прокинулась стара та й перехрестилась. Через годину все поснуло, навіть сни поснули в душі, побитій горем та нуждою. Один тільки цвіркун цвірчав у куточку під полом. (1:56)

[Meanwhile, before the old woman's sleepy eyes flashed the fresh face of Vasyl', like a freshly blossomed flower, and behind him in a corner appeared the face of a young maid. The old woman sits on a bed rocking a young grandson in her arms while her daughter-in-law busies herself around the oven. And she felt light-hearted, so light-hearted, as if her better, younger years had returned, as if she were born again into the world. And in her dream she imagines herself young and beautiful again, working in her own home while her late husband, young and handsome, is sitting on the bench and speaking to her. The old woman awoke and made the sign of the cross. In an hour everything was sleeping, even her dreams were asleep in her soul, burdened and downtrodden with cares and poverty. Only the cricket was chirping in the corner beneath the floorboards.]

The contrast between Vasyl''s story of hardships in the army and Khomykha's daydream is a familiar component of realist fiction – the hopes and dreams of the lower classes are shattered by the reality of their difficult lives. But the juxtaposition also tells us something about the mother's eternal hopefulness, her desire to imagine a better world than the one at hand. She is happy to follow her son's advice: he won't talk about the hardships of military life, she won't cry. But there's something more than that too.

Nechui lets the narrative move quickly from the army hardships to the imagined family bliss. There is, perhaps, just a slight suggestion that the mother is not deeply moved or surprised by her son's suffering as a soldier. Most importantly, the imagined family bliss is not focused on her son. Her son's face briefly flashes (мигнуло) in her dream only to be replaced by images from which he is entirely absent. Grandma cradles the baby. The young wife (молода молодиця) manages the household (a benefit to the grandmother, who is no longer required to do this). These are images that reflect the satisfaction that Khomykha can experience because her son has returned home and, she hopes, will marry and start a family. But the next images in her daydream go beyond anything directly tied to Vasyl'. The scenes of a happy family life evoke Khomykha's memories of her own early married life when she and her husband, both still young and good-looking, spent time alone together. These are not the kind of thoughts we expect from a mother contemplating the joys associated with the return of her son from military service. No wonder she superstitiously makes the sign of the cross to chase away the evil one! Her emotions have followed a transition from sympathetic sorrow at her son's suffering through a happy expectation of a pleasant and easier home life with her son's family to a recollection of her own early marriage. The explicit description of both her and her husband as young and good-looking (молода й хороша, молодий та гарний) clearly suggests an amorous, even a sexual relationship. This is not merely a recollection of a quiet simple peaceful moment from her youth. It evokes passion, fulfilment, and pleasure.

Khomykha's dream at the end of the very first chapter of Nechui's earliest work signals the importance of one key motif of his entire oeuvre: women's joy. Throughout his career as a writer, and with remarkable consistency – though certainly not in every work, nor to the same degree in all those works where it occurs – Nechui likes to depict the world through the eyes of women. But what's even more remarkable, in his representation of this feminine perspective, Nechui very often depicts the lives of women as a struggle to achieve personal happiness, as a pursuit of pleasure and joy. Of course, this is not a formula that applies to all his female characters – women appear in a variety of roles in his works. But there is a noticeable pattern of building plots and situations around the idea of women seeking joy. In "Dvi moskovky," as we saw earlier, Nechui divides Shevchenko's Kateryna between two women: Hanna, the dutiful, reliable, and long-suffering victim, and Maryna, the carefree, outgoing pleasure seeker. But such a characterization is misleading. Although Maryna is an extrovert and somewhat unconstrained by social conventions of women's behaviour, she is a good-hearted woman and a very loyal friend. Nechui devotes most of the second chapter of the story to the comparison between the two women among whom Vasyl' must choose. Hanna is short with brown hair. Maryna is angular with thick black hair. Like Kobylians'ka's Tetiana in *V nediliu rano zillia kopala* (On Sunday morning she gathered herbs), Maryna is called a gypsy. Hanna is quiet and melancholy. Maryna is daring and agile. The contrast is one of character types, not of moral absolutes. Both girls appear in church for Vasyl' to see them. Both girls actively pursue Vasyl', although in different ways. Hanna shows up at his mother's house on the day he arrives, pretending to need a hot ember to light a fire. At that point, an uninterested Vasyl' doesn't even ask her name. She's the one pursuing him. Later, at the customary nightly village revels, Maryna is the life of the party (Hanna does not participate). In Vasyl''s eyes, the two girls are two types of flowers: Hanna is a rose, Maryna is a peony or poppy. He must make a choice, and it falls on the rose.

What's crucial here is Nechui's avoidance of a moral judgment. This is not in fact a contrast between a virtuous and a wicked girl. Indeed, Nechui makes them both victims. In chapter 3 we find the usual folkloric elements of a betrothal. Vasyl' sends matchmakers and Hanna and her family must make their choice. Nechui presents the familiar dilemma, should she marry a "moskal'," with the virtual widowhood that marrying a soldier entails? On the other hand, she will become a free person and, since Vasyl' is an only child, they will not need to divide the property he will inherit with siblings. This dilemma casts the wedding in a sombre light, and Nechui adds a traditional folk song about the bitter tears of a newlywed wife. He then adds: "І заплакала гірко, тільки не Ганнуся, а Марина" (1:63) [And she cried bitter tears, but not Hanna, rather Maryna]. Nechui uses an unexpected juxtaposition to turn the familiar marriage ritual on its head. Hanna's marriage may be a potential source of woe to the bride, but it is an unmitigated emotional disaster for the friend who will be her bridesmaid, Maryna, who must watch her own happiness disappear as her beloved Vasyl' marries another woman. What's more, she can't even express her own misery and is harshly and mistakenly judged by the community: "Плаче, бо заміж хоче, та ніхто не сватає! А ніхто більше не винен, як стара мати! Таки розпустила дочку ще змалечку" (1:64) [She's crying because she wants to get married, but no one is asking her! And it's all her mother's fault for letting her run loose from an early age].

As in Khomykha's reverie on her own youthful bliss, so, too, in Maryna's sorrow at Hanna's marriage Nechui deliberately reverses familiar stereotypes and thus gives a sympathetic depiction of a woman's desire for personal satisfaction. In both cases, there is an undertone of forbidden pleasure. A woman's sexuality is notoriously problematical in most cultural traditions, including the Ukrainian one. So Khomykha must chase away the evil spirit and Maryna is condemned by her neighbours. But Nechui's voice is not part of the chorus of condemnation even after the story takes its inevitable turn towards misfortune and misery. Nechui deliberately juxtaposes the idyllic life of Hanna and Vasyl', based on hard work and fulfilling social expectations, with Maryna's carefree enjoyment of life:

> Після Василевого весілля смуткувала Марина осінь, смуткувала й зиму, а на різдво вже й розвеселилась! Знов держить вона перед чи на весіллях, чи на музиках. Хлопці липнуть до неї, як бджоли до меду, та не сватають, бо матері заказали їм старостів слати до Марини. А Марина знов весела та співуча!

З гарними хлопцями жартує, і постоїть, і побалакає, а поганому часом і по щоці дасть нишком та тишком. Чи на музиках, чи на весіллях увивається коло Марини чорнобривий ткач Микола, і почав ходити до неї, стежку топтати ...

Зацокотіли молодиці по селу, що Марина й сяка й така. Марина постояла з хлопцем під вишнями, а слава пішла по селу, що Марині парубки ніби хотіли косу одрізати, що Марина швидко покриткою стане. (1:68)

[After Vasyl''s wedding Maryna was gloomy through the autumn, she was gloomy in the winter too, but at Christmas she cheered up. Once again she is the life of the party at weddings and at dances. Boys stick to her like bees stick to honey, but they don't dare propose marriage, because their mothers have forbidden them to send matchmakers to Maryna. But Maryna is again happy and full of song. She jokes around with the nice boys, hangs around with them and talks to them. The bad boys sometimes get a quiet slap in the face. At dances and at weddings the black-browed weaver Mykyta has been favouring Maryna and he's started beating a path to her door ...

The young wives of the village have begun to chatter about Maryna, saying she's this and that. Maryna had a conversation with a boy under the cherry tree and already her fame has spread across the whole village, the boys even contemplating cutting off her braid since she's likely to have a bastard soon.]

Unlike Shevchenko's Kateryna, however, Nechui's Maryna is not pregnant. There is no real scandal – only the wagging tongues of the village matrons. Nechui resolutely neither defends nor condemns Maryna. But in the climate of cavillous village gossip, his silence is almost an endorsement. In any event, the gossip prompts Maryna to get married after all, but she marries another soldier, Mykyta, a man she doesn't love. Nechui, to the degree the modest, old-fashioned sensibilities of the times allow, makes clear that Maryna feels a physical revulsion to him:

Москаль жартує, дивиться їй любо в вічі, бере її за руку. А Марині світ немилий! Покладе їй руку на шию, а їй здається, що він вірьовкою обвив її горло; схилиться він на плече, голова його важка, як камінь, поцілує – неначе гадина яка, холодна й слизька, доторкнеться до її лиця, гарячого й молодого, а його вус кудлатий – неначе здоровий павук лазить по її лиці. (1:70)

[The soldier jokes, looks lovingly into her eyes, holds her hand. But everything displeases Maryna. He puts his hand on her neck and she feels a noose tightening around her throat; he bends down to her shoulder – his head feels as heavy as a stone; he kisses her and it's as if a snake, cold and slimy, were touching her hot and youthful face; and his bushy moustache feels like a large spider crawling on her face.]

While Hanna's relations with Vasyl' were structured by the successful development of a family – a situation where happiness is measured by the level of material and spiritual comfort its members enjoy – Maryna's world revolves around sensual pleasure, or, in this case, the absence of such pleasure

The comparison between the two women continues after their husbands depart, but now the situation is reversed. Hanna is miserable, and her household has sunk into poverty, loneliness, and anguish. Maryna, on the other hand, is happy to be rid of her unloved husband. She even does her best to cheer up her friend Hanna, but the dutiful woman cannot be cheered. Her happiness has vanished along with her husband, she tells her friend. The stark contrast between the sources of happiness these women experience is made explicit in their dialogue:

– Бог зна, що ти оце верзеш, Марино! – одказала Ганна. – Я тоді тільки щаслива, як піду до церкви та помолюся богу за свого Василя ...

– А я й богові молюся, і на хлопців дивлюся! Мені шкода моєї молодої краси, моєї коси. Нехай цвіте, не марніє моє лице, не линяють брови! Нехай люблять мене хлопці молоді й хороші! Я молода, хочу всмак нажитись в світі, хочу бути щаслива і весела.

Ото мені щастя, Ганно, як я стою ввечері під вишнями та дожидаю мого милого, чорнобривого, як він свисне тричі за ставком між вербами, подаючи мені звістку. А в мене серце холоне й душа холоне! І добре мені, і страшно мені, аж прихилюся я до вишні ... А тут чую, шелеснуло через тин, шелестить лист гарбузовий, гойдається висока кукурудза й соняшники. А милий випливає звідтіль, як ясний місяць сходить, наближається до мене, моє серце, мліє, умліває ... Чи то ж не щастя, Ганно, ввечері, обнявшись з милим, слухати, як щебече соловейко? Чи то ж не доля, як пригорне милий до свого серденька, як дивитись йому в вічі, цілувати його брови, його очі?

Марина положила обидві руки на Ганнині плечі і припала головою до її плеча.

– І годі, Марино, – одказала Ганна. – Не задля мене жарти та сміхи! Не задля мене чорніють брови та очі. Минулося моє кохання, моє женихання! Помандрувало моє щастя з Василем в далеку сторононьку.

– Але ж ти нажилася з милим, Ганно! А я пішла заміж за нелюба і не зазнаю такого щастя, як тобі судилося … Я й не накохалась, я й не навтішалась! (1:78–9)

["What kind of nonsense are you prattling," replied Hanna. "The only happiness I have is when I go to church and say a prayer to God for my Vasyl'."

"I both pray to God, and stare at the boys! Why should I forsake my youthful beauty and my braid? Let my face flower, rather than wither. May my brows not fade. Let the young and handsome boys love me. I'm still young and I want to enjoy my life in this world, to be happy and gay.

"My happiness, Hanna, is standing in the evening under the cherries and waiting for my handsome, dark-browed lover to whistle three times from beyond the pond, among the willows, giving me the signal. My heart stops and my soul chills. It's so wonderful and so frightening that I need the cherry tree to lean on. And I listen, and I hear someone by the fence, and the melon leaves rustle and my lover floats out from the twilight, like a bright moon rising. He approaches me, my heart faints and tightens … Is that not happiness, Hanna, to listen to the nightingale sing in the evening in the arms of your lover? Is that not good fortune, when your lover holds you close to his heart and you look into his eyes, kissing his brows, his eyes?"

Maryna put both her hands on Hanna's shoulders and dropped her head on her shoulder.

"Enough, Maryna," said Hanna. "Not for me these jokes and laughter. Black brows and black eyes are not for me. My days for love are over, for courting and wooing. My happiness has wandered off with Vasyl' into a distant land."

"But you had a life with your beloved, Hanna! I married a man I didn't love, and I'll never know such happiness as you were given. I haven't yet had my share of love or my share of joy."]

The remainder of chapter 5 is devoted to examining Maryna's immodest behaviour and her self-doubt. She feels entitled to enjoy her life, but at the same time she sees that happiness has passed her by. She chases boys and throws parties in her home, but she also works to maintain good relations with Hanna, whose strict morality condemns Maryna's dissolute lifestyle. But by putting the condemnation of Maryna in Hanna's mouth, Nechui reduces its moral authority. The pious, dutiful, and suffering Hanna is no better off for her virtues. Her son grows up and becomes another source of misery for her. Significantly, when the selfish son asks his mother to sell her house for his material benefit, Maryna, the shameless free spirit yet loyal friend to Hanna, offers the same advice as the village priest: don't do it. Hanna finally does something for herself alone – she keeps the house – but she soon dies of want and poverty anyway. As Maryna gets older, she can no longer find satisfaction in her old habits in the village and she moves to Kyiv where, unkempt and bedraggled, she can dance all night in bars with soldiers. The pernicious effects of the military are once again centre stage. Conscription has destroyed the lives of two more women, or, more precisely, two types of women, one dutiful and the other fun-loving. But the social dimension of the problem presented in this story further highlights the particular psychological profile that Nechui portrays in the character of a licentious woman. Just before her death, Maryna imagines herself walking the streets of the capital, which is shining brightly with the blinding glow of sunlight reflected on the golden domes of churches, with tall stalks of wheat, ready for reaping, growing along the streets of the city. The image morphs into her native village, and she stands by the pond as a young woman. She hears her own mother calling her and Vasyl' approaching her with a smile in his eyes (1:100). Moments before her death Maryna is still remembering her youthful amorous ideal. The road to social decay, moral dissolution, and urban vulgarity begins with an idyllic quest for joy, a woman's simple pursuit of sensual pleasure. When word reaches her native village that Maryna has died, Nechui tells us, even her enemies cross themselves and say a prayer: "Не втекла, – кажуть, – таки од свого лиха, і не загуляла, й не заспівала, й не затанцювала його навіть в Києві" (1:101) ["She could not run away," they say, "from her fate, and she couldn't out-party it, out-sing it, or out-dance it, even in Kyiv"]. In Nechui's Ukraine, a woman's quest for joy may lead to sin and misery, but it evokes sympathy.

The delineation of women's characters in "Dvi moskovky" sets the stage for much of what will appear in Nechui's later works. In the simplest terms, a woman's world is divided between duty and domestic responsibility, on one hand, and sensuality, pleasure-seeking, and joy on the other. This is a familiar division, particularly when viewed from a backward-looking feminist perspective that understands this traditional categorization of women into either sacred mothers or profane harlots as a fundamental historical injustice. Nechui is no feminist, although he does tell Natalia Kobryns'ka in a letter of 31 March 1893 that he is "well-disposed to the women's question" (10:339). His works are not the place to seek radical new views of women's roles in society. But they do reflect the changing views on this issue in Nechui's time and, what's more, a peculiar concentration on women's perspectives along with deliberately ambiguous depictions of traditional women's roles. The dutiful wife and mother seldom appears in Nechui's works in the idealized version embodied by Hanna in "Dvi moskovky." There are few children in Nechui's works, and when they do appear, they are more often than not adult children of either sex. The relations their mothers have with these offspring are not characterized by nurturing or education, but rather by meddling and chastisement. Such is the case in *Kaidasheva sim'ia*, *Starosvits'ki batiushky ta matushky*, and *Neodnakovymy stezhkamy*, to name just a few of the best-known works. What is even more typical of Nechui's good matrons is that their role in the household includes not only responsibility for domestic management, but also authority over all domestic circumstances. Since Nechui's world is largely composed of domestic situations, women generally hold authority over men, particularly their husbands. In the predominantly comic mode of his writing, this means that men are often reduced to weak characters who are subservient to their wives. This is what we find in the three works just mentioned.

Perhaps the most iconic such portrait occurs in the opening pages of *Prychepa*, where the two clerical neighbours, Father Moisei and Father Khvedor, spend the evening in friendly conversation accompanied by strong drink. When their carafe runs dry, Father Khvedor is reduced to sneaking into his own living room in the dark so as not to awaken his wife while he gets more vodka. In their relations with their wives, Nechui's husbands are often depicted as something equivalent to mischievous children, badly in need of firm guidance and control. Alternatively, they are – like Vasyl' Dashkovych, the ivory-tower professor in *Khmary* – too weak, uninterested, or timid to restrain their domineering wives. Of course, Nechui is aware of the real possibility of husbands dominating and even mistreating their wives, as he shows in the incident of a peasant beating his wife in *Khmary* and in the relationship between Elpidyfor Vanatovych and Liuba Svatkivs'ka in *Neodnakovymy stezhkamy*, but when such situations occur, Nechui treats them as specific social ills that are explicitly outside the social norm. The domineering matron represents a comic "normal" state of affairs.

To be fair, not all of the women in Nechui's works fit these two stereotypes. There are even a few, although rare, examples of independent women. There is Melaniia Ulasevych in "Vol'ne kokhannia," a wealthy woman who lives as she pleases in Kyiv, having sold off the family estate she inherited. In *Khmary*, readers encounter the widow Turman, born the Marquise de Pourverser, and her sister, who direct the Institute for Noble Girls. Of course, these two women are negative characters in the novel. They are foreign (both Russian and French). They are pretentiously (and falsely) aristocratic. And they are rude, mean, and foolish. But they are unencumbered women who present a very strong role model for the two daughters who are put in their care. In *Nad Chornym Morem*, Nechui presents a threesome of more-or-less independent women: the widow Zoia Murashkova; her daughter, Nadezhda, who works in a bank; and the schoolteacher Sania Navrots'ka. True, the fate of the younger two women is still tied to their search for a marriage partner, but they are given a relatively large degree of independence. Also noteworthy in this novel is Khrystyna Borodavkina, an aristocratic landowner's daughter who fled through her window from her odious father into the hands of a waiting fiancé, who has since passed away. This woman, whom Nechui calls a free bird of the steppes, is extraordinarily free in her behaviour, but her field of activity and interests is limited to epicureanism and coquetry. She appears again in *Navizhena*, where she shares the stage with Marta Karalaieva, a widow who is intent on getting married for a second time before her daughter gets married.

There are not many such independent women in Nechui's works, nor would there have been very many in the society of his day. More common are the female characters who exhibit, in one way or another, a free spirit and a certain degree of independence in their behaviour. This group includes a very large percentage of Nechui's female characters. First and foremost are the inseparable comic neighbours, Paraska Hryshykha and Palazhka Solov'ikha, better known as Baba Paraska and Baba Palazhka, who were, in their own day, among the best-known literary characters in all of Ukrainian literature. It is worth noting that practically no one remembers the names of their husbands (Omel'ko Hryshenko, Tereshko Soloveiko), who are mentioned by name only once or twice in the series of stories. Of course, these two women can be called independent only provisionally and in a purely psychological context. They are more or less free to pursue their malevolence against each other, but only to the point where their fellow villagers or family intercede. Nevertheless, readers certainly perceive them as dominant individuals in their own setting. They may be satirized, but they are strong, wilful women who do not bend – or at least try not to bend – to the will of their husbands and male neighbours. They are personally responsible for their own fate.

In his depictions of women whose strong personalities allow them to control their own fate and even, occasionally, to dominate the men in their circle, Nechui usually focuses on two specific motives: ambition and pleasure. This corresponds to the division in "Dvi moskovky," except that over the course of his development as a writer, Nechui will adjust the balance between these two motives and reduce the impact of social problems on the women thus depicted. In "Dvi moskovky," Hanna's ambition was reduced to the minimum desire for a materially secure life. A similar outlook characterizes Hania, Father Khvedor's daughter in *Prychepa*. But in this novel, Hania's antagonist, Zosia, is not just a reproduction of Maryna from the earlier story. Zosia is both a pleasure-seeking, debauched woman and a social climber with ambition for aristocratic wealth and pretensions of aristocratic honour. Unlike Maryna, she gets none of the author's or reader's sympathy. In *Khmary*, the significance of the contrast between dutiful and profligate women is reduced, even though there are at least three pairs of women in the novel where some form of this contrast is evident: Marta and Stepanyda (and their daughters), Halia Masiuk and Ol'ha Dashkovych, and Oleksandra Masiuk (Halia's mother) and Nadezhda Iskra-Radiuk (Pavlo's mother). The vices displayed by the second woman in all these pairings are social and material rather than sensual. In *Mykola Dzheria*, however, Nechui returns to the contrast between a dutiful, self-effacing wife and an assertive, pleasure-seeking competitor. While the abandoned Nymydora goes on a religious pilgrimage to Kyiv, seeking divine intervention for the return of her husband, Mokryna Kovbanenko shamelessly chases Mykola, even after she learns that he is already married. Her father, the captain of the fishing crew, scolds her for this, but he nevertheless appoints Mykola as his assistant, signalling, as it were, a lenient moral judgment, one very different from the reaction of Kateryna's parents in Shevchenko's poem.

In the early part of his writing career, Nechui focused largely on uncovering social and national injustice. The overall tenor of his works is judgmental. So, too, is the depiction of women. Strong women are often characterized by sensuality and licentiousness, which, even if not condemned outright, is still presented as an inappropriate trait that leaves an indelible moral taint on a woman. In the next period of his creativity there is a greater emphasis on painting a broad canvas of society in Ukraine. In these works, women (and men, too!) are less likely to be victims of social ills than of their own quirky or dysfunctional personalities. They are also unlikely to suffer injustice in silence. Motria Dovbysh-Kaidash in *Kaidasheva sim'ia* is a good example. After she marries Karpo and moves in with his family, Marusia Kaidash, now her mother-in-law, treats her like a domestic servant. Marusia assumes that the purpose of her son's marriage was to allow her to kick back her heels and watch someone else do the household chores while she reaps all the benefits. It's pride and material interest that lead to the confrontation between the mother and the new bride. While Nechui does not really take sides in this conflict – both parties are objects of his satire – the language he uses shows two peculiarities. The material desires of both women are tied to their *amour propre*, to their appearance. In the case of the younger woman, this desire to appear attractive is presented with some sympathy by the author. When the older woman returns from market with a sombre-looking kerchief, Motria complains:

> – Мабуть, хочете мене в черниці постригти, – сказала Мотря й кинула хустку на стіл. Вона глянула на матерію, набрану на спідницю; матерія була убога, темненька, з червоними краплями. Мотря навіть не розгорнула її та й одійшла од стола.
>
> – Я знала, що тобі не вгоджу. Я не знаю, хто тобі й вгодить, – сказала Кайдашиха, розсердившись, – де ж пак! зросла в такій розкоші.
>
> Мотря мовчала. А для неї, молодої, так хотілось зав'язать на празник голову розкішною червоною хусткою. Вона тільки легко зітхнула.
>
> "Не моя воля волить в цій хаті", – подумала вона. І для неї схотілось волі та своєї хати. (3:334)

["You probably want to cut my hair and send me off to a convent," said Motria, and threw the kerchief on the table. She glanced at the material intended for her skirt – it was dowdy, dark, with red splashes. Motria didn't even examine it and stepped away from the table.

"I knew I couldn't satisfy you. I don't know who could satisfy you," said Mrs Kaidash, getting angry. "What do you expect, when she grows up in the lap of luxury."

Motria was silent. She was young and just wanted to put on a fine red kerchief for the holiday. She only sighed gently.

"It's not my will [воля] that has power [волить] in this house," she thought. And now she wanted freedom [воля] and her own house.]

Nechui's deliberate pun on the word воля (both will and freedom) is a tacit endorsement of a woman's freedom. Just because Motria is a married woman, why shouldn't she enjoy her youth, her good looks, and a house of her own? By depicting the older woman as a tyrant, Nechui manipulates the reader to partially approve Motria's rebelliousness, vanity, and materialism.

The relationship between Motria and Marusia is, thus, a variant of the rebellious vs dutiful pattern established in "Dvi moskovky." Both poles of the dualism have been significantly scaled back. The sinful or sexual undercurrent of Motria's rebellion is almost entirely absent, in sharp contrast to Maryna in the earlier work. As an example of the "dutiful" woman, Marusia is a far cry from Hanna. In this new pattern of contrasting female characters, the dutiful (usually suffering) woman has been transformed into an upholder of her own traditional authority and comfortable entitlements. These women don't earn the respect of their community – they exercise their dominant status. Nechui's satire consistently undermines their arrogance and presumption. When Marusia Kaidash visits the Balash home to meet the impoverished parents of her younger son's bride, she bangs her head against the low door frame (3:361). The bump on her head and the blow to her ego will require constant retribution in the form of persistent denigration and abuse of Melashka, the second daughter-in-law, which provokes the latter into her own rebellion: on a pilgrimage to Kyiv, she stays behind and doesn't return to the family home until they come looking for her. But the differences between Motria and Melashka, on the one hand, and their mother-in-law, on the other eventually evolve into a new relationship. All three women become equal partners in the same world that Marusia Kaidash lives in. The two young families end up in an eternal quarrel, in which the materialism and arrogance of the wives spreads contagiously to all the members of the family, including the two brothers.

This is the mode for Nechui's presentation of women in a number of his major works, including *Starosvits'ki batiushky ta matushky, Pomizh vorohamy,* and even, to a certain extent, in *Neodnakovymy stezhkamy,* where mothers and wives control their husbands and children and often ruin the lives of these men and women through their own arrogance and meddling. They are eternally in search of good marriages for their children and material comforts for themselves. They are particularly preoccupied with maintaining social appearances and proprieties. Often, as was the case with Marusia Kaidash, they are influenced by exposure to aristocratic customs and tastes and try to emulate these in their own households, but they lack both the money and the aesthetic sensibility to accomplish this. But even in these essentially descriptive satiric works, Nechui is never very far from the contrast between dutiful and rebellious or even licentious women that he had established in his earlier work. In *Starosvits'ki batiushky ta matushky* Onysia Mossakovs'ka and Olena Balabukha both dominate their respective households and terrorize their husbands and children, but Olena is also an unfaithful wife and would have had an affair with a military officer, Ivan Kazantsev, except that he abandons her in shame. Vatia, the female half of the young pair who find themselves "among enemies" in *Pomizh vorohamy,* is a far more temperate woman, but when she finally realizes that her chances of marrying Leonid Pasenko are hopelessly compromised by her parents' enmity with Leonid's in-laws, even she contemplates a mini-rebellion. At first she contemplates entering a monastery, since she feels she is already living "as if in a monastery" (6:292). Then she changes her mind and considers attending women's courses in St Petersburg that would prepare her for making an independent living. Finally, she and her friend Antosia (who will end up marrying Leonid) decide that the best course is to study music at the Kyiv conservatory and pursue professional careers. Antosia even imagines herself playing the innocent Marguerite seduced by Faust in Charles Gounod's opera. Her career path and her preening before a mirror (6:296) suggest a search for sensual rather than material pleasures. Among the characters in *Neodnakovymy stezhkamy,* too, there are women who think of their own pleasure in sensual terms. Nadezhda Ladkovs'ka may be a clergyman's wife, but that does not stop her from flirting with the doctor, deliberately speaking to him about "women's maladies," showing off her command of horses, and leaving behind her handkerchief in his quarters, all in an effort to attract him to her person. There's also Maria Pokotylovs'ka, a woman no longer very young, who is nicknamed the Marquise Kakadu for her showy, fun-loving, and parrot-like manners.

Even in *Kaidasheva sim'ia* Nechui leaves a small hint of his interest in women's pursuit of sensual gratification. When Melashka Kaidash stays behind in Kyiv and fails to return to her husband and her family, the reason for her behaviour is made explicit: "Третій день прожила Мелашка в Києві, як у раї ... Вона в Києві не бачила ні свекрухи, ні свекра, ні Мотрі, не чула ні од кого лихого слова. Ніхто не гриз їй тут голови" (3:381–2) [In Kyiv Melashka had spent three days as if in paradise ... She had not seen her mother-in-law, her father-in-law, or Motria, she had not heard a single harsh word. No one was nagging her here].

The simple-minded and credulous Melashka is very impressed with Kyiv's urban religious sites and stays behind to avoid harsh treatment from her in-laws, rather than to escape her husband, whom she loves. But Nechui throws in a comic scene that hints at another possibility. On Good Friday, the pilgrims lie down to sleep on the grounds of the Brotherhood Monastery, on the grass directly in front of the building housing the monks. One of the monks is struck by Melashka's beauty and makes a mental note when she lies down second from the end of the row. But when another late-coming pilgrim lies down at the end of that row, Melashka becomes third and Baba Palazhka second. The lustful monk ends up kissing Baba Palazhka, who in turn has a nightmare in which she sees herself crushed by a large church bell falling off the bell tower. Thus, without casting any doubt on Melashka's innocence, Nechui adds a little comic spice to a topic that he explores elsewhere in his works: women who leave their husbands. Melashka's sexual fidelity is further emphasized in the description of her decision to return home. She longs for her husband, and when he and his mother, along with her own mother, come to Kyiv to look for her, she does not put up any resistance and agrees to return, although with some trepidation. Their meeting takes place in a cemetery, and there is no jubilant reunion or celebration of the return home.

This incident with Melashka resembles another event described in a prose work entitled "Neslukhniana zhinka" (The disobedient wife). This brief sketch has the character of a diary entry or notation from a writer's working notebook. The editors of the ten-volume edition do not give any particular information about this item, not even if the title is theirs or Nechui's. The sketch is not dated, but it is likely from the years shortly before the outbreak of the First World War. In the narrative, Nechui describes himself on a holiday in Bila Tserkva, where he encounters a growing crowd of people at the bazaar listening to an argument between a mother, Maryna Zharka, her daughter Varka, and the daughter's husband, Onys'ko. Nechui recognizes the principals and gets involved in the conversation. Varka has left her husband because he bosses her around like a servant, telling her to do things that he could just as well do himself. Onys'ko defends himself on the grounds that it is a husband's place to give his wife commands, not the other way around. Maryna is trying to mediate the conflict, urging her daughter to go back to her own home and suggesting to Onys'ko that he should stop pestering his wife. Nechui adds his own voice to the conversation, suggesting that the two should reconcile and that Varka should go home before her clumsy-fingered husband breaks the rest of the kitchenware that he has now come to the bazaar to replace. Like the similar scene in *Kaidasheva sim'ia*, the conflict is resolved amicably. Varka decides to go back home, and Nechui quickly extricates himself from the situation that has attracted a large crowd, including a policeman.

The sketch "Neslukhniana zhinka" merits attention for three reasons. The fact that Nechui returns to a description of a scene that he has already included in a published novel (*Kaidasheva sim'ia*) clearly indicates that he sees something particularly significant or intriguing in this situation. Repetition, as we have seen, is a staple of Nechui's aesthetic method, but in this instance, the matter is a question of his psychological predispositions, rather than his aesthetic tastes. Rebellious women, understood as those who are willing to endure the personal, social, and moral consequences of transgressing against oppressive social strictures on women, are a topic Nechui keeps revisiting. He is neither a moral philosopher nor a profound social critic, so his approach to this issue does not lead to noteworthy assertions or condemnatory judgments. But he is aware of the significance of the issue.

The second reason why this sketch commands more interest that its modest size and stature would suggest is hidden in what is absent from this traditional folkloric situation: the wife in question here, as in *Kaidasheva sim'ia*, is not the victim of a husband's abuse. The husband in this sketch, Onys'ko, who remains without a surname, may have medieval ideas about a wife's subservience to her husband, but he does not use violence against her. Nechui had depicted such a husband in *Khmary*, so he certainly could have added that to the list of the abused woman's grievances. But Varka has left her husband not because he beat her or because she wanted another man, but because her dignity was challenged. Melashka in *Kaidasheva sim'ia* has more reasons – her husband's family treats her badly – but she, too, is not physically abused nor sexually promiscuous. The reference to the policeman at the end of "Neslukhniana zhinka" raises a number of possible interpretations, but at the level of simple facts there is no wrongdoing, legal or moral, for which to censure either woman. Nechui is not simply depicting a well-established problem about how the social code allows the wholesale abuse of women. His interest is in a finer point: a woman's right to dignity and respect.

The third point of interest is a dialectical expansion of the first two points. In the sketch Nechui (as a personage in his own story) tells his friend Maryna Zharka, the mother of the aggrieved wife, that her daughter abandoned Onys'ko just like Solomiia in Nechui's novel *Ne toi stav*, which, adds Nechui as a character in the sketch, he had given Maryna's husband as a gift. So Nechui is not just returning to a scene he has used: he is self-consciously returning to this scene (and he has used it more than just once). What's more, he is calling attention to the fact that he has used this scene before. This is more than just an indication of a writer's propensity for a certain topic. The writer is signalling this propensity. And, by pointing at *Ne toi stav* Nechui is also signalling that the matter is larger than dignity and respect. That novel is a remarkable experiment in Nechui's thematic repertoire and, indeed, in the thematic repertoire of Ukrainian literature in the nineteenth century. Although the title *Ne toi stav* (He's not the same) refers to a male character, this is a novel about women and how they struggle to achieve something more than mere dignity – they are struggling for their own happiness, for their own pleasure, for their own understanding as women of what they want in their lives.

The fact that Nechui wrote a whole novel about women is not as surprising as it may seem. In an important sense, all his works are to a great extent about women. This is particularly true of the narrative perspective. As customary in the narrative style of most nineteenth-century realists, Nechui chooses and alters the narrator's perspective in accordance with the general intentions and needs of the plot. The perspective varies from an omniscient, ubiquitous, anonymous narrator, which is the most common situation in Nechui's works, to a variety of narrower points of view that are more or less circumscribed and identified by the points of view of individual characters in the story – in other words, in focalized narration, using Genette's terminology. In Nechui's works, narration focalized on a female character is unusually common. In chapter 5 of *Kaidasheva sim'ia*, the Kaidash family visit their future in-laws, the Balashes. The action centres on Mrs Kaidash. It is she who goes flying out of the wagon on the way to the Balash home. She is the one who hits her head on the low door frame of the modest Balash home. It is about her that the Balash children whisper their unflattering commentary. As readers, we are tied to the experiences of her person: we see with her eyes, we hear with her ears, and it is through her consciousness that we understand what is going on in this home. About Mr Kaidash we know only that he drank vodka and spoke with Mr Balash. The other characters are given one sentence each. Something similar occurs in the second chapter of *Starosvits'ki batiushky ta matushky* when the timid Kharytin Mossakovs'kyi arrives at the home of Onysia Prokopovychivna for their betrothal. Nechui doesn't even bother to recount the conversation between the young man and his future father-in-law. Instead, he shows us the mother and daughter climbing a chair in the kitchen to sneak a peek at the suitor through the transom. Focalization through female characters is a constant feature of Nechui's writing.

Another quality of Nechui's narration that is closely tied to female focalization is the overwhelming preponderance of "women's" themes, subjects, and situations in his plots and his narration. Of course, the notion of "women's themes" is entirely subjective. But in the context of nineteenth-century Ukrainian society, a typical woman's life would, in practice, involve activities that were deemed her responsibility by dint of her gender. Furthermore, in his works, Nechui emphasizes those aspects of human life that are common to both men and women, or are unique to women. A great deal of attention is given to love, courting, betrothal, weddings, care of children, and household and domestic chores and responsibilities. On the other hand, very little attention in his works is devoted to those tasks that separate men from women. Very rarely do we find descriptions of the professional or income-producing activities of men, where they would be less likely to encounter women.

A great many of Nechui's significant male characters are priests, but the reader sees almost nothing of a priest's work. Among the roster of religious activities he depicts there are many and various celebrations, usually of a public character and including women as homemakers and cooks. But we have very few instances of the ordinary working lives of priests or any other men that would be conducted in private or away from their families. By and large, Nechui's priests do not say mass, they do not write sermons, they do not perform marriages, baptisms, or funerals, they do not pray, and they invariably leave the administration of their homes and property to their wives. When we consider that Nechui's father was a priest, the absence of these functions becomes even more noticeable. Other males are similarly treated. Teachers are not depicted in schools, bankers do not appear near banks, students are seldom in a classroom, administrators don't seem to have anything to administer, civil servants have no specific duties, and opera singers don't sing on stage.

In the novel *Khmary*, for example, the two main characters are professors of the Kyiv Academy. Nechui tells us very little about these two professors' professional lives. We learn little about their academic duties and obligations, although we do learn of Daskovych's scholarly interest in Japanese culture. In this regard, Mykola Dzheria, protagonist of Nechui's eponymous novel, is something of an anomaly, since we do know a good deal about his employment, whether in a factory or on a fishing boat, much more than we do about most of Nechui's male characters. But then, Dzheria had to run away from his wife to make this possible! There is no other male character in Nechui's works similar to Dzheria. There are also no widowers in Nechui, except as potential candidates for marriage to a widow. Widows, on the other hand, are common in Nechui's works, and they have very prominent roles. Old Mrs Kaidash is widowed for a good part of that novel. In *Starosvits'ki batiushky ta matushky*, Kharytin Mossakovs'kyi dies at the beginning of the ninth chapter, while his widow, Onysia Stepanivna, goes on fighting for herself and her children until the end of the novel in the eleventh chapter.

The prominence of women and of a woman's perspective is strengthened by yet another factor, which we might call the emasculation of men. As mentioned above, male roles in Nechui's works are presented in a limited perspective. But where these roles are given a wider canvas, they acquire a comic and pejorative colouring. With the exception, once again, of Mykola Dzheria, whenever a male character is presented in an independent role or activity, this activity is depicted as something of little value. This is particularly true of intellectual activity. As the critic Nila Zborovs'ka argued, the favourite activity of clergymen in Nechui's works is sleeping.[2] Scholarly work is also seen in a negative light. The novel *Khmary* overflows with examples. The whole academy is depicted very contemptuously, nowhere more strikingly than in the scene where the metropolitan argues that Hegel is an idiot because he is a heretic. Similarly, although Vasyl' Dashovych and Pavlo Radiuk are unquestionably positive heroes, they are incapable of making any significant contribution to social or political change. They are just scholars in their own private ivory towers. Something similar is observed in the characters of Vasyl' Komashko and Kharyton Navrots'kyi in *Nad Chornym Morem*. This weakness of Nechui's intellectuals is also evident in their relations with women and in their family lives, where they invariably play a secondary role. When set beside a sleeping clergyman, or a professor befuddled by the philosophy of Asia, homemaker wives, by choice or by default, take over the governance of the family and its possessions, and, therefore, appear more active and effective in worldly affairs.

Of course, not all of Nechui's male characters are weak, but the strong willed are often depicted as negative characters. In *Nad Chornym Morem*, the Greek skirt-chaser, Selabros, and the overly ambitious Fesenko both take personal and financial (but not sexual) advantage of women in amorous situations. Furthermore, their masculine power is limited to their relations with women. Selabros has no interests at all other than chasing women. Fesenko is a pitiful opportunist who consistently elicits scorn from the narrator. Even Mykola Dzheria is not without ambivalent qualities. His masculine strength and forcefulness are presented as positive traits, but these very traits rob him of any chance for a normal, peaceful life with his wife and with his family.

In general then, Nechui depicts the relationship between men and women according to the model of an emasculated man and a dominant woman, usually his wife. Where this model is reversed – where the man is dominant – Nechui generally sees unfavourable consequences: unhappiness, abuse, violence, and even, in the case of the love triangle in the historical novel *Kniaz' Ieremiia Vyshnevets'kyi* (Prince Ieremiia Vyshnevets'kyi), sexual pathology. But in the novel *Ne toi stav*, Nechui goes far beyond this model. He doesn't just present the world from a woman's point of view, he doesn't just elevate women by denigrating men, he presents a case study of women successfully asserting themselves into a male world.

As in other works, so too in this novel there is a contrast between a dutiful woman and a sensual one. Zin'ka Mysanka is a devout widow. Solomiia Chechit is the fun-loving young wife of Zin'ka's son, Roman. Both women are depicted in conflicts with men. In her dreams Zin'ka hears the voice of her late mother instructing her to institute a celebration of the feast of the myrrh-bearing women. The second Sunday after Easter in Orthodoxy is dedicated to these women, who came to Christ's grave the morning after his crucifixion and burial. Although the holiday may not be very well known, the religious context here is unexceptional and in keeping with Orthodox tradition. In a gender studies context, however, the feast of the myrrh-bearing women is the Orthodox equivalent of a feminist rally. This is a women's holiday that celebrates women and has special meaning for the female parishioners. The men in the parish treat the idea of the feast, and the feast itself when it is instituted, with derision and scorn precisely because it is a holiday for women. Thus, Zin'ka's efforts to institute such a feast is an act of social upheaval. Nechui is not one to delve deeply into the psychology of his characters, so there is little in the novel that elaborates, motivates, or explains Zin'ka's desire. The idea comes to her from a repeated dream in which her late mother, literally a ghost from the past, instructs her to institute such a celebration. Nechui is at pains to avoid any appearance of rebelliousness in Zin'ka's behaviour. Her encounter with Father Harasym makes this clear. Zin'ka is a large woman whose physical presence commands respect, while Father Harasym is a slight man. Nechui reverses the presumed authority of the two characters:

> Здавалося, ніби не баба прийшла по ділу до отця Герасима, а навзворіт: ніби отець Гарасим прийшов до баби Зіньки, і поважна баба вітала його, як господиня.
>
> – Сідай, Зінько, – промовив отець Гарасим. Він нікого з молодиць та бабів не просив сідати в себе, але це була баба Зіня. Треба було її посадовити, бо баба Зіня мала великий вплив на всіх бабів в селі. Зінька була баба над бабами. Її в селі усі поважали.
>
> Баба Зінька і не одмагалась, і не одмовлялась. Вона неначе знала собі ціну і просто сіла на канапці, котра стояла під грубою. Батюшка сів на стільці коло столика. (6:322)

> [It seemed that it wasn't the matron who had come to Father Herasym on business, but the other way around: as if Father Herasym had come to Zin'ka and the serious matron was welcoming him as the mistress of the household.
>
> "Sit down, Zin'ka," said Father Herasym. He never invited girls or women to sit down in his home, but this was Zin'ka. She had to be given a seat because Zin'ka had a great influence over all the matrons in the village. She was the first matron among the matrons. Everyone in the village respected her.
>
> Zin'ka did not dispute or refuse the offer. She seemed to know her own worth and merely sat down on the sofa that stood beside the fireplace. The pastor sat down on a chair by the table.]

When it comes to her request for the holiday, however, Father Herasym can barely suppress a laugh. He is an intellectual pragmatist with little tolerance for a silly imperative transmitted through an old woman's dreams. He will go along with her request because her social position in the village demands respect, and because this additional holiday will also improve his own income. Her victory is a simple power play. She even conveys a subtle threat. When she perceives the priest is contemplating a refusal, she once again mentions her dream visions of her mother:

– Ой, прошу вашої милості і я, і моя сестра, і старостиха, усі просимо вас: і дозвольте, і допоможіть нам, бо першого разу снилась мені мати веселою та ласкавою, а цей раз снилась вже неласкавою. Їй-богу моєму! аж сердито глянула мені в вічі … А вид в неї такий чорний став, неначе землею припав. Я аж затрусилась, як прокинулася … Боюся, батюшко! Знаю, що знов прийде вона до мене у сні ...

– Як прийде знов твоя мати, то ще й поб'є тебе. Ну-ну, Зінько! Нехай вже буде так, як ти кажеш, – обізвався отець Гарасим і глянув їй в вічі гострим поглядом.

Чорні, гострі бабині очі стали зразу спокійні; чималі, виразно обведені й випнуті уста весело осміхнулись, а з-під уст забіліли усі цілісінькі довгі міцні зуби, вже трохи пожовклі. Зінька підвела вгору свою чималу, як у чоловіка, голову. Білі широкі кінці намітки заворушились на широких плечах. Довгобразий, схожий на грецький вид її став веселий. (6:324)

["Oh, I beg your reverence, I beg, and my sister begs, and the headmistress begs, we all beg you: allow us and help us. The first time my mother appeared in my dream she was cheerful and gracious, but this time she was not cordial in the dream. As God is my witness she looked me in the eye angrily, and her face became black, as if covered with earth. It made me shiver and I awoke. I'm scared, father. I know she will come to me in my dreams again.

"If your mother comes again, she likely will give you a beating. Well, well, Zin'ka. Let it be your way," spoke up Father Herasym and raised his eyes to hers with a sharp glance.

The matron's black, sharp eyes immediately became calm, her large, clearly outlined and full lips smiled cheerfully, and from beneath her lips her full row of strong, somewhat yellowed teeth gleamed brightly. Zin'ka raised up her head, as large as a man's. The broad white ends of her cap slid up her broad shoulders. Her Greek-looking, long face beamed with happiness.]

If power is measured in gender terms, Nechui is on the mark in comparing Zin'ka's head to a man's. Her wily diplomacy has outsmarted the priest, who is shown to be an intelligent and level-headed man, and thus a formidable opponent. What is missing in all this, however, is any sense of rebellion or impropriety.

Ne toi stav is constructed around the contrast of supposedly rebellious acts. Zin'ka's conversation with the priest concludes with a series of evaluations. Father Herasym asks her about the other women who will help her collect funds for the holiday preparations. One by one Zin'ka diplomatically rejects his suggestions with the narrator's explanations that this one drinks, that one is unreliable, and yet another has poor judgment. The overall effect is to enhance Zin'ka's image as a serious, reliable, level-headed woman. And here Nechui introduces her presumed opposite, Solomiia. Zin'ka asks the priest for his opinion of the young girl that her son wishes to marry. The priest is a reasonable man to ask, because the girl was a nanny for his children. The serious, pious Zin'ka is worried that Solomiia is too impulsive and frivolous:

> А вона якась стрибка та проворна.
>
> – Та вона проворна: це правда, але, сказати по правді, дуже робоча, робить діло швидко, скрізь встигне; що не загадай – скрізь увинеться. Та й на вдачу вона добра, не сердита.
>
> – Ой батюшко! А я боюсь, що вона дуже вже любить ті співи, танці та смішки. Крутілка, та й годі!
>
> – Це не вадить, бо вона молода. Адже ж, Зінько, і ти колись співала та крутилась, як була молодою.
>
> – Ой, співала! Нема що казати, – промовила Зінька осміхаючись.
>
> Вона махнула рукою і потім поклала руку на коліно. На білій свиті її здорова, як у чоловіка, рука з дуже довгими товстими пальцями чорніла, неначе вилита з заліза.
>
> – Соломія, бабо, з таких, що "на улиці перед веде, а на полі серпом гуде," як приказують люде: вона з півроку була в мене за няньку, а півроку за куховарку. Дітей вона добре гляділа й жалувала. Видко, що вона серцем добра, хоч і крутілка, як ти кажеш.
>
> Зінька встала, випросталась на цілий свій зріст. Намітка на плечах загойдалась. Встав і батюшка. І здавалось, що не батюшка випроваджує Зіньку, а поважна Зінька випроваджує з своєї господи отця Гарасима.
>
> Зінька узяла в свою кремезну руку невеличку сухорляву білу руку отця Гарасима, поцілувала й розпрощалась. (6:326)

> [She seems somehow jumpy and frisky.
>
> "She is frisky, that's true, but to be honest, she is a good worker. She works quickly, she finishes on time, whatever you ask her she'll manage to get done. And she's good-hearted, not mean."
>
> "Oh, Father, I'm afraid that she likes singing, dancing, and joking around too much. She's high-spirited."
>
> "That's not a serious fault – she's still young. Remember, Zin'ka, that you used to sing and dance too, when you were young."

"Oh, I did indeed sing, there's no two words about that," said Zin'ka, smiling.

She waved her hand and put it down on her knee. Against her white mantle her hand, as big as a man's, with thick black fingers, looked as if it were cast in iron.

"Solomiia, my good woman, is one of those who 'parties hard and works harder,' as folks say. She was a nanny for me for half a year and then another half year she was our cook. She looked after the children very well and she was kind to them. It's clear she has a good heart, even if she's high-spirited, as you say."

Zin'ka got up and stretched out to her full height. The cap on her head was loose and shook slightly. The priest got up too. And it seemed that it wasn't the priest escorting Zin'ka to the door, but the stately Zin'ka bidding him farewell from her household.

Into her powerful hand Zin'ka took Father Herasym's small white hand, kissed it, and parted.]

With the addition of yet another gender reversal for Zin'ka (this time, her hands), Nechui establishes but then swiftly dismisses a contrast between the dutiful Zin'ka and the licentious Solomiia. Yes, Solomiia is a fun-loving girl, but the village priest himself gives her a clean bill of moral health. Zin'ka, whose opinion the reader has been led to trust even more than the priest's, accepts this verdict, and any doubts about Solomiia's undesirable, rebellious character are laid to rest. This absolution will be critical in the reader's judgment of her subsequent actions.

Nechui does not let the search for potential rebels end here. There is, indeed, a real rebel in the story. Zin'ka's daughter, Nastia is also looking for a partner, and her choice falls on Denys Odnosumenko, a friend of Roman, her brother. Denys is not at all like Roman, however:

Денис був жвавий, проворний; парубок з його вийшов крутий на вдачу, запеклий, непокірливий і неслухняний. Він не міг ні в кого вибути й півроку на службі, бо не любив покорятись; навіть не все слухав свого батька, а про матір і вухом не вів. Денис часто сміявся з Романа, що він слухає матері, усе ходить до церкви, співає й читає на криласі, не їсть скоромного в піст. (6:316)

[Denys was a lively, frisky young man. He was high-spirited by nature, fiery, headstrong, and defiant. He couldn't last even a half year in someone's employ, because he wouldn't take instruction; he didn't even always obey his father, and as for his mother, well, his ear was deaf. Denys often jibed Roman for obeying his mother, going to church, singing psalms and following the service, and abiding by fast days.]

Here, at last, is a real rebel! Although some of the words in the description are identical to those used for Solomiia (проворний, крутий), Denys is a real rule-breaker. He disobeys his parents, he doesn't go to church, he doesn't keep the fast, and he can't hold down a job. Denys even organizes a group of young men who attack the village reeve and bailiff in retribution for the repeated disbanding of the village revels. For this assault Denys is imprisoned for a few days, cementing his reputation as a rascal and miscreant. The stern Zin'ka is not about to let her daughter marry such a fellow.

But Denys's qualities are not all bad. He is deliberately contrasted with his friend Roman. In school, Nechui tells the reader, Denys would, like Roman, borrow religious books from the priest. But whereas Roman found great delight in religious writings, Denys showed no interest in the subject (6:317). On the other hand, when Denys visits the newly married Roman and Solomiia, he brings a book to read. Where Roman spent time alone reading religious books, Denys reads from Ivan Kotliarevs'kyi's *Natalka Poltavka* to the young couple and Nastia. Even Zin'ka comes over to listen to the reading of this classic work of Ukrainian literature. Evidently, even here, Nechui is confusing the question of what constitutes rebellious behaviour. If rebels read Kotliarevs'kyi, then perhaps rebellion is not as bad as it's made out to be? In a world of value reversals, perhaps it's the traditional virtues that need re-examination?

The reader first meets Roman Mysanka in this novel in a scene cited above,[3] when the young man enters his mother's home carrying a bunch of flowers. His mother asks if he has gathered some stalks for the pigs. No, he says, the flowers are to decorate the icons in the house (6:301–2). We are also told that the painted flowers above the hearth are the work of both Roman and his sister. Though not very dramatic, this is a reversal of gender roles. Decoration in a village home is generally women's business. Roman is being depicted as something of an oddball. His interests are aesthetic, intellectual, and religious. Measured in traditional terms, his masculinity, like that of Father Herasym, is soft, particularly when compared to Denys, who has served his military duty and is capable of initiating a punitive beating of the village reeve. But the priest has normal relations with women, as his interview with Zin'ka shows. Not so Roman. He's shy and although he likes Solomiia, he doesn't come out for the evening revels. When they meet at the well, she is the one who initiates contact and makes jokes at his expense. This is a familiar ritual in Nechui's works and in Ukrainian literature as a whole. Men are often depicted as helpless fools in the game of romance. But Roman's reticence is twofold. On the one hand, he is the familiar, thunderstruck lover who can't find the means to express his emotions. On the other hand, he is a dreamy intellectual idler who loses track of his work and avoids other people. In the end, this latter quality leads him into religious obscurantism, solitude, and a virtual abandonment of his role as a husband.

Solomiia and her mother-in-law both conduct campaigns to achieve their goals. Zin'ka must get permission, raise funds, and make preparations for the holiday, always facing the ridicule and interference of the men in the village. Where Zin'ka struggles in public view, her daughter-in-law wages a private, hidden war with her husband. After their marriage and the birth of two children, Roman further develops his great interest in scholarly and intellectual religious matters. He studies and reads books and neglects his family, his farm, his domestic chores, and his wife. Even his physical appearance changes for the worse: he lets his hair grow long and wears an unkempt full beard. Nechui, usually reticent and discreet in these matters, emphasizes that Roman no longer sleeps in the same bed with his wife. Happy, playful, carefree Solomiia tries to renew their marriage and conjugal relationship. She teases her husband coquettishly and tries to divert his attention away from his books and back onto her. Frustrated by her husband's lack of attention to herself, their family, and their home, Solomiia literally attacks her husband. In an already tense and angry conversation, Solomiia asks whom she is supposed to love (since her husband is lost to his books). He answers: "No one." Enraged by such a response, she lunges at him with scissors and cuts off part of his beard and hair (6:395). At a party that evening in a game where the women play with a doll and pretend it's a baby, Solomiia throws the doll head first to the floor: "Коли твій батько не любить твоєї матері, то й я тебе не буду любити! Оце тобі за батька така смерть! – крикнула Соломія і знов зареготалась голосно на всю хату чудно й дико, як часом регочуться божевільні" (6:397) ["If your father doesn't love your mother, then I won't love you either. And here is your death on your father's account," yelled Solomiia, and again began laughing loudly through the whole house, in a laugh like those sometimes heard from the insane].

Here at last, it seems, is real rebellion and transgression by a woman! A village Delilah, lusting for happiness and for her husband, assaults his person, symbolically emasculates him, and then expresses her despair by figuratively killing a child. Indeed, the other women at the party are taken aback by her behaviour, but this is temporary. In the very next scene Nechui shows Solomiia ready to leave home and abandon her husband, but her plan is derailed by an act of charity. On this cold and wet day, she runs outdoors in her bare feed to help a poor Jew, Avrum, push his wagon out of the mud. She falls ill and almost dies. Without excusing her behaviour, without endorsing her intended abandonment of her family, Nechui immediately and almost magically turns condemnation into sympathy. Furthermore, as Solomiia recovers, the plot of the novel turns against her husband. He and Solomiia's father, Fylon Chechit, who is a foolish old religious fanatic, are elected village judges. Because of the devout piety of these two religious men, the villagers feel their new judges will not be susceptible to intrigue and manipulation. But as with the old judges, so with Roman and Fylon: the endless stream of judicial affairs pulls the two away from their domestic responsibilities, and, since judicial matters always require a conversation at the tavern, turns them into drunkards. Ironically, the previously unreliable Denys gets elected treasurer at the same time, but he is uncorrupted by his public duties. The drunk Roman constantly badgers Solomiia that she is only interested in showy clothing and parties. "Їй аби вертітись та крутитись. Так, так! Я вже добре знаю. Знаємо ми вас!" (6:405) [She just wants to be active and high-spirited. Yes, yes! Now I understand. We know your types], he tells her, repeating words used earlier in the story, but this time using the plural pronoun, as if he represented all men and she all women. Finally, Solomiia can stand it no more and leaves the home, telling her mother-in-law: "Роман вже давно мені не чоловік, а я йому не жінка" (6:407) [For a long time now, Roman has not been my husband, nor I his wife].

This is the incident to which Nechui refers in his conversation with Maryna Zharka in "Neslukhniana zhinka." The reference adds a great deal to our understanding of the situation in the novel, or more precisely, to our understanding of how Nechui sees it. It is not just a matter of a husband's disrespect for his wife. It is an exploration of a woman's right to happiness in life, whether she is married or not. *Ne toi stav* is built around a consistent pattern of reversals and contrasts. We have already observed a few of the gender reversals in the text. There are also the reversals of reliable and unreliable men: Denys, Roman, Filon.

There is a consistent pattern of questioning the authority of religious sentiments. The women's holiday focuses this questioning on the relationship between women's rights and religion. And, of course, there is the question of a woman's role in a marriage, whether a woman has the same rights as a man to seek happiness, and whether a woman is entitled to her husband's attention.

At the heart of this series of contrasts is the opposition between duty and pleasure. Zin'ka finds her pleasure by instituting a religious feast that has a special resonance for women. Solomiia seeks pleasure of a more direct kind. She wants to enjoy herself and to enjoy her husband's company. To achieve their ends, both women must struggle against the unwillingness of men to cede an equal place in the world to women. Thus they are both, in fact, rebels. By deliberately setting their rebellions side by side, by giving them equal positions in the construction of the story line, Nechui returns again to the question he had raised in "Dvi moskovky": is a woman justified in seeking her own pleasure? This time, however, Nechui removes the additional factor of illicit, extramarital sex. Solomiia's desires, however they may be judged, are within the social norms of an accepted marriage, just as Zin'ka's feminist holiday is entirely legitimate in Orthodox Christianity. Whereas the tragic end of Maryna in "Dvi moskovky" can be interpreted as an emblem of the just fate that awaits licentious women, Solomiia's death frames her as a martyr and community benefactor. Her first brush with death comes in assisting Avrum, who represents the most underprivileged member of society. Then, in contrast to her husband, whose service to the community turned him into a drunkard, Solomiia dies from injuries received in helping her neighbours fight a fire, literally, while saving the icons from the burning home. To make an unmistakable link between her public service and her personality, Nechui offers the following dialogue between Roman and Father Herasym, where Solomia's instinct to help others is described with the same words that were used earlier to characterize her impulsiveness:

> – І як вона вбігла в те полум'я? І чом вона не остереглася? Хіба ж вона не бачила, що в сінях вже горить покрівля? – питав священик.
>
> – А бог її зна. Хіба ж я, батюшко, посилав її лізти в полум'я? Така вона вже зроду метка та проворна, а до помочі людям так і кидається, неначе їй паморoки забиває людське нещастя. Цілий вік пурхала, як та птиця, і в полум'я кинулась, мов та птиця. Така вже їй доля судилась, – говорив Роман. (6:416–17)

["How could she run into such flames? Why wasn't she careful? Couldn't she see that the thatch in the vestibule was already aflame?" asked the priest.

"Heaven only knows. Father – do you think I told her to climb into the fire? She was like that by nature, vivacious and frisky, and when it came to helping people, she would just jump in, as if she were made dizzy by people's suffering. All her life she was flighty, like a bird, and she jumped into the fire like a bird. I guess that was her fate," Roman said.]

Ne toi stav leaves no doubt that Nechui sympathizes with a woman's pursuit of happiness and pleasure both in the public and the private sphere. Solomiia's pursuit of her own joy is tied to her willingness to help others. But whether in this novel or in Nechui's works as a whole, the unusual tendency to reflect women's sensibilities and a woman's search for happiness cries out for further exploration and analysis.

In the history of Nechui studies, there have been very few acknowledgments of this proclivity on the part of the author, and even fewer analyses of its significance. By far the most important occurs in the essay by Valerian Pidmohyl'nyi cited above in chapter 1, that discusses Nechui as an example of the Oedipal complex. In that essay Pidmohyl'nyi discusses a number of biographical facts about Nechui, but stops short of discussing the features of his literary works that might corroborate this speculative deduction. He refers only to one incident, Vasylyna's infanticide in *Burlachka,* which he interprets as Nechui's revenge for his mother's death in childbirth. Perhaps more significant is his citation of an observation about Nechui's relations with women:

"Ів. Сем. більше любив балакати з бабами, ніж з чоловіками, бо краще вмів заставити (їх) повести розмову в бажаному напрямі" – тоб-то з бабами йому легше було знайти спільну мову, і з цієї, суто-бабської, властивости його й народилися потім не тільки знамениті його "Баби," але й багато инших жіночих постатів його творів.

["Iv[an] Sem[enovych] liked to talk to women more than he liked to talk with men, because he was better at making them take the conversation in the desired direction," that is, he was more likely to find common ground with women and from this essentially female quality of his were born not only his famous Babas [i.e., the characters of Baba Palazhka and Baba Paraska] but also many other female characters in his works.][4]

The observation speaks to the recognition of a particular aptitude on the part of Nechui to create female characters and attributes this aptitude to qualities of his personality. While the quoted remark does not specify the particular qualities of Nechui's fictional women made possible by the author's presumed facility at conversing with women, clearly Pidmohyl'nyi sees, as I have argued, that women have a disproportionately important place in Nechui's works. In Pidmohyl'nyi's essay, this is another argument in support of the thesis that Nechui was a homosexual. His relationship to his father, discussed previously, is another important factor. But in the absence of any scientific methodology or clinical rigour, and with absurdly simplistic conclusions drawn from incomplete facts from Nechui's biography, the psychoanalytic conclusions that Pidmohyl'nyi reaches are not matter for serious discussion. They simply cannot be justified by the evidence presented. But the essay is important because it attempts to link the peculiarities of Nechui's works with the personality of the author. Nechui's depiction of women and their concerns are clearly more than figments of a reader's interpretation, but they are also less than consciously held dogmatic positions the author is attempting to articulate.

Another attempt to understand Nechui's presentation of women is Nila Zborovs'ka's essay "Ukrains'kyi svit Nechuia-Levyts'koho: Gendernyi pidkhid" (The Ukrainian world of Nechui-Levyts'kyi: a gender approach), which appeared in her collection of essays, *Feministychni rozdumy* (Feminist musings).[5] As the title itself indicates, Zborovs'ka is tying together two important factors that play a significant role in Nechui's works: nation and gender. To Zborovs'ka's credit, in this essay she manages to show, on the basis of a mere handful of Nechui's works, how important a topic the depiction of women is in Nechui's works and how important this topic is for researchers working on Nechui. Using the ideological terminology and methods of contemporary gender studies, Zborovs'ka sees in Nechui the symptoms of a dominant paternalism and the influence of the quiet sexual revolution of the nineteenth century. But the characteristic contrast in Nechui's works between a passive male and a strong, dominant female is, for Zborovs'ka, an outgrowth of the Ukrainian national character, or of a Jungian collective unconscious of the Ukrainian nation. Assuming that patriarchal attitudes are primary and dominant, she concludes that the image of a strong woman and a passive man in Nechui's works is a condemnation of sexuality.[6] Such a conclusion leads her to question and condemn any attempts to see in Nechui any evidence of homosexuality.

Zborovs'ka views Nechui's works from the perspective of a collective national consciousness. She is certainly right in claiming that Nechui depicts male sexuality negatively, as a form of brutality. But the same is not true, as we have seen, of his presentation of female sexuality. Her essay points to some very interesting gender issues in Nechui's works, but her programmatic conclusion that these peculiarities are the product of a national rather than a personal psychology seems to be more directly motivated by a fervent desire to slay the mythical dragon of Nechui's supposed homosexuality than by any real connections to collective myths. Whether or not Levyts'kyi was a homosexual has no bearing on the possible role of Jungian collective myths in shaping Nechui's works. Conversely, while Pidmohyl'nyi's bald assertion of Nechui's homosexuality is certainly unconvincing and unsupportable, his focus on the relationship between the personality of the author and the peculiarities of his works offers far more promise as a methodological tool than do historical paternalism and Jungian psychology. In short, the depiction of women in Nechui's work is clearly a result of Nechui's own psychic distinctiveness.

Judging by its reflection in his works, the central element of Nechui's personality is joy.[7] From the happiest moments of pure ecstasy to the most miserable suffering, with dollops of comedy and satire in between, the primary colours on Nechui's palette are bright and cheerful. He is forever searching for the light-hearted view. Unhappy and suffering characters are almost always contrasted with cheerful, easy-going counterparts. Negative characters, with a few important exceptions, are depicted mainly as projections of human foibles and foolishness, rather than as having evil motives attributed to them. Even some of the wicked characters are simply taking advantage of the foolishness of others. Almost invariably, characters are motivated by a desire for their own happiness rather than real malice towards others, even in cases like that of the feuding Baba Paraska and Baba Palazhka, who are more ridiculous than evil. Even in *Mykola Dzheria*, a novel that depicts the tragedy of a bitter man whose righteous anger strips him of the possibility of happiness, numerous passages emphasize a more joyous, more light-hearted perspective. Petro Dzheria's negotiations with the priest, Mykola's relationship with Mokryna, his experience as a fisherman, the comic description of the sudden disappearance of people whose names the refugees had adopted – all these point to an alternative perspective in the novel. Even more important, the thematic focus of the story is precisely on Mykola's lost joy, the anger that rips apart his quiet (though unjustly oppressed) existence and sends him on a life journey where the possibility of happiness is negated by his undefined legal status and emotional disposition. Mykola is that very rare character in Nechui's works who pursues a goal other than his own pleasure and fulfilment.

Of course, not all of Nechui's characters are happy, regardless of their pursuit of this quality. Some fail to achieve it because they are prevented by others. Others fail because the happiness they seek is unattainable. But it isn't success or failure to achieve happiness that is uppermost in Nechui's universe – it is the nature of the joy his characters seek, the source of the pleasure they expect to experience. Surprisingly, this distinction, as we have seen in "Dvi moskovky," is not about social or religious prohibitions. Nechui does not condemn the joys of sinful pleasure. He condemns those joys that derive not from a character's innate feelings, but from that character's pretensions and feelings of superiority over others. The faults of Zosia Pshepshyns'ka and Ias' Seredyns'kyi lie not in their illicit love affair but in their feelings of entitlement because they are Polish gentry. The competing mothers in *Starosvits'ki batiushky ta matushky* are not judged poorly for their clingy affection towards their sons but for their pretensions to a better social status for themselves and their offspring. Marusia Kaidash, like many upright, dutiful women in Nechui's works, is an unfailing champion of her own superiority. The joys she seeks are built on the diminution of others. The opposite of pretension in Nechui is the joy of pure merriment. The ultimate embodiment of this virtue is surely Father Mel'khyzedek in *Starosvits'ki batiushky ta matushky*, who seeks the simplest of pleasures in pranks with potatoes and crayfish. Here, too, are all the tipsy priests and partying peasants, the jokesters and pranksters, the gossips and chatterers, the shirkers and sleepers, the dreamers and storytellers, the singers and dancers that populate the background of so much of Nechui's writing. They all seek the most direct forms of pleasure, unmediated by the views or the prohibitions of others. Here, too, on a different level, are all the idealists who struggle to make a better world for themselves and for others: Pavlo Radiuk (*Khmary*), Viktor Komashko (*Nad Chornym Morem*), Iakiv Ulasevych (*Neodnakovymy stezhkamy*), and Zin'ka Mysanka (*Ne toi stav*). Their motives are personal, sincere, and authentic, rather than public, pretentious, and acquired. Whether or not they are successful in their endeavours, Nechui treats characters who seek such personal fulfilment and pleasure with sympathy and respect. This is the source of happiness and good cheer in his world.

The notion that happiness constitutes the core value in Nechui's world flies in the face of a great deal of received opinion about the writer. How could this irascible old curmudgeon, this stubborn, conservative anachronism, this aesthetic and intellectual dinosaur from a gloomy age long passed be a man of principled merriment and joy? Here lies the great harm, the pernicious legacy of Iefremov's biography and the language wars that Nechui so vehemently pursued in his latter years. The generation that succeeded him remembered him as the crusty old prophet of linguistic purity, the author of stinging jeremiads against real or imagined enemies or sinners. Iefremov codified this view in his biography. Lost in this flood of bad memories is the image of the writer as a life-affirming, good-natured, friendly cheerleader for all things literary and Ukrainian. His biographical writings and his epistolary heritage (excepting, of course, those on matters of orthography) paint a portrait of a happy, quiet workaholic, somewhat reclusive and certainly quirky (as solitary men often are), but very open to friendship and to good cheer. In his own life, and in the personalities of his characters, particularly women, the pursuit of happiness and pleasure is a fundamental principle, even when it involves a struggle against public opinion and social authority.

The exploration of a woman's search for love, for the pleasure of romantic engagement, occupies a surprisingly large place in the thematic universe of Nechui's later works. Even before *Ne toi stav*, which was written in 1894, Nechui had sketched a group of characters in *Nad Chornym Morem* that consisted of middle-class men and women engaged in a variety of hedonistic or idealistic pursuits. The central character, Viktor Komashko, an idealistic champion of Ukrainian schooling, is contrasted with a group of men and women whose chief interest is in playful merriment and romance. Komashko is also contrasted with Sania Navrots'ka, his future wife, who is also an idealistic teacher at a school for Jewish girls, but not particularly interested in the status of Ukrainian culture. She, in turn, is contrasted again with the group of light-hearted men and particularly women, whose primary interest is romance and pleasure. Sania is one of Nechui's rare examples of a positive urban female, and her interest in the social and political advancement of women is seen in a very favourable light in the novel, particularly in contrast to the frivolity and self-gratification of Khrystyna Mylashkevych and her sister-in-law Motrona Borodavkin. Significantly, however, these women are seen as mere innocents, shallow individuals who do not share the values of the protagonists in the story. The villains of the story are Fesenko and Navrots'kyi, who actively obstruct the virtuous program that Viktor and Sania wish to implement. The hedonistic women themselves are not condemned for their behaviour.

As with a number of his other fictional characters (most notably Baba Palazhka), so with Khrystyna Mylashkevych, Nechui gives in to the temptation to reprise a successful comic character. She reappears a few years later in a short novel entitled *Navizhena* as the matchmaker and experienced romantic advisor to two young lovers. Dem'ian Lomyts'kyi is a caricature of an apathetic lover. He isn't sure whether he would rather sleep or visit the woman he loves. Marusia Karalaieva, his beloved, is a very proper and conservative young lady who faces a very peculiar romantic problem. Her mother, Marta, will not allow her daughter to get married until she herself remarries. Old Mrs Karalaiev is a widow who wants to re-experience the passion of her youth. Her father refused permission for her marriage to Platon Bychkovs'kyi because the suitor was poor. Bychkovs'kyi, in his turn, wouldn't take her up on her suggestion that they elope. So she married Karalaiev, whom she didn't love, but now Marta is a widow looking to rekindle the feelings in her heart:

> Щоки в Марти Кирилівни спахнули, її лице стало таке червоне, як півонія. Очі запалились і заблищали. І дух весняний, і дівочий чистий колорит неба, і недавній візит молодого гарного хлопця розбуркали в її серці незамерлі дрімаючі інстинкти жіночої душі, невдоволеного жіночого серця, розбудили дрімаючу гарячу потребу палкої вдачі, потребу любити, вгамувати пал своєї вдачі, невдоволеної в свій час. (6:17–18)

> [Marta Kyrylivna's cheeks flushed, her face became as red as a peony. Her eyes were aflame and glowing. The spirit of spring, the girlish clear colour of the sky, and the recent visit of the handsome young boy had kindled in her heart the unextinguished sleeping instincts of the female soul, of the unsatisfied heart of a woman. They had awakened the dormant burning desire of a passionate personality, a desire to love, to quench the flame of her personality, unfulfilled in its own time.]

These characters – Marta, Marusia, Khrystyna, Dem'ian, and Platon – recreate familiar contrasts from Nechui's earlier works. Weak, emasculated men are contrasted with domineering, self-centred women. There's also a contrast between a proper, dutiful woman and a licentious, pleasure-seeking one. By endowing the elder woman with the "instincts of the female soul," Nechui reverses the usual comic relation between a thoughtful, cautious mother and a passionate, reckless daughter. Although the title of the work (*navizhena* = crazy) clearly delivers a judgment about the behaviour of Marta Karalaieva, the text does not carry the same indictment. Eventually, the reader cannot help but sympathize with Marta, as her once youthful lover, Platon Bychkovs'kyi, forgets to show up for Marusia's wedding, where Marta expects them to formalize their own wedding plans. What's more, in the final chapter the newlyweds set up their very proper household at some distance from their "crazy" mother, but their quiet, stable, and unobjectionable married life brings out an entirely unexpected sentiment from the young husband: "Отут, в цій хатині моїй, в цьому засохлому, пожовклому садочку панує моральна й соціальна моя смерть … Я заперся тут, неначе в домовині", – подумав Ломицький" (6:91) ["Here, then, in my own home, in this withered, yellowed orchard, I am fated to meet my moral and social death. I have locked myself up here, as if in a coffin," thought Lomyts'kyi]. Nechui further drives home his point by having the young couple receive a letter from a socially active, rebellious colleague. The contrast between his activism and their complacency condemns their quiescence and endorses, in some measure, Marta Karaleieva's active pursuit of her own pleasure.

As the nineteenth century gave way to the twentieth, the issues associated with women's rights and with relaxed social norms regarding sexuality became matters of frequent public debate and agitation. No doubt Nechui also felt the influence of these public debates. As we have seen, he reacted critically to modernist aesthetics, which he, like many other critics of modernism, associated with pornography. But in his own fictional works written in the new century, the depiction of women who transgress against traditional social norms in marriage is, for the most part, far more tolerant – indeed, it shows a relatively sympathetic view that is in line with the views on women's joy that were evident in earlier works. This is true even where Nechui explicitly ties the transgression to modernist literature.

There are four works among those written after 1900 that directly involve women who disregard marital fidelity. Two of them are built on related material. *Na gastroliakh v Mykytianakh* and "Gastroli" are built on the same principal characters: the operatic singer Flegont Litoshevs'kyi and his wife, Sofiia. In the first of these short novels, the urban couple go out to the village for a relaxing summer, visiting with the singer's brother, a priest in the village, who lets them live in the schoolhouse.

In the second work, it's springtime, and the couple are resting in their own country home, which they are remodelling into an urban palace in the countryside (a phenomenon repeating itself in many Ukrainian villages today). In both works, it's the husband who has a romanticized view of rural life. He enjoys the countryside, hunting, and a slow, carefree existence. His wife, on the other hand, is a true urban woman. She is from St. Petersburg, a middle-class daughter of a government clerk, but she has a democratic view of the rural classes and even tries to learn Ukrainian, unlike her pretentious Kyiv cook, Masha. This contrast with her cook is significant and allows Nechui to give a rather strong endorsement of Sofiia, whose willingness to learn Ukrainian, despite being both Russian and urban, makes her a unique individual among Nechui's characters:

> – А я й сама радніша б навчиться говорити по-українській, та в Києві не навчусь од Маші й од людей. От і добре, що мій син принаймні добре навчиться говорити тутечки на селі українською мовою.
>
> Софія Леонівна й справді згодом потім нахапалася слів на селі й навчилась таки добре говорити по-українській. Як цікава столична людина, вона зацікавилась українськими книжками й читала їх залюбки. Пробуваючи на селі в Флегонтового батька, вона вже й тепер добре розуміла українську мову й не забороняла синкові говорить з селянами по-українській, як звичайно забороняють у нас батьки своїм дітям, нехтуючи народну мову й народ. (8:13)
>
> ["I would be happy to learn to speak Ukrainian, but I won't learn it in Kyiv, neither from Masha nor from other people. At least here, in the village, my son will learn to speak Ukrainian well."
>
> Sofiia Leonivna truly did, over time, pick up various words in the village and eventually she did learn to speak Ukrainian well. As an inquisitive woman from the capital, she became interested in Ukrainian books and enjoyed reading them. Having spent time with Flegont's father in the village, she already understood Ukrainian very well and did not forbid her son to speak Ukrainian with the villagers, as is usually the case with parents nowadays, scorning the common language and the common people.]

The constellation of values that define Nechui's later works on women's behaviour are characterized by the urban-rural divide and by aesthetic sensibilities. In both *Na gastroliakh v Mykytianakh* and "Gastroli" Nechui gives a great deal of attention to the physical space the urbanites inhabit in the village: the schoolhouse that needs so much repair in the first novel, the village dacha that will be remodelled in the second. Urban tastes and styles – at least in architecture and interior decorations – have entered the traditional Ukrainian village. On the material side, it is the buildings that get altered, but in the psychological dimension it is the urban visitors who are reconstructed. The urban women who come to the village are out of place there. For better or worse – no, invariably for the worse – they are infected by the beauty and freedom of the village. Their own aesthetic sensibilities, their desire for beauty, their unconstrained freedom, and the absence of a strong social grounding in the village lead them into ruinous love affairs. When Flegont is off hunting or called up to the city to sing, Sofiia is left lonely and without activity, ready to fill her days with emotional adventure.

A key ingredient in this incompatible mix of city and village is art. Flegont is an opera star, and other characters also have connections to music. In both works there is considerable attention to singing, including some terrible noise when the two brothers and their cousin sing a trio from Karl Maria von Weber's *Der Freischütz* so badly that Ol'ha Litoshevs'ka is forced to cover her ears (8:31). But art in the countryside is not just music. Ol'ha's brother is a landscape painter. In general the urban visitors see art and poetry at every turn in the village, but they often ignore the actual inhabitants, behaving as if they were alone in the wild. This aesthetic romanticization of the countryside is an important factor in the licentious behaviour of Sofiia. In both of the novels she behaves immodestly, first flirting publicly and then, in each of the works, falling into an illicit affair with the available young man. Although he brands her a Messalina, using the name of the notoriously licentious third wife of the Roman emperor Claudius as an indictment for sexual promiscuity, Nechui takes unusually elaborate steps to explain and thereby partially to excuse Ol'ha's actions. Even the priest's wife is affected by the poetry of the romantic scene of peasants singing at sunset:

> Сонце заходило, неначе падало в зелену безодню на далеких очеретах та гаях. Пишнота на рожевому заході, в синьому небі, на зелених лиснючих луках, в синій далечі лісів, на горбах знов викликала в співунів хіть до співів. Надворі було тихо, як у покоях. Шум та гам на селі стишувавсь і ніби замирав. Зелена земля й синє небо неначе дрімали в легеньких сутінках. Надворі потрошку смеркало. Вечірня поезія махнула крилом над садком, над річкою та зеленими очеретами. Потоптаний закаблуками канупер та м'ята

розливали пахощі. Резеда ніби розливала тонкий ароматичний солодкий дух, що промикувавсь в повітря поміж гіллям. Співаки затягли чудової арії в тріо. І чудові були їх співи не для публіки, а для себе! Скільки щирого почування, скільки поезії виливалось з їх молодих душ під синім небом! То були щирі й поетичні співи поетичних на вдачу душ, співи щирого артизма й штучннцтва, а не співового байдужного ремества, як здебільшого буває в театрах на сцені, де часто співці одбувають повинність, як селяни одбували колись панщанну повинність.

І Софія Леонівна, і Ольга Павлівна, під подихом поетичного вечора та співів, несамохіть слухали, не розмовляли, неначе зчамріли од співу. Вони обидві позадумувались. Ольга Павлівна зітхнула. На той час вона забулась і за гармидер в покоях, і за клопіт в пекарні. Тихі мелодії, чарівні, як синє небо та рожевий захід, навели на клопотливу та запопадну господиню тиху задуму й поезію. В неї серце несамохіть взрушилось. Щось миле, приємне заворушилось в її серці, в її уяві. Їй чогось згадались і ніби привиджувались давніші часи, молоді літа. Ніби промайнули перед нею чиїсь тіні, приємні, милі, як ті співи, і ніби визирнули з давнини. Задзвеніли чиїсь давні молоді голоси, неначе вони одгукувались з давньої давнини її молодих літ, ніби десь з неба. Вона ніби почула з далекого гаю, як там щебетали пташки, співав соловейко, кувала зозуля, – але десь далеко-далеко … І з тієї далекої далечі неначе на неї повіяло духом зеленої весни … Вона згорнула руки й задумалась, згадуючи свою молодість, згадуючи поезію свого дівування. (8:36–7)

[The sun was setting, as if falling into a green abyss, on the distant reeds and groves. The majesty of the pink sunset against a blue sky, of the fading green meadows against the blue forest, of the hills, once again called out the song in the singers. Outdoors it was as quiet as indoors. The hustle and bustle of the village was fading and dying out. The green earth and the blue sky seemed to be sleeping in the soft twilight. Night was slowly falling. The poetry of eventide spread its wing over the orchard, over the river, and over the green marsh. The balsam herb and mint, trampled by many shoes, gave off their fragrance. Resedas seemed to spray its thin, sweet, aromatic mist into the air among the branches. The singers took up a few beautiful arias as a trio. They sang beautifully, not for an audience, but for themselves. So much sincere feeling, so much poetry poured forth from their young souls beneath the blue sky! This was the sincere, poetical singing of artistically inclined souls, songs of true feeling and poetical art, not the carelessness of professional craft, as is the usual case on stage in the theaters, where singers are often merely fulfilling their obligations, like peasants once fulfilled their feudal obligations to their masters.

In the atmosphere of the poetical evening and the singing, Sofiia Leonivna and Ol'ha Pavlivna were both silent, listening motionlessly as if stupefied. They were both lost in thought. Ol'ha Pavlivna sighed. For a moment, she forgot all about the disorder in the house and the obligations in the kitchen. The quiet, magical melodies, like the blue sky and the pink sunset, put the thoughtful and anxious mistress of the home into a quiet reverie of poetry. Her heart stirred involuntarily. Something pleasant and enjoyable aroused her feelings and her imagination. She remembered and seemed to visualize things from the past, from her youth. Someone's shadows from the past seemed to flit before her eyes, shadows pleasing and joyful, like the singing. Young voices from the past rang out, calling from the distant past of her youth, as if from somewhere in heaven. She seemed to hear, as if from a distant meadow, the chirping of birds, the song of the nightingale, the call of the cuckoo, but all far, far away … And from that distant past, it was as if she felt a breath of green spring in her spirit … She folded her hands, contemplating, remembering her youth, recalling the poetry of her maidenhood.]

Sofiia is also affected by the romantic mood of the evening, but her thoughts go further than her sister-in-law's:

Майнули чиїсь густі чорні брови. Вона згадала красуня студента, Наркиса Назарова, його чорні очі, захищені довгими кучерявими віями, згадала й зітхнула. Він був далеко од неї ...

Вона так само запрошувала й його прибуть до неї в гості на село на дачу. І їй чогось в цей час заманулось, щоб він прибув оце зараз, таки цього вечора … щоб подивиться на ті пишні очі отутечки, під цим зеленим гіллям, під тихим сяєвом вечірнього неба. Вона насамохіть зітхнула. Поезія співів, поезія вечора промкнулась і в матеріальну душу, і в серце цієї Мессаліни під гіллястою грушею.

А співаки доводили до кінця свої співи. Арія наприкінці пішла в піано, а далі в піаніссімо, тихе, делікатне, замираюче. Співи неначе впадали в дрімоту і ніби засипали од солодкої втоми солодким сном, і вже лунали снами мрій та чарів, золотих, легеньких, як марево, гарячих літніх днів. (8:37)

[Someone's thick black brow flitted before her eyes. She recalled the handsome student, Narkys Nazarov, his black eyes protected by curly lashes. She remembered and sighed. He was far from her now.

She had invited him to visit her at the cottage in the village, as well. And now she felt that she wanted him to come right away, this very evening, so that she could look at those wonderful eyes here, beneath these green boughs, under the quiet light of the moonlit sky. She sighed involuntarily. The poetry of the singing, the poetry of the evening, had penetrated the materialist soul and the heart of this Messalina under the boughs of the pear tree.

The singers were bringing their song to its end. The aria drifted into piano, then pianissimo, quiet, delicate, fading. The singing became like a dream and everyone seemed to be overcome with sweet languor and sweet sleep. They were in the land of magical dreams – golden, soft illusions born of hot summer days.]

Nechui's understanding of the power of love on a woman's behaviour combines a number of factors, including the sociology of the urban-rural divide, the modern romanticization of the countryside, the stimulating power of aesthetic perception, the psychology of ennui, as well as a healthy portion of traditional comic caricature. There is also a clear sense of moral condemnation. Sofiia and the other women he describes are not innocent victims of circumstances. They are responsible women who consciously ignore social conventions and their own vows to pursue their own amorous pleasure. But what is certainly missing in Nechui's depiction of these women is any sense of righteous indignation. There is no moralizing of either a religious or a secular flavour. More than anything else, Nechui seems to empathize with their dilemma: Why can't a woman enjoy the happiness she seeks?

In a story that Nechui wrote in 1912 entitled "Kokhannia z prytychynamy" (A romance with impediments) he returns to the general theme of the "Gastroli" stories. Nastia Leheza, a young teacher, comes from Kyiv to a village to take charge of the local school. Many of the motifs from the earlier works are repeated here, including the role of the village priest and his wife, the dilapidated schoolhouse, the schoolhouse caretaker, and music. After a long and hard winter, the schoolteacher, Nastia, struck by the beauty of spring in the village, starts flirting with a married violinist. When the violinist's wife has had enough, she attacks her husband with a rolling pin as he comes home. The village folk laugh at the affair, the violinist can't play for a while because of his injuries, and Nastia returns to the city, where she eventually dies. The story does not add anything substantially new to the pattern already observed, but this time the woman is not married and the musician's wife puts a quick end to the affair, showing another side of a woman's love. Nastia is not nearly as sympathetic a character as Sofiia, but her love, like Sofiia's, is given a sensitive hearing: "Молоде серце забажало кохання, любові раптово, несподівано" (9:149) [Suddenly, unexpectedly, the young heart wanted love and romance]. Even in a simple comic genre, Nechui treats women's amorous feelings with compassion and without belligerence.

The closest Nechui comes to an outright condemnation of licentious women is in the story "Vol'ne kokhannia" (Free love). As the title suggests, the topic is viewed in the context of contemporary social debates on liberal ideological positions, particularly regarding feminist and sexual issues. In this story, Melania Ulasevych, a wealthy grass widow (her husband isn't dead – he simply left), lives her life as she pleases. This character is another of Nechui's attempts to depict a decadent lifestyle. Melania and her friend, the divorcee Iryna Zabolotna, enjoy the company of a widower and a few young unmarried men. The atmosphere and the conversation are piquant. The company discuss the old widower's youthful abduction of a woman from her tyrannical father, they discuss the events of the 1905 revolution, they discuss the question of free love. All this takes place in an urban aristocratic setting full of current cultural allusions. As the revolutionary disarray settles, they all move back out to the village, where they find the local gentry not up to their refined standards in politics, culture, or decadent lifestyle. Eventually, Iryna, bored with the provinces, engages the son of the widower in an affair, and they run off together to Petersburg while his father, the widower, is busy in political meetings of the local duma assembly. But the affair ends badly, Iryna runs off with yet another man and the son comes home to beg daddy's forgiveness.

Where in the "Gastroli" stories Nechui deliberately vacillated between depictions of Solomiia's sincerity and her pretensions, in "Vol'ne kokhannia" there is no longer any doubt. Melania and Iryna are spoiled aristocrats. They are not artistic souls who are overwhelmed by the natural beauty of the countryside. But this story is neither a satire nor a morality play. It is an exercise in realist contrasts between revolutionary politics and social mores, between new aesthetic principles (modernism) and decadent lifestyles. Nechui, as we have seen in the previous chapter, was no friend of modernism in literature. But this story, unlike "Bez puttia," is not an attack against modernism *per se*, but against insincerity, false illusions, and frivolity. Nechui sees a woman's feelings as a powerful force that arises from real circumstances and one that has real consequences, both positive and negative. Feelings are not a matter for trivial psychologizing, as practised by the spoiled children in his satiric version of modernist love, "Bez puttia." Women's feelings, whether honourable or dishonorable, are expressions of a psychic condition that women experience with their full being. Nechui does not condemn sincere feelings. Sincere and authentic feelings are the cornerstone of his joyful world view.

6 Nechui's Historical Writing

Within the complete oeuvre of Nechui's writing there are four general categories of works. The first and certainly the most important is his belletristic work, the subject of the preceding four chapters. Another category consists of his personal papers – his letters, autobiographical writings, notebooks, sketches, and other writings not necessarily intended for publication. These were of concern to us in chapter 1 to illuminate his biography, but otherwise they are not examined in this study. The third category is his published work on language and on a range of cultural subjects. Nechui's cultural essays were examined where appropriate in previous chapters. His linguistic efforts, which include a grammar of Ukrainian and various essays expressing his views on orthographic matters, are of only incidental interest to scholars and students of Ukrainian literature and have been explored elsewhere.[1] That leaves an important fourth category: historical writing.

Nechui's historical writing is largely unknown, and some of his published historical works are available only in archival collections in Ukraine. Unless a major effort is mounted to bring together all of his writings in a scholarly edition, these historical works, never republished, are likely to remain in obscurity. But Nechui was not a historian, and his history writing attracts attention only insofar as it is the work of Ivan Nechui-Levyts'kyi, not for its historical arguments or factual details.

Over the course of his long career as a writer, Nechui produced a variety of works on historical subjects. They can be classified by subject, by genre, and by length. The most important works are the belletristic ones. He wrote two historical novels, one about Iarema (Ieremiia) Vyshnevets'kyi (Jeremi Wiśniowiecki) and the other about Hetman Ivan

Vyhovs'kyi. He wrote two plays on historical subjects as well: *Marusia Bohuslavka*, about the legendary (and therefore not quite historical)[2] favourite of the Ottoman sultan who freed captive Ukrainian cossacks, and *V dymu ta polum'ï* (In smoke and flame), about Hetman Vyhovs'kyi. In addition to these works, Nechui also wrote a short story entitled "Zaporozhtsi" (Zaporozhian cossacks), which could be considered historical, although – unlike the works on Vyshnevets'kyi and Vyhovs'kyi – it doesn't actually relate historical events. With the exception of the novel on Hetman Vyhovs'kyi, these belletristic works were included in the ten-volume edition of Nechui's works and are thus generally available. The historical novel about Ivan Vyhovs'kyi was not republished in Soviet times and was mentioned by only two or three Nechui scholars. It finally reappeared in print after Ukraine's independence in a volume together with the novel about Vyshnevets'kyi.

A different situation exists in regard to Nechui's attempts at historical essays. According to the best existing bibliography of his works, he wrote and published a dozen of these treatises between 1875 and 1915. They were a part of the Kyiv Hromada's cultural outreach program.[3] The treatises range in size from a small brochure of twenty pages to short monographs of 150 pages. There are essentially two topics. The first is cossack history, specifically the events before, during, and after the Khmel'nyts'kyi revolt in the mid-seventeenth century. This topic receives the bulk of Nechui's attention. The second topic is Kyivan Rus', that is, early Ukrainian history in general. This category includes an essay on Ukrainian folk beliefs entitled *Svitohliad ukrains'koho narodu: Eskiz ukrains'koi mifolohii* (The world view of the Ukrainian people: an outline of Ukrainian mythology), first published in 1876 in Lviv. Of the dozen or so works described in bibliographies, I have seen and examined only about half of the titles.

In recent years Nechui's historical writing has attracted the attention of a number of scholars who have written dissertations and shorter essays on the subject. Olena Poda,[4] Alla Kalynchuk,[5] Iulia Volynets',[6] and others have examined in considerable detail the sources, substance, and style of Nechui's historical writing, and they have shown that in the works on cossack history Nechui is largely repeating the ideas and facts presented by Mykola Kostomarov. Nechui did not, of course, do any original research. He did not try to establish any striking new interpretations of Ukrainian history. His work is derivative and compilatory. His historical essays are largely attempts to retell significant moments in Ukrainian history in a popular manner and in a somewhat informal style. As noted in chapter 1, these historical essays were part of the program of the Kyiv Hromada to popularize Ukrainian history among a wider reading audience of Ukrainians. Nechui shapes his writing to such a purpose. He sticks closely to the facts, which he gathers from Kostomarov or a limited but mostly reliable body of histories and well-known primary sources, such as the cossack chronicles. Although he makes no effort to document his facts or to cite his sources, he often makes it clear in his texts that the facts are taken from a particular source.

His approach to telling history is quite simple. He narrates historical developments as stories, focusing on events that illuminate history as a process that reflects the will of specific individuals. These individuals become the focus of the narrative, and the narrative itself is enlivened by the personalities of these characters and the colourful language that Nechui uses both in the narrative and in interpolated conversations. In short, Nechui uses a familiar and traditional mode of retelling popular history, much like modern television dramas on historical subjects. In his explicitly fictional works, Nechui, like most writers of historical fiction, tries even further to flesh out historical events, to give them a human face, to examine the people involved in the historical events, and to give them a visual, psychological, personal, and material reality that may not be directly recorded as historical fact. This combination of conjecture and invention distinguishes Nechui's historical fiction from his historical non-fiction. Otherwise, the two genres share very much in common.

For a Ukrainian writer or intellectual in the late nineteenth century, history was a common concern. A number of prominent historians, most notably Volodymyr Antonovych and his students, including Hrushevs'kyi and Bahalii, were raising the standards of historical research and writing and focusing public attention on the Ukrainian past. But the importance of the past was not lost on earlier generations, either. The entire Ukrainian revival of the nineteenth century, from Kotliarevs'kyi's Trojan cossacks onward, had a very strong connection with Ukrainian history. Many of the most prominent figures in this revival movement were serious historians, such as Kostomarov and Kulish. Many writers, among them Shevchenko and Gogol, had portrayed historical figures and events in their works. Nechui's outlook on Ukrainian cultural and national identity is shaped to a considerable degree by this earlier period. He shows direct influences from Shevchenko, and he was, to some extent, a protégé of Panteleimon Kulish, so the interest in history is easily understood as a shared understanding of the importance of historical memory for Ukrainian identity. In small and subtle ways, however, Nechui and the members of the Hromada who encouraged and supported his historical writing were moving beyond the understanding of history that was common among the romantics of the previous generation.

The first difference lies in the uses of history. In keeping with the more scrupulous approach of the new generation of academic historians, Nechui treats history as an intellectual subject. In his essays and his fiction, history is a lesson to be presented to an audience of readers. Nechui, who was a teacher for twenty years, packages history as a schoolroom subject. It consists mostly of facts with explanations for the motives of various individuals. The narrative in the non-fiction essays is enlivened with occasional epithets characterizing the actions of the various individuals, but these additions are mostly just colourful expressions rather than interpretations of historical facts. The area where Nechui allows himself some originality in these historical essays is in the sequencing of the narrative. As in his writing in general, so too in the historical essays Nechui tells stories in linear segments that are interrupted by flashbacks, parallel stories, and repetitions from a different angle. Thus the plot lines of his historical essays have some of the qualities of a slowly winding tale rather than a direct, purposeful exposition.

This pedagogical quality underscores another important quality of history writing in the latter years of the nineteenth century, namely, its overtly nationalizing purpose. In the works of earlier writers – Shevchenko or other romantic writers – history was a shared past that the artist invoked for any number of reasons and ideological messages, but the presumed view of the audience placed them within the same circle as the author. That is not the case in later historical works. Nechui's audience is learning: they are not hearing a shared familiar story, they are being told the facts. The narrative is partisan: it is clearly intended to reinforce group identity, as were the historical writings of the earlier generation, but it also sets out to establish this identity and to identify the historical knowledge that accompanies it. These essays and stories have far more detail and far more authenticity as historical writing than did the works of the earlier romantics. Inasmuch as national identity is related to a knowledge of history, the reader is in an inferior position to the narrator of the text. These texts do not simply reinforce a shared identity: they push the reader into one. One of their goals is to indoctrinate the reader into that sense of shared historical identity that earlier texts had been content to assume.

Of course, this is not unexpected when the situation is viewed from a wider perspective, with an awareness of what is going on elsewhere in Europe in the latter decades of the nineteenth century. Ukrainians are not the only national minority whose cultural world is moving into an increasingly unambiguous proclamation of national values, and for all these groups, history, particularly when seen in a positivist, determinist spirit, is a crucial weapon in the formation of an assertive and righteous national spirit. Even the Russians are doing something similar. But the crucial comparisons, as far as Ukraine is concerned, are in Poland. There, not only is history an important factor in maintaining popular patriotism, but this history is often closely associated with Ukrainian history. In particular, in the 1880s Henryk Sienkiewicz is writing a trilogy of very popular works on the dark days of Poland in the mid-seventeenth century. The first of these, entitled *Ogniem i mieczem* (With fire and sword), was a presentation of the Khmel'nyts'kyi revolt from a Polish point of view.

Nechui was certainly influenced by Sienkiewicz, particularly in his later works (one of Nechui's nephews wrote him a letter about how "we have to fight back against Sienkiewicz"[7]), but Nechui's first historical essays date back to 1875 and his larger historical works about the Khmel'nyts'kyi revolt are from 1879, well before Sienkiewicz's novel of 1883. So Nechui and the Polish novelist are actually parallel examples of the importance and popularity of historical writing. They also both exemplify the nationalizing function of historical writing. But whereas Sienkiewicz's trilogy can realistically be called an unbridled glorification of its heroic figures (against a background of very difficult times for Poland as a whole), Nechui's view of Ukrainian history is far more problematical. And that is not just because Nechui has a less glorious Ukrainian history to work with. Sienkiewicz is also trying to make the best of a bad situation in Polish history. But Nechui, unlike his Polish counterpart, deliberately focuses on topics that do not give him positive characters. In depicting a period of general decline for Poland, Sienkiewicz is happy to invent heroic characters with chivalric, knightly qualities to serve as protagonists and to substitute or augment the positive values of the actual historical figures he depicts. In Nechui's case the situation is somewhat different. Because he focuses on the primary actors, on the major historical personages in his writing, he does not take advantage of the possibility to substitute a wholly positive secondary fictional character for the actual but flawed historical heroes. This ambivalence is related, in part, to his non-purposeful narrative style, which is still present, though somewhat less forcefully, in his historical writing.

But the disposition of positive heroes in Nechui's historical works is not merely a question of his habits in constructing narratives and his desire to stick to the historical facts. Nechui chooses to portray figures of ambiguous qualities. Among his essays is one on the events surrounding Khmel'nyts'kyi's military victories in the siege of Zbarazh and the battle of Zboriv,[8] which led to the treaty of Zboriv, one of Khmel'nyts'kyi's major victories and presented as such by Nechui. But another essay is on the conflict between the competing Left-Bank and Right-Bank hetmans, Briukhovets'kyi and Teteria.[9] It narrates the historic events in both halves of Ukraine following the Black Council of 1663 until the death of Briukhovets'kyi in 1668. The traditional view of this period in Ukrainian history is of a dark period of woe, and Nechui conforms to this view. His narrative voice is very dry, generally avoiding his characteristic light-hearted turns of phrase. Russians and Poles are presented as equal enemies, but the central story that Nechui tells is not of battles between Ukrainians and Russians or Poles but of internecine strife and of overriding ambition on the part of the hetmans and their unwillingness to serve the general interests of the population of Ukraine. Nechui does not editorialize anywhere in this essay. The ironies of intersecting betrayals of Ukrainian interests by the two hetmans who align with each other's enemies are underscored by the sequence in which Nechui tells the events, but the narrator's voice is silent insofar as any conclusions or lessons to be drawn. Furthermore, Nechui does not even side with the general population against its leaders. Popular sentiment is seen to be a volatile factor, moving one way or another depending on events and perceptions. The nationalizing program in this essay is certainly not a matter of patriotic pride in the accomplishments of the past, or even a dissociation from the enemies of the past, since there are no positive characters and the protagonists are equally culpable; but the degree of their culpability is too small, their circumstances too constrained, to transform them into negative rallying figures. Nechui's nationalizing program here is entirely contained in the two features that are central to his historical perspective: first, the desire or need to tell the story at all, that is, the need to know Ukrainian history; and second, the unabashedly – and somewhat anachronistically – all-Ukrainian perspective that is maintained throughout. He presents a view of authentic Ukrainian interests as embodied in unity and a clear identity that distinguishes both Russians and Poles as enemies, something much more appropriate to the 1890s than to the 1660s.

The peculiarity of Nechui's choices for historical subjects is even more evident in his choice of subjects for his two novels. His first historical novel was composed in 1895, well after the publication of Sienkiewicz's trilogy, and focuses on Hetman Ivan Vyhovs'kyi. This was not a new topic for Nechui. He had already written a play, entitled *V dymu ta polum'ï*, in 1875 about Vyhovs'kyi, although it was not published until 1910, and in 1879 he had written an essay about the hetman. A modern audience might assume that Nechui writes about Vyhovs'kyi for the same reason that Dmytro Dontsov or Bohdan Lepkyi write about him, as the hetman who tried to undo Khmel'nyts'kyi's treaty with the Russian tsar. But Nechui, in keeping with the bulk of Ukrainian historiography before the twentieth century, sees Vyhovs'kyi as a very problematical figure, not very far removed from being considered a traitor. It is only later generations of Ukrainian historians from the nationalist camp that will elevate Vyhovs'kyi to the status of a hero. The Vyhovs'kyi Nechui depicts in his essay about him is not very different from the self-serving hetmans Briukhovets'kyi and Teteria.[10]

In the novel *Hetman Ivan Vyhovs'kyi*, written in 1895 and published in 1899, Nechui goes one step further by enhancing his portrait with a glimpse of Vyhovs'kyi's private life. Nechui carefully ascribes and elaborates two elements of the protagonist's personality – his pretentious ambition and his calculating intelligence. In order to demonstrate these qualities, Nechui presents two parallel aspects of the hetman's activities. On the one hand, the reader sees Vyhovs'kyi as a wise, calculating, but also ruthless politician and leader. This part of the novel is very largely based on historical sources, particularly Kostomarov and the cossack chronicles. On the other hand, we see the hetman surrounded by his family and retinue, where he and particularly his wife display their sense of superiority to the common man. Here Nechui, allowing himself some poetic licence, invents the person and family of Demko Liutai, a retired old cossack whose son marries a cousin of Vyhovs'kyi's wife. The Liutais are the opposites of Vyhovs'kyi in their cultural and social orientation. They are simple folk with old-fashioned ways and habits. Their weather-worn but cosy old house, with its small windows and tilted porch, has sunk directly into the earth, like its inhabitants, who are also rooted in the local customs and culture. Like most of the cossacks, the Liutais are fiercely Orthodox and anti-Polish. When Vyhovs'kyi signs the treaty of Hadiach, returning Ukrainian cossack lands to Polish sovereignty, the Liutais are active organizers of the rebellion against him.

This view of Vyhovs'kyi was already a partial vindication of the hetman, relative to the traditional view of him in Ukraine, but at the time of its writing, Nechui's novel could already provoke opposition based on an even more favourable view. In a letter to Mykhailo Hrushevs'kyi, Nechui recounts that Orest Levyts'kyi (no relation) refused to publish the manuscript in the journal *Kievskaia starina*. Orest Levyts'kyi, says Nechui,

> Написав до мене, що я в повісті дуже вже принизив Виговського … Тим часом, на мій погляд, Орест Іванович вже без міри піднімає його вгору до небес, на що він не заслуговує, і пише до мене, що усі ті, котрі ставали йому в опозицію, себто мої повістярські герої, "люде неможливі." А в мене в повісті поставлені в опозицію навіть не Мартин Пушкар з Чорнотою, а місцеві чигиринські козаки та народ, котрі носом почутили, що Виговський хотів завести на Україні шляхетський, аристократичний уклад старої Польщі з його темними перспективами, що й сталось на Західній Україні після Андрусівської умови, коли […], за Дніпром, в Гетьманщині, запанував демократичний уклад […] схожий на сучасний уклад в Норвегії, Швейцарії, а потроху навіть в Америці. (10:354, letter of 2 January 1899)

> [wrote to me and said I demean Vyhovs'kyi excessively … Meanwhile, in my view, it's Orest Ivanovych who exalts him beyond measure to the heavens, to a degree that Vyhovs'kyi does not deserve. He further writes that all those who rose in opposition to him, that is, the heroes of my novel, are "implausible people." But in my novel it isn't even Martyn Pushkar and the rabble whom I portray as the hetman's antagonists, but the local cossacks and common people of Chyhyryn, whose noses could smell out the fact that Vyhovs'kyi wanted to introduce in Ukraine the *shliakhta*, the aristocratic social order of old Poland, which is indeed what happened in Right-Bank Ukraine after the treaty of Andrusovo, while […] in the Hetman state a democratic order came into being […] that was similar to the current social order in Norway, Switzerland, and even somewhat in America.]

This justification of his position in the novel may not be a very convincing argument for a historian today, but the fact is that in his own time Nechui's view of the hetman was more or less reasonable and a plausible balance of national and social considerations. In choosing an ambiguous figure for the hero of his novel, Nechui signals that his understanding of the nationalizing function of historical fiction is not merely patriotic chest-thumping. This issue becomes even more acute in his second historical novel, which was written just two years after the first (in 1897) but remained unpublished until 1932.

The subject of this second novel, *Kniaz' Ieremiia Vyshnevets'kyi*, is far more surprising than the first. By the usual standards of patriotic history, Vyshnevets'kyi (1612–51) is not at all a suitable topic for a Ukrainian writer. Although he was the grandson of Dmytro Baida Vyshnevets'kyi (1516?–63), the legendary founder of the Zaporozhzhian Sich, he was also the father of the Polish king, Michał Korybut Wiśniowiecki (1640–73, ruled 1669–73). But his own accomplishment lies in his considerable military prowess, demonstrated most critically on behalf of the Polish crown during the Khmel'nyts'kyi uprising. He was a very rich magnate with immense and thriving landholdings throughout Ukraine, including the Left Bank. He obtained an education in Western Europe and converted to Catholicism and was a very powerful figure in Polish political life. But in the traditional schemes of Ukrainian history passed down through the cossack chronicles and in folklore, Iarema Vyshnevets'kyi is presented as nothing short of a monster. Not only was he a traitor to Ukraine and to Orthodoxy (despite the fact that his mother was Metropolitan Petro Mohyla's sister), but he was a merciless scourge of rebellious Ukrainian cossacks and peasants, notorious for ordering barbaric public tortures of cossack and peasant leaders who dared to rise up against him. Of course, barbaric killings were common on all sides during these wars, but in the popular imagination, Vyshnevets'kyi, perhaps because he was a rich, well-educated aristocrat, was held more culpable for these acts than were others. In any case, Nechui starts out with a protagonist Ukrainians universally consider odious.[11] Perhaps Nechui's interest in this character was also stimulated by Sienkiewicz's *Ogniem i mieczem*, in which Jeremi Wiśniowiecki is a major figure.

As in the case of Vyhovs'kyi, so too with Vyshnevets'kyi, Nechui presents his hero mostly in a traditional valuation, with only modest attempts to show different aspects of his character. The original working title of this novel was "Pereverten'" (The traitor), so there was clearly never any intention of presenting Ieremiia as a positive figure. But if the patriotic message of this novel relied on the bloodthirsty, inhuman Ukrainophobic tyrant galvanizing the faithful Ukrainian readers into patriotism by the pure, unadulterated evil of his ways, this novel would give nationalists no satisfaction. Of course, Nechui depicts his dark hero as a monster – even Sienkiewicz depicts Wiśniowiecki as a heartlessly cruel scourge of rebel sentiments. Ieremiia detests the peasant and cossack rabble that opposes him, and his cruel violence is underscored at every turn of the plot. But Nechui also allows his hero to be an effective military commander and a man whose wealth and high station have not turned him into a pampered nobleman. Nechui takes pains in the novel to show Vyshnevets'kyi associating with ordinary soldiers, sharing with them the hardships of military camp life, and recoiling from the frippery and ostentation of the threesome of Polish military commanders known as "peryna, latyna, i dytyna" (duvet, Latinist, and the child: i.e., Prince Wladyslaw-Dominik Zaslawski, Mikolaj Ostroróg, and Aleksander Koniecpolski). Ieremiia is a prince, but he is something of a regular guy, an ordinary man. That quality is also emphasized in his relations with women.

The historical Vyshnevets'kyi was married to Gryzelda Zamoyska, daughter of a prominent Polish nobleman. Nechui presents her as a materialist spoiled brat, an inveterate Polonizer, and a trophy wife whom Vyshnevets'kyi likes to have on display, but with whom he shares little affection. In keeping with the common male stereotype, Nechui invents a "hot, red-blooded woman" who can bring out the aggressive and passionate "real man" in his protagonist. Of course, this contrast between a dutiful and a passionate woman is familiar in Nechui's other works.

Todozia Svitailivna, the "red-blooded other woman" in Vyshnevets'kyi's life, offers a stark contrast to the cold, stately Gryzelda. Todozia is a passionate, physical woman. Nechui's description of her emphasizes her physical features rather than her clothing, as was the case with Gryzelda. Furthermore, Nechui makes the connection between violence and sexual passion. Todozia is the widow of a registered cossack. When Ieremiia learns this, he asks if he had killed her former husband. No, Todozia tells him, her husband was killed in a war with the Tatars, but the very fact that Ieremiia poses the question suggests that Nechui is drawing a deliberate connection between his protagonist's attraction to this woman and his violent, cruel character. The first love scene between them is described in terms that suggest something close to rape. But for all that Nechui allows Todozia some sympathy, she is not a victim here, but a willing participant. She is clearly smitten by Vyshnevets'kyi's very masculinity, his strength, his power. And what's more, as in the case of other licentious women, so here too Nechui does not scold her or depict her as a traitor.

There is something of tragedy in her love for the ruthless enemy of her people. As Nechui explains to Ivan Belei in a letter of 13 February 1902, the model for his depiction of Vyshnevets'kyi's amorous conquests is borrowed from the biography of Napoleon Bonaparte. For Vyshnevets'kyi as for Bonaparte, ruthless power is associated with instinctual gratification of passion; men are sexual beasts and women are attracted to this wild passion, which they, too, share.

In contrast to this instinctual carnality, Nechui depicts scenes in which Vyshnevets'kyi is repulsed by what is explicitly described as effeminacy in men. In this novel Nechui divides the world between manly men, whose military and sexual prowess are tied to instinctive and violent urges, and unmanly men, who fail at war and at sex because their attention is turned to aristocratic splendour and amusements, or religion, or learning. Such is the threesome of Polish commanders – peryna, dytyna, and latyna – to whose foolish excesses Nechui devotes an entire chapter in the novel. The manly Vyshnevets'kyi is, of course, repulsed by their behaviour, particularly after the undiplomatic Liash tells him that the aristocrats were confused by the lack of adornments at his military camp and thought they might have mistakenly come upon a lower-class camp of the Ukrainian cossacks. Vyshnevets'kyi may hate the rebellious cossacks, but in both Nechui's and Vyshnevets'kyi's system of values they are good, manly warriors, and the absence of ostentation is a positive indicator. The opposite quality is associated on a number of occasions with Polish characters in the novel. In the novel's first chapter, the young Vyshnevets'kyi is being welcomed into the Jesuit college in Lviv by its rector:

> І патер Вінцентій обняв молодого Єремію і щільно й гаряче й з притиском цмокнув його в обидві щоки і в чоло.
>
> Єремії не сподобалися ті поцілунки. Він не любив пестощів ще гірше, ніж усякого напутіння та докорів. Як патер розняв свої гладкі та гарячі руки, Єремія одвернув голову набік, неначе боявся, щоб ті противні руки не лапнули його й не обхопили його плечей вдруге. (7:13)

[Father Vincentii embraced the young Ieremiia and kissed him warmly and energetically on both cheeks and on the forehead.

Ieremiia did not like these kisses. He detested coddling even more than he did instruction and complaining. When the priest opened his smooth, warm arms, Ieremiia turned his head aside, as if afraid that those despicable arms might cling to him and embrace his shoulders again.]

An even more explicit allusion occurs in chapter 12, when Vyshnevets'kyi in his military camp greets a messenger from Warsaw, a nobleman named Dzen'kovs'kyi. Even before Dzen'kovs'kyi tells Ieremiia the bad news that the Polish Diet has not appointed him military commander, Vyshnevets'kyi is already forming a negative judgment of the messenger:

> [Єремія став непорушно і втирив очі в Дзеньковського. Дзеньковський був ще молодий пан, випещений, вигодований, з білими повними щоками, з розкішними русявими вусами. Дівочі рум'янці грали на повних щоках, уста чевоніли під вусами, як калина. Єремія слухав шляхтича й несамохіть приглядався до повновидого круглого лиця шляхтича. Єремії чогось став противний той випещений свіжий панянський вид шляхтича, стали противні стримкі пухлі русяві вуса, став гидкий самий тоненький голос, що подавав йому неприємні звістки з Варшави. (7:212)

> [Ieremiia stood motionless and buried his eyes in Dzen'kovs'kyi. Dzen'kovs'kyi was still a young lord, spoiled and fattened, with white full cheeks and a thick ruddy moustache. Girlish rosy cheeks lit up his face, his red lips stood out beneath his moustache like holly. Ieremiia listened to the aristocrat and unconsciously stared at his full, round face. For some reason this pampered fresh look, like that of an aristocratic young girl, was unpleasant to Ieremiia. He found the groomed, rich, ruddy moustache unpleasant too, as he also found unpleasant the thin voice itself, which was bringing him the bad news from Warsaw.]

As this and the previous passage show, Nechui associates Poles, nobility, and hedonistic excess with androgyny and, conversely, Ukrainians, violence, and the underclass with traditional and exploitative sexuality. This is a set of characteristics that, as I have argued in the preceeding chapter, can be tracked throughout Nechui's works, not just in his historical writing. Another aspect of this inclination, also readily apparent in his historical writing, is the attention he gives to women as the carriers of both the narrative focus in his writings and the symbolic argument as well. In *Kniaz' Ieremiia Vyshnevets'kyi* there is far more attention in the narrative to the clothes that women (and effeminate men) wear than there is to the military encounters on which Vyshnevets'kyi's actual historical reputation rests. In this quality, Nechui even outdoes Sienkiewicz, who also gives very prominent attention to women and love in his novels. The symbolic conflict in Nechui's novel about

Vyshnevets'kyi is embodied in the conflict that Ieremiia experiences in his love life. He is married to Gryzelda, but his passion is awakened by Todozia. Ieremiia is a traitor, of course, and an inhuman monster. The underlying problem, however, is one that Nechui sees, in his historical works as elsewhere in his writing, as a common problem in Ukrainian culture: loyalty to a Ukrainian cultural and national ideal is continually challenged by personal interests in the social, professional, and material worlds. Vyshnevets'kyi is a monster whose motives are very familiar. He is clearly an anti-hero, but he – like Vyhovs'kyi – is also a characteristic embodiment of the national dilemma as it is faced by the Ukrainian upper classes.

When Nechui turns to historical writing, his nationalizing program is not a matter of putting the best face on heroic periods of Ukrainian history. As I have said, he is not a deep thinker on historical questions and he does not look for strikingly original new interpretations of historical events. He focuses on individuals who are challenged by the inherent problems of national identity as they arise throughout various periods of Ukrainian history. Nechui examines these issues not from a nationalist or a cosmopolitan perspective, but rather from a personal perspective that focuses on the personality traits that are central throughout his literary oeuvre. For him, the uses of history are personal and creative. The nationalizing mission is central, but its parameters are those of Nechui's own vision, not that of an ideological dogma defined by any of the numerous political spin doctors in his world or in the generation immediately succeeding his, who took Nechui's views on the inherent problems in Ukrainian national identity and transformed them into rigid judgments. In Nechui's world and in his works, patriotism was an absolute virtue, but its absence was, if not excusable and if not reasonable, at least understandable and subject to creative depiction.

Conclusion

Ivan Nechui-Levyts'kyi is the central figure in Ukrainian literature in the Russian Empire from the time of of Taras Shevchenko's death to the end of the nineteenth century. This is a smaller claim than it may seem. His obvious competitors are disqualified on technicalities: Ivan Franko lived in a different empire; Mykhailo Drahomanov was not actually a literary figure; Panteleimon Kulish really belongs in an earlier period, even though a strong case can be made for his importance after Shevchenko's death. The only serious contender is Panas Myrnyi, and he's just not as important as Nechui. But it is not the negative argument, it's not the default victory that makes Nechui worthy of our attention. Nechui represents and dominates the post-Shevchenko era in Ukrainian literature because he moves Ukrainian literature in a new direction, because he overcomes a new set of challenges and obstacles, because he writes in a unique and deliberate style, because he depicts a world that no other writer dared to describe, because he dared to write literature in a language that had been banned by an empire bent on exterminating what he held sacred, and because he revised the argument about Ukrainian identity from a plaintive romantic cry of the doomed to a powerful and self-confident (if often sarcastic) assertion of the inherent humanity and dignity of his nation.

After Shevchenko's death Ukrainian literature faced an entirely new landscape, shaped on one hand by Shevchenko's enormous accomplishments and on the other by the new repressive measures (the Valuev circular and the Ems Ukaz) implemented by the state. As the readership for Ukrainian writing grew in size and in its downward social reach, the importance (and quality) of poetry diminished, while prose, particularly the novel, was developing into the primary genre of literary consumption. But since the government was interfering in this process, only certain individuals could, or would, continue writing Ukrainian prose. In this regard Nechui was in a fortunate position. His teaching assignment in the western reaches of the Russian Empire provided him with the connections and encouragement that allowed him to establish himself as a Ukrainian writer. His profession and solitary life afforded him ample leisure time to pursue this calling with few distractions. His early retirement also helped. His summer trips home while he was still a teacher facilitated contacts with the Kyiv Hromada, a key connection in his battle to advance Ukrainian literature. Nechui's earnest and positive outlook, his humour and joyful disposition, gave him the perseverance and personal stamina to continue this struggle against difficult odds and trying circumstances. In other words, Nechui was fortuitously placed and constitutionally disposed to become the leading figure in Ukrainian belles-lettres in this period. To be sure, the field was not densely packed with competitors – there weren't many other potential writers willing and able to make the commitment he made. Had there been, perhaps his role would have been smaller. In any event, it was Nechui's novels that defined the post-Shevchenko period in Ukrainian literature, and it was Nechui's novels that framed the debate for the next generation of writers, who, inevitably, would turn against their old-fashioned predecessors to establish a new paradigm.

This is the point at which this book began. Nechui lived long enough to outlive his own epoch. Even before he died, he was already seen as something of a literary dinosaur, a figure from a previous age, still highly respected as a writer, still popular with many readers, but clearly a representative of the aesthetic tastes of an earlier generation. By that time, modernists had overrun the literary landscape of the trendy educated public, and a new brand of politicized populists had replaced the cultural philanthropists of the past, whose circumspect approach to political involvement had been a hallmark of the previous era. Nechui's reputation among both these groups was not improved by his intemperate rants on linguistic purity and the accusations of orthographic treason and phonetic terrorism against some of the leading public figures of the day. Yet in the normal course of events these anachronistic biases and the recollections of Nechui's irascible antics would have faded over time, allowing a more balanced and nuanced understanding of his creativity to establish itself in literary history. But that did not happen. The peculiar cultural atmosphere of the 1920s in Soviet Ukraine followed by the Stalinist ideological ossification of the Ukrainian literary canon and literary history did not allow a normal re-evaluation of Nechui to take place.

The key figure in this matter was Serhii Iefremov, a man of prodigious energy and resolve whose enormous contribution to the study of Ukrainian literature in the difficult atmosphere of the early Soviet period laid a lasting and vital foundation for all of the students of Ukrainian literature in the twentieth century. But where he was wrong, or biased, or hasty, or unseeing, those errors, biases, and faults acquired outsized importance because of the stagnation that Soviet practices brought to the study of Ukrainian culture. Almost a century after Iefremov's biography of Nechui, this study aims to undo the faults of Iefremov's legacy, to open Nechui to a fresh understanding, and to attract new attention to this interesting and important writer.

A fresh understanding of Nechui begins with a clear assessment of what he writes about. That subject is Ukraine, which Nechui understands as a place, a people, and a culture. Nechui's goal is to describe this national group and to defend it, that is, to identify the various forces that endanger its existence. In simple terms, he is a Ukrainian nationalist. A century after his death, however, such a designation evokes all the wrong associations. In the aftermath of the First World War, Ukrainian nationalism has acquired – particularly among those who are antipathetic to Ukrainian statehood for various reasons – an image of racism and intolerance, particularly anti-Semitism. This has naturally led to a focus on evaluative judgments. Expressions of Ukrainian nationalism are commonly measured against a modern liberal standard of inclusivity and civic nationalism. National feelings are judged to be good or bad, progressive or reactionary, redemptive or reprehensible. But such an approach to Nechui's nationalism is both anachronistic and counterproductive. So too are approaches based on modern theories of nationalism. Applying the ideas of Gellner, Hroch, Anderson, or any other modern theorist is entirely unlikely to illuminate Nechui's writing. His understanding of a Ukrainian nation is both irridentist and inclusive at the same time. The Russians, Poles, Jews, Greeks, and others who inhabit his novels are all Ukrainians, part of the human landscape of Ukraine. But they are also foreigners, since they are not Ukrainians. Since denationalization is one of his major topics, anything and anyone who endangers the national identity of Ukrainians is a villain. So Russians and Poles are often portrayed as enemies. Jews are in a different category. They are economic exploiters rather than forces of denationalization. Like many realist writers, Nechui uses handy national stereotypes to depict his characters, heroes and villains alike. Many of his Ukrainian characters are also products of such national stereotypes, which he often applies for satiric effect. But the transition from these national types to ideas about the role of nationality in state-building is entirely missing in Nechui's work. Beyond a broad and unspecified condemnation of social injustice, there are no explicitly political notions in his works. What's more, for Nechui the greatest evil is found in the hearts of men and women, not in national categories. And denationalization, the greatest threat to his beloved Ukrainian nation, is most commonly presented as an inferiority complex of Ukrainians themselves. It is an image for which he is justifiably famous, although its most successful presentation is in Mykhailo Staryts'kyi's *Za dvoma zaitsiamy* (Chasing two hares), an adaptation of a play Nechui wrote under the title *Na kozhum'iakakh* (In Kozhumiaky [= a Kyiv neighbourhood]).

The ideas presented in this book regarding Nechui's depiction and defence of Ukraine are largely in keeping with the spirit and substance of earlier studies, albeit with a clearer understanding of the national question than was possible during Soviet times. As the focus moves from "what he writes about" to "how he writes" the connection to previous studies of Nechui largely disappears. Nechui's technique as a writer engenders a long series of questions, difficulties, and paradoxes. The first of these is his position in the history of literature, which boils down to a discussion of literary realism. Readers who seek a clear, succinct, and authoritative exposition of the development of Ukrainian realism and Nechui's role in it will be disappointed by the present study, particularly those who want a measure of the distance between Russian and Ukrainian novelists. Ukrainian realist literature is a complex phenomenon that requires its own monograph rather than a few pages in a study of Nechui, and such a work has yet to be written. A comparison with Russian realism will prove very revealing, but mostly in the absence of actual influence. A philosophical analysis along the lines practised by postmodernist or deconstructivist critics will certainly succeed in demonstrating that Ukrainian realists are only sketchily realistic in their depiction of Ukrainian society. Indeed, the entire enterprise of Ukrainian realist literature is open to question. The prohibitions on Ukrainian literature in the Russian Empire and the resulting paucity of works and absence of a critical discourse meant that Ukrainian realist prose developed very unevenly and unsystematically. That is why my own approach to Nechui's writing focuses on his peculiarities rather than on his position in a larger cultural system.

If realism is defined in terms of a focus on social issues, then Nechui more or less fits the bill. If realism is identified with a penchant for descriptiveness and attention to the details of everyday life, then, too, Nechui is comfortably at home. But if realism means unadorned composition and objective narrative techniques, if it means a positivist certainty in reason and logic, if it means bourgeois values, then Nechui (and quite a few other writers from this era) are sooner found outside looking in. The key features of Nechui's writing style are repetition and non-purposeful narration. It is these qualities more than any others that give shape and texture to Nechui's prose. He uses repetition for rhetorical purposes, he uses repetition for emphasis, he uses repetition for symbolic and melodramatic highlighting, he uses repetition for narrative pacing, and he uses repetition because he likes to use repetition, because it offers him a simple and convenient tool to enhance the aesthetic qualities of the text he is shaping. Repetition is also related to his meandering narrative style and his non-purposeful narrative construction. In these qualities he is profoundly different from other Ukrainian realists, such as Panas Myrnyi and Ivan Franko, whose focused arguments – derived from social theories – dominate the construction and often the texture of their writing. These unique features of Nechui's writing – repetition and non-purposefulness – are not universally regarded as successful characteristics of a literary text, but they are an indisputable marker of the aesthetic, rather than ideological, function that for him is the basic principle of literary art.

Another unique and surprising feature of Nechui's writing is its feminine focalization. Nechui consistently looks at the world from a domestic perspective, seldom entering the space where people work. In nineteenth-century Ukraine, the home was mostly a woman's world. But Nechui's "feminine" focus is not dictated by domestic space – it is a deliberate choice. Even the lives of priests and bureaucrats are seen mostly through a woman's eyes. Some of this is tied to the author's satiric inclination: it is easier to lampoon the powerful and arrogant from the presumably subaltern, deferential, and submissive female perspective. But Nechui's female characters are not usually very deferential and submissive. What's more, their perspective is almost invariably tied to personal happiness, which Nechui surprisingly endorses, even when it challenges well-established social conventions and sexual norms. This "feminine" predilection begs for an incisive psychological study of Nechui as a person and as a social entity. Previous efforts in this vein are largely inadequate because the evidence available from Nechui's biography simply doesn't offer enough detail to draw serious conclusions. Clearly, there is more work to be done.

My general goal in this monograph was to produce a synthetic portrait of Ivan Nechui-Levyts'kyi, one of the most important figures in Ukrainian literature. My particular goal was to uncover the Nechui who has remained largely unknown and misunderstood, not only in the English-speaking world, where he is almost entirely unknown, but also in the familiar world of Ukrainian literary studies, where he has languished beneath layers of distorted and atrophied opinion. Yet Nechui was not only an important writer but a prolific one as well, and a single monograph cannot accomplish all the tasks that cry out for attention. There is much that needs to be done. Nechui's biography has far too many lacunae. Surely more information can be found, but it will require diligent and persistent research in places beyond the obvious range of sources. There is a need for an exploration of Nechui's place in the development of Ukrainian realism where the focus is not on his peculiarities but on the patterns and features that link the various writers of this period. This topic would go well beyond a study of Nechui alone, but he would certainly play a major role in it. Another area for further work lies in studies of the many works that have not found their place in this book: Nechui's plays, his short stories, his humorous anecdotes. The wave of dissertations on Nechui's historical fiction that was mentioned in chapter 6 represents something of a fortuitous exception to the stagnation in Nechui studies, but even there, the focus is traditional and largely ideological, rather than innovative and insightful. Future studies of Nechui must examine his works and person with a clear sense of the foundational role of his national commitment, with an understanding of his unique methods, and without the ideological prejudices, whether positive or negative, that characterize so much of the writing about him.

Nechui's nationalizing mission was to promote, understand, and present national identity, not necessarily to create an ideological framework around it. Whether his subject was historical or contemporary, whether his characters were aristocrats, priests, peasants, or intellectuals, whether his argument was social, national, cultural, or personal, Nechui's entire creative oeuvre is largely of one piece. His topic is Ukraine, his method is repetition, and his perspective is that of women. This combination of qualities makes him a unique figure in Ukrainian literature and a figure whose significance goes far beyond his role as a pillar of the realist era. Disencumbered of the interference of aesthetic, ideological, and anachronistic prejudice, stripped of the noise of received opinion, Nechui's unheard and unknown voice is an inexhaustible source of aesthetic pleasure, of literary joy, of national pride, and of delightful and enlightening scholarly exploration.

Notes

Introduction

1 Kharkiv: Maidan, 2012.
2 My Internet library of Ukrainian literary texts, the *Electronic Library of Ukrainian Literature*, now has a substantial collection of Nechui's writings, including some that are not readily available in North American scholarly libraries. Cf. http://sites.utoronto.ca/elul/.
3 Iefremov's biography of Myrnyi is a vital source for Ushkalov's monograph.
4 Serhii Iefremov, *Vybrane: Statti, naukovi rozvidky, monohrafii* (Kyiv: Naukova dumka, 2002), p. 479. In the original, 1924 edition, p. 165.
5 Ivan Franko, "Iuvilei Ivana Levyts'koho (Nechuia)," in his *Zibrannia tvoriv u p' iatdesiaty tomakh*, vol. 35 (Kyiv: Naukova dumka, 1980), 374.

1 The Unknown Nechui

1 Serhii Iefremov, *Ivan Levyts'kyi Nechui* (Leipzig: Ukrains'ka nakladnia, 1924). This monograph is reprinted in Serhii Iefremov, *Vybrane: Statti, naukovi rozvidky, monohrafii* (Kyiv: Naukova dumka, 2002), 396–494.
2 Iefremov, *Vybrane*, 396. 1924:5.
3 Iefremov, *Vybrane*, 398 (1924:8), citing Iefremov, *Vybrane*, 235. Letter to Volodymyr Hnatiuk, 8 September 1905. *Mykhailo Kotsiubyns'kyi. Tvory v semy tomakh.* Volume 6 (Kyiv: Naukova dumka, 1975), 33.
4 Beyond the various publications of his many works of fiction and journalism, which offer tantalizing clues about Nechui but little direct evidence about his life, there are only a few primary sources for his biographers, all included in the ten-volume edition: *I.S. Nechui-Levyts'kyi: Zibrannia tvoriv u desiaty tomakh*, 10 vols. Kyiv: Naukova dumka, 1965–8;

hereafter identified by reference to volume and page number in parentheses, e.g., (10:255), i.e., volume 10, page 255, where Nechui's letters begin. There are 166 letters written by Nechui to various correspondents from 1872 to 1917. They are published in volume 10. Four memoirs or autobiographical essays appear in the same volume: (1) "Zhyttiepys' Ivana Levyts'koho (Nechuia) napysana nym samym" (The biography of Ivan Levyts'kyi [Nechui] written by himself), which was published in the Lviv journal *Svit* in 1881 as a capsule introduction to one of the publication's popular authors; (2) "Uryvky z moikh memuariv ta zhadok: V Bohuslavs'kim uchylyshchi" (Excerpts from my memoirs and reminiscences: In the Bohuslav school), which was written in 1914 apparently in answer to a suggestion from a reader, but not published until half a century later; (3) a biographical sketch in a letter to Oleksander Konys'kyi from 19 April 1876, intended for an anthology Konys'kyi was preparing that did not appear because of the Ems Ukaz; and (4) another biographical sketch in two letters from 12 and 28 July 1890 to Omelian Ohonovs'kyi, who was writing his history of Ukrainian literature. There are only a few public documents relating to Nechui's life, such as the employment certificate issued to him on his retirement. Most are unpublished but have been incorporated into Nechui studies.

Indirect witnesses of Nechui's life are also unusually rare. Of course, letters written to him by various correspondents can be found in the published works of those correspondents. There has been no systematic effort to assemble this evidence in a single collection, but they are familiar to those who write about Nechui. More numerous but less well known are the letters written by various individuals to others about Nechui. The correspondence of Drahomanov, Franko, Meliton Buchyns'kyj, Barvins'kyi, Kulish, Hrinchenko, and the various members of the Kyiv Hromada contain references to Nechui in different contexts that are helpful in illuminating his biography. This is an area of research that deserves much more attention, although it is not likely to produce startlingly new facts about the writer. Finally, there are also a number of memoiristic recollections of Nechui by friends and acquaintances; the most important are essays by Hrinchenkova, Kobryns'ka, Krotevych, and Siryi.

5 Levyts'kyi's genealogy is presented in great detail by Ievhen Chernets'kyi in a brochure entitled *Studii nad zhyttiepysom Ivana Nechuia-Levyts'koho* (Bila Tserkva: Tovarystvo okhorony starozhytnostei Kyivshchyny, 2000). The family history summarized below is gleaned from this brochure.

6 In the aftermath of the Polish uprising of 1830, *szlachta* status was devalued.

7 See http://uk.wikipedia.org/wiki/Стеблів, accessed 15 June 2012.

8 "Opisanie svad'by i svadebnykh obriadov ukrainskikh malorossian (v Bohuslave). Sostavleno sviashchennikom sela Stebleva Simeonom

Levitskim," 1845. Rept. in Oleksii Dei, "Vesillia, zapysane 1845 roku bat'kt'kom I. Nechuia-Levyts'koho," *Narodna tvorchist' ta etnohrafiia*, 1972, 2: 85–99.

9 *Pravda*, 1870, 3:98. "Колись давно п. Куліш, їздивши і ходивши пішки по Київщині, спізнавсь із розумним одним попом сільським. Опісля той піп збирав для п. Куліша між народом пісні, приказки, перекази і т. ін. та й давав переписувати малому синкові, щоб посилати через пошту. Оцей же то синок, набравшись у народу смаку словесного, об'явивсь тепер славним Нечуєм." Editorial note to Vsevolod Kokhovs'kyi's story entitled "Pan Komarchuk." Quoted in Oleksii Dei, ibid., 86.

10 Ibid.

11 Pavlo Klebanovs'kyi, however, a pupil at the Bohuslav school eight years after Nechui, complains in his memoirs about poor students stealing his books. Pavlo Klebanovskii, "Bohuslavskoe dukhovnoe uchylyshche," *Kievskaia starina*, 1894, 9: 420–1.

12 Mykola Mandryka. "Do biohrafii I.S. Nechuia-Levyts'koho (Roky navchannia pys'mennyka)," *Radians'ke literaturoznavstvo*, 1968, 12:35.

13 Mandryka, ibid., 38–40.

14 Klebanovskyii, "Bohuslavskoe dukhovnoe uchylyshche," 1894, 10:32–3; 11:272–3.

15 Mandryka, "Do biohrafii I.S. Nechuia-Levyts'koho," 38.

16 Mandryka, ibid., 40.

17 I.A. Zubkovs'kyi, "I.S. Levyts'kyi-Nechui na Poltavshchyni (Uryvok zi spohadiv)," *Kul'tura i pobut* (A weekly supplement to the newspaper *Visti VUTSVK*), 23 June 1928: 3.

18 Serhii Plokhy, *Unmaking Imperial Russia: Mykhailo Hrushevsky and the Writing of Ukrainian History* (Toronto: University of Toronto Press, 2005), 436. Plokhy is citing Theodore Weeks, *Nation and State in Late Imperial Russia: Nationalism and Russification on the Western Frontier, 1863–1914* (Dekalb: Northern Illinois University Press, 1996), 128.

19 Iefremov, *Vybrane*, 409.

20 Kyrylo Studyns'kyi, comp., *Halychyna i Ukraina v lystuvanni 1862–1884 rr. Materiialy do istorii ukrains'koi kul'tury v Halychyni ta ii zv'iazkiv z Ukrainoiu* (Kyiv: Proletar, 1931), 143; a letter (no. 128) from Mykhailo Podolyns'kyi to Volodymyr Navrots'kyi dated 12 January 1870.

21 The text of the circular, with an English translation, can be found in Alexei Miller, *The Ukrainian Question: The Russian Empire and Nationalism in the Nineteenth Century*, trans. Olga Poato (Budapest: Central European University Press, 2003), 263–6. Johannes Remy discusses the ambiguity of the circular's instructions in his "The Valuev Circular and Censorship of Ukrainian Publications in the Russian Empire (1863–1876): Intention and

Practice," *Canadian Slavonic Papers*, 2007, 1–2: 97. For a fuller discussion of the role of the Valuev Circular in Nechui's career, see my article "Ivan Nečuj-Levyc'kyj and the Prohibitions on Publishing Ukrainian Literature" which is to appear in a forthcoming collection on the Valuev Circular edited by Michael Moser.

22 Johannes Remy, ibid.

23 This is one of the principle arguments in his "Antrakt z istorii ukrainofil'stva (1863–1872)," which first appeared in *Pravda* in 1876. It appears in Mykhailo Drahomanov, *Vybrane ... mii zadum zlozhyty ocherk istorii tsyvilizatsii na Ukraini* (Kyiv: Lybid', 1991), 204–33; cf. 218–20.

24 Efimii Kryzhanovs'kyi, "Kniaz' V. A. Cherkasskii i kholmskie greko-uniaty," *Ruskoe zabuz'e (Kholmshchina i Podliash'e)* (St Petersburg: Mirnyi trud," 1911), 351.

25 This letter and an extensive commentary to it were published by Oles' Fedoruk in his "Nevidomyi lyst-spohad I. Nechuia-Levyts'koho pro P. Kulisha," in *Panteleimon Kulish: Materialy i doslidzhennia* eds. Mykola Zhulyns'kyi, et al. (Lviv: M.P. Kots, 2000), pp. 277–96. I follow Fedoruk in correcting the obviously incorrect date (1869) given in the letter and in filling in the details of the relations between the two men.

26 I. Shenrok, "P.A. Kulish (Biohraficheskii ocherk')," *Kievskaia starina* 1901, 2:153–79; 3:461–92; 4:126–48; 5:183–213; 6:344–82; 7/8:46–102; 9:304–30; 10:18–44.

27 Fedoruk, "Nevidomyi lyst-spohad I. Nechuia-Levyts'koho pro P. Kulisha," 279n.7. He is citing Studyns'kyi, comp. *Halychyna i Ukraina v lystuvanni*, 88, which is a letter (no. 79) from Osyp Barvins'kyi to Danylo Taniachkevych from July 1868.

28 Valeriian Pidmohyl'nyi, "Ivan Levyts'kyi-Nechui (Sproba psykhoanalizy tvorchosty)," *Zhyttia i revoliutsiia* 1927, 9:295–303.

29 Mykola Taranenko, "Do kharakterystyky sedlets'koho periodu tvorchoi biohrafii I. Nechuia-Levytskoho," *Radians'ke literaturoznavstvo* 1971, 6:37, citing item 27929 in the Manuscript division of the Vernadsky Library.

30 Taranenko, ibid., p. 37, citing an unpublished manuscript in Russian on "The Ukrainian literary language." Verndadsky, no. 27798.

31 Mykhailo Vozniak, "Kulish iak redaktor *Prychepy* Levyts'koho," *Zapysky Naukovoho tovarystva im. Shevchenka*, 1928, vol. 148:1–54.

32 *Perepyska Mykhaila Drahomanova z Melitonom Buchyns'kym 1871–1877*, ed. Mykhailo Pavlyk (Lviv: NTSh, 1910), 107.

33 Mykhailo Vozniak, "Prymitky Ivana Nechuia-Levyts'koho do perekladu *Malorosii* Pryzhova," *Literaturnyi arkhiv*, 1930, 1/2: 138–43.

34 Studyns'kyi, comp., *Halychyna i Ukraina v lystuvanni*, 99, a letter (no. 91) from Osyp Barvins'kyi to his brother, 10 March 1870.

35 Its first publication was in the ten-volume *Zibrannia tvoriv* (2:369–76).
36 "Mandrivka na ukrainske Pidliassia," *Pravda* 1872, 7 (October 15): 310–17; 8 (November 30): 373–82; 9 (December 27): 423–31.
37 Cf. Taranenko, "Do kharakterystyky," 38–9.
38 Taranenko, "Do kharakterystyky," 31–2.
39 Serhii Khavrus', director of the Ivan Nechui-Levyts'kyi museum in Stebliv, collected memoiristic recollections of Nechui's unfulfilled amorous hopes: Serhii Khavrus', "Do obrazu narodnoho pys'mennyka," *Vitchyzna*, 1978, 11: 165–73.
40 Maria Hrinchenkova, "Spohady pro Ivana Nechuia-Levyts'koho," *Ukraina*, 1924, 4: 124.
41 Studyns'kyi, comp., *Halychyna i Ukraina v lystuvanni*, 91, 143, 417; *Perepyska Drahomanova z Buchyns'kym*, 108.
42 Ibid., 41.
43 Ibid., 54–5.
44 Ibid., 263.
45 Mykola Taranenko, *I.S. Nechui-Levyts'kyi. Seminarii* (Kyiv: Vyshcha shkola, 1984), 104.
46 *Arkhiv Mykhaila Drahomanova. Tom 1. Lystuvannia kyivs'koi staroi hromady z M. Drahomanovym (1870–1895 r.r.)*, ed. Roman Smal'-Stots'kyi (Warsaw: Ukrains'kyi naukovyi instytut, 1937), 122.
47 The early history of the Kyiv Hromada and particularly the Sunday schools are described in Ihnat Zhytets'kyi, "Kyivs'ka hromada za 60-ykh rokiv," *Ukraina*, 1928, 1: 91–125. Ihnat was the son of Pavlo Zhytets'kyi.
48 *Mykola V. Lysenko. Lysty*, comp. Ostap Lysenko (Kyiv: Mystetstvo, 1964), 112–24.
49 Ibid., 117.
50 The picture is reproduced in *Arkhiv Mykhaila Drahomanova. Tom 1*, facing page 128.
51 Fedir Savchenko compiled the list of Hromada members and the dates when they were formally accepted into the organization based on the archived minutes of the meetings of the Southwestern (Kyiv) Branch of the Russian Imperial Geographical Society. These were, as he shows, actually meetings of the Kyiv Hromada. Fedir Savchenko, *Zaborona ukrainstva 1876 r.* (Kyiv: DVU, 1930), 95–100, and the list of members, 271–5. Rept. Fedir Savčenko, *The Suppression of the Ukrainian Activities* [*sic*], Harvard Series in Ukrainian Studies 14 (Munich: Wilhelm Fink, 1970).
52 S.M. Kuz'menko, "I. Nechui-Levyts'kyi v Kyshynevi (Z novykh arkhivnykh materialiv)," *Radians'ke literaturoznavstvo*, 1966, 6: 70.
53 Ibid., 70.

54 Staryts'kyi's letter to Nechui from 17 March 1883 details some of the changes. Mykhailo Staryts'kyi, *Tvory u vos'my tomakh*, vol. 8 (Kyiv: Dnipro, 1965), 464–5.
55 Ostap Lysenko, "M.V. Lysenko i I.S. Nechui-Levyts'kyi," *Dnipro*, 1959, 4: 141.
56 Remy, "The Valuev Circular and Censorship," 106–9.
57 In 1874, Nechui's satiric sketch "Ne mozhna Babi Parastsi vderzhatysia na seli" (Baba Paraska can't hold on in the village) appeared in *Kievlianin*, in a separate brochure, and in a volume with *Khmary*. A Russian translation of his "Rybalka Panas Krut'" had earlier appeared in *Kievlianin*.
58 The Russian text of the edict is reproduced in *Savchenko, Zaborona ukrainstva*, 381–3. An English translation (and the Russian original) can be found in Miller, *The Ukrainian Question*, 267–72.
59 *Arkhiv Mykhaila Drahomanova*, 209 and 411 (letter 102n.18).
60 Iefremov, *Vybrane*, 413n.2, 1924: 39n.1. These materials have not been cited by susbsequent scholars, perhaps they have not survived.
61 Kuz'menko, "I. Nechui-Levyts'kyi u Kyshynevi," 71.
62 Oleksander Bilets'kyi, "Ivan Semenovych Levyts'kyi (Nechui)," *Zibrannia prats'*, vol. 2. *Ukrains'ka literatura XIX – pochatku XX stolittia* (Kyiv: Naukova dumka, 1965), 334.
63 This polemic is discussed in chapter 3, below.
64 Tsvitkivs'kyi's letter to Drahomanov of 9 December 1876 mentions that Nechui is composing such a work and gives a brief plot summary; *Arkhiv Mykhaila Drahomanova*, 209.
65 *Pravda*, 31 (19) July 1876 (no. 13–14): 500–5.
66 Kuz'menko, "I. Nechui-Levyts'jkyi u Kyshynevi," 70.
67 See his letters to Hrinchenko (10:287–91) and to Mykhailo Hrushevs'kyi (10: 295–308).
68 The archival documents are cited in Kuz'menko, "I. Nechui-Levyts'jkyi u Kyshynevi," 71.
69 Bilets'kyi, "Ivan Semenovych Levyts'kyi (Nechui)," 320.
70 Kuz'menko, "I. Nechui-Levyts'jkyi u Kyshynevi," 71.
71 "Sluzhbu ia pokynuv shche pislia rizdva" (I left the service shortly after Christmas), he says in a letter of 11 May 1885 (10: 299)
72 Liudmyla Staryts'ka-Cherniakhivs'ka, "V.I. Samiilenko (Pamiati tovarysha)," in her *Vybrani tvory* (Kyiv: Naukova dumka, 2000), 805.
73 The novel is further discussed in chapter 5, below.
74 *Lysenko. Lysty*, 236, 237, 240.
75 *Zoria*, 1894 (XV), 23 (Dec. 1), 508.
76 *Lysenko. Lysty*, 223.
77 Taranenko, *Nechui-Levyts'kyi. Seminarii*, 114.

78 Ibid., 111.

79 Iefremov, *Vybrane*, 418. 1924:48.

80 Iefremov, *Vybrane*, 419. 1924:49.

81 Panas Myrnyi, *Zibrannia tvoriv u semy tomakh*, vol. 7 (Kyiv: Naukova dumka, 1971), 472. The subsequent letter to Iefremov from 22 March 1901 again uses Nechui's volumes for comparison, this time for financial considerations. Myrnyi, a professional accountant, was making sure he got his fair share from sales of the books.

82 Iefremov is citing a letter to Stebnyts'kyi from 2 February 1899. There is a published letter to Stebnyts'kyi from 9 February 1899. It seems unlikely that Nechui would write two letters to the same addressee in the span of a single week. Iefremov cites this same unknown letter elsewhere in his text and that citation too cannot be found in published letters. Although the Soviet editors of Nechui's 10-volume works where the letters are published deliberately hide Iefremov's name (he is omitted from the index and his biography is cited anonymously) they are clearly aware of his text and make use of it.

83 Iefremov, *Vybrane*, 419. 1924:51.

84 Mykhailo Kotsiubyns'kyi, *Tvory v semy tomakh*, vol. 5 (Kyiv: Naukova dumka, 1974), 388.

85 In a letter to Volodymyr Hnatiuk from 24 January 1904, he calls it weak (*slabe*): Kotsiubyns'kyi, *Tvory*, vol. 5, 307.

86 Kotsiubyns'kyi, *Tvory*, vol. 6:11.

87 Cf. Kotsiubyns'kyi, *Tvory*, vol. 5:180.

88 Kotsiubyns'kyi, *Tvory*, vol. 6:54–5.

89 *Kievskaia starina*, 1903 (vol. 83), Oct., 19.

90 Mykola Taranenko, "Do istorii vysvitlennia 35-richnoho iuvileiu I.S. Nechuia-Levyts'koho," *Ukrains'ke literaturoznavstvo*, 19 (1973): 110–15.

91 Hrinchenkova, "Spohady ...," 114–15.

92 Although he did not come to Kyiv, Franko published his jubilee greeting in the *Literaturno-naukovyi visnyk*, 1905, vol. 29, bk. 1, 36–42.

93 Serhii Khavrus', "Zhandarms'ki dokumenty pro I.S. Nechuia-Levyts'koho," *Ukrains'kyi istorychnyi zhurnal*, 1968, 11: 136–8.

94 These celebratory events resembled the Russian "banquet campaign" of 1904–5 and the character and form of both was shaped by the legal constraints that the tsarist government enacted to restrict political opposition.

95 For more details, see Taranenko, "Do istorii vysvitlennia ...," and the anonymous account of the jubilee that appeared in *Kievskaia starina*, 1905, vol. 88, bk. 1, part 2, 19–23.

96 In a letter to Hrinchenko in 1902 Nechui says he never drank: "horilky iz rodu ne pyv" (10: 398–9). The stomach ailment that he frequently complained about likely played a role in his abstinence.
97 *Kievskaia starina*, 1905, vol. 88, bk. 2, part 2, 163.
98 For a detailed list of publications and a general account of the significance of this event, see Olga Andriewsky, "The Politics of National Identity: The Ukranian Question in Russia, 1904–1912" (PhD diss., Harvard University, 1991) 168, particularly footnote 74.
99 Hrinchenkova, "Spohady …," 116.
100 See George Y. Shevelov, *The Ukrainian Language in the First Half of the Twentieth Century (1900–1941): Its State and Status* (Cambridge, MA: Harvard Ukrainian Research Institute, 1989). See in particular chapter 2, 21–66, where Nechui's views are discussed, 59–64.
101 Remarkably little is written about Nechui's peculiar linguistic prescriptions. Cf. George Shevelov, *The Ukrainian Language in the First Half of the Twentieth Century*, 63–4; George Shevelov, *Die Ukrainische Schriftsprache 1798–1965: Ihre Entwicklung unter dem Einfluss der Dialekte* (Wiesbaden: Otto Harrassowitz, 1966), 84–91; 138–47; Ivan Bilodid, *Istoriia ukrains'koi literaturnoi movy*, in his *Vybrani pratsi v tr'ox tomakh*, vol. 2 (Kyiv: Naukova dumka, 1986), 104–7.
102 That he did not quite understand what was new and what was old is an entirely different matter .
103 "S'ohochasna chasopysna mova na Ukraini," *Ukraina*, 1907, vol. 1, bk. 1, 1–49; bk. 2, 183–237; bk. 3, 280–331.
104 Shevelov, *Die Ukrainische Schriftsprache*, 85–6.
105 Mykhailo Zhovtobriukh, "Ukrains'ka hramatyka I.S. Nechuia-Levyts'koho," *Movoznavstvo*, 1989, 1: 33–7
106 Ievhen Krotevych, *Kyivs'ki zustrichi* (Kyiv: Molod', 1963), 70.
107 Hryhorii Kovalenko-Kolomats'kyi, "Vystavka pam'iaty Iv. Levyts'koho-Nechuia," *Chervonyi shliakh*, 1929, 1: 242–4.
108 Iurii Siryi, "Z moikh zustrichiv. 2. I.S. Nechui-Levyts'kyi," *Literaturno-naukovyi zbirnyk*, vol. 3 (Hannover: K.N.V., 1948), 60–9.
109 Siryi, "Z moihk zustrichiv," 67.
110 Oleksander Lotots'kyi, "I.S. Levyts'kyi," in his *Storinky mynuloho*, Pt 1 (Warsaw: Ukrains'kyi naukovyi instytut, 1932), 186.
111 Fedir Sarana, "Iz neopublikovanykh spohadiv pro I. Nechuia-Levyts'koho," *Literaturna Ukraina*, 18 June 1999, 5.
112 Hrinchenkova, "Spohady …," 126–7. She emphasizes that Dehteriv had a very bad reputation.
113 *Literaturno-naukovyi visnyk*, 1918 (69), 2–3: 113–15.

2 Describing Ukraine

1 Таким фокусом для своєї громади повинен бути реальний художник-письальник, таким осередком випнутого або увігнутого скла повинен бути і український художник-писальник для України. В його душі повинна одсвітитись і перетворитись українська жизнь, що кипить або що пліснє кругом його. Коли писальник хоч трошки чує себе українським громадянином, часткою українського народу й українського громадянства, він повинен мати за святу повинність одсвічувати в своїй фантазії, в свойому серці ту громаду, що роїться кругом його, радіти її радістю, плакати її слізьми, а не перелазити в чужі городи і підставляти свою душу під картини чужої, неукраїнської жизні. Український писальник не повинен клопотатись, що йому буде мало роботи на Україні. Українська жизнь – то непочатий рудник, що лежить десь під землею, хоч за його вже брались і такі високі таланти, як Шевченко; то безконечний матеріял, що тільки ще жде робітників, цілих шкіл робітників на літературному полі. От перед ним розгортується широким-широким полотнищем народна, мужицька жизнь од Кавказу й Волги до самого лиману Дунаю, до Карпат і за Карпати, до далекого Гроднянського та Мінського полісся. Нам скажуть, що народ дає убогий матеріал для літератури, що в ньому мало розвита індивідуальність, що поет не знайде в ньому багато усяких типів та характерів, що народна жизнь дуже стихійна, а селяни похожі один на другого, як одна комашка на другу. Нехай буде й так, але український народ все-таки дасть багато матеріялу для українських писальників. Од Кавказу за Карпати не може бути жизнь народу зовсім однакова. Кубанський козак, потомок запорожців, саратовський та астраханський селянин дуже одрізняється од венгерського. Карпатський гуцул, лемко та бойко дуже одрізняється од хлібороба киянина та полтавця, бо на Карпатах навіть не сіють, ні жнуть, а збирають в свої житниці – сир та масло, як давні патріярхи. Гроднянський, мінський, могилівський, волинський, сідлецький поліщук вже й костюмом мало похожий на свого земляка наддніпрянця, в своїх рудих або білих магерках, в своїх сірих свитках, в узеньких штанах та в личаках. Повісті Осипа Федьковича, в котрих описується жизнь українських селян на Буковині, на Карпатах, показують, що їх бит дуже не похожий на бит степових українців. Український народ, розкинутий на такому широкому просторі, може бути широким сюжетом українського писальника-реаліста. Ivan Nechui-Levyts'kyi, *Ukrainstvo na literaturnykh pozvakh z Moskovshchynoiu* (Lviv: Kameniar, 1988), 71.

2 Я згоджуюсь з Вами, що українським письменникам не можна омежовуватись обписуванням одного селянського життя,… А тим часом українська книжка в наші часи має багато інтелігентного читальника. Треба

для нього постачати й утворів, де б було обписувано й його самого з шкурою та кістками, правдиво й реально, який він є. … Натурально, що нашим письменникам треба дбати про свій край, обписувати усі верстви, усе життя, усіх людей, які тільки є на території українського плем'я. (10:400)

3 *Kyivs'ka oblast. Istoriia mist i sil Ukrains'koi RSR* (Kyiv: Akademiia nauk, 1971), 146.

4 Bilets'kyi, "Ivan Semenovych Levyts'kyi (Nechui)," 326.

5 Serhii Khavrus', "Zapovitnymy stezhkamy Stebleva," *Ukrainska mova i literatura v shkoli*, 1986, no. 3 (349): 69–74 and his "Sered narodu: Stebliv u zhytti ta tvorchosti I.S. Nechuia-Levyts'koho," *Prapor*, 1968, 11: 87–8.

6 Iefremov. *Vybrane*, 467 (1924:142).

7 Iefremov, *Vybrane*, 415 (1924:42).

8 For more on Nechui's personalization of landscape, see L.H. Bykova, "Iz sposterezhen' nad osoblyvostiamy peizazhnoho zhyvopysu I.S. Nechuia-Levyts'koho," *Ukrainska mova i literatura v shkoli*, 1972 (22), 7: 18–24.

9 Iefremov, *Vybrane*, 399–401 and 457–8 (1924:11–13; 122–5).

10 The scene is in chapter 4 of part 1 of Svydnyts'kyi's novel.

11 Even serious critics such as Oleksander Bilets'kyi exaggerate Nechui's negative depiction of religion. In keeping with Soviet Marxist categories of analysis and bibliography, Mykola Taranenko's guidebook, *I.S. Nechui-Levyts'kyi. Seminarii*, has a chapter entitled "Atheistic Themes in Nechui's Works," while Mykola Moroz's bibliography of Nechui has a section (dictated by Soviet bibliographic norms) entitled "Atheistic Ideas in the Works of I.S. Nechui-Levyts'kyi." *I.S. Nechui-Levyts'kyi. Tvory v tr'okh tomakh* (Kyiv: Dnipro, 1988), vol. 3, 608–9. L. Fedosov's essay "Antyklerykal'ni motyvy u povistiakh Nechuia-Levyts'koho," *Radians'ke literaturoznavstvo* 1963, 1: 27–41, is a good example of just how blunt a tool this pseudo-scholarly analysis can become.

12 Valerian Pidmohyl'nyi, "Ivan Levyts'kyi-Nechui (Sproba psykhoanalizy tvorchosty)," *Zhyttia i revoliutsiia*, 1927, 9: 295–303. Available on the Internet at http://sites.utoronto.ca/elul/Nechui/nech-psyx-orig.pdf.

13 See chapter 1, p. 19, above.

14 Ivan Nechui-Levyts'kyi, *Svitohliad ukrains'koho narodu: Eskiz ukrains'koi mifolohii*, originally published in *Pravda* between 1868 and 1876, then published in 1876 in a single volume at the print shop of the Shevchenko Society in Lviv, and reprinted in Kyiv by Oberehy publishers in 1992 and then again in 2003.

15 Ivan Nechui-Levyts'kyi, *Ukrainstvo na literaturnykh pozvakh z Moskovshcynoiu. Kul'turolohichni traktaty*, ed. Mykhailo Chornopys'kyi (Lviv: Kameniar, 1998), 73–5.

16 Discussed in chapter 5, below, p. 307.

17 Gounod's *Faust* (or perhaps not the opera but Goethe's play itself) is also mentioned in *Neodnakovymy stezhkamy* (8:463; 8:468) and in *Na gastroliakh v Mykytianakh* (8:107). Nechui wrote all these works in 1902–3.

3. Defending Ukraine

1 Nechui gives no explanation for this leave. Vasyl' is returning home "по білету" [with a document] after only five years of service. Service would have normally been for twelve years at this time. For a general account of conscription practices, see Dana M. Ohren, "All the Tsars Men: Minorities and Military Conscription in Imperial Russia, 1874–1905" (PhD diss., Indiana University, 2006), chapter 2, 32–42 and concerning the reforms of the early 1860s, 87–9. See http://search.proquest.com/docview/305335965 (accessed 14 May 2012).

2 Shevchenko's use of "moskal" here is famously ambiguous. Does he mean soldiers, or does he mean outsiders, Russians, Muscovites, people from somewhere else who aren't part of our community? Or are the two meanings blended together?

3 У залі стало тихо. Василина стояла й хлипала. Вона трохи опам'яталась у тиші й почала розглядати горницю, мебіль, фортеп'ян, дзеркала. Все приймало перед нею якийсь фантастичний вид. Фортеп'ян здавався для неї якимсь звіром на чотирьох коротких ногах, стільці здавались сухими людськими кістками; важка софа неначе була схожа на домовину, а з здорових дзеркал неначе виглядали на неї якісь страшні упирі (3:202).

4 Napping is a finishing process that raises the surface fibres of a fabric by means of passage over rapidly revolving cylinders covered with metal points or burrs.

5 Serhii Iefremov makes this point in his monograph on Nechui (Iefremov, *Vybrane*, 453; 1924:115). Soviet critics frequently disputed it, without actually naming Iefremov as the source. In particular, Oleksander Bilets'kyi makes a reasonable argument that Nechui depicts a variety of Ukrainians as exploiters in positions of minor authority (village priest, secretary) and a few denationalized Ukrainians as major exploiters in higher office; nevertheless, the clear tendency is to associate exploitation with non-Ukrainians. Cf. Bilets'kyi, "Ivan Semenovych Levyts'kyi (Nechui)," 350.

6 Myroslav Shkandrij. *Jews in Ukrainian Literature: Representation and Identity* (New Haven, CT: Yale University Press, 2009).

7 Review of Myroslav Shkandrij, *Jews in Ukrainian Literature: Representation and Identity*, *Journal of Ukrainian Studies*, 35–6 (2010–11), 340.

8 A similar contrast between the beauty of nature and the griminess of Jews' lives occurs in the story "Zhyvtsem pokhovani," in the description

of the town square before the train station in Bila Tserkva. The poetry of the flower-bedecked square is spoiled by the disheveled appearance of the Jewish carriage drivers waiting for fares (7:262). In this story, probably from the 1890s, Nechui already uses the word *ievrei*, which was being introduced into Ukrainian to replace *zhyd* which was increasingly perceived as pejorative. Nechui, however, did not stop using *zhyd* but rather used both words interchangeably.

9 Clear examples of genuine goodwill toward Jews can be found in the portrait of Avrum in the novel *Ne toi stav* and in the words of Nykon Kuchma in *Neodnakovymy stezhkamy* (8:328).

10 Ivan Nechuy-Levitsky, *Mikola Dzherya: A Long Story* [*sic*], trans. Oles Kovalenko (Kyiv: Dnipro, 1985).

11 Nechuy-Levitsky, *Mikola Dzherya*, trans. Kovalenko, 72. I have modified the translation to reflect the original text more closely.

12 Chapter 2, p. 125.

13 Soviet critics like L. Fedosov cite Nechui's words to Ivan Puliui in a letter of 14 January 1904 (10:409) that scholarship has not fared well under Eastern Christianity as evidence of anti-religious sentiments. But this remark is specifically about the Synod of the Russian Orthodox Church that had denied and continued to refuse permission for the publication of the Bible in Ukrainian translation. He might have also mentioned Galileo and other examples, but that would still not make him an atheist or an opponent of Christianity.

14 Chapter 1, p. 52.

15 *Ukrainstvo na literaturnykh pozvakh z Moskovshchynoiu*, ed. Chornopys'kyi, 73.

16 *Ukrainstvo na literaturnykh pozvakh z Moskovshchynoiu*, ed. Chornopys'kyi, 83.

17 *Ukrainstvo na literaturnykh pozvakh z Moskovshchynoiu*, ed. Chornopys'kyi, 84.

18 Nechui praises Pypin in the essay for his sympathy to and familiarity with Ukrainian issues. He also speaks favorably of Pypin in letters to Volodymyr Barvins'kyi on 1 March 1879 (10:275) and Mykhailo Komarov on 13 October 1879 (10:278).

19 For more on Franciszek Duchiński, see Ivan L. Rudnytsky, "Franciszek Duchiński and His Impact on Ukrainian Political Thought," *Harvard Ukrainian Studies* III/IV(*Eucharisterion*, pt. 2): 690–705.

20 Letter of 10 August 1881 (10:289).

21 *Kievsii telgraf* 1875, 30 (March 9).

22 "Радюк просто смішний дурень!" Mykhailo Drahomanov, *Lysty na naddniprians'ku Ukrainu*, letter 4, in Borys Hrinchenko, Mykhailo Drahomanov, *Dialohy pro ukrains'ky natsional'nu spravu* (Kyiv: Natsionalna Akademiia Nauk Ukrainy, 1994), 131.

23 O. Koshovyi (=Oleksander Konys'kyi), "Koly zh vyiasnyt'sia? (Za provodom povisty I. Levitskoho *Khmary*," *Pravda* 8 (1875): 768–74; 807–13.

24 Iefremov, *Vybrane*, 461. 1924:130.

25 "Жоден навіть найактивніший персонаж Левицького далі палких промов, далі теоретизування не йде." Iurii Mezhenko, "Ivan Semenovych Nechui-Levyts'kyi. Literaturnyi narys," *I.S. Nechui-Levyts'kyi. Tvory*, Volume 1 (Kharkiv: DVU, 1926), 5–18.

26 O. Koshovyi, "Koly zh vyiasnyt'sia?" 809 and passim.

27 Miller, *The Ukrainian Question*, chapter 8.

28 *Perepyska Drahomanova z Buchyns'kym*, 306. Cf. Ksenya Kiebuzinski, *Paris to Poltava: Ukrainian Cossacks as an Imagined Community in Nineteenth-Century French Culture* (PhD diss., Brandeis University, 2002), 244–6.

29 It is likely that Drahomanov did write to Nechui, since he asks Buchyns'kyi for Nechui's address in a letter of 16 November 1871, *Perepyska Drahomanova z Buchyns'kym*, 54–5.

30 *Perepyska Drahomanova z Buchyns'kym*, 263.

31 *Perepyska Drahomanova z Buchyns'kym*, 307.

32 *Perepyska Drahomanova z Buchyns'kym*, 307.

33 Ivan Franko, "Literatura, ii zavdannia i naivazhnishi tsikhy (*Pravda, chast' literaturno-naukova*. Knyzhka druha. "S'ohochasne literaturne priamuvannia)," in his *Zibrannia tvoriv u p'iatdesiaty tomakh*, vol. 26 (Kyiv: Naudova dumka, 1980), 7–8. This essay is a review of Nechui's culturological essay. Although Nechui's essay was published annonymously, Franko knew at the time he was writing the review, that the author of the essay he was reviewing was Nechui. See his letter of 26 Dec 1878 to Ol'ha Roshkevych, *Zibrannia tvoriv*, vol. 48, 133.

34 *Mykhailo Petrovych Drahomanov: Literaturno-publitsystychni pratsi v dvokh tomakh* (Kyiv: Naukova dumka, 1970), vol. 2, 308.

35 *Drahomanov: Literaturno-publitsystychni pratsi*, vol. 2, 310.

36 *Drahomanov: Literaturno-publitsystychni pratsi*, vol. 2, 310.

37 *Drahomanov: Literaturno-publitsystychni pratsi*, vol. 2, 311.

38 *Lesia Ukrainka: Zibrannia tvoriv v dvanadsiaty tomakh* (Kyiv: Naukova dumka, 1975–9), vol. 10, 109.

39 *Drahomanov: Literaturno-publitsystychni pratsi*, vol. 2, 311.

40 *Drahomanov: Literaturno-publitsystychni pratsi*, vol. 1, 292–5.

41 *Drahomanov: Literaturno-publitsystychni pratsi*, vol. 1, 294.

42 *Drahomanov: Literaturno-publitsystychni pratsi*, vol. 1, 295.

43 For more about the conflicts surrounding methods in the Sunday Schools, see Syl'vestr Hlushko, "Drahomanov i nedil'ni shkoly," *Ukraina*, 1924, no. 4, 35–42.

4 Realism, Rhetoric, and Repetition

1 For a comparison of Nechui's and Vovchok's prose, see Nina Krutikova, *Tvorchist' I.S. Nechuia-Levyts'koho* (Kyiv: Akademiia nauk URSR, 1961), 7–20.

2 A good example of the problem can be seen in Mykhailo Markovs'kyi's study of Nechui and Turgenev, written in 1925, long before Soviet Orthodoxy prescribed a specific approach to both writers. Contrary to the author's intentions, it establishes that the similarity between them is mostly illusory. Mykhailo Markovs'kyi, "Literaturni paraleli. I.S. Levyts'kyi i I.S. Turhenev," *Ukraina*, 1925, 3: 130–4.

3 *Ukrainstvo na literaturnykh pozvakh z Moskovshchynoiu*, ed. Chornopys'kyi, 70–1.

4 Many studies of Nechui's language take a very simplistic approach and are often aimed at providing tools for the high school teacher who is presenting Nechui as part of the school curriculum. Nevertheless, there is useful descriptive information in such studies as: Halyna Izhakevych, "Mova tvoriv I. Nechuia-Levyts'koho," *Kurs istorii ukrains'koi literaturnoi movy*, Tom. 1 (Kyiv: Akademiia nauk, 1858), 435–55; D.M. Bilets'kyi, "Vyvchennia movy povisti I.S. Nechuia-Levyts'koho *Mykola Dzheria*," *Ukrains'ka mova v shkoli*, 1959, 3:40–3; and L.P. Kulyns'ka, "Mova povisti *Kaidasheva sim'ia* I.S. Nechuia-Levyts'koho," *Ukrains'ka mova v shkoli*, 1959, 3:44–9.

5 Shevelov, *Die Ukrainische Schriftsprache*, 84–91.

6 Izhakevych, "Mova tvoriv I. Nechuia-Levyts'koho," 443–5.

7 Ivan Franko, "Iuvilei Ivana Levyts'koho (Nechuia)," *Zibrannia tvoriv*, vol. 35, 376.

8 The phrase is from *Prychepa*, chap. 11. The published text has з'явився instead of показався. The phrase translates as "there was a crack, a flash, and a bluish tuft of smoke appeared."

9 *Ukrainstvo na literaturnykh pozvakh z Moskovshchynoiu*, ed. Chornopys'kyi, 77.

10 *Ukrainstvo na literaturnykh pozvakh z Moskovshchynoiu*, ed. Chornopys'kyi, 77.

11 Izhakevych, "Mova tvoriv I. Nechuia-Levyts'koho," 451.

12 Discussed in chapter 2, p. 144 ff.

13 Izhakevych, "Mova tvoriv I. Nechuia-Levyts'koho," 437.

14 Vasyl' Vlasenko, *Khudozhnia maisternist' I.S. Nechuia-Levyts'koho*. Kyiv: Radians'ka shkola, 1969, p. 27.

15 Iefremov, *Vybrane*, 444. 1924:97–8.

16 Iefremov, *Vybrane*, 442. 1924:93.

17 Iefremov, *Vybrane*, 440. 1924:89. Actually, by my count the phrase occurs 31 times in the entire 10-volume collected works, usually more than once in longer works.

18 The phrase comes from Andrii Nikovs'kyi's introduction to Nechui's *Mykola Dzheria*, discussed below.
19 Valerian Pidmohyl'nyi, "Ivan Nechui-Levyts'kyi," introduction to Ivan Nechui-Levyts'kyi, *Vybrani tvory* (Kyiv: Chas, 1927), vol. 1, vii. The phrase "descriptive genealogy" refers specifically to Nechui's *Starosvits'ki batiushky ta matushky*.
20 Pidmohyl'nyi, "Ivan Nechui-Levyts'kyi," x.
21 Pidmohyl'nyi, "Ivan Nechui-Levyts'kyi," x.
22 Pidmohyl'nyi, "Ivan Nechui-Levyts'kyi," x.
23 Pidmohyl'nyi, "Ivan Nechui-Levyts'kyi," x.
24 Nechuy-Levitsky. *Mikola Dzherya*, trans. Kovalenko, 3.
25 The translator, Oles Kovalenko, has smoothed out the text and undone some of this repetition, particularly in the second and third sentence. A more literal translation might read: "In the valley stood green, luxurious, rich, and tall willows, where the village of Willow-ville seemed to drown in the willows. Among the willows there shone very clearly in the sun a tall white church with three domes ..."
26 "Good fences make good neighbors," "Mending Wall," 1914.
27 Rootedness is discussed in chapter 2, above, p. 93.
28 J. Hillis Miller asserts that "The reader's identification of recurrences may be deliberate or spontaneous, self-conscious or unreflective," in his *Fiction and Repetition: Seven English Novels* (Cambridge, MA: Harvard University Press, 1982), 2. This may be true, but nevertheless there must be an identification of the recurrence. The unreflective identification of repetition cannot be understood as a total unawareness of the recurrence. There can be no emphatic function without this recognition. The subjective nature of this recognition also helps to explain the variability of the effect of repetition on readers and of their judgment of its rhetorical efficacy. A very attentive reader may find an instance of repetition annoying because the emphasis it provides was already evident. A very inattentive reader may not notice the repetition at all, or may fail to appreciate the relevance of the emphasis in a particular text. For a wide discussion of repetition as a linguistic and rhetorical device, see the essays collected in *Repetition*, ed. Andreas Fischer, *Swiss Papers in English Language and Literature*, 7:1994 (Tübingen: Gunter Narr Verlag, 1994), particularly Jean Aitchison "'Say, Say it Again Sam':The Treatment of Repetition in Linguistics," 15–34, and Brian Vickers, "Repetition and Emphasis in Rhetoric: Theory and Practice," 85–114.
29 It must not go unnoticed that in this fifth paragraph, Nechui introduces a new and different image of the valley as a space flooded with sea water that has suddenly crystalized in tall waves of green. This image belongs to

a different kind of non-rhetorical repetitive sequence that points forward to Mykola's sojourn on the shores of the Black Sea as a fisherman.

30 Pidmohyl'nyi, "Ivan Nechui-Levyts'kyi," xii. "Читаємо далі сторінку – немає нічого про той другий глиняник; на половині другої сторінки, посердившись на автора за недоцільні деталі, про глиняника з білою глиною, зрештою, забуваємо, і раптом, звернувши на третю сторінку, бачимо: 'Карпо обернувся, щоб не замазать чобіт, і зачепив п'ятою другого глиняника з білою глиною'!" (3:311).

31 Andrii Nikovs'kyi. "*Mykola Dzheria.* (A literary analysis)," introduction to a reprint of the novel, I. Nechui-Levyts'kyi, *Mykola Dzheria* (Kyiv: Knyhospilka, 1926), xii. Nikovs'kyi echoes Mykola Kostomarov's famous phrase about the Ukrainian language, which was suitable only for "domestic usage," as opposed to Russian, which had a general utility.

32 Nikovs'kyi, "*Mykola Dzheria,*" 18–19.

33 Nikovs'kyi, "*Mykola Dzheria,*" xix–xxi.

34 Nikovs'kyi, "*Mykola Dzheria,*" xli.

35 Chapter 3, p. 250.

36 Matthew Beaumont cautions: "It is important not to fall into the trap of congratulating a realist novel ... for being proto-modernist or proto-postmodernist, largely on the grounds that it has demonstrated an intuitive, if ultimately dim-witted understanding of its own formal limitations." See "Introduction: Reclaiming Realism," in *Adventures in Realism*, ed. Matthew Beaumont (Malden, MA: Blackwell Publishing, 2007), 6.

37 George Levine speaks of a "tendency of realism to formless and plotless detailist representation of character." *Adventures in Realism*, 18.

38 Nechuy-Levitsky, *Mikola Dzherya*, trans. Kovalenko, 11.

39 *Lesia Ukrainka: Zibrannia tvoriv v dvanadsiaty tomakh*, vol. 10, 113. The key portion of this letter, in her uncle's transcription, is cited in chapter 3, p. 219.

40 Визволення плоті (10, 193). Nechui attributes the phrase to Max Nordau.

41 Vasyl' Vlasenko suggests that Nechui saw decadence as a response to a domineering Christian morality but this is most unlikely. Vasyl' Vlasenko, *Khudozhnia maisternist'*, 16.

42 Letter to Natalia Kobryns'ka, 13 September 1900 (OS).

43 Iurii Mezhenko, "Khronolohiia artystychnoi diialnosti M.L. Kropyvnyts'koho (Materialy do biohrafii)," in *Marko Lukych Kropyvnyts'kyi. Zbirnyk stattei, spohadiv, i materialiv* (Kyiv: Mystetstvo, 1955), 471. Petro Rulin, "Persha drama Lesi Ukrainky," *Lesia Ukrainka. Tvory* (New York: Tyshchenko & Bilous, 1954), vol. 5, 12.

44 Roman Weretelnyk, *A Feminist Reading of Lesia Ukrainka's Dramas* (PhD thesis, University of Ottawa, 1989), 36–7.

45 For general evaluations of Lesia Ukrainka, including specific references to this play, see Solomiia Pavlychko, *Dyskurs modernizmu v ukrains'kii literaturi* (Kyiv: Lybid', 1999), 243–6; Vira Aheieva, *Poetesa zlamu stolit': Tvorchist' Lesi Ukrainky v postmodernii interpretatsii* (Kyiv: Lybid', 1999), 91–112; Nila Zborovs'ka, *Moia Lesia Ukrainka: Esei* (Ternopil': Dzhura, 2002), 112–22; Tamara Hundorova, *ProIavlennia slova: Dyskursiia rann'oho ukrains'kohi modernizmu. Postmoderna interpretatsiia* (Lviv: Tsentr humanitarnykh doslidzhen', 1997), 244; Lesia Dems'ka-Buzuliak, "Kryza zhinochoi identychnosti v konteksti 'novoi ievropeis'koi dramy,'" in *Lesia Ukrainka i suchasnist'* (Luts'k: Volyns'ka oblasna drukania, 2006), vol. 3, 136–49.

46 Lidia Zelins'ka, "*Blakytna troianda* Lesi Ukrainky: Problema dyskursu i metodu," *Lesia Ukrainka i suchasnist. Zbirnyk naukovykh prats'*, vol 4, bk. 1, 69; http://dspace.nbuv.gov.ua/bitstream/handle/123456789/17764/04-Zelinska.pdf. Accessed 12 June 2012 under a different URL.

47 See the accounts presented in Oleh Babyshkin, *Dramaturhiia Lesi Ukrainky* (Kyiv: Derzhavne vydavnytstvo obrazotvorchoho mystetstva i muzychnoi literatury, 1963), 26–31; Abram Hozenpud, *Poetychnyi teatr: Dramatychni tvory Lesi Ukrainky* (Kyiv: Mystetstvo, 1947), 26–9; and, of course, Petro Rulin, "Persha drama Lesi Ukrainky," *Lesia Ukrainka: Tvory v 12 tomakh*, vol. 5, pp. 7–28.

48 Petro Rulin, "Persha drama Lesi Ukrainky."

49 Petro Rulin, "Persha drama Lesi Ukrainky," 11.

50 *Lesia Ukrainka: Zibrannia tvoriv v dvanadsiaty tomakh*, vol. 11, p. 200.

5 Nechui's Characters: Women and Joy

1 See the discussion of "Dvi moskovky" at the beginning of chapter 3, p. 157.

2 Nila Zborovs'ka / Maria Il'nyts'ka, *Feministychni rozdumy: Na karnavali mertvykh potsilunkiv* (Lviv: Litopys, 1999), 62.

3 In chapter 2, p. 113.

4 Pidmohyl'nyi, "Ivan Levyts'kyi-Nechui (Sproba psykhoanalizy tvorchosty)," 301. In Pidmohyl'nyi's essay, this sentiment is attributed to a correspondent of Iurii Mezhenko named Velykokhat'ko (perhaps the ichthyologist Fedir Velykokhat'ko, 1894–1987?). The letter is cited from Mezhenko's archive.

5 Zborovs'ka, *Feministychni rozdumy*, 54–72.

6 Ibid., 69.

7 Biographical manifestations of Nechui's joyfulness are discussed in chapter 1, p. 23.

6 Nechui's Historical Writing

1 Maxim Tarnawsky, "Orthography, Copyright, and Legendary Anecdotes. The Story of Nečuj's Linguistic Peculiarities," in *Studien zu Sprache, Literatur und Kultur bei den Slaven: Gedenkenschrift für George Y. Shevelov aus Anlas seines 100. Geburstages und 10. Todestages*, eds. Andrii Danylenko and Serhii Vakulenko (Munich: Otto Sagner, 2012), 295–308.
2 But often deliberately synthesized with the historical Roxolana, wife of Suleiman the Magnificent.
3 See the discussion of the Hromada metelyky in chapter 1, p. 48.
4 Olena Poda, Problema transformatsii istorychnoi pravdy u tvorchosti I.S. Nechuia-Levyts'koho (Kandydat degree diss., Zaporizhzhiia State University, 2000).
5 Alla Kalynchuk, Istorychni romany I. Nechuia-Levyts'koho: Osoblyvosti poetyky, Avtoreferat (Kandydat degree Diss. summary, Institute of Literature, Academy of Sciences, 2001).
6 Iulia Volynets', "Postat' Bohdana KhMel'nyts'koho v narysakh Mykoly Kostomarova ta Ivana Nechuia-Levyts'koho," Literaturoznavstvo, *fol'klorystyka, kul'turolohiia: Zbirnyk naukovykh prats*, Cherkasy: Cherkasy State University, 2009. Available online at http://kulk.ck.ua/files/visnuk-18.pdf#page=11. Accessed 8 June 2012.
7 Letter from O. Radzievs'kyi to Nechui in 1895, Instytut Rukopysiv Tsentral'noi Naukovoi Biblioteky im. Vernads'koho, Fond 1, no. 27979. Quoted in her kandydatska dissertation by Olena Iuriivna Poda, "Problemy transformatsii istorychnoi pravdy u tvorchosti I.S. Nechuia-Levyts'koho" (Kandydat degree diss., Zaporizhzhia State University, 2000), 62.
8 Pobida Khmelnyts'koho pid Zbarazhem i Zborovom: Opovidanniie iz davnikh chasiv (Kolomyia: Vydavnycha spilka ukrains'kykh uchyteliv, 1910). Now available on the Internet: http://sites.utoronto.ca/elul/Nechui/nech-xmel-title.html. This is, no doubt, a re-edition of the original 1885 publication which appeard in an annual almanac.
9 *Ukrainski hetmany Brukhovets'kyi ta Teteria* (Lviv: Ruslan, 1899).
10 For an account of Nechui's depiction of Vyhovs'kyi, see part 2 of chapter 4 in Olena Poda's dissertation, 131–75. See also the brochure by schoolteacher turned politician and OUN leader, Bohdan Chervak, Obraz het'mana Vyhovs'koho v ukrains'kii literaturi (Drohobych: Vidrodzhennia, 1993), also available on the Internet at http://aphy.net/publicism/70-publi/215-2009-08-01-10-56-37.
11 With the exception of Iurii Rudnyts'kyi, Ieremiia Vyshnevets'kyi: Sproba Reabilitatsii (Eseistychna Rozvidka) (Lviv: Piramida, 2008).

Bibliography

Abramova, Inna. "Bilia vytokiv ukrains'koi idei (Nechui-Levyts'kyi i 'formalno-natsional'nyi' napriam)" *Slovo i chas*. 1999, 12: 56–8.

Aheieva, Vira. *Poetesa zlamu stolit': Tvorchist' Lesi Ukrainky v postmodernii interpretatsii*. Kyiv: Lybid', 1999.

Andriewsky, Olga. "The Politics of National Identity: The Ukranian Question in Russia, 1904–1912." PhD diss., Harvard University, 1991.

Anonymous. "Iubylei Y.S. Levytskaho v' Kieve." *Kievskaia staryna*. 1905, Vol. 88, Bk. 1: 19–23.

Anonymous. "Nad svizhoiu mohyloiu." *Literaturno-naukovyi visnyk*, 1918 (69), 2–3: 113–15.

Antonovych, Marko. "P. Kulish v otsintsi I. Nechuia-Levyts'koho." *Ukrains'kyi istoryk*, 1969 (6), 4 (24): 38–46.

Babyshkin, Oleh. *Dramaturhiia Lesi Ukrainky*. Kyiv: Derzhavne vydavnytstvo obrazotvorchoho mystetstva i muzychnoi literatury, 1963.

Barvins'kyi, Oleksander. "Pochyn pys'mennyts'koi tvorchosty Ivana Nechuia-Levyts'koho." *Literaturno-naukovyi vistnyk*. 1926. Vol. 89: 233–8.

Beaumont, Matthew, ed. *Adventures in Realism*. Malden, MA: Blackwell Publishing, 2007.

Bernshtein, Mykhailo Davydovych. "Do kharakterystyky svitohliadu rann'oho I.S. Nechuia-Levyts'koho." *Radians'ke literaturoznavstvo*, 1966, 9: 34–47.

Bilets'kyi, D.M. "Vyvchennia movy povisti I.S. Nechuia-Levyts'koho 'Mykola Dzheria'." *Ukrains'ka mova v shkoli*. 1959, 3: 40–3.

Bilets'kyi, Oleksander. "Ivan Semenovych Levyts'kyi (Nechui)," *Zibrannia prats'*, Tom 2. *Ukrains'ka literatura XIX – pochatku XX stolittia*. Kyiv: Naukova dumka, 1965. 317–67.

Biliavs'ka, O.O. "Deiaki krytychni vidhuky pro I.S. Nechuia-Levyts'koho (Kinets' XIX – pochatok XX st.)." *Radians'ke literaturoznavstvo*, 1979, 12 (228): 62–7.

Bilodid, Ivan. *Istoriia ukrains'koi literaturnoi movy*, in his *Vybrani pratsi v tr'ox tomakh*, vol. 2. Kyiv: Naukova dumka, 1986.

Bohdan, M.M. "Frazeolohiia prozovykh tvoriv I.S. Nechuia-Levyts'koho (sklad i sposoby vykorystannia)." *Naukovi zapysky*. Zhytomyrs'kyi derzhavnyi pedahohichnyi instytut. Seriia Linhvistychna. Volume XVII. Zhytomyr: Zhytomyrs'kyi derzhavnyi pedahohichnyi instytut, 1962. 19–31.

Buhaiko, F.F. "Vyvchennia opysiv khudozhn'oho tvoru." *Ukrains'ka mova i literatura v shkoli*, 1972 (22), 1: 40–4.

Burlaka, Halyna. "'Shchyro kokhaty stav ia otchyznu svoiu Ukrainu ... ' (Lysty m. Hrushevs'koho do I. Nechuia-Levyts'koho)." *Slovo i chas*, 1996, 10: 18–27.

Burtyn, M.L. "I.S. Nechui-Levyts'kyi u bibliohrafii." *Ukrains'ke literaturoznavstvo*, 1990 (55): 126–30.

Bykova, L.H. "Iz sposterezhen' nad osoblyvostiamy peizazhnoho zhyvopysu I.S. Nechuia-Levyts'koho." *Ukrains'ka mova i literatura v shkoli*, 1972 (22), 7: 18–24.

Chernets'kyi, Ievhen. *Studii nad zhyttiepysom Ivana Nechuia-Levyts'koho*. Bila Tserkva: Tovarystvo okhorony starozhytnostei Kyivshchyny, 2000.

Chervak, Bohdan. *Obraz het'mana Vyhovs'koho v ukrains'kii literaturi*. Drohobych: Vidrodzhennia, 1993.

Chornopyskyi, Mykhailo. "Kul'turolohichni traktaty Ivana Nechuia-Levyts'koho. Traktat pershyi." *Dyvoslovo*, 2001, 12 (538): 6–9.

– "Kul'turolohichni traktaty Ivana Nechuia-Levyts'koho. Traktat druhyi." *Dyvoslovo*, 2002, 1 (539): 3–6.

– "Kul'turolohichni traktaty Ivana Nechuia-Levyts'koho. Traktat tretii." *Dyvoslovo*, 2002, 2 (540): 6–10.

Dei, Oleksii I. "Nevidomi statti I. Nechuia-Levyts'koho pro narodnu shkolu." *Radians'ke literaturoznavstvo* 1967, 2: 74–7.

– "Tsinnyi dokument mystets'kykh zatsikavlen' I. Nechuia-Levyts'koho." *Radians'ke literaturoznavstvo*, 1977, 5: 69–71.

– "Vesillia, zapysane 1845 roku bat'kom I. Nechuia-Levyts'koho." *Narodna tvorchist' ta etnohrafiia*, 1972, 2: 85–99.

Dems'ka-Buzuliak, Lesia. "Kryza zhinochoi identychnosti v konteksti 'novoi ievropeis'koi dramy'." *Lesia Ukrainka i suchasnist'*. Luts'k: Volyns'ka oblasna drukania, 2006. Vol. 3, 136–49.

Doroshkevych, Oleksander. "Ideolohichni postati v ukrains'kii literaturi pislia Shevchenka (Sposterezhennia i uvahy)." *Chervonyi shliakh*, 1923, 3: 216–26.

Drahomanov, Mykhailo Petrovych. *Literaturno-publitsystychni pratsi v dvokh tomakh*. Kyiv: Naukova dumka, 1970.

Drahomanov, Mykhailo. *See also* Hrinchenko, Borys; Pavlyk, Mykhailo; Smal'-Stots'kyi, Roman; and Studyns'kyi, Kyrylo.

Fedoruk, Oles'. "Nevidomyi lyst-spohad I. Nechuia-Levyts'koho pro P. Kulisha." *Panteleimon Kulish: Materialy i dosldidzhennia*. Lviv: M.P. Kots', 2000. 278–96.

Fedosov, L.P. "Antyklerykal'ni motyvy u povistiakh Nechuia-Levyts'koho." *Radians'ke literaturoznavstvo*, 1963, 1: 27–41.

– "Narodnopoetychni dzherela humoru i satyry I.S. Nechuia-Levyts'koho." *Radians'ke literaturoznavstvo*, 1969 (13), 7: 50–63.

– "Shevchenkivs'ki tradytsii v satyri I.S. Nechuia-Levyts'koho." *Zbirnyk prats' dvanadtsiatoi naukovoi shevchenkivs'koi konferentsii*. Kyiv: Naukova dumka, 1964. 226–40.

– "Zhyvyi, nev'ianuchyi humor." *Radians'ke literaturoznavstvo*, 1968, 4: 62–9.

Fischer, Andreas, ed. *Repetition. Swiss Papers in English Language and Literature*, 7. Tübingen: Gunter Narr Verlag, 1994.

Franko, Ivan. Retsenziia na "*Ukraina, naukovyi ta literaturno-publitsystychnyi shchomisiachnyi zhurnal*. Rik pershyi, tom 1. U Kyivi 1907 r." *Literaturno-naukovyi visnyk*, 1907 (38), 6: 506–12.

– *Zibrannia tvoriv u p'iatdesiaty tomakh*. Kyiv: Naudova dumka, 1976–86.

Hlobenko, Mykola. "Zabutyi," in his *Z literaturoznavchoi spadshchyny*. Paris: Natsionalistychne vydavnytstvo v Evropi, 1961. 133–9 [reprint from the newspaper *Ukrains'ka trybuna*, 30 May 1948].

Hlushko, Syl'vestr. "Drahomanov i nedil'ni shkoly." *Ukraina*, 1924, no. 4, 35–42.

Hmyr, I.S. "Systema urokiv vyvchennia povisti I.S. Nechuia-Levyts'koho *Mykola Dzheria*." *Ukrains'ka mova i literatura v shkoli*, 1976, 11: 41–52.

Hol'berh, M. Ia., and D.M. Kuzyk. "I.S. Nechui-Levyts'kyi i Bairon." *Ukrains'ke literaturoznavstvo*, 1971 (12): 34–9.

Hozenpud, Abram. *Poetychnyi teatr: Dramatychni tvory Lesi Ukrainky*. Kyiv: Mystetstvo, 1947.

Hrinchenkova, Mariia. "Spohady pro Ivana Nechuia-Levyts'koho." *Ukraina*, 1924, 4: 111–27.

Hrinchenko, Borys, and Mykhailo Drahomanov, *Dialohy pro ukrains'ku natsional'nu spravu*. Kyiv: Natsionalna Akademiia Nauk Ukrainy, 1994.

Hrushevs'kyi, Oleksandr. "Ivan Levyts'kyi-Nechui. Suchasne ukrains'ke pys'menstvo v ioho typovyykh predstavnykakh." *Literaturno-naukovyi vistnyk*, 1907, Volume 37 [February]: 243–56.

Hryhorovych, I.O. "A. Iu. Kryms'kyi ta I.S. Nechui-Levyts'kyi." *Radians'ke literaturoznavstvo*, 1980, 2 (230): 77–80.

Hundorova, Tamara. *ProIavlennia slova: Dyskursiia rann'oho ukrains'koho modernizmu. Postmoderna interpretatsiia*. Lviv: Tsentr humanitarnykh doslidzhen', 1997.

Iakymovych, S. "Do kompozytsii romaniv Nechuia-Levyts'koho." *Chevonyi shliakh*, 1925, 3: 208–17.

Iefremov, Serhii. *Ivan Levyts'kyi Nechui*. Leipzig: Ukrains'ka nakladnia, 1924.

– "Vidhuky z zhyttia i pys'menstva. Pro kazku bezkoneshnyk." *Literaturno-naukovyi vistnyk*, 1907 (10), Vol. 38: 331–9.

– *Vybrane: Statti, naukovi rozvidky, monohrafii*. Kyiv: Naukova dumka, 2002.

Ïzhakevych, Halyna P. "Mova tvoriv I. Nechuia-Levyts'koho." *Kurs istorii ukrains'koi literaturnoi movy. Volume 1. Dozhovtnevyi period*. Edited by Ivan Kostiantynovych Bilodid. Kyiv: Akademiia nauk, 1958. 435–55.

Izotov, I. "Do svitohliadu Iv. Nechuia-Levyts'koho." *Literaturnyi arkhiv* (Kharkiv), 1931, 6: 49–82.

Kalenychenko, Nina Lukivna. "I.S. Nechui-Levyts'kyi pro literaturu." *Radians'ke literaturoznavstvo*, 1969, 12: 48–56.

Kalynchuk, Alla. *Istorychni romany I. Nechuia-Levyts'koho: Osoblyvosti poetyky*, Avtoreferat. Kandydat degree Diss. summary, Institute of Literature, Academy of Sciences, 2001.

– "Moral'no-etychna problematyka istorychnykh tvoriv I. Nechuia-Levyts'koho ta A. Malyshka (na materiali romanu *Het'man Ivan Vyhov'kyi* ta poemy 'Duma pro kozaka Danyla')." *Materialy Vseukrains'koi mizhvuzivs'koi naukovoi konferentsii, prysviachenoi 85-richchiu vid dnia narodzhennia A.S. Malyshka*. Kyiv: RVTs "Kyivs'kyi universytet," 1997. 34–6.

– "Osoblyvosti kharakterotvorennia v istorychnykh romanakh I.S. Nechuia-Levyts'koho." *Slovo i chas*, 2000, 11: 26–31.

– "Poetyka istorychnykh romaniv I.S. Nechuia-Levyts'koho." *Literaturoznavchi obrii: Pratsi molodykh uchenykh ukrainy*. Vypusk 1. Kyiv: Natsional'na akademiia nauk, 2000. 12–19.

Kawin, Bruce. *Telling it Again and Again: Repetition in Literature and Film*. Ithaca, NY: Cornell University Press, 1972.

Khavrus', Serhii. "Do obrazu narodnoho pys'mennyka. Nechui-Levyts'kyi u spohadakh suchasnykiv." *Vitchyzna*, 1978, 11: 165–73.

– "Ivan Semenovych Nechui-Levyts'kyi (Do 130-richchia z dnia narodzhennia)." [Zhandarms'ki dokumenty pro I.S. Nechuia-Levyts'koho] *Ukrains'kyi istorychnyi zhurnal*, 1968, 11: 136–8.

– "Oberezhno: Ob'iektyvnist'!" *Vitchyzna*, 1971, 1: 213–14.

– "Sered narodu." *Prapor*, 1968, 11: 87–8.

– "Zapovitnymy stezhkamy Stebleva." *Ukrains'ka mova i literatura v shkoli*, 1986, 3 (349): 69–74.

Khropko, Petro. "I. Franko i zhurnal 'Pravda' (Do pytannia pro polemiku I. Franka z I.S. Nechuiem-Levyts'kym ta T. Zin'kivs'kym)." *Ukrains'ke literaturoznavstvo*, 1993, 58: 152–60.

– "Romany I. Nechuia-Levyts'koho z zhyttia intelihentsii." *Ukrains'ka mova i literatura v shkoli*, 1988, 11: 3–10.

Kiebuzinski, Ksenya. *Paris to Poltava: Ukrainian cossacks as an Imagined Community in Nineteenth-Century French Culture*. PhD diss., Brandeis University, 2002.

Klebanovskyi, Pavlo, "Bohuslavskoe dukhovnoe uchylyshche." *Kievskaia starina*, 1894, 9: 415–33; 1994, 10: 25–39; 1994, 11: 271–8.

Kobryns'ka, Natalia. "U Nechuia." *Natalia Kobryns'ka. Vybrani tvory*. Kyiv: Derzhavne vydavnytstvo khudozhn'oi literatury, 1958. 364–6.

Koshovyi, O. (=Oleksander Konys'kyi). "Koly zh vyiasnyt'sia? (Za provodom povisty Y. Levitskoho *Khmary*.)." *Pravda*, 8 (1875): 768–74; 807–13.

Kotsiubyns'kyi, Mykhailo. *Tvory v semy tomakh*. Kyiv: Naukova dumka, 1973–5.

Kovalenko-Kolomats'kyi, Hryhorii Andriiovych. Review of "Akad. Serhii Iefremov. *Ivan Levyts'kyi-Nechui*. Kyiv: Slovo, 1925. storin 190." *Chervonyi shliakh*, 1925, 8 (29): 236–7.

– "Vystavka pam'iaty Iv. Lyvyts'koho-Nechuia." *Chervonyi shliakh*, 1929, 1 (70): 242–4.

Kravets', H.A. "Deiaki osoblyvosti realizmu iak tvorchoho metodu ukrains'koi prozy 70-kh rokiv XIX st. u svitli lenins'kykh nastanov z literatury." *Ukrains'ke literaturoznavstvo*, 1971 (12): 9–14.

– "Nechui-Levyts'kyi i Turheniev." *Ukrains'ke literaturoznavstvo*, 1971 (13): 30–6.

Kril', K.A. "Lystuvannia N. Kobryns'koi z Nechuiem-Levyts'kym ta Borysom Hrinchenkom." *Ukrains'ke literaturoznavstvo*, 1970 (10): 120–8.

Krotevych, Ievhen. *Kyivs'ki zustrichi*. Kyiv: Molod', 1963.

Krutikova, Nina Ievhenivna. "Bez uperedzhen'." *Radians'ke literaturoznavstvo*, 1970, 12: 67–9.

– "Entsyklopediia narodnoho zhyttia." *Vitchyzna*, 1968 (36), 9: 178–84.

– *Tvorchist' I.S. Nechuia-Levyts'koho*. Kyiv: Akademiia nauk URSR, 1961.

"U sviti khudozhn'oi pravdy i krasy." *I.S. Nechui-Levyts'kyi. Tvory. U 3 tomakh*. Kyiv: Dnipro, 1987, tom 1: 5–28.

Kryzhanovs'kyi, Efimii. "Kniaz' V.A. Cherkasskii i kholmskie greko-uniaty," *Ruskoe zabuz'e (Kholmshchina i Podliash'e)*. St Petersburg: Mirnyi trud, 1911.

Kulyns'ka L.P. "Mova povisti *Kaidasheva sim'ia* I.S. Nechuia-Levyts'koho." *Ukrains'ka mova v shkoli*. 1959, 3: 44–9.

Kurochkin, Oleksandr . "Etnohrafichni interesy I.S. Nechuia-Levyts'koho." *Narodna tvorchist' ta etnohrafiia*, 1974, 4: 91–5.

– "Ivan Nechui-Levyts'kyi pro antyklerykalizm i stykhiinyi materializm ukrains'koho narodu." *Narodna tvorchist' ta etnohrafiia*, 1971, 6: 54–8.

Kuz'menko, S.M. "I. Nechui-Levyts'kyi v Kyshynevi." *Radians'ke literaturoznavstvo*, 1966, 6: 69–72.

Kyryliuk, Ievhen. "Vydannia *Tvoriv* Nechuia-Levyts'koho." *Zhyttia i revoliutsiia*, 1930, 5: 183–7.

Leonova, M.V. "Movna kharakterystyka personazhiv povisti *Kaidasheva sim'ia*. *Literatura v shkoli*, 1960, 1: 57–62.

Levyts'ka, V.A. "Iz spadshchyny I.S. Nechuia-Levyts'koho." *Radians'ke literaturoznavstvo*, 1978, 12 (216): 65–73. Vydannia opovidannia "Iak sakharni holovy litaly v povitri."

Levyts'kyi, Modest. "De-shcho do spravy pro vkrains'ku pys'mennyts'ku movu." *Literaturno-naukovyi visnyk*, 1909 (47), 8: 238–51.

Levyts'kyi, Semen. "Opisanie svad'by i svadebnykh obriadov ukrainskikh malorossian (v Bohuslave). Sostavleno sviashchennikom sela Stebleva Simeonom Levitskim," 1845. Rept. in Oleksii Dei, "Vesillia, zapysane 1845 roku bat'kom I. Nechuia-Levyts'koho," *Narodna tvorchist' ta etnohrafiia*, 1972, 2: 85–99.

Lisovyi, I.A. "'Ellins'kyi kul'turnyi typ' I.S. Nechuia-Levyts'koho." *Ukrains'ke literaturoznavstvo*, 1976 (27): 103–8.

Lisovyi, P.M. "I. Franko pro I. Nechuia-Levyts'koho." *Radians'ke literaturoznavstvo*, 1968, 2: 26–30.

Lotots'kyi, Oleksander. "I.S. Levyts'kyi," in his *Storinky mynuloho*, Pt. 1. Warsaw: Ukrains'kyi naukovyi instytut, 1932. 186–8.

Luts'kyi, Iurii. "Vid Nechuia do Etvud." *Suchasnist'*, 1979, 3: 116–23.

Lysenko, Mykola V. *Lysty*. comp. Ostap Lysenko. Kyiv: Mystetstvo, 1964.

Lysenko, Ostap. "M.V. Lysenko i I.S. Nechui-Levyts'kyi." *Dnipro*, 1959, 4: 139–45.

Mandryka, Mykola. "Do biohrafii I.S. Nechuia-Levyts'koho (Roky navchannia pys'mennyka)." *Radians'ke literaturoznavstvo*, 1968, 2: 31–40.

– "I.S. Nechui-Levyts'kyi sered Halychan." *Zhovten'*, 1968, 4: 121–8.

– "Ivan Nechui i tsars'ka okhrana: Do 130-richchia vid dnia narodzhennia I.S. Nechuia-Levyts'koho." *Dnipro*, 1968 (42), 10: 139–45. [Look under Sereda. 3 essays in one issue.]

– "Nechui-Levyts'kyi – perekladach." *Vitchyzna*, 1983, 11: 172–5.

– "'... bahato zavziatosti i protestu proty usiakoi liuds'koi kryvdy' (I. Nechui-Levyts'kyi pro zarubizhne pys'menstvo)." *Slovo i chas*, 1998, 11: 10–12.

– "Khronolohiia artystychnoi diialnosti M.L. Kropyvnyts'koho (Materialy do biohrafii)." *Marko Lukych Kropyvnyts'kyi. Zbirnyk stattei, spohadiv, i materialiv*. Kyiv: Mystetstvo, 1955. 379–504.

– "Literaturni paraleli. I.S. Nechui-Levyts'kyi i I.S. Turhenev." *Ukraina*, 1925, 3: 130–4.

– "Nove vydannia tvoriv I.S. Nechuia-Levyts'koho." *Radians'ke literaturoznavstvo*, 1965, 4: 95.

– "Z lystuvannia I.S. Nechuia-Levyts'koho." *Radians'ke literaturoznavstvo*, 1988, 11: 53–69. [Look under Sereda. 3 essays in one issue.]

Mezhenko, Iurii. "Ivan Semenovych Nechui-Levyts'kyi. Literaturnyi narys." *I.S. Nechui-Levyts'kyi. Tvory*, Volume 1. Kharkiv: DVU, 1926. 5–18.

Miller, Alexei. *The Ukrainian Question: The Russian Empire and Nationalism in the Nineteenth Century*. Trans. Olga Poato. Budapest: Central European University Press, 2003.

Miller, J. Hillis. *Fiction and Repetition: Seven English Novels*. Cambridge, MA: Harvard University Press, 1982.

Mishchuk, R.S. "Pro humanizm tvorchosti I. Nechuia-Levyts'koho." *Radians'ke literaturoznavstvo*, 1987, 5: 26–35.

Moroz, Mykola. "Bibliohrafichnyi pokazhchyk." *I.S. Nechui-Levyts'kyi. Tvory v tr'okh tomakh*. Kyiv: Dnipro, 1988. Vol. 3, 556–636.

Muratov, Ihor. "Klasychnyi realizm u rozvytku." *Prapor*, 1972, 1: 81–5. [Review of H.A. Kravets', *Piznaval'ne ta vykhovne znachennia ukrains'koi klasychnoi literatury*. Kharkiv: Kharkivs'ky instytut kul'tury, 1970.]

Myrnyi, Panas. *Zibrannia tvoriv u semy tomakh*. Kyiv: Naukova dumka, 1968–71.

Nechui-Levyts'kyi, Ivan. "Iak sakharni holovy litaly v povitri." *Radians'ke literaturoznavstvo*, 1978, 12 (216): 66–73. See Levyts'ka, V.A. 1978.

– *Mikola Dzherya: A Long Story* [*sic*]. Trans. Oles Kovalenko. Kyiv: Dnipro, 1985.

– *Pobida Khmelnyts'koho pid Zbarazhem i Zborovom: Opovidanniie iz davnikh chasiv*. Kolomyia: Vydavnycha spilka ukrains'kykh uchyteliv, 1910. Available on the Internet in the Electronic Library of Ukrainian Literature.

– "S'ohochasna chasopysna mova na Ukraini." *Ukraina*, 1907, Vol. 1, Bk. 1, 1–49; Bk. 2, 183–237; Bk. 3, 280–331. Available on the Internet in the Electronic Library of Ukrainian Literature.

– *Svitohliad ukrains'koho narodu: Eskiz ukrains'koi mifolohii*. Kyiv: Oberehy, 1992; rpt. 2003.

– *Ukrainski hetmany Brukhovets'kyi ta Teteria*. Lviv: Ruslan, 1899. Available on the Internet in the Electronic Library of Ukrainian Literature.

– *Ukrainstvo na literaturnykh pozvakh z Moskovshchynoiu*. Lviv: Kameniar, 1988. Available on the Internet in the Electronic Library of Ukrainian Literature.

– *Zibrannia tvoriv u 10 t*. Kyiv: Naukova dumka, 1965–8.

Nikovs'kyi, Andrii. "*Mykola Dzheria*. (Literaturnyi analiz)." In I. Nechui-Levyts'kyi, *Mykola Dzheria*. Kyiv: Knyhospilka, 1926. vii–xlv.

Ohren, Dana M. "All the Tsars Men: Minorities and Military Conscription in Imperial Russia, 1874–1905." PhD diss., Indiana University, 2006.

Pashkovs'ka, Hanna Volodymyrivna. *Ivan Nechui-Levyts'kyi i normy ukrains'koi movy*. Uman: PP Zhovtyi, 2009.

Pavlychko, Solomiia. *Dyskurs modernizmu v ukrains'kii literaturi*. Kyiv: Lybid', 1999.

Pavlyk, Mykhailo, ed. *Perepyska Mykhaila Drahomanova z Melitonom Buchyns'kym 1871–1877*. Lviv: NTSh, 1910.

Pidmohyl'nyi, Valeriian. "Ivan Levyts'kyi-Nechui (sproba psykhoanalizy tvorchosty)," *Zhyttia i revoliutsiia* 1927, 9: 295–303. Available on the Internet in the Electronic Library of Ukrainian Literature.

– "Peredmova." *Ivan Nechui-Levyts'kyi. Vybrani tvory*. Kyiv: Chas, 1927, Vol. 1, v–xvi; Vol. 2, v–viii. Available on the Internet in the Electronic Library of Ukrainian Literature.

Plokhy, Serhii. *Unmaking Imperial Russia: Mykhailo Hrushevsky and the Writing of Ukrainian History*. Toronto: University of Toronto Press, 2005.

Poda, Olena *Problema transformatsii istorychnoi pravdy u tvorchosti I.S. Nechuia-Levyts'koho*. Kandydat degree diss., Zaporizhzhiia State University, 2000.

Polishchuk Volodymyr. "Do 150-richchia z dnia narodzhennia I.S. Nechuia-Levyts'koho." *Radians'ke literaturoznavstvo*, 1989, 5 (341): 65–9.

– *Ivan Nechui-Levyts'kyi: Postat' i tvorchist'. Zbirnyk prats' Vseukrains'koi naukovoi konferencii 25–27 veresnia 2008 roku*. Cherkasy: Iu. Chabanenko, 2008.

Pustova, F.D. "Tvorchist' Nechuia-Levyts'koho v otsintsi I. Franka." *Ukrains'ke literaturoznavstvo*, 1978 (30): 25–35.

Remy, Johannes. "The Valuev Circular and Censorship of Ukrainian Publications in the Russian Empire (1863–1876): Intention and Practice," *Canadian Slavonic Papers*, 2007, 1–2: 87–110.

Rubchak, Bohdan. "Heroizm malykh dil: Sytuatsiia ukrains'koi literatury navkolo 1878 roku." *Suchasnist'*, 1979, 3 (219): 61–90.

Rudenko, M.A. "Rozhliad povisti I.S. Nechuia-Levyts'koho 'Burlachka'." *Ukrains'ka mova i literatura v shkoli*, 1975, 10 (294): 49–53.

Rudnyts'kyi, Iurii. *Ieremiia Vyshnevets'kyi: Sproba Reabilitatsii (Eseistychna Rozvidka)*. Lviv: Piramida, 2008.

Rudnytsky, Ivan L. "Franciszek Duchiński and His Impact on Ukrainian Political Thought," *Harvard Ukrainian Studies* III/IV(*Eucharisterion*, pt. 2, 1980): 690–705.

Rudych, Feliks Mikhailovich, ed. *Kyivs'ka oblast. Istoriia mist i sil Ukrains'koi RSR*. Kyiv: Akademiia nauk, 1971.

Rulin, Petro. "Persha drama Lesi Ukrainky." *Lesia Ukrainka. Tvory*. New York: Tyshchenko & Bilous, 1954, Vol. 5, 7–28.

Sarana, Fedir. "Iz neopublikovanykh spohadiv pro I. Nechuia-Levyts'koho," *Literaturna Ukraina*, 18 June 1999, 5.

Savchenko, Fedir. *Zaborona ukrainstva 1876 r.* Kyiv: DVU, 1930; rept. Fedir Savčenko, *The Suppression of the Ukrainian Activities* [*sic*], Harvard Series in Ukrainian Studies 14. Munich: Wilhelm Fink, 1970.

Sereda, V.T. "Vytoky styl'ovoi manery vydatnoho prozaika." *Radians'ke literaturoznavstvo*, 1988, 11: 43–8.

Shavlovs'kyi, Ivan. "Bez uperedzhen' i nalychok." *Vitchyzna*, 1970, 8: 175–80.

Shenrok, I. "P.A. Kulish (Biohraficheskii ocherk')," *Kievskaia starina*, 1901, 2: 153–79; 3: 461–92; 4: 126–48; 5: 183–213; 6: 344–82; 7/8: 46–102; 9: 304–30; 10: 18–44.

Shevelov, George Y. *Die Ukrainische Schriftsprache 1798–1965: Ihre Entwicklung unter dem Einfluss der Dialekte.* Wiesbaden: Otto Harrassowitz, 1966.

– *The Ukrainian Language in the First Half of the Twentieth Century (1900–1941): Its State and Status.* Cambridge, MA: Harvard Ukrainian Research Institute, 1989.

Shkandrij, Myroslav. *Jews in Ukrainian Literature: Representation and Identity.* New Haven, CT: Yale University Press, 2009.

Siryi, Iurii. "Z moikh zustrichiv. 2. I.S. Nechui-Levyts'kyi." *Lieraturno-naukovyi zbirnyk*, ch. 3, Hannover: K.N.V., 1948. 54–69.

Smal'-Stots'kyi, Roman, ed. *Arkhiv Mykhaila Drahomanova. Tom 1. Lystuvannia kyivs'koi staroi hromady z M. Drahomanovym (1870–1895 r.r.).* Warsaw: Ukrains'kyi naukovyi instytut, 1937.

Staryts'ka-Cherniakhivs'ka, Liudmyla. Review of "Ivan Nechui-Levyts'kyi. *Povysty i opovydannia. T. II. Starosvyts'ky Batiushky ta Matushky.* Z' portretom' avtora. Kiev. 1900." *Literaturno-naukovyi vistnyk*, 1900 (3), Vol. 12, pt. 11: 115–20.

Staryts'kyi, Mykhailo. *Tvory u vos'my tomakh.* Kyiv: Dnipro, 1963–5.

Studyns'kyi, Kyrylo, comp. "Perepyska M. Drahomanova z V. Navrots'kym (Z pochatkiv sotsiialistychnoho rukhu v Halychyni)." *Za sto lit: Materialy z hromads'koho i literaturnoho zhyttia Ukrainy XIX i pochatkiv XX stolittia.* Book 1. Kyiv: Derzhavne vydavnytstvo Ukrainy, 1927, pp. 83–154. http://sites.utoronto.ca/elul/Documents/Za_sto_lit/Za_sto_lit_I.djvu?djvuopts&page=93 or http://sites.utoronto.ca/elul/Documents/Za_sto_lit/Za_sto_lit_I.pdf#page=93.

– *Halychyna i Ukraina v lystuvanni 1862–1884 rr. Materiialy do istorii ukrains'koi kul'tury v Halychyni ta ii zv'iazkiv z Ukrainoiu.* Kyiv: Proletar, 1931.

Syvachenko, M. Ie. "Pro knyhu N. Ie. Krutikovoi *Tvorchist' I.S. Nechuia-Levyts'koho.*" *Radians'ke literaturoznavstvo*, 1962, 6: 139–45.

Syvokin', H.M. Ukrains'kyi chytach Nechuia." *Radians'ke literaturoznavstvo*, 1988, 11: 48–53.

Taranenko Mykola Panasovych [Nykolai Afanas'evych]. "Bilia dzherel robitnychoi tematyky v ukrains'kii literaturi." *Ukrains'ka mova i literatura v shkoli*, 1972 (22) 8: 13–22.

– "Do istorii vysvitlennia 35-richnoho iuvileiu I.S. Nechui-Levyts'koho." *Ukrains'ke literaturoznavstvo*, 1973 (19): 110–15.
– "Do kharakterystyky sedlets'koho periodu tvorchoi biohrafii Nechuia-Levyts'koho." *Radians'ke literaturoznavstvo*, 1971, 6: 30–9.
– "I. Franko pro tvorchist' I. Nechuia-Levyts'koho." *Ukrains'ke literaturoznavstvo*, 1981 (36): 90–6.
– "I. Franko v otsintsi I. Nechuia-Levyts'koho." *Radians'ke literaturoznavstvo*, 1967 (11), 2: 46–55.
– *I.S. Nechui-Levyts'kyi. Seminarii*. Kyiv: Vyshcha shkola, 1984.
– Retsenziia na "*I.S. Nechui-Levyts'kyi. Zibrannia tvoriv u desiaty tomakh*, K. Naukova dumka, 1965–1968." *Radians'ke literaturoznavstvo*, 1969, 11: 81–5.
– "Shevchenko v otsintsi Iv. Nechuia-Levyts'koho." *Zbirnyk prats' odynadtsiatoi naukovoi shevchenkivs'koi konferentsii*. Kyiv: Akademiia nauk, 1963. 158–78.
Tarnawsky, Maxim. "Ivan Nečuj-Levyc'kyj's Realism." *Adelphotes: A Tribute to Omeljan Pritsak by his Students; Harvard Ukrainian Studies* 14, No. 3/4 (December 1990): 608–22.
– "Orthography, Copyright, and Legendary Anecdotes. The Story of Nečuj's Linguistic Peculiarities." *Studien zu Sprache, Literatur und Kultur bei den Slaven: Gedenkenschrift für George Y. Shevelov aus Anlas seines 100. Geburstages und 10. Todestages*, ed. Andrii Danylenko and Serhii Vakulenko. Munich: Otto Sagner, 2012. 295–308.
– "Zhinka v tvorakh Nechuia-Levyts'koho." Published in an internet journal. *Vydnokola*. No. 3 http://sites.utoronto.ca/elul/Nechui/Vydnokola-nechui-women.html.
Ukrainka, Lesia. *Zibrannia tvoriv v dvanadsiaty tomakh*. Kyiv: Naukova dumka, 1975–9.
Ushkalov, Leonid. *Realizm–tse eskhatolohiia: Panas Myrnyi*. Kharkiv: Maidan, 2012.
Vertii, Oleksii Ivanovych. "Narodni dzherela psykholohizmu tvoriv I.S. Nechuia-Levyts'koho." *Narodna tvorchist' ta etnohrafiia*, 1988, 6: 9–18.
Vizyr, Mykola i Kolesnychenko, Iurii. "Nespravdzhenyi namir." *Ukraina*, 1967, 6: 17.
Vlasenko, Vasyl' Onufriievych. "Do pytannia pro psykholohichnyi analiz u tvorchosti I.S. Nechuia-Levyts'koho." *Radians'ke literaturoznavstvo*, 1968 (12), 10: 61–8.
– "I.S. Nechui-Levyts'kyi i tsars'ka tsenzura." *Radians'ke literaturoznavstvo*, 1965, 4: 80–4.
– *Khudozhnia maisternist' I.S. Nechuia-Levyts'koho*. Kyiv: Radians'ka shkola, 1969.
– "Problemy typolohii ukrains'koho sotsial'noho romanu XIX stolittia (Na dopomohu studentovi-zaochnyku)." *Ukrains'ka mova i literatura v shkoli*, 1974, 7 (279): 14–21.

– "Zasoby psykholohichnoi kharakterystyky u tvorakh I.S. Nechuia-Levyts'koho." *Ukrains'ka mova i literatura v shkoli*, 1968 (18), 11: 18–21.

Volynets', Iuliia. "Postat' Bohdana Khmel'nyts'koho v narysakh Mykoly Kostomarova ta Ivana Nechuia-Levyts'koho." *Literaturoznavstvo. Fol'klorystyka. Kul'turolohiia. Zbirnyk naukovykh prats'*.. Naukovi zapysky kafedry ukr. lit-ry ta komparatyvistyky, Cherkas'kyi natsional'nyi universytet imeni Bohdana Khmel'nyts'koho. Vypusk 8. Cherkasy: Brama, 2009. 11–20. http://kulk.ck.ua/files/visnuk-18.pdf#page=11.

Vozniak, Mykhailo. "Do znosyn Iv. Levyts'koho z Halychanamy (Desiat' ioho lystiv do Iv. Puliuia)." *Literaturnyi arkhiv* (Kharkiv), 1931, 1 / 2: 142–53.

– "Kulish iak redaktor "Prychepy" Levyts'koho." *Zapysky NTSh* (Lviv, 1928) Vol. 148: 1–54.

– "Prymitky Ivana Nechuia-Levyts'koho do perekladu 'Malorossii' Pryzhova." *Literaturnyi arkhiv* (Kharkiv), 1930, 1 / 2: 138–43.

– "Z lystuvannia Ivana Nechuia-Levyts'koho z Halychanamy." *Naukovyi zbirnyk za rik 1927* (Zapysky ukrains'koho naukovoho tovarystva v Kyivi teper istorychnoi sektsii vseukrains'koi akademii nauk [=Zapysky Istorychno-filolohichnoho viddilu], Vol. 24) edited by Mykhailo Hrushevs'kyi. Kyiv, DVU, 1927. 97–133.

Weretelnyk, Roman. "A Feminist Reading of Lesia Ukrainka's Dramas." PhD diss., University of Ottawa, 1989.

Zaklyns'kyi, Roman. "U mene pered ochyma. Iz neopublikovanykh spohadiv pro I.S. Nechuia-Levyts'koho." (Foreword by Fedir Sarana) *Literaturna Ukraina*, 18 June 1992, 5.

Zborovs'ka, Nila / Maria Il'nyts'ka. *Feministychni rozdumy: Na karnavali mertvykh potsilunkiv*. Lviv: Litopys, 1999.

Zborovs'ka, Nila. *Moia Lesia Ukrainka: Esei*. Ternopil': Dzhura, 2002.

Zelins'ka, Lidia. "*Blakytna troianda* Lesi Ukrainky: Problema dyskursu i metodu," *Lesia Ukrainka i suchasnist. Zbirnyk naukovykh prats'*, Vol 4, Bk. 1, 59–72. Available on the Internet at http://dspace.nbuv.gov.ua/bitstream/handle/123456789/17764/04-Zelinska.pdf.

Zhovtobriukh, M.A. "Ukrains'ka hramatyka I.S. Nechuia-Levyts'koho." *Movoznavstvo*, 1989, 1: 33–7.

Zhytets'kyi, Ihnat. "Kyivs'ka hromada za 60-ykh rokiv." *Ukraina*, 1928, 1: 91–125.

Zinchenko, N.I. "Meta iasna i prosta – narod i Ukraina. (Intelihent-demokrat u tvorakh I. Nechuia-Levyts'koho)." *Slovo i chas*, 1991, 8: 42–7.

Zubkovs'kyi, I.A. "I.S. Nechui-Levyts'kyi na Poltavshchyni. (Uryvok iz spohadiv)." *Kul'tura i pobut* [Visti VUTsVK], 1928, 25 (23. chervnia 1928): 3.

Index

www.ingramcontent.com/pod-product-compliance
Lightning Source LLC
LaVergne TN
LVHW090147080826
844660LV00013B/709/J

* 9 7 8 1 4 4 2 6 5 0 0 8 4 *